REX CONWAY'S
WESTERN
STEAM JOURNEY

THE LOCAL HISTORY COMPANY

First published in the United Kingdom in 2008 by
The Local History Company, an imprint of The History Press
Cirencester Road · Chalford · Stroud · Gloucestershire · GL6 8PE

British Library Cataloguing in Publication Data
A catalogue record for this book is available from the British Library.

ISBN 978-0-7509-4798-5

Typeset in 10/12pt Palatino.
Typesetting and origination by
The History Press.
Printed and bound in England by Ashford Colour Press Ltd., Gosport, Hants.

Contents

Map   iv

Introduction   v

Rex Conway's Western Steam Journey   1

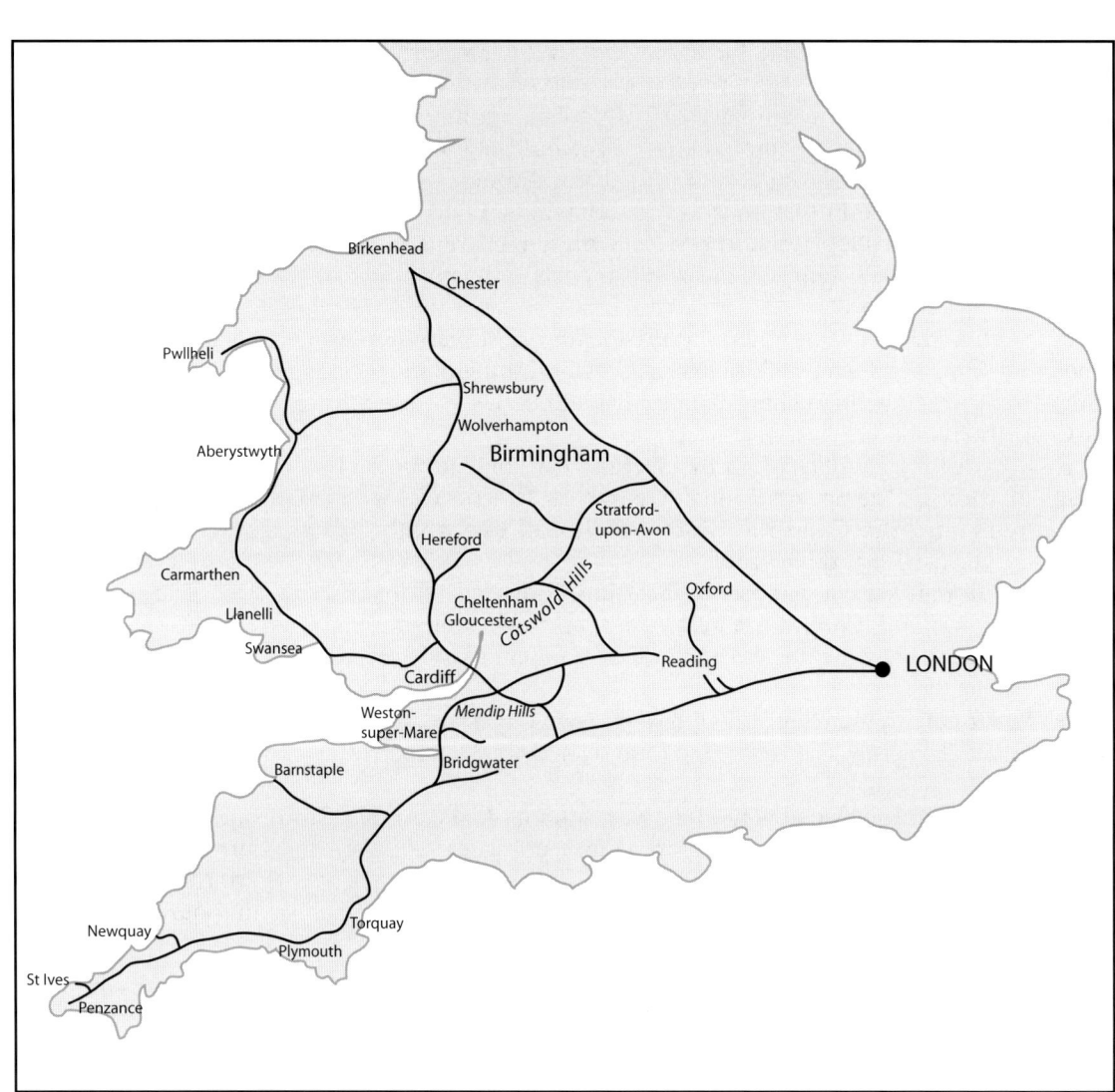

Introduction

In this book I intend to take the reader on a Western journey from Paddington to Penzance through the medium of steam photographs. I know it will be impossible to achieve complete coverage as I would need a vastly bigger collection than the 60,000 negatives I have, and it would probably run to many more pages than would fit into one volume.

On this journey we will travel to Birmingham, through Chester to Birkenhead, then return to the mainline and take in Oxford and the Cotswolds, Didcot and continue to Cheltenham and Gloucester, and take a look at the works in Swindon. Beyond Swindon is the junction at Wootton Bassett where we will temporarily leave the main Bristol line to take the Badminton route through to Stoke Gifford.

We return to the mainline and on to Bristol, and at Bathampton we take another junction, this time to Westbury and eventually Weymouth. Continuing along we arrive in the historic town of Bath and we are now but a short distance from Bristol, the end of the first part of our journey to the Cornish Riviera.

Leaving Bristol we will head north, meeting with the Badminton line at Patchway to the north of Bristol, through the Severn Tunnel, we bypass Newport by the Maindy Curve and head for Shrewsbury and the Cambrian line, which will eventually bring us back to Bristol via Aberystwyth, Cardiff and Newport.

Leaving Bristol we once more are heading westward to the holiday destinations through Taunton, Exeter and along the much-loved and well-photographed Teignmouth and Dawlish where travellers get a wonderful view of the sea, and waves have been known to wash over carriages.

There are many branch lines to holiday areas on our route, and we shall visit several, but soon we arrive in Plymouth. On again, we pass over Brunel's superb Royal Albert Bridge and into Cornwall.

Now we feel journey's end is not far away, through Liskeard, Par, Truro, and now the journey is almost over, past the loco depot and into the terminus of Penzance, and journey's end.

I have tried to use mainline post-1948 photographs, but where necessary for continuity I have resorted to pre-1948, so there has to be a little bit of imagination to believe this journey could be made in one day.

The biggest problem with an archive is lack of information with negatives that are donated or bought. Very often the photographer is no longer with us or not even known – the result being that you then have a lovely photograph but you have to do some detective work and try to identify location and date – though I must admit I enjoy this work.

If any fellow enthusiast can offer accurate information, please contact me via the publishers. I would also like to make an appeal on behalf of my archive: if anyone reading this book has negatives that they no longer want, I will clean the dust off and add them to my archive. It is only through the generosity of many fellow enthusiasts that I have been able to make this journey. Who knows, perhaps I can make a Midland, Eastern, Southern or even a Scottish journey.

Rex Conway, 2008

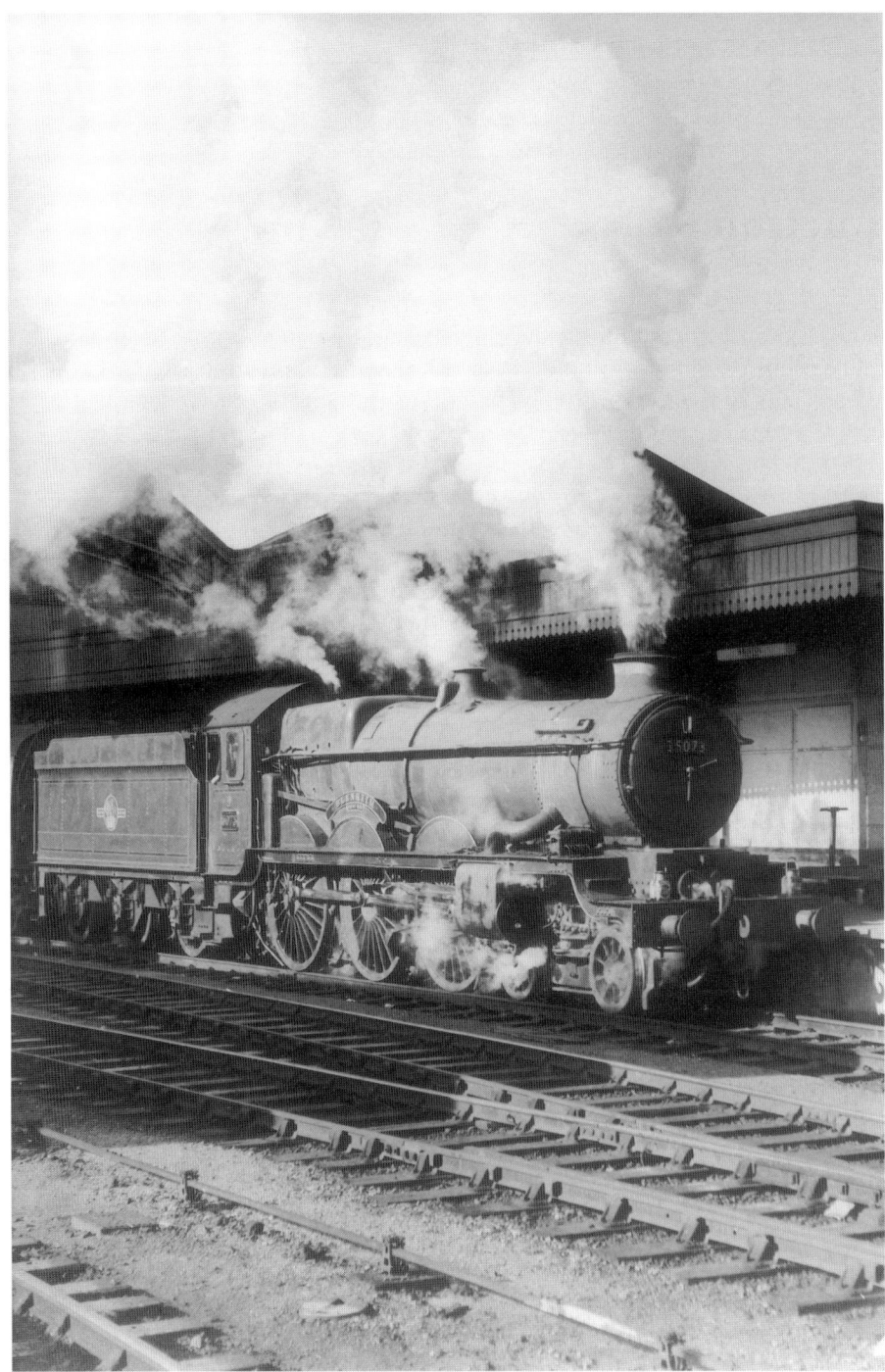

I was quite young when I made my first journey to Paddington, at around twelve years old, but in this day and age, regrettably, it would be considered too dangerous for a young lad of that age to travel alone. In those days it was an adventure.

I was up early, camera checked, a supply of films in hand, very limited pocket money, a pile of sandwiches and fizzy drinks, all put into a shoulder bag, then off to catch the bus to Temple Meads in time to board the 8.30 am to Paddington. This view is of no. 5073 *Blenheim* leaving platform 9 with the 8.30 am to London in 1958. I captured this image on a much better camera than a twelve-year-old could afford in 1949.

Rex Conway's Western Steam Journey

A journey has to start somewhere, and what better place to start than Paddington? I have fond memories of the times I went to London as a schoolboy trainspotter, and on later journeys with my camera. I always caught the 8.30 am from Bristol Temple Meads, arriving at Paddington at around 11 a.m., as far as I can remember. On arrival it was a rush to the underground train and onto foreign territory: Kings Cross, Euston, etc, but that's another story.

On arrival back at Paddington from foreign tracks, there was usually an hour or so to take a few more photographs. There were so many areas at Paddington that choosing photographs which give the atmosphere of such a huge station is difficult. I have included pictures that show the everyday work: a pannier bringing empty stock into a departure platform, a suburban train, and of course I had to include 'Castles', as no enthusiast would deny that in their early spotting days the sight of a 'King' or 'Castle' was a cop that made their day. I can still remember that feeling, and I am not ashamed to admit that I have a similar feeling when I get a new negative for my archive that fills a gap, as I know many enthusiasts who collect photographs share the same sentiment.

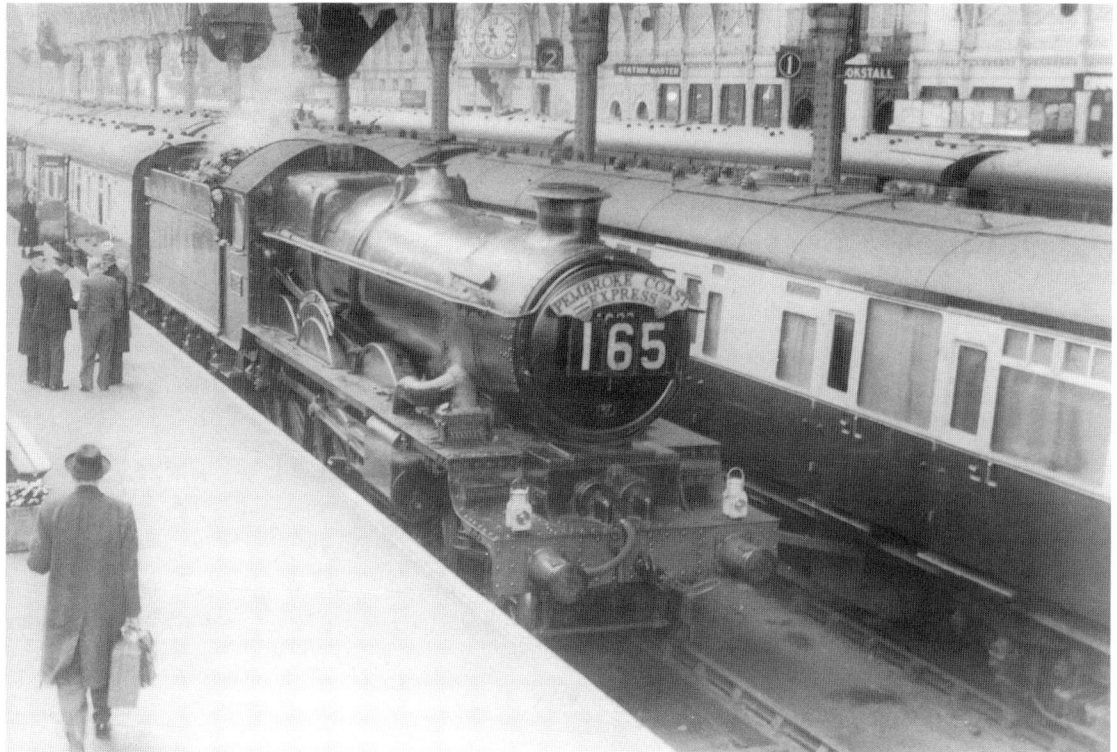

No. 4088 *Dartmouth Castle* on arrival at Paddington with the 'Pembroke Coast Express', July 1957.

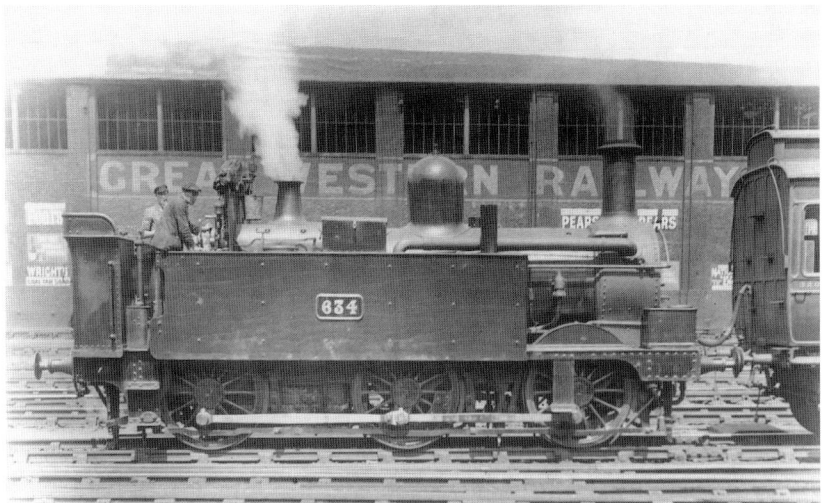

0–6–0T no. 634 was built by Armstrong in 1871. Its weight was around 38 tons but it had surprising power and was used on empty stock shunting at Paddington. It was scrapped in about 1930. This picture was taken in the early 1900s.

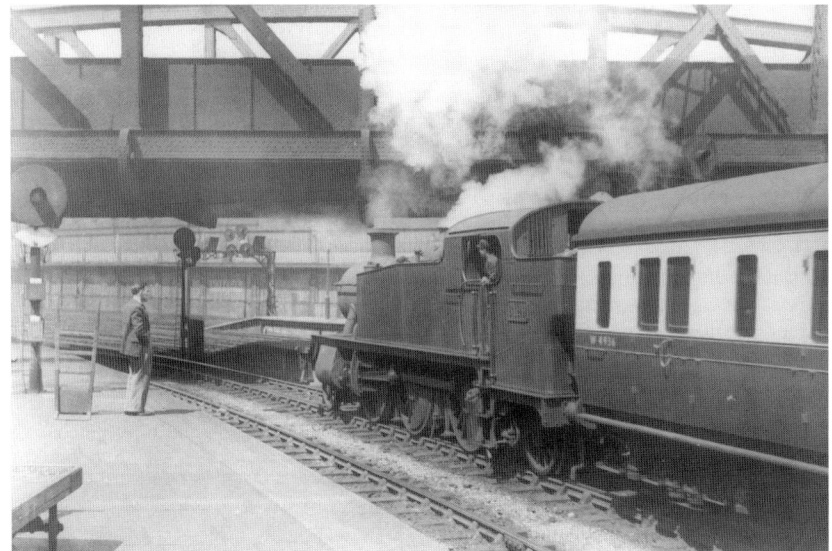

Prairie tank no. 6129 departs with a suburban train, possibly heading for Reading via Slough. These locos were very popular working local trains.

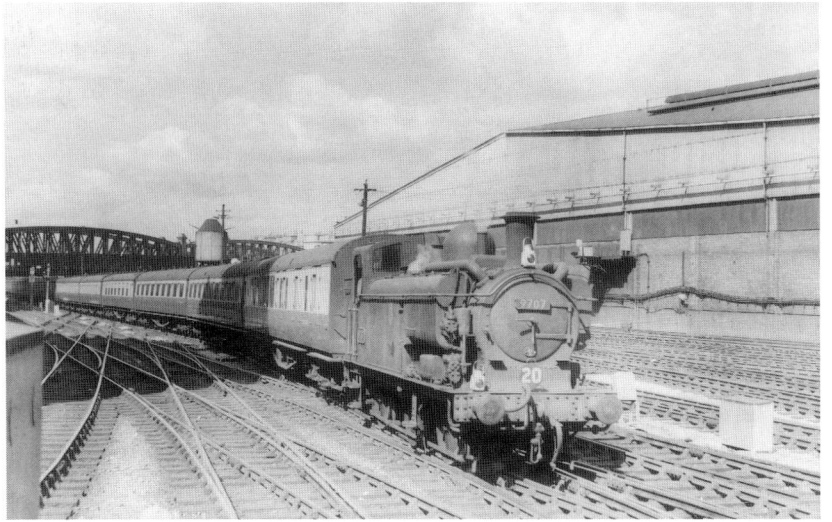

Another tank loco, this time one of a small number that were fitted with condensing apparatus for working through underground tunnels to Smithfield Market. This view is of no. 9707 bringing empty stock into Paddington.

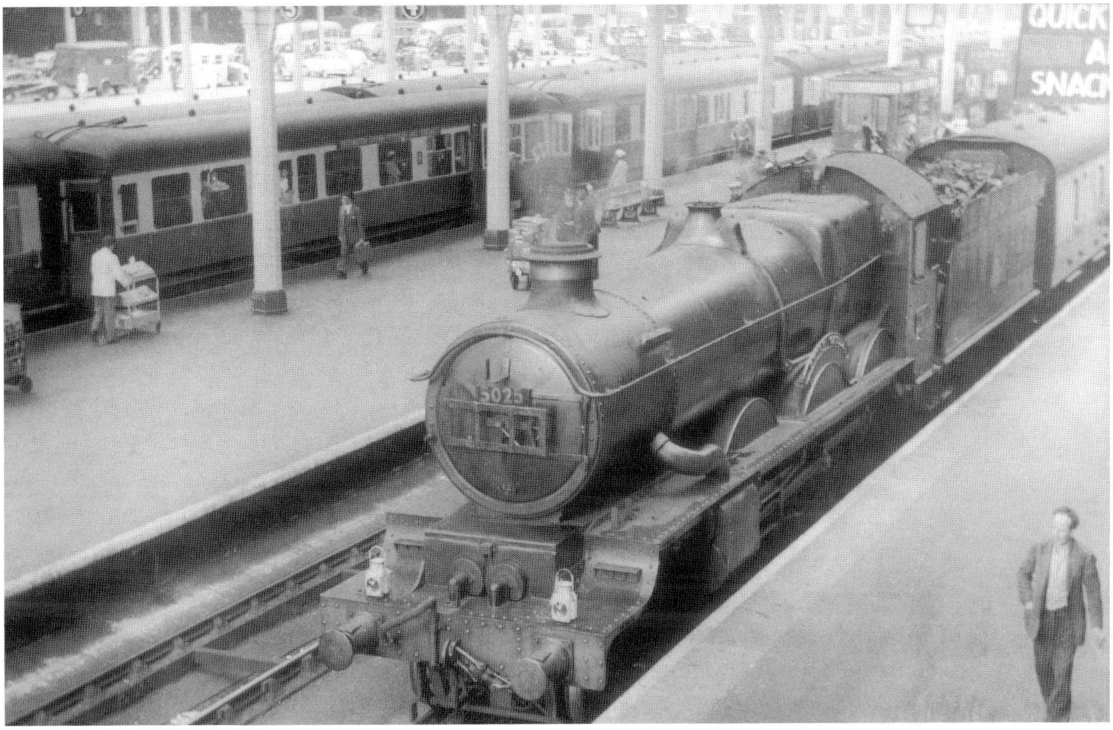

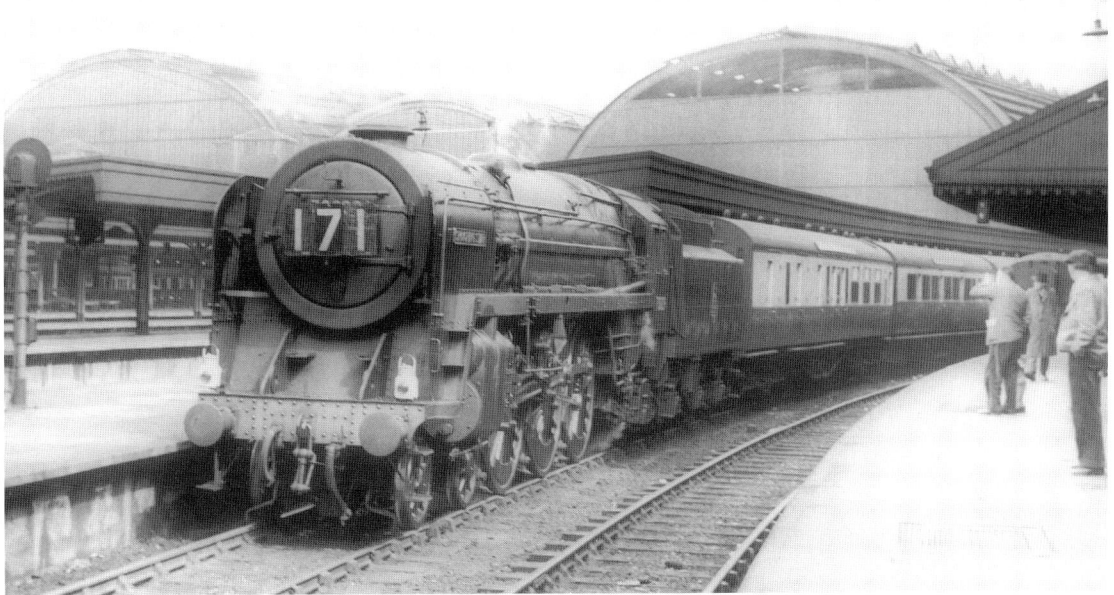

No. 5025 *Chirk Castle* has arrived with an express from the west, but without identification numbers. It would be a guess – a calculated guess on my part – that it was from South Wales, because I photographed it many times at one of my favourite locations, Patchway, near Bristol. The carriages in the background carry destination boards which read Paddington, Exeter, Plymouth and Penzance ,so let us get aboard and start our journey.

'Britannia' no. 70029 *Shooting Star* starts us on our journey. There is a slightly jerky motion in the carriages and the squeal of the wheels on the rails as they follow the curves out of Paddington. At this point if we look out of the left-hand window we will see Ranelagh Bridge.

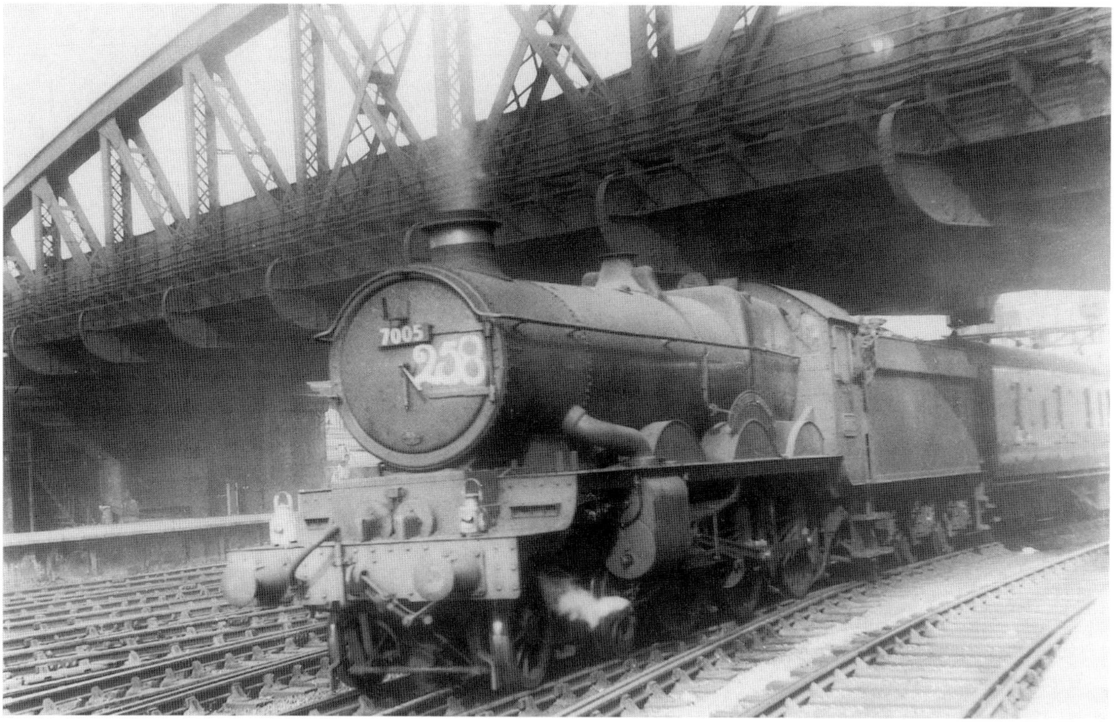

Shortly after departure we pass under the girder bridge which carries Bishop Road over the railway and which features in so many photographs taken at Paddington. Here no. 7005 *Lamphey Castle* departs with an express and a little further on we pass Ranelagh stabling point where locomotives were serviced, turned, and made ready for another duty. Below is a pre-war view of 'Bulldog' no. 3705 *Mauritius* with a pile of coal in the tender and the safety valve lifting gently. It is obviously ready to back down to Paddington, but not before the crew have smiled for the camera.

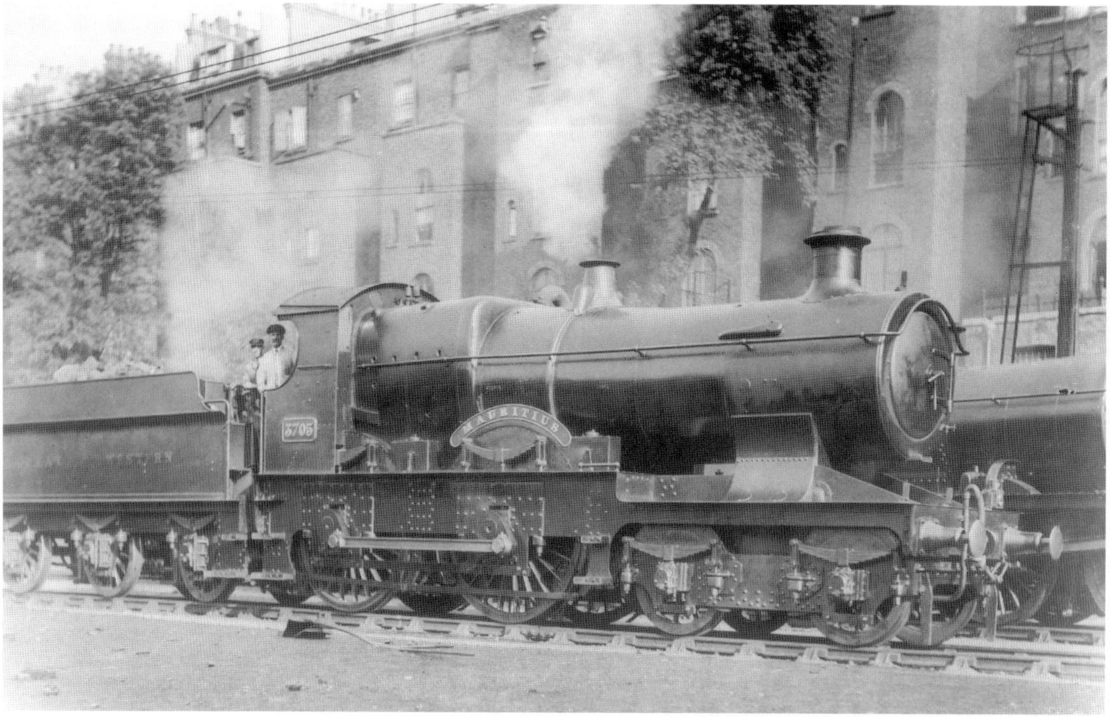

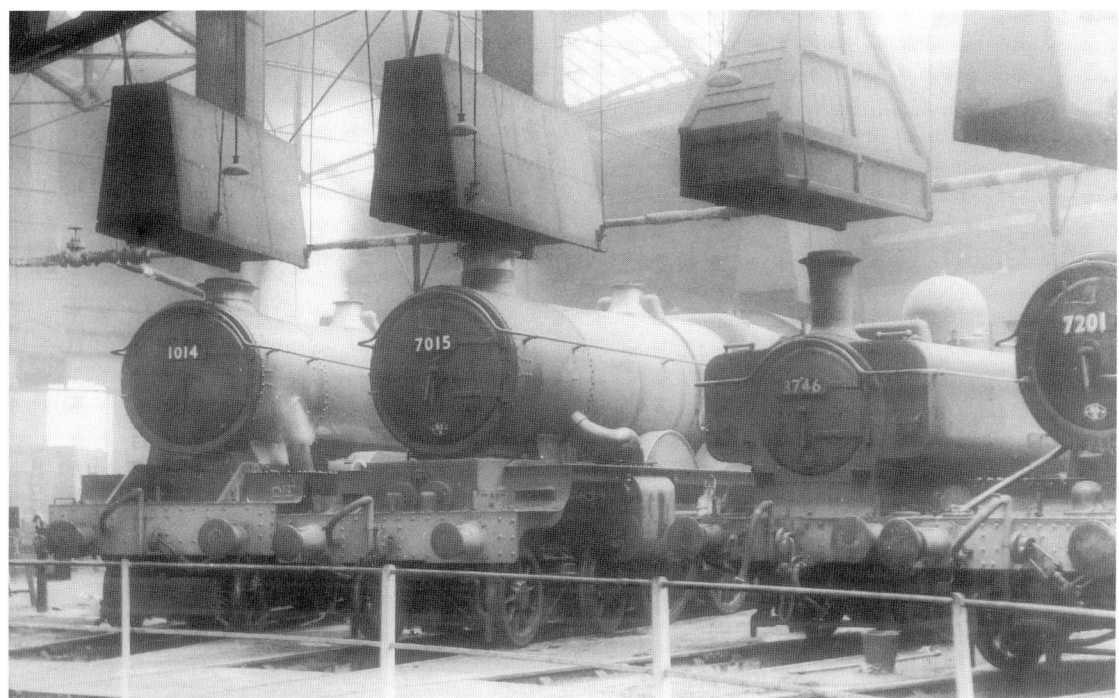

After Ranelagh speed starts to pick up, past all the houses whose windows look down on such a wonderful mainline. As an enthusiast who has looked out of the carriage window I dreamed of living in such a house, trainspotting from the comfort of my own room. No more frozen fingers hardly able to operate a camera, rain dripping down your neck, trying to keep camera and record books dry under your coat, and food, drink and home comforts when they are required. The irony of it is that most of those who live in what is an idyllic location to us probably curse the railways – constant noise, soot and cinders. Onward we go, the sound of the engine's exhaust bouncing back from these houses, past Royal Oak and Westbourne Park. Looking out of the window to the right we see the carriage sidings at Old Oak Common shed, home of many of the mighty 'Kings' and 'Castles'. Above, round the turntable, left to right in no. 1014 *County of Glamorgan*, no. 7015 *Carn Brea Castle*, pannier tanks nos 3746 and 7201 which have most likely worked a coal train from South Wales to Acton. Also in the roundhouse (below) is no. 4934 *Hindlip Hall*.

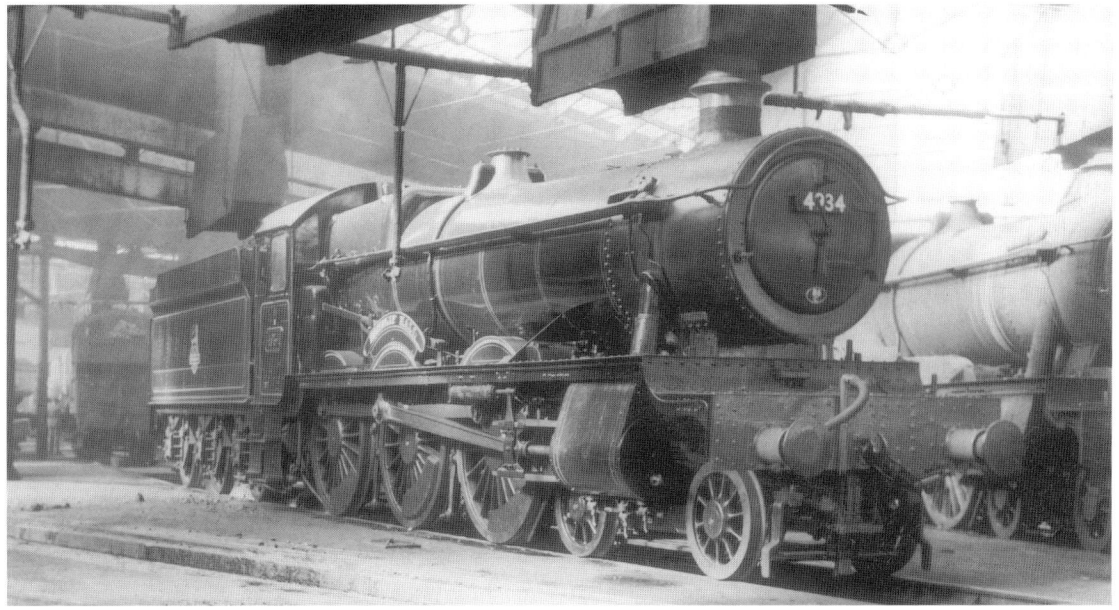

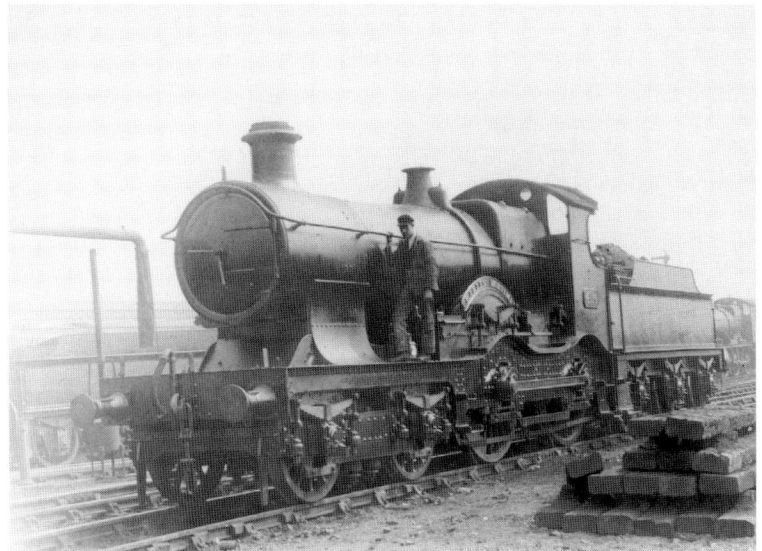

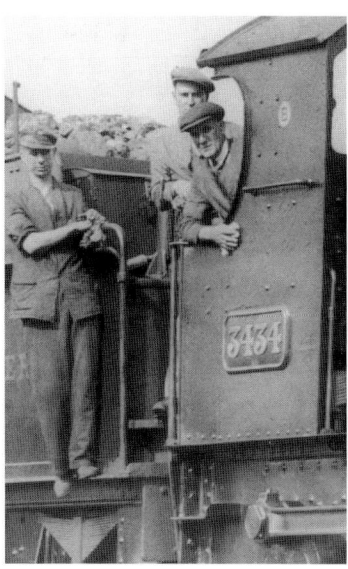

We are still at Old Oak Common, but we have now gone back in time. This view of 'Badminton' no. 4110 *Charles Mortimer* was taken in the early part of the 1900s. There is a pile of coal in the tender and the fireman is making the final checks so it must be ready to back down to Paddington.

The crew of 'Bulldog' no. 3434 *Joseph Shaw* pose for the camera.

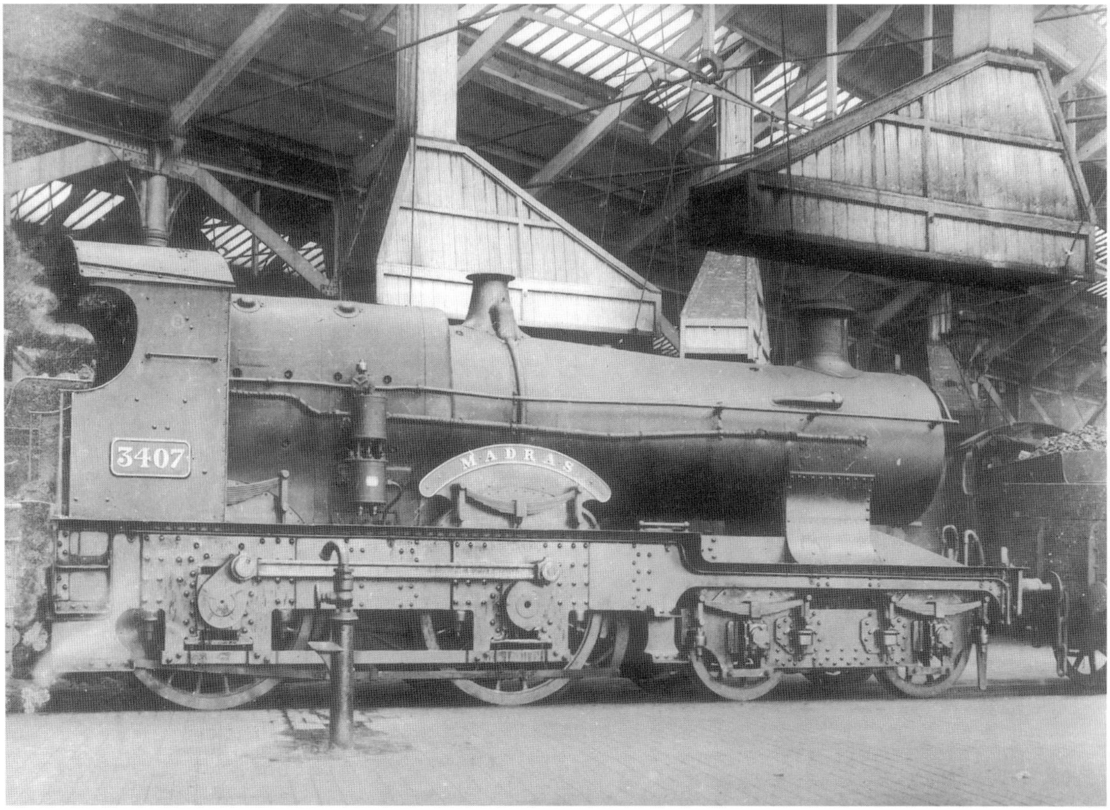

'Bulldog' no. 3407 *Madras* was a Didcot engine which saw an active life for many years until after the Second World War.

Back on our journey, we now leave the Bristol Line and head for Birmingham.
This was a great line for seeing 'Kings' and 'Castles' heading two-hour expresses.

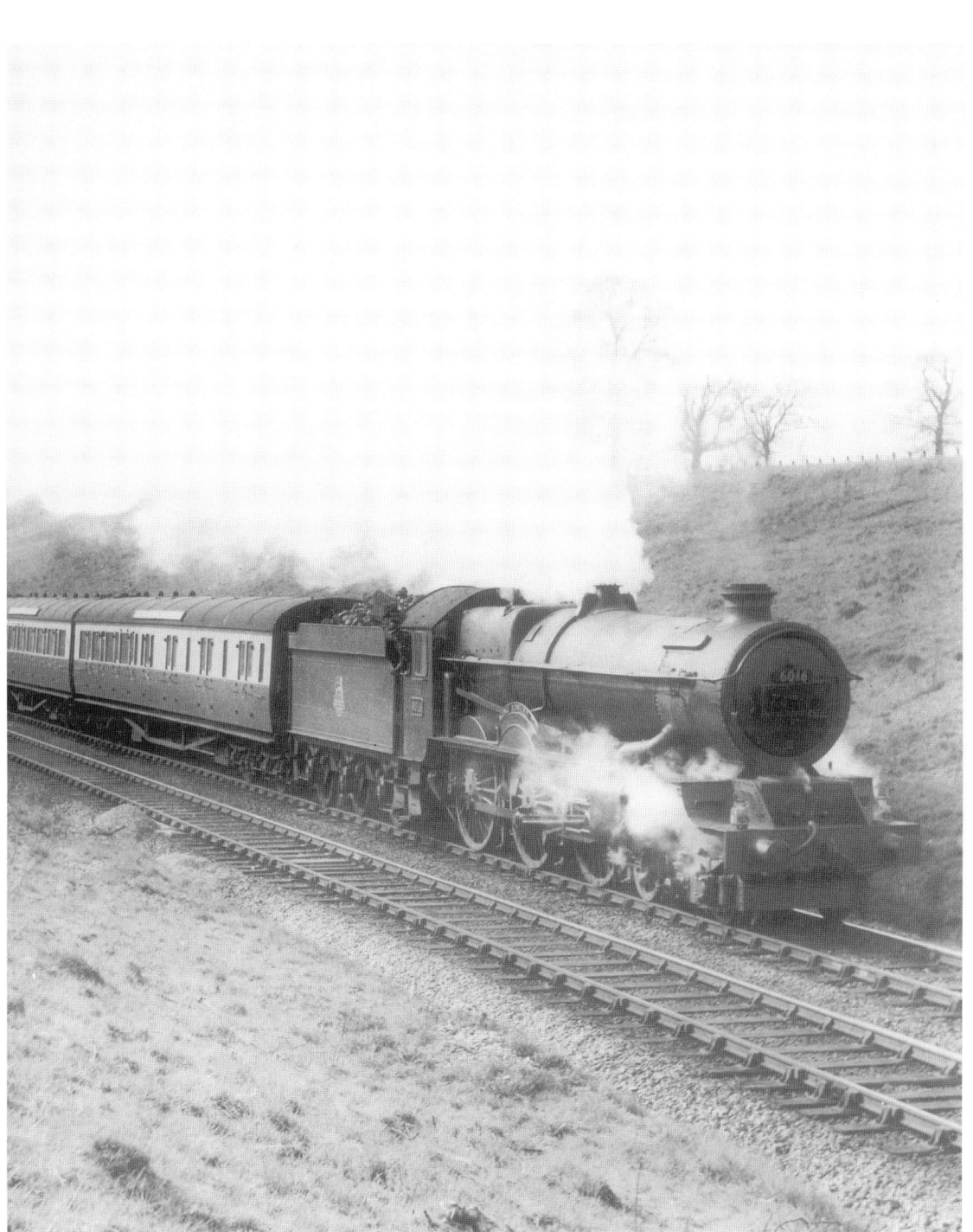

No. 6016 *King Edward V* shortly after leaving the West of England Main Line, with a Birkenhead train in the early 1950s.

We are picking up speed nicely now, past Brentham, Perivale and Greenford.
There is a junction at Greenford which goes south and joins the West of England at West Ealing,
on towards Birmingham again, through Northolt and South Ruislip. It is here that the
Metropolitan and Piccadilly goes under the main line and heads to Uxbridge.

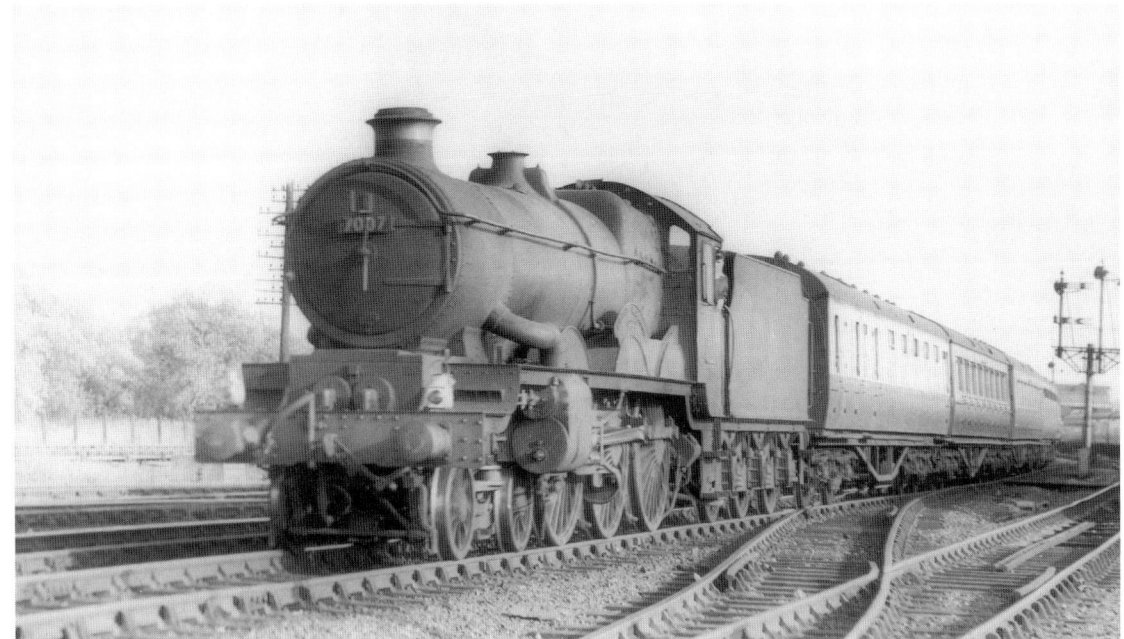

'Castle' class no. 7007 *Great Western* at speed near Greenford, August 1955.

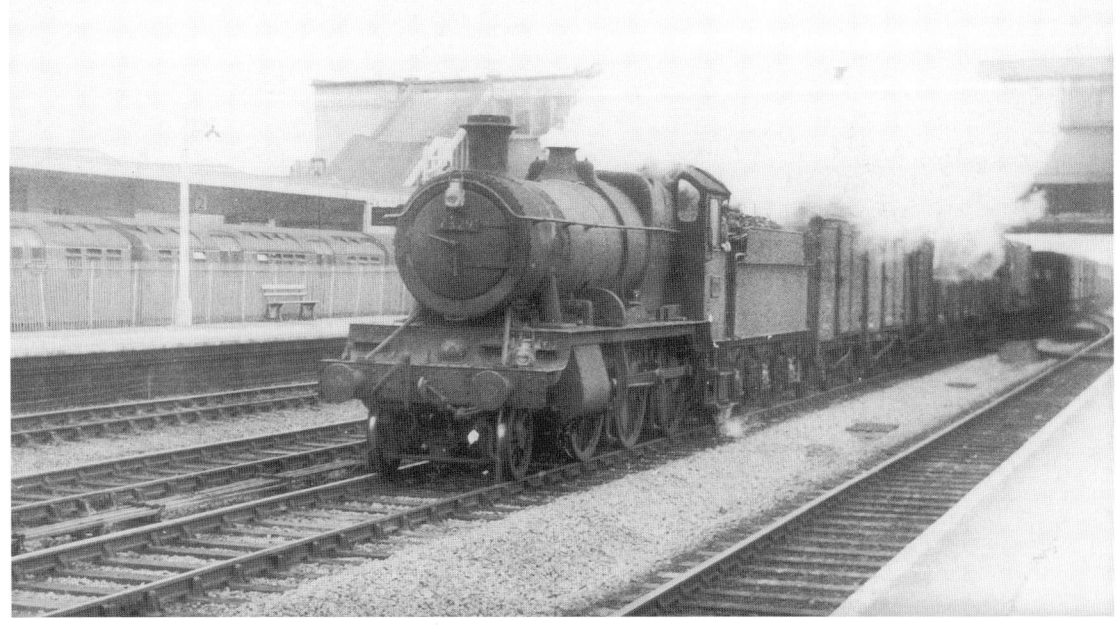

No. 7329 heads a freight working through Ruislip. In the background can be seen a Metropolitan and
Piccadilly train.

Through West Ruislip we come to a branch line to Uxbridge High Street. I have never been to Uxbridge, and looking at a railway map it appears to be a terminus. A short distance away seems to be another terminus, Uxbridge Vine Street. Both stations are listed as Great Western, so either the map is wrong or the Great Western had some reason to build two stations and break a line from the Birmingham Mainline to the West of England Mainline – perhaps a reader knows the answer? The next location is Denham, a popular spot for photographers.

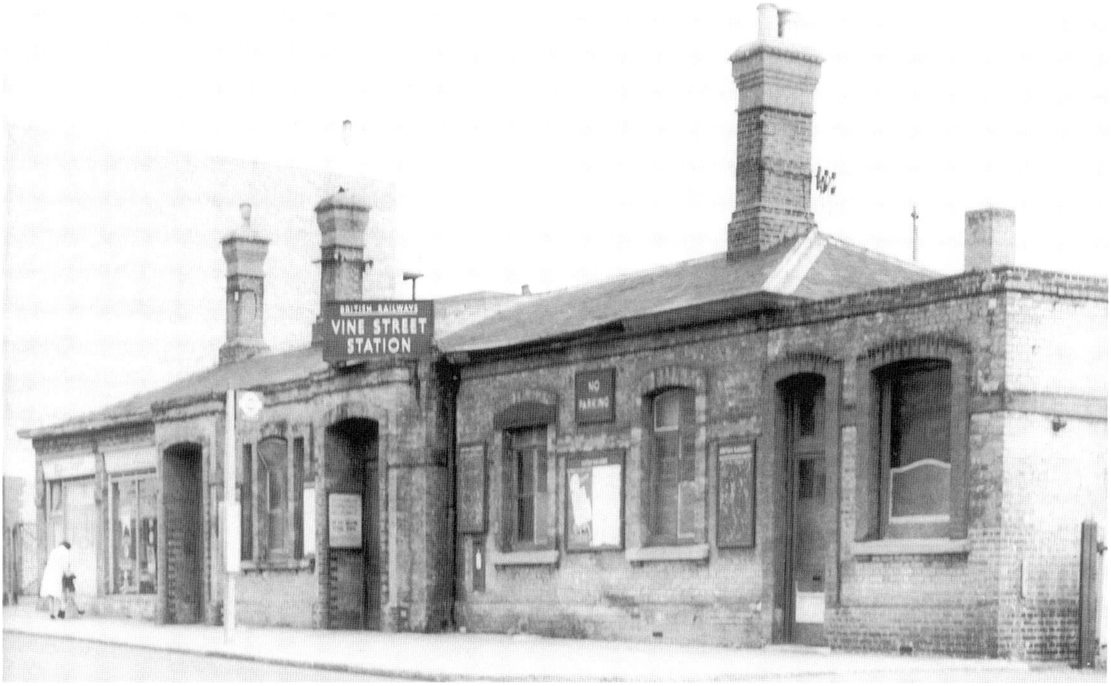

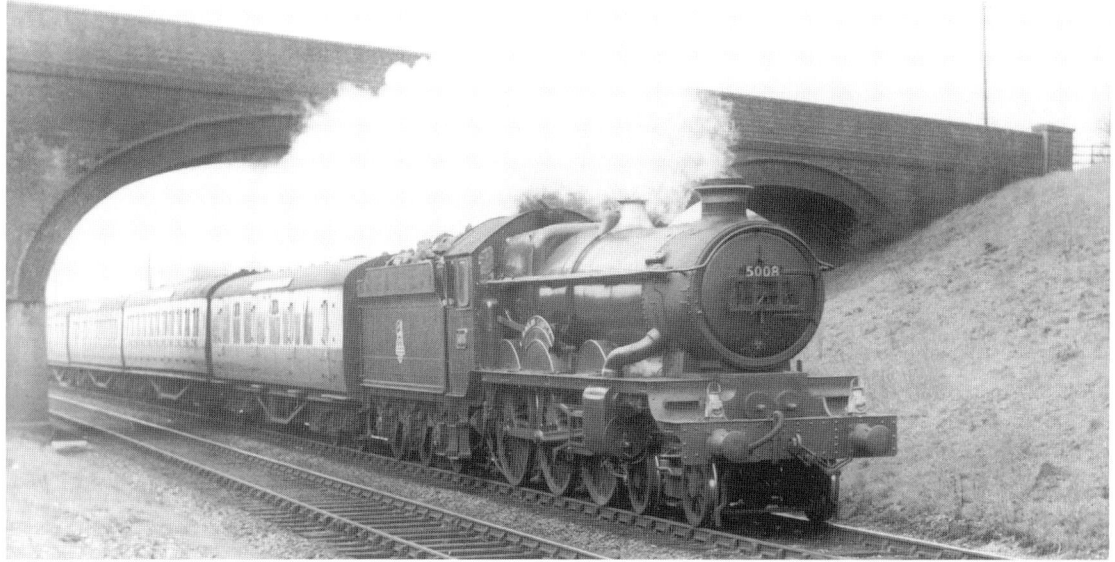

Uxbridge Vine Street station in the 1950s.

No. 5008 *Raglan Castle* at Denham with an express for Birmingham in the mid-1950s.

Our journey continues through Denham to Gerrard's Cross, Seer Green, Beaconsfield, and just before High Wycombe another junction that went south through Loudwater, Bourne End and on to join the West of England Mainline at Maidenhead. We then travel into High Wycombe.

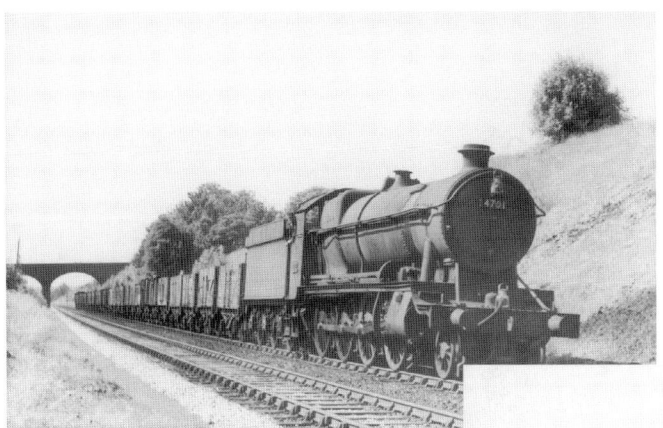

No. 4701, one of Churchwards massive 2–8–0 mixed traffic locos built for working heavy freight, but equally at home on express passenger workings, is photographed at Seer Green in 1953.

Pannier tank no. 5424 arriving at High Wycombe. It carries an 84C shedplate which denotes Banbury, so it seems to be a long way from its home in this 1953 view.

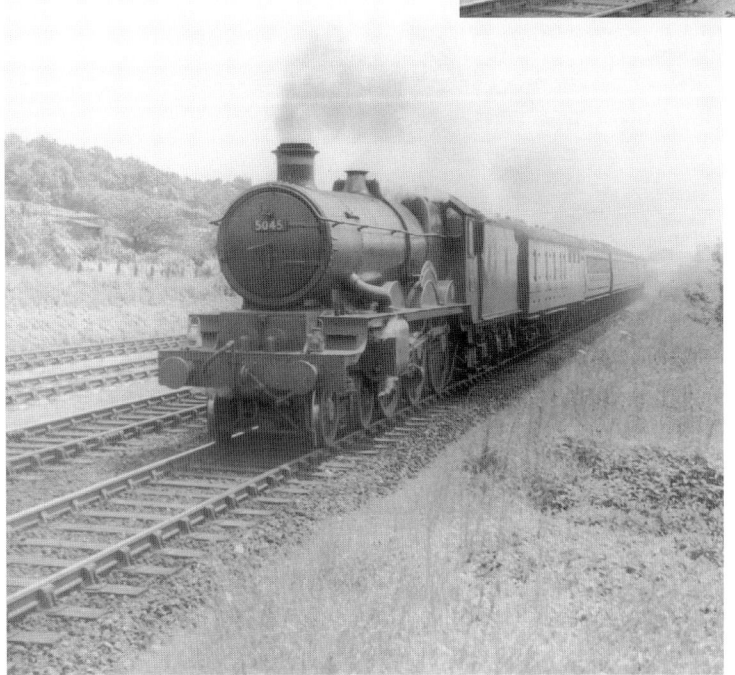

No. 5045 *Earl of Dudley* near High Wycombe. An appropriately named engine to be heading an express to Birmingham.

Next comes West Wycombe, then Saunderton and into Princes Risborough. I remember listening to recordings of 'Castles' and 'Kings' at this well known location. There is also a branch to Watlington, passing through Chinnor and just past this branch the main line continues to Oxford.

No. 6159 leaving West Wycombe in 1955.

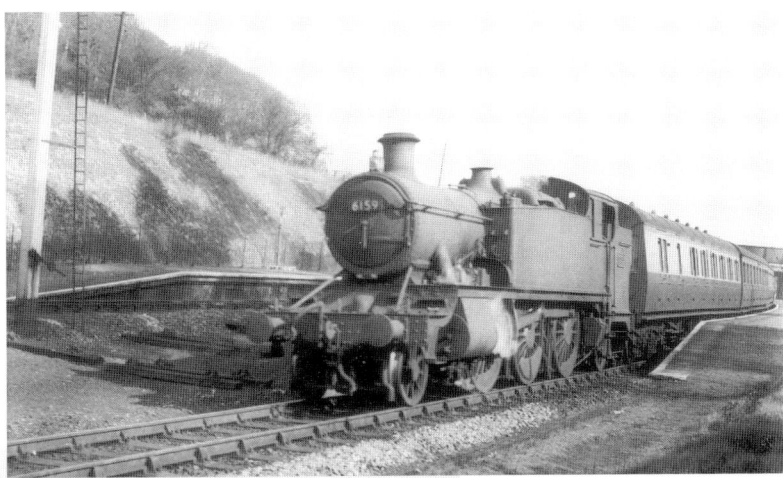

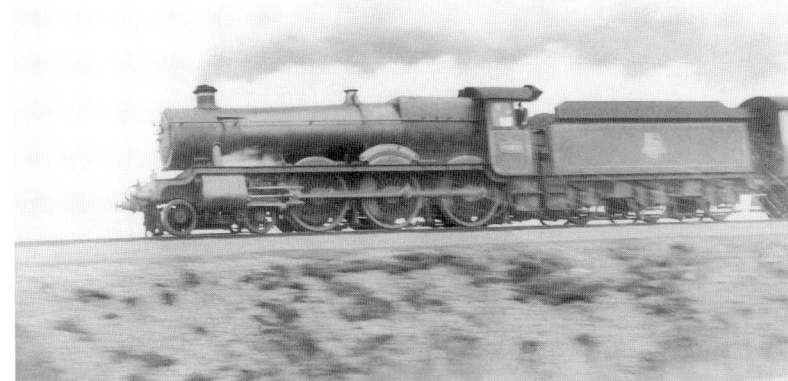

No. 4967 *Shirenewton Hall* near Princes Risborough.

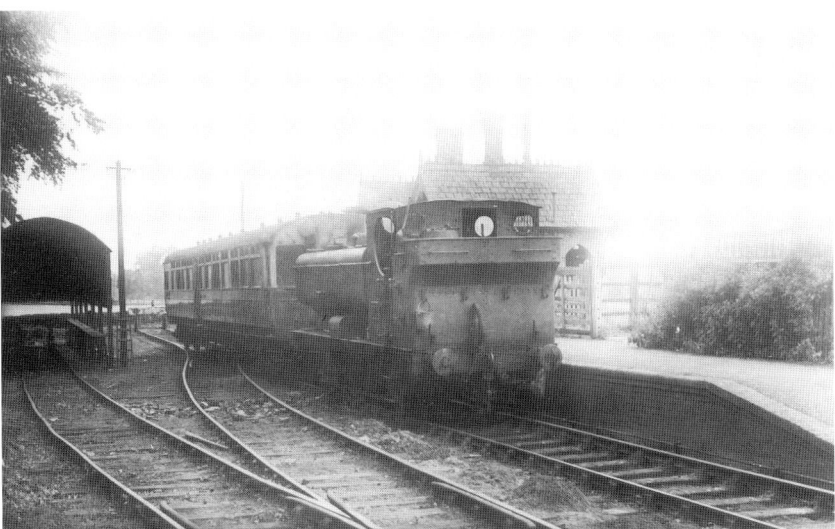

Watlington station opened in the 1870s and it survived for early ninety years, finally closing in 1957.

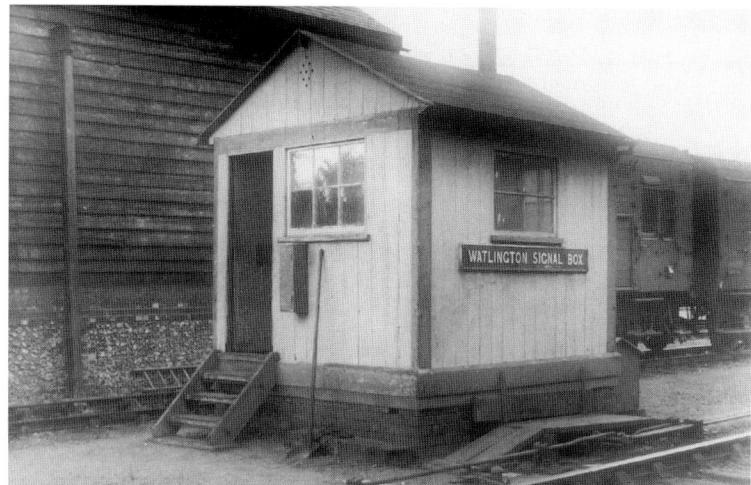

Watlington signal-box is not much bigger than a garden shed. There could not have been many levers, although there is a chimney. One can assume from the fact that the cabin is kept warm that there must have been a resident signalman, or possibly a signalman-porter. Both these views were taken in about 1950.

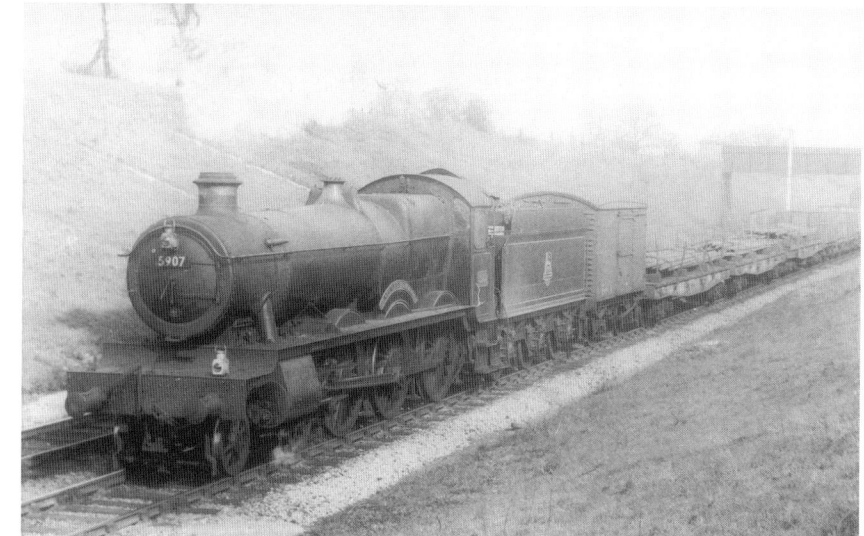

Leaving Princes Risborough on time, we are making good progress on our journey, through Haddenham, Wotton, Rill, and now Bicester. It is here that the main line to Birmingham crosses the Oxford Bletchley line. The first view is of no. 5907 *Marble Hall* with a mixed freight somewhere between Princes Risborough and Wotton, 1953.
The lower picture is of no. 5985 *Mostyn Hall* in the Bicester area. I am sorry information is a little sketchy on a lot of of the views on the Birmingham Line. I received the negatives from a elderly gentleman with very limited details, and before I could gain more, he sadly passed away.

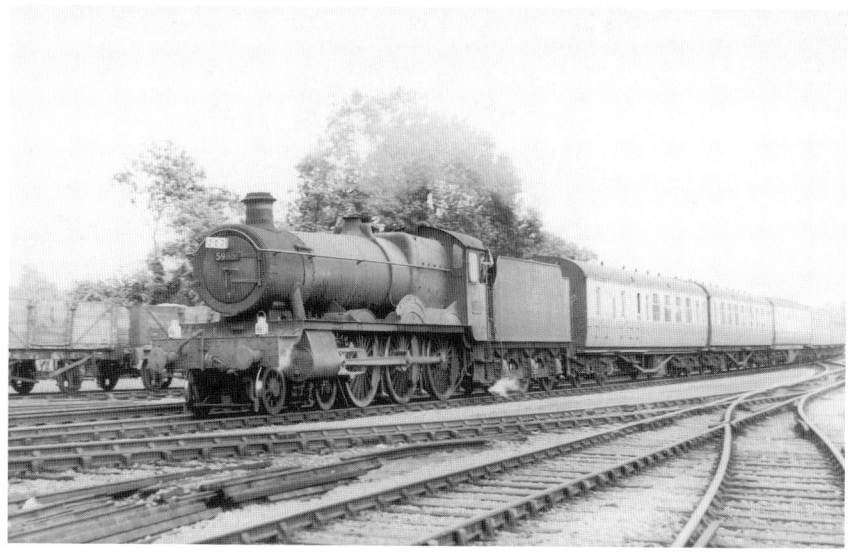

We are speeding along nicely now, first to Ardley and then Aynho Junction. This is where we join the line that comes up from Oxford and further on comes King's Sutton.

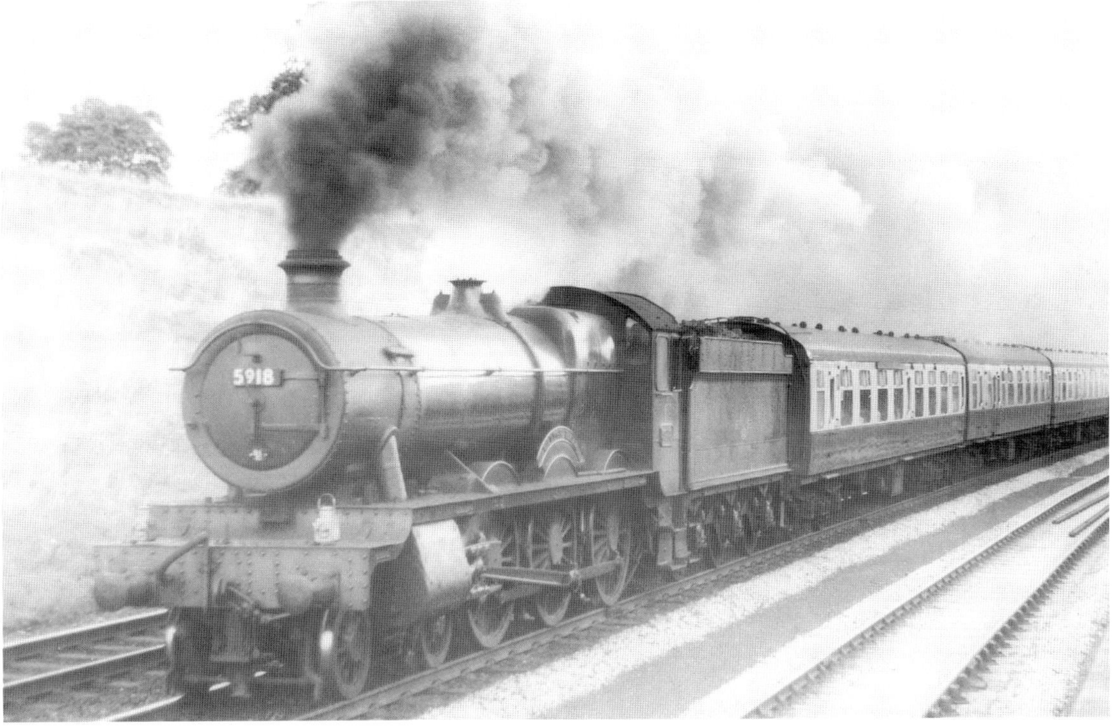

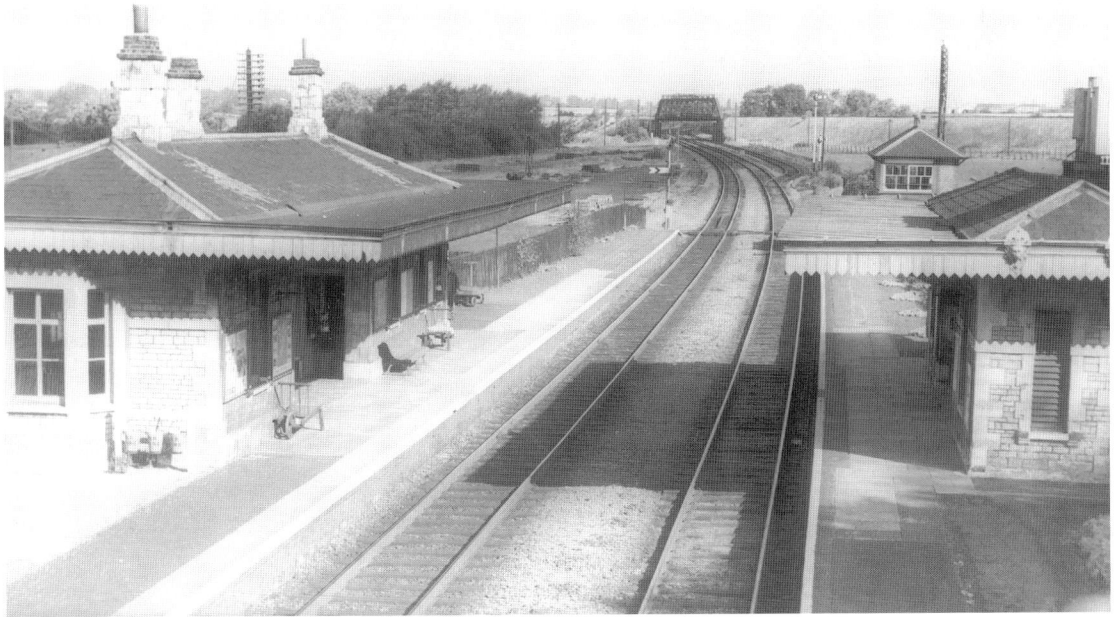

No. 5918 *Walton Hall* near Aynho.

Aynho Junction picutured in the 1950s.

King's Sutton is where we will make a diversion onto the main line that branches from the Birmingham line, and will take us to Stratford-upon-Avon, Cheltenham, Gloucester and into the beautiful Cotswolds. We could spend a long time in this lovely part of the world, but it must be short visit or we shall never finish our journey. It won't be a high-speed run, but a steady rural pace through lovely scenery, passing through a number of stations, including Chipping Norton. We then arrive at Kingham Junction where we will head north for Stratford-upon-Avon, or south to the Cotswolds.

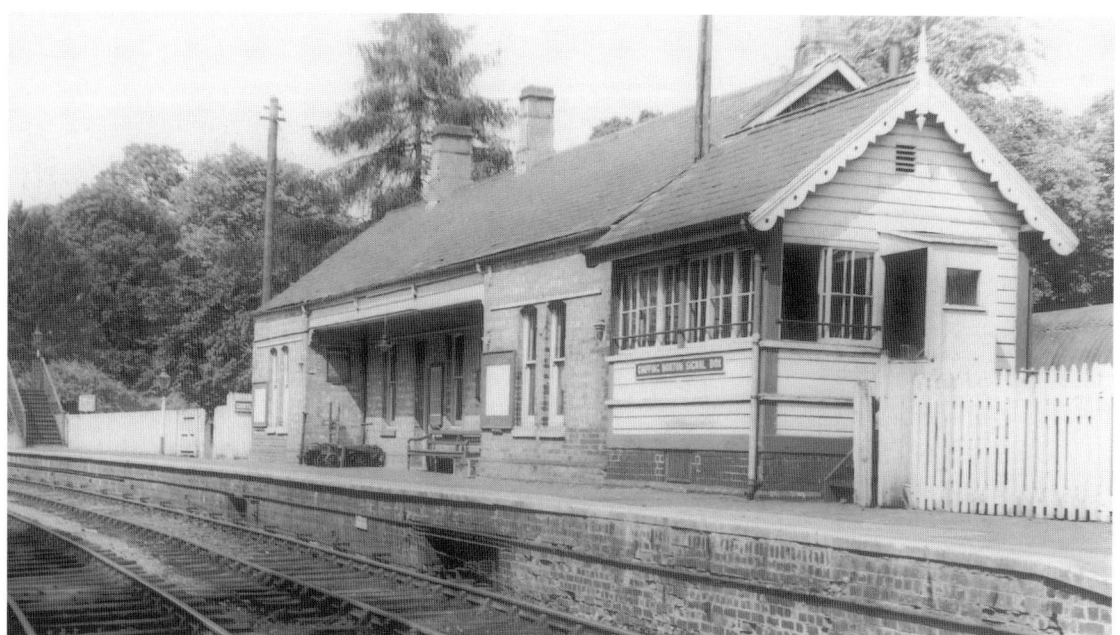

Chipping Norton station.

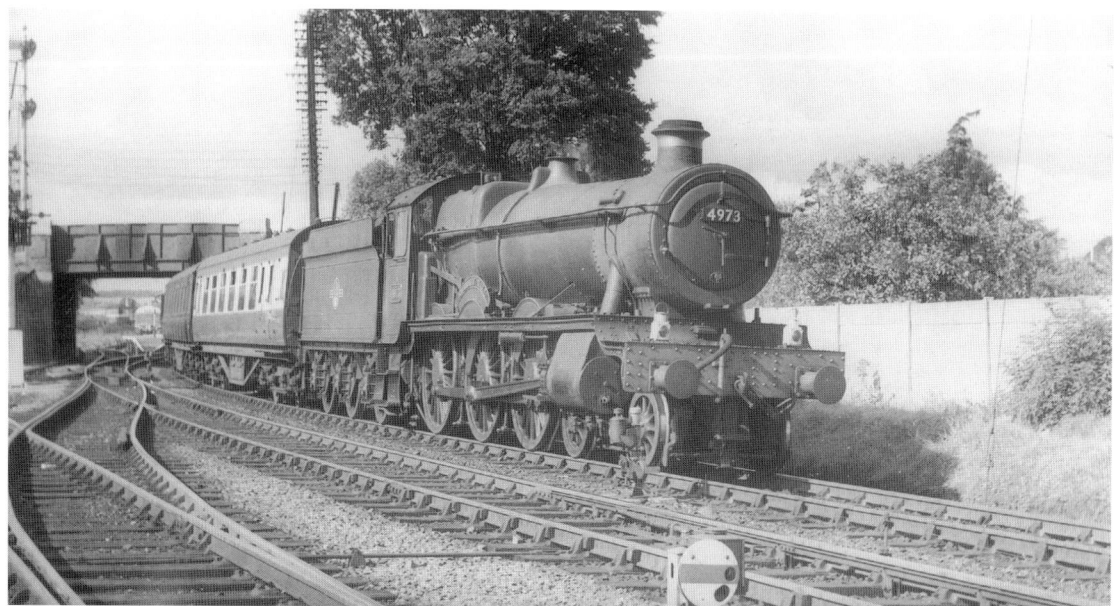

No. 4973 *Sweeney Hall* at Stratford-upon-Avon in 1958.

On leaving Stratford-upon-Avon we take the direct route to Cheltenham passing through Broadway and Toddington to name but two of the stations on this route. We arrive at the spa town of Cheltenham, which was important to the railway enthusiast because at one time it had the world's fastest train leaving here for Paddington – 'The Cheltenham Flyer'.
From Cheltenham to Swindon it was fairly fast, but from Swindon to Paddington it truly lived up to its name. It was recorded as covering the 77 miles from Swindon to the capital at the incredible average of 81 mph. There was nearly always a 'Castle' in charge.

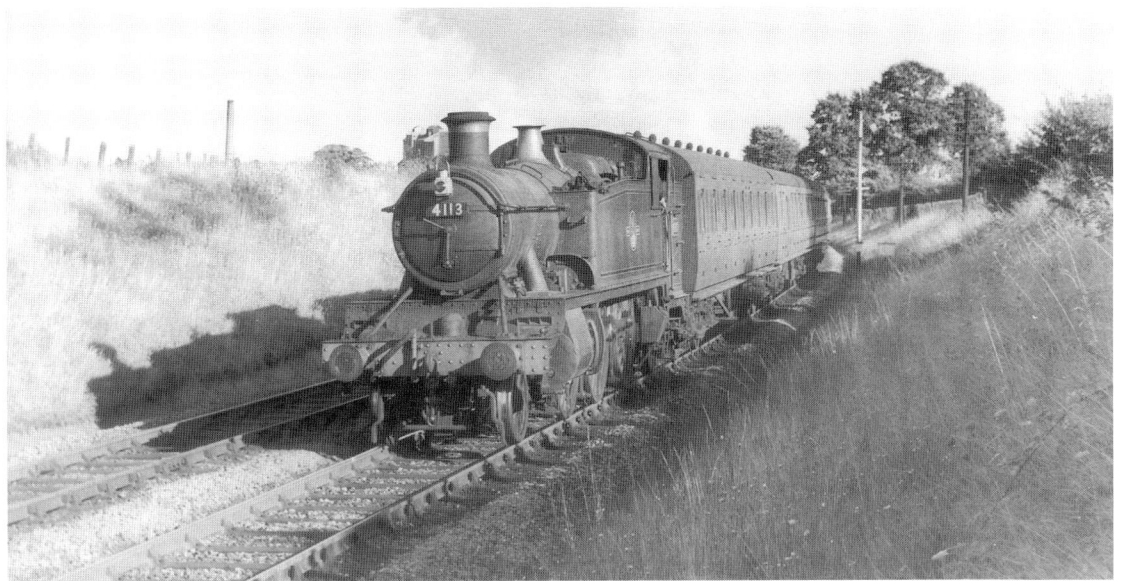

No. 4113 on the Stratford–Cheltenham line with a local stopping train in the late 1950s.

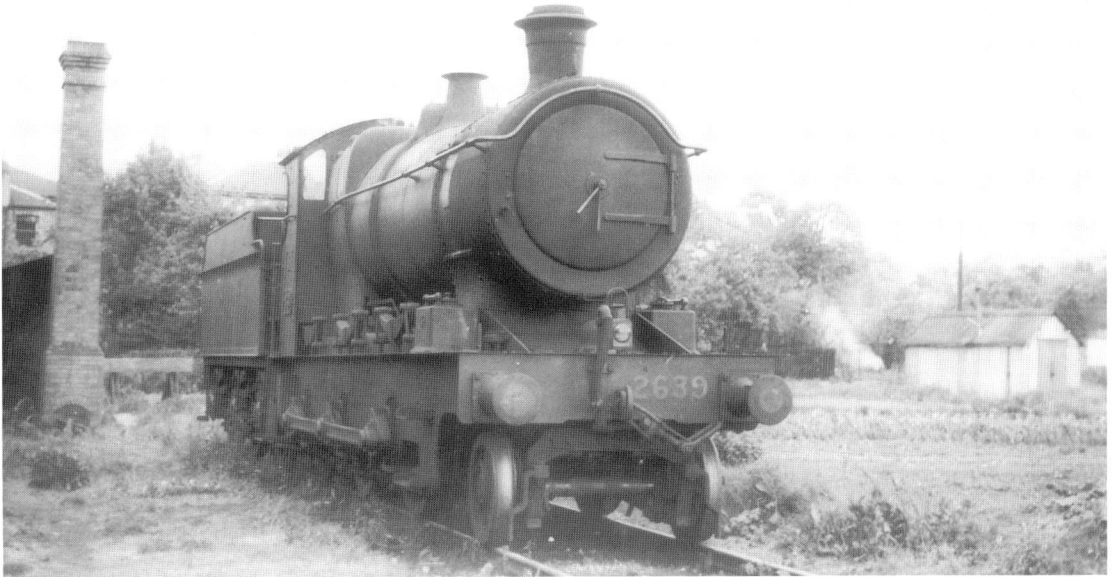

In the 1930s no. 2639 *Aberdare* had failed at Cheltenham and appears to have been put out in the fields to the back of Cheltenham shed.

From Cheltenham to Gloucester the Western and Midland region share the track, diverging to their separate stations at Tramway Junction, the Midland to Eastgate, the Western to Central.

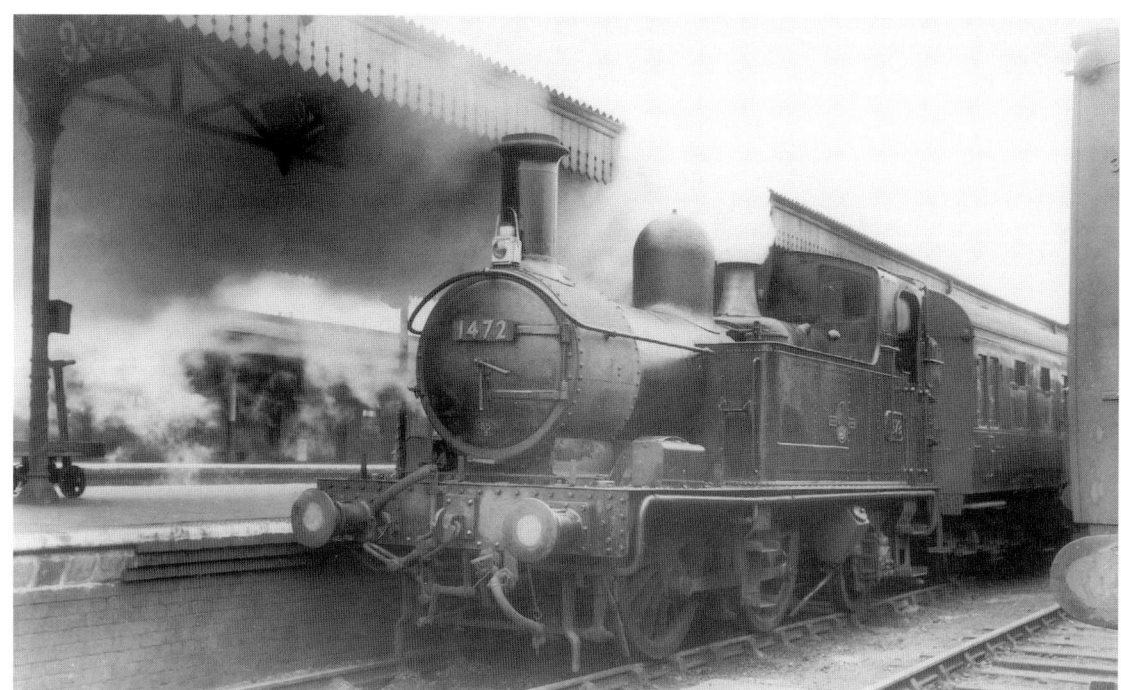

0–4–2T no. 1472 prepares to leave Gloucester Central with a local to Stroud, 1960.

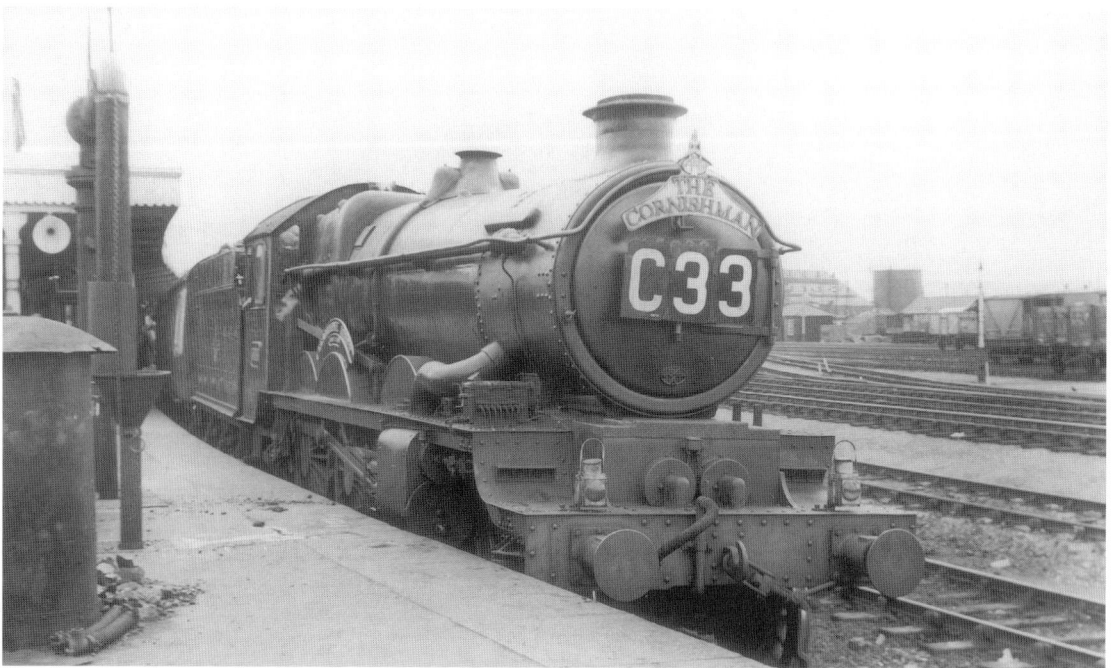

'Castle' class no. 5088 *Llanthony Abbey* with 'The Cornishman' at Eastgate station, 1960. It will use the Midland Line to Bristol from here.

We must hurry back to the main line to Birmingham, as we have a lot of track to cover. We rejoin it at King's Sutton. The next stations we will stop at are Banbury and then Leamington.

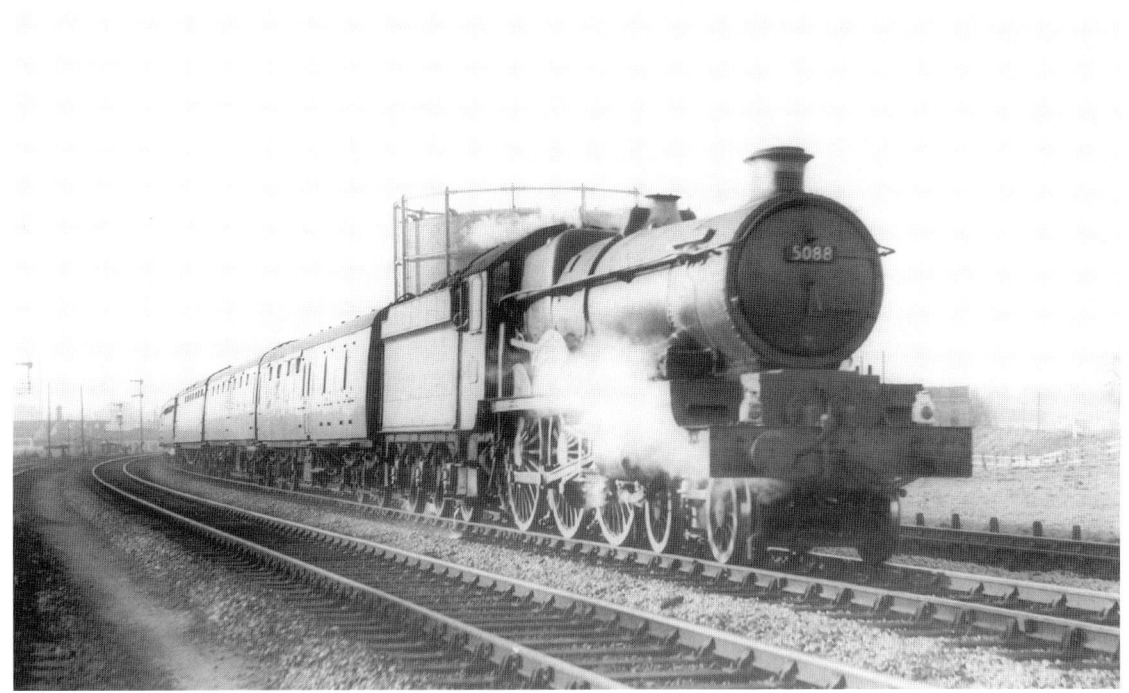

Another view of 'Castle' no. 5088 *Llanthony Abbey*, this time leaving Banbury in 1959.

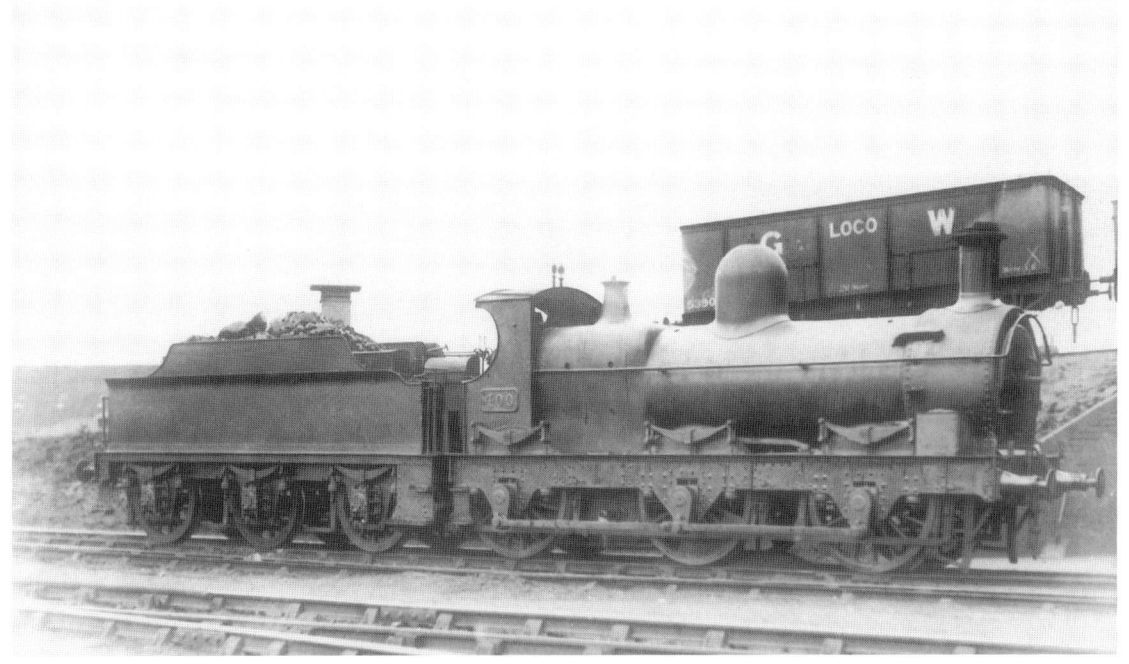

A much earlier view at Leamington 0–6–0 outside crank, GWR 400, on shed in the early 1930s.

We are now approaching Warwick and will soon be into the suburbs of Birmingham. Just before Warwick we run close to the LMS line from Warwick Milverton to Rugby, not much further we pass Hatton and then Lapworth. There are many branch lines and other main lines that we could explore but we cannot spare the time, so we will continue to Snow Hill.

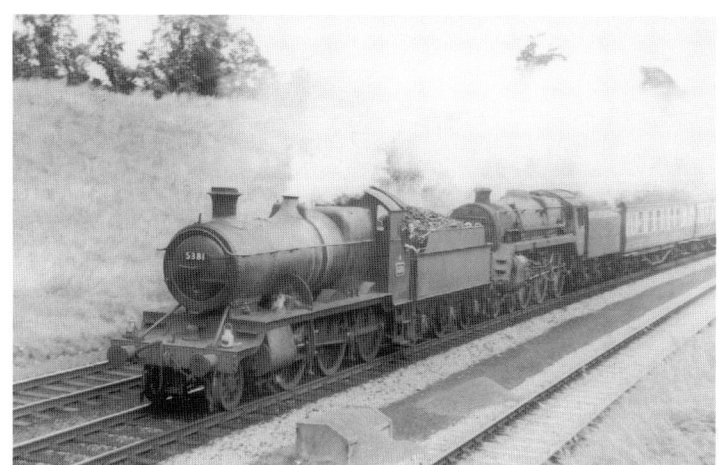

No. 5381, a 2–6–0 'Mogul' double-headed with a 'Standard' 4–6–0 in 1959.

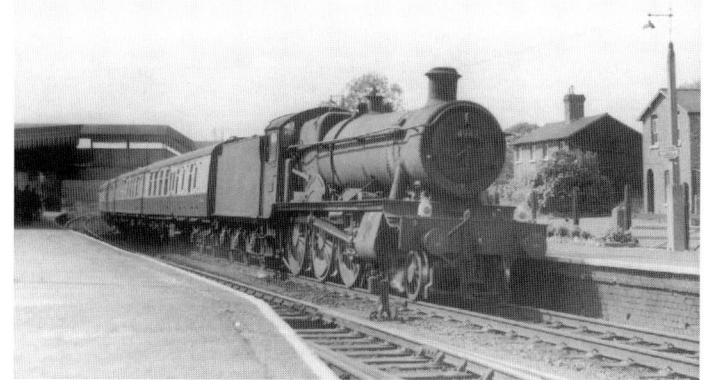

This photograph of no. 4942 *Maindy Hall* was taken at Hatton in the 1950s.

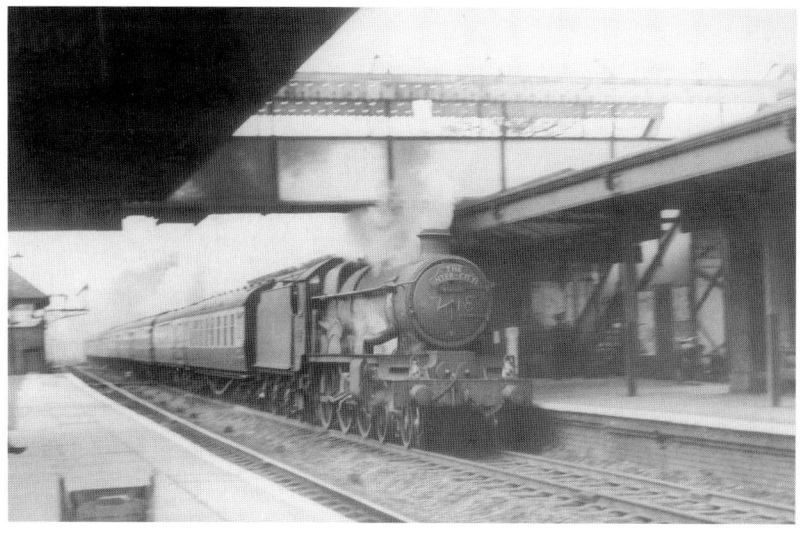

'The Inter City' with no. 4089 *Donnington Castle* at its head, roars through Lapworth in 19

After Lapworth comes Knowle and Dorridge. The scenery is certainly changing now, and there are far more signs of civilisation. We shall be passing through Solihull, Acocks Green and then Tyseley.

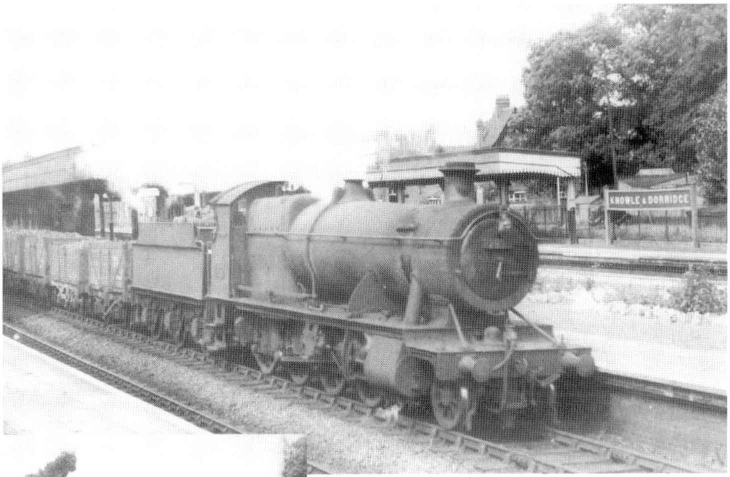

Churchwards powerful 2–8–0 no. 2833 is seen hereworking its way through Knowle and Dorridge in 1951.

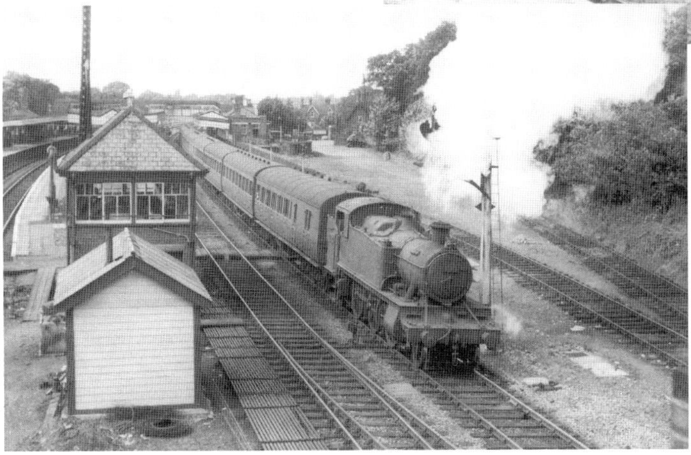

A local stopping train headed by no. 4119 leaves Knowle and Dorridge, 1953.

A rare picture in my archive, a Great Western loco showing black smoke. Either there was an inexperienced fireman on board or they had been given some real rubbish to put in the firebox! No. 2830 is the loco struggling near Solihull.

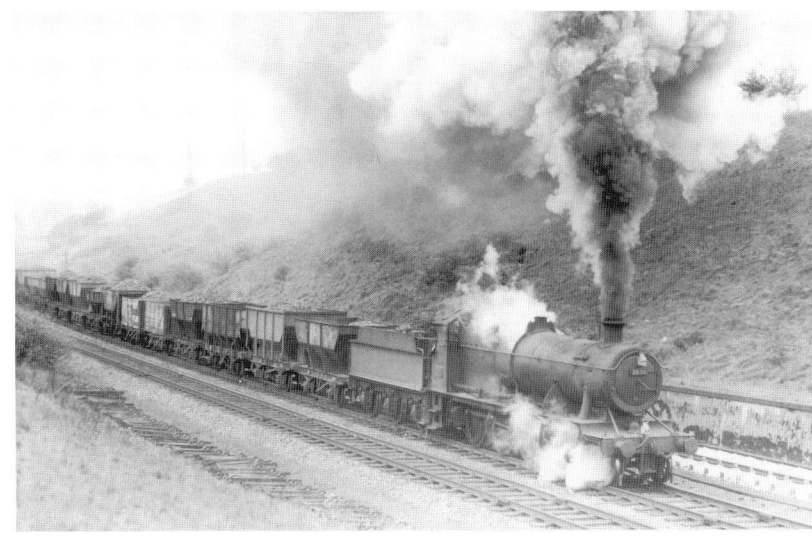

Leaving Tyseley we continue on through Small Heath. We know we are in the city now as there are houses on all sides. Now comes Bordesley and we pass the small spur to Moor Street terminus, through the smoke-filled tunnel and into Snow Hill.

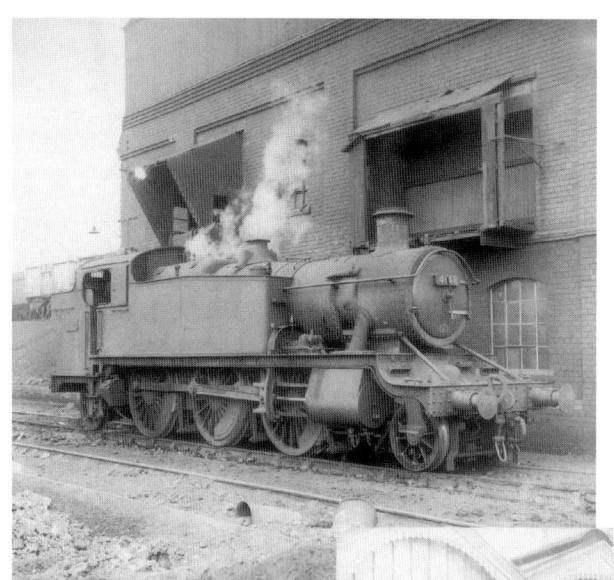

A 2–6–2T Prairie tank no. 4148 being called on Tyseley depot.

At Moor Street, no. 6694, an 0–6–2T used mainly on freight, seems to be carrying an express passenger headlamp code, I wonder why?

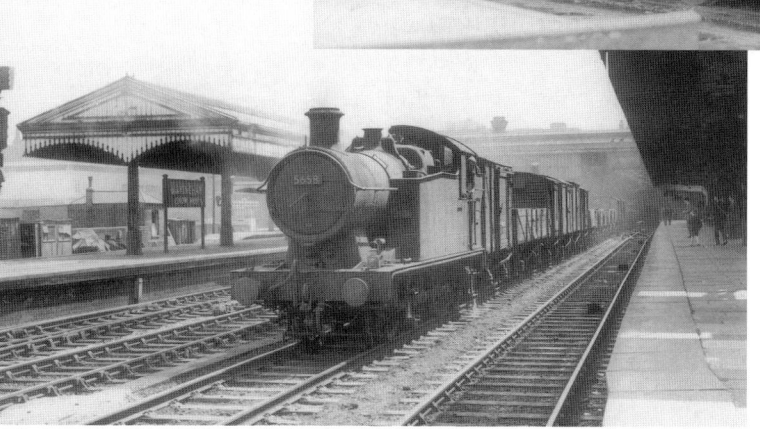

No. 5658 passing through Snow Hill in 1955.

This is the view all railway enthusiasts who visited Snow Hill in steam days wanted to see: the mighty 'Kings'. The platform end would be crowded with spotters and enthusiasts with cameras. This was in the days when porters and managers would pass the time of day with us. They probably couldn't understand why we crowded there, sometimes in the bitter cold, pouring rain or boiling heat, but they didn't mind our presence; not like staff today who think it's a criminal offence to want to photograph trains. Here no. 6006 *King George I* arrives at Snow Hill with a train for London in 1953.

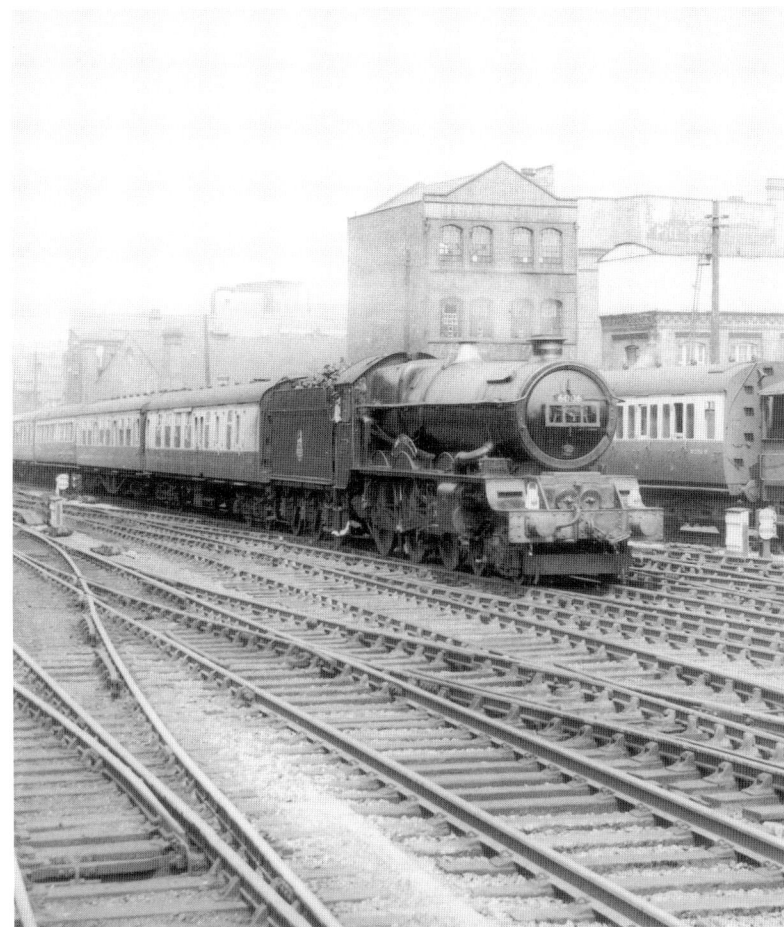

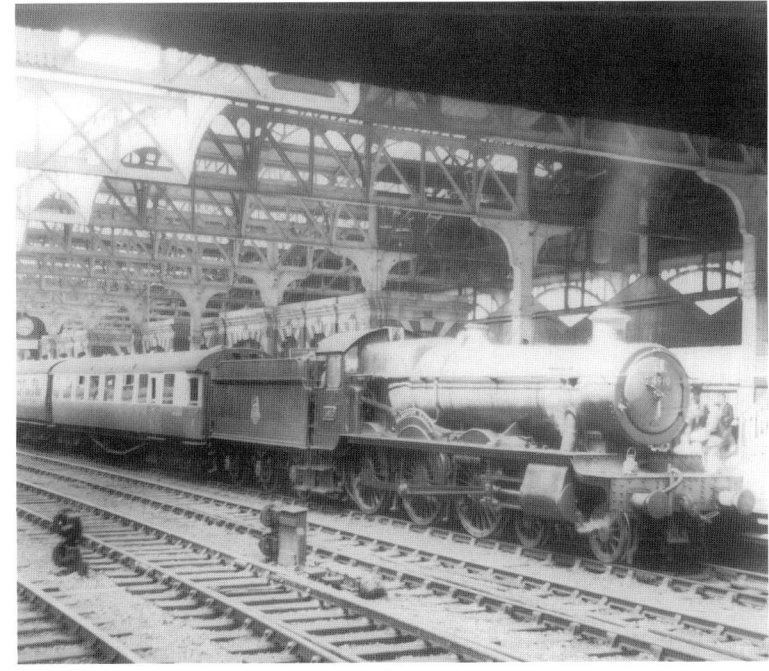

Arriving in Snow Hill is no. 4910 *Blaisdon Hall*, 1954. It could be a difficult station to take photographs at if the sun was bright, as can be seen in this photograph where the sun is catching the top of the boiler.

Leaving Snow Hill we make our way to Wolverhampton. As would be expected in a city the size of Birmingham there are a mass of lines, freight and passenger, far too numerous to go into on our journey, but mention can be made of the few stations we pass through. The first after Snow Hill is Hockley, then Handsworth, West Bromwich and into Wolverhampton.

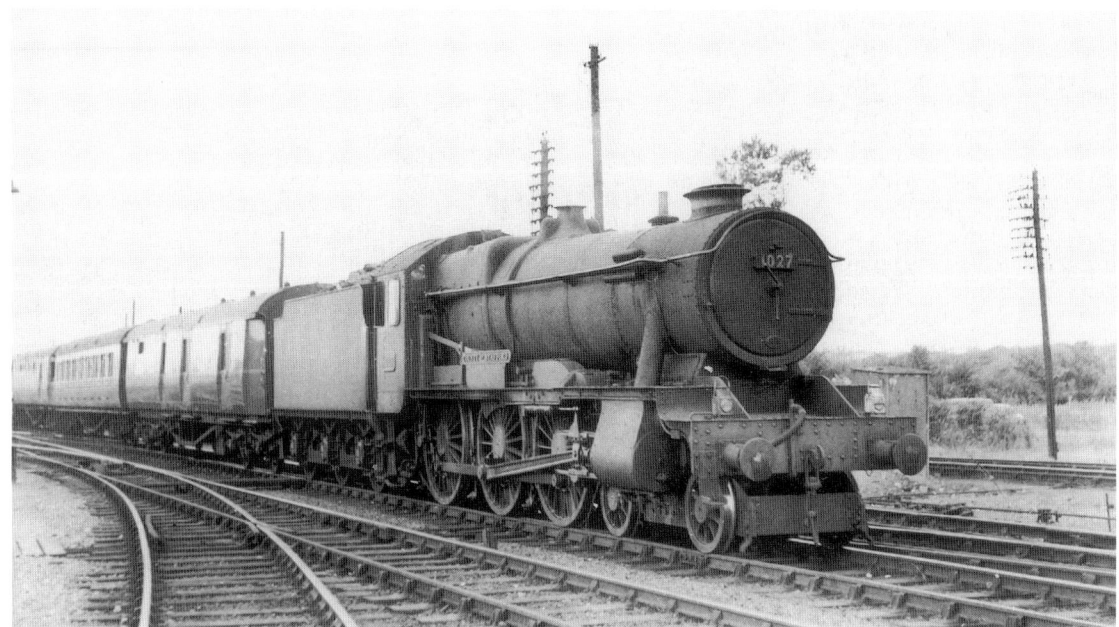

No. 1027 *County of Stafford* near Wolverhampton, 1955.

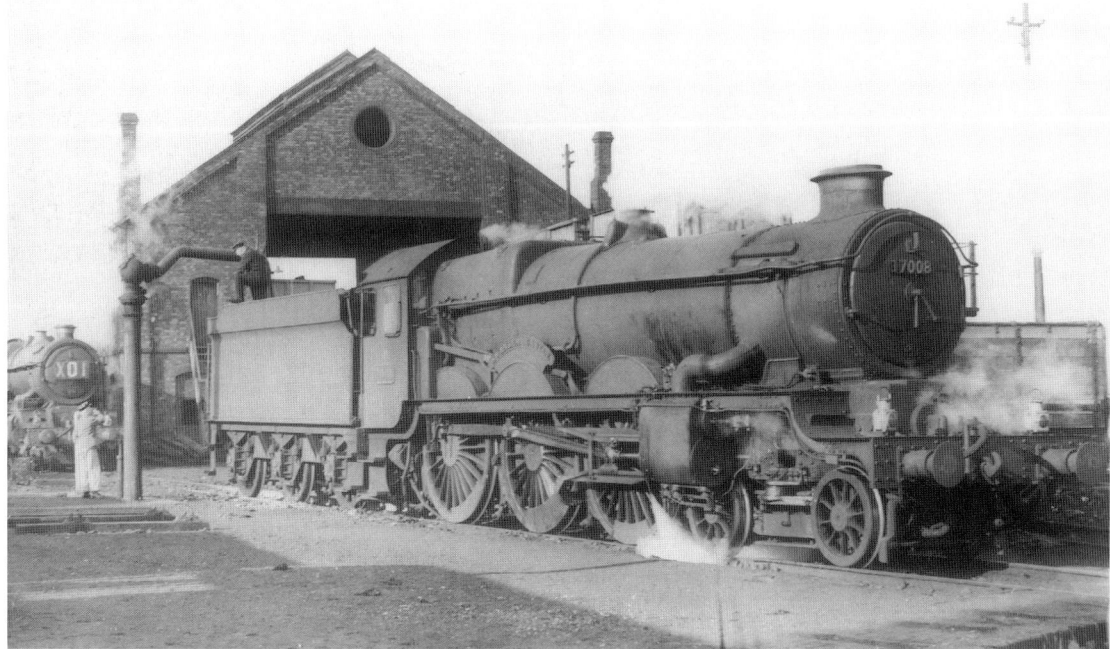

'Castle' class no. 7008 *Swansea Castle* is serviced and prepared for its next duty – probably an express to London. This view is at 84A Stafford Road shed in 1958.

Trains run right through to Birkenhead from Paddington, via Shrewsbury and Chester. Birkenhead on the Wirral peninsula opposite Liverpool, with docks on the Mersey, is about as far north as the GWR ventured. I don't think we can afford the time to go all the way to Birkenhead, as we must get back to the West of England Main Line.

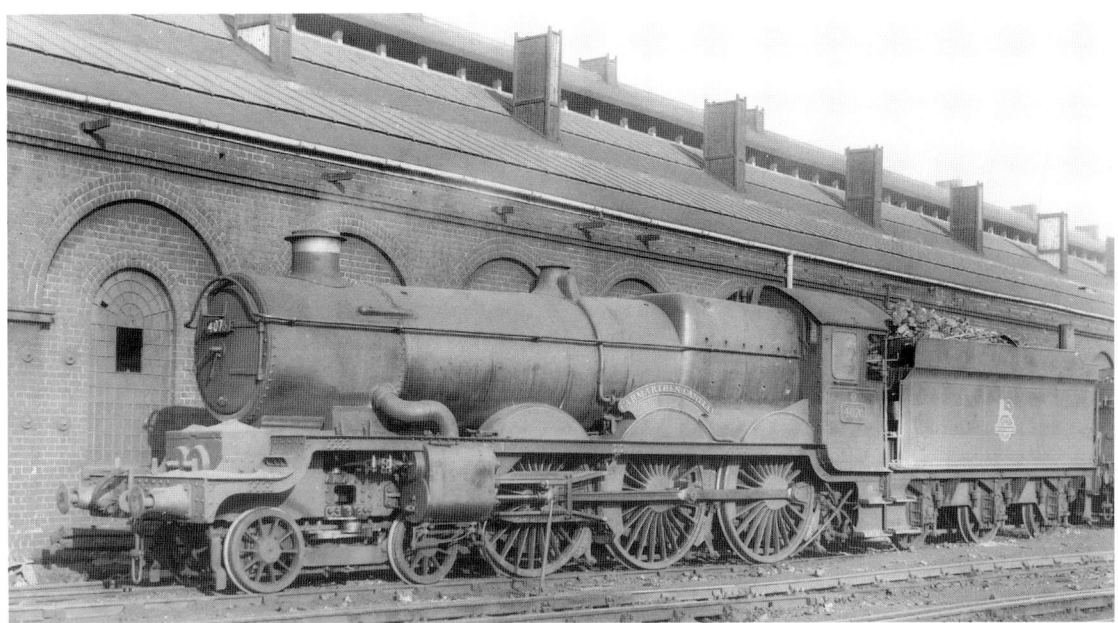

No. 4076 *Carmarthen Castle* at Chester shed, 1954. A big stack of coal in the tender is obviously simmering quietly awaiting its next duty

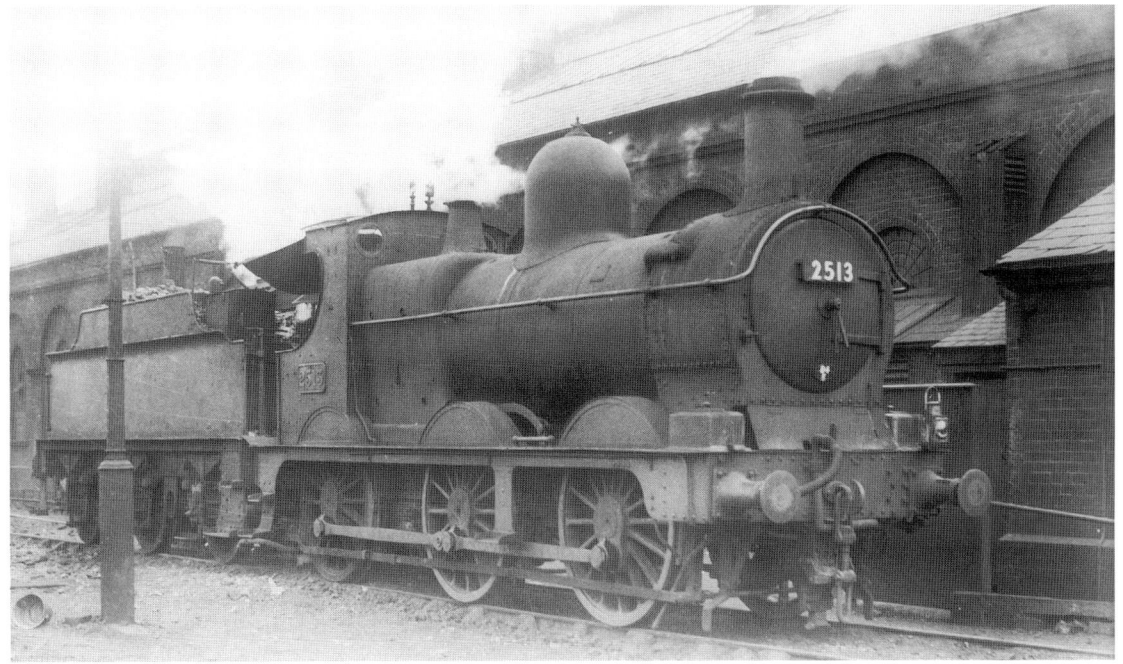

No. 2513, introduced in 1883 and designed by Dean, is seen here at Chester shed in 1952.

Back on the West of England Main Line no. 5019 *Treago Castle* picks up speed on its way to Bristol, 1954.

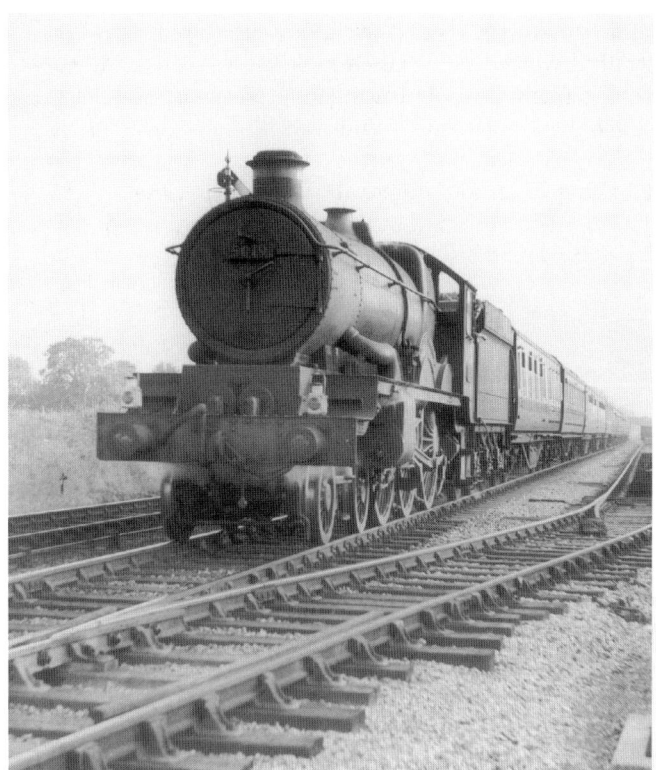

Acton Main Line station opened in 1868 as Acton. It acquired the name Acton Main Line when the railways were nationalised in 1948. I am not sure when this photograph was taken, but the board at the top of the building reads 'T.E. Scudder Ltd for demolition', and the station has rather a sad look.

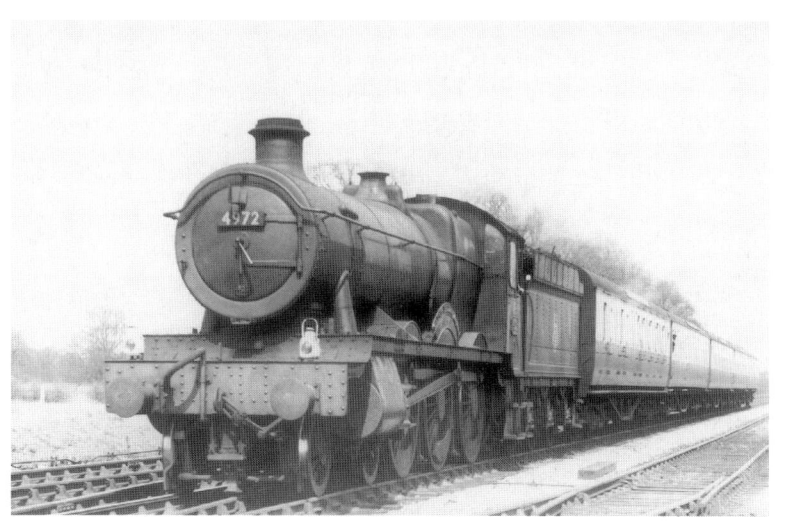

No. 4972 *Saint Brides Hall* not far from Acton in 1954.

Our train is moving nicely now, with smoke drifting past and the sun flickering through the windows. There won't be much in the way of locomotives to see for a few miles, so we can settle back in our seats and reflect on our journey to Birmingham, making sure our record books are safe, checking the films that we have are labelled and secured and putting them somewhere safe. We can now get ourselves ready for the next part of our journey, fresh pages in the record book, checking the cameras are in good working order and above all making sure we have film – if not sufficient we shall have to nip out at the next stop and buy some at the station bookstall; Smiths or John Menzies. We are now approaching Ealing Broadway.

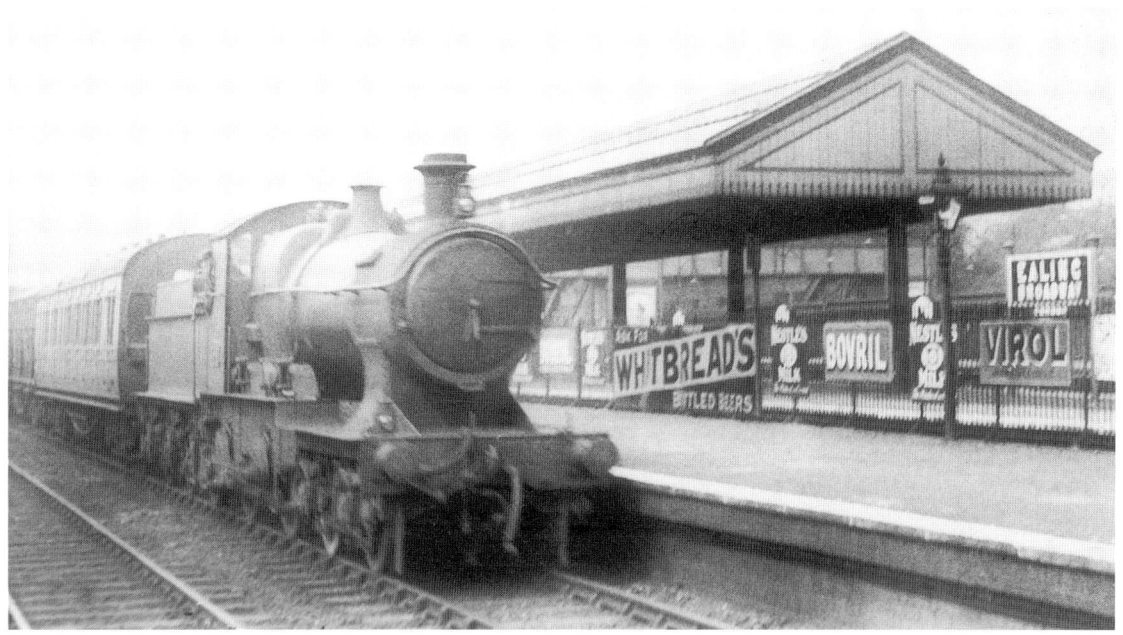

An unidentified 'Bulldog' heads a local stopping train through Ealing Broadway in the 1920s.

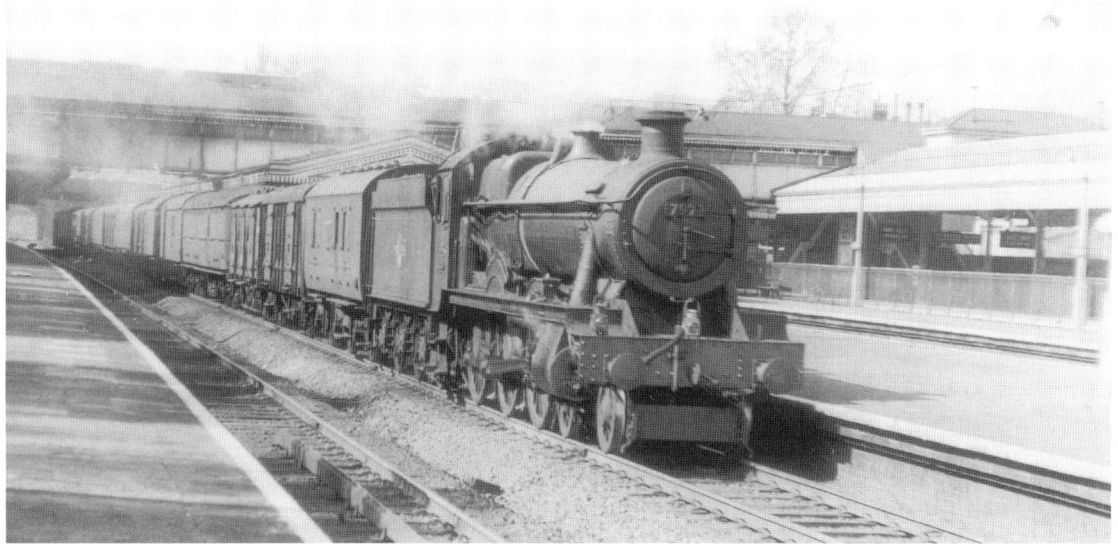

At almost the same spot a modified 'Hall' no. 7923 *Speke Hall*, is photographed about thirty-five years later.

On to West Ealing and just past the station there is a branch to Greenford, which would take us back onto the main Birmingham line that we have not long left. The brakes are coming on gently as we are approaching Southall.

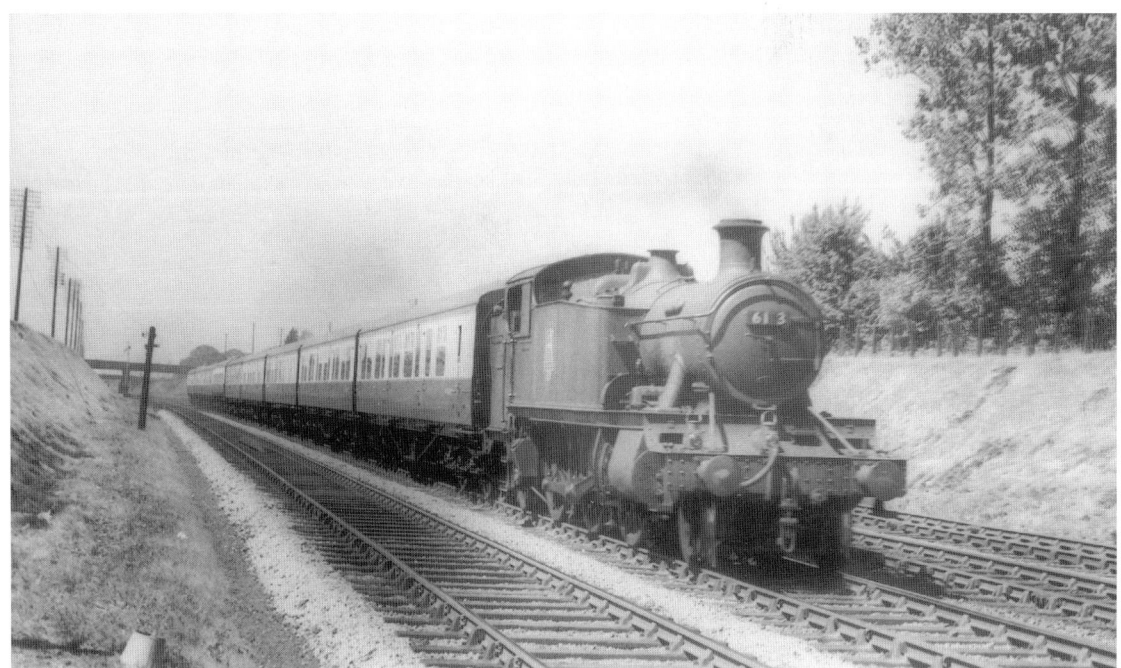

No. 6113 2–6–2T near West Ealing. These locos were very common between Didcot and Paddington as they were ideal for working commuter trains. They had good acceleration and were quite powerful and with 5ft 8in driving wheels, they were quite fast.

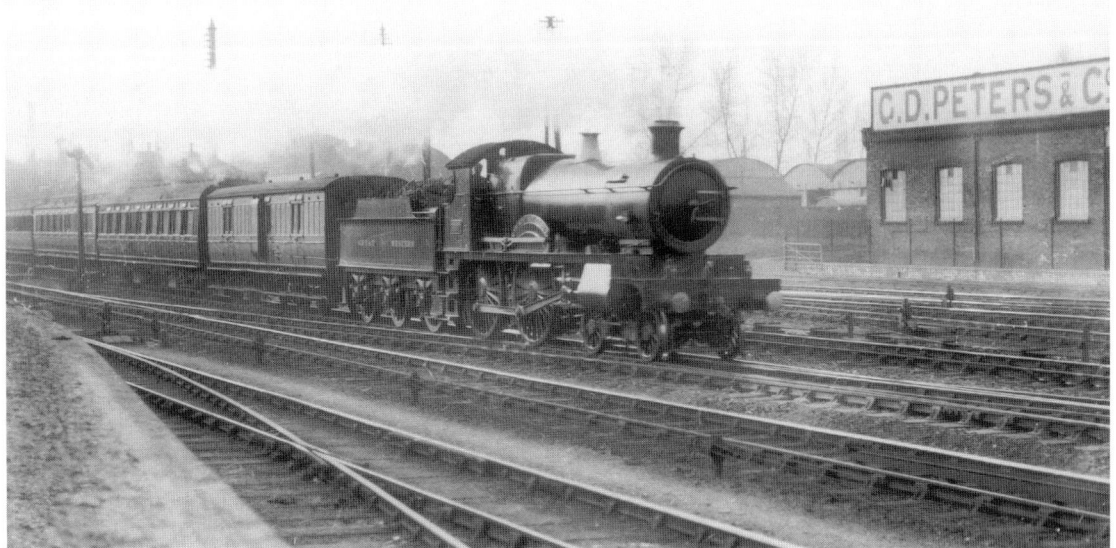

GWR 'County' no. 3807 *County Kilkenny* approaches Southall in 1922. One of Churchwards 4–4–0s with 6ft 8in driving wheels, they were built for express working. They lasted from the early 1900s to the early 1930s.

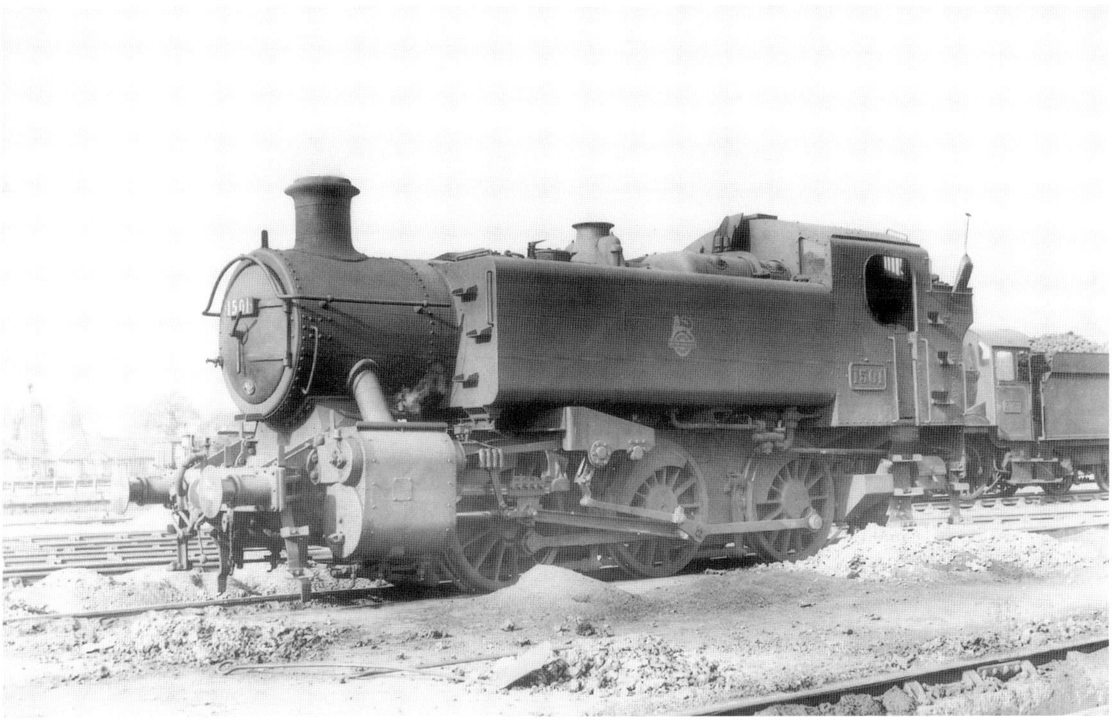

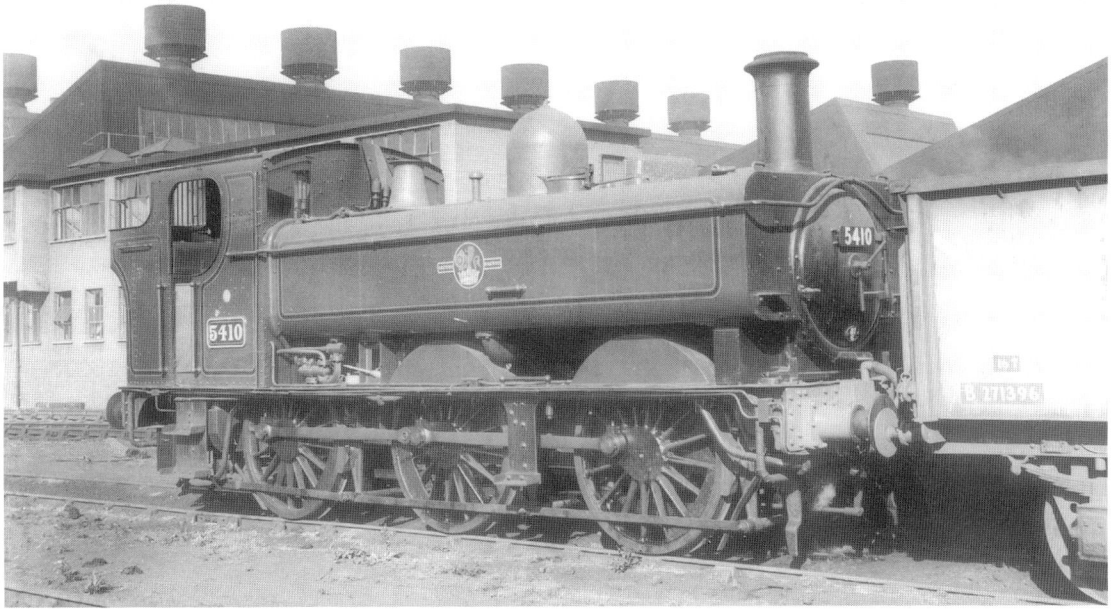

Hawksworth introduced ten of these heavy shunting engines in 1949, so strictly speaking they are British Railways locos, although I don't think anyone would argue that they looked anything other than pure GWR. They were mainly to be seen in the London area and this is no. 1501 at Southall in 1956.

An immaculate green painted pannier tank no. 5410 at Southall shed in 1959.

Leaving Southall, we have the feeling we are still in the suburbs of London. Soon we are through Hayes and approaching West Drayton where there is a branch to Uxbridge and also Staines.

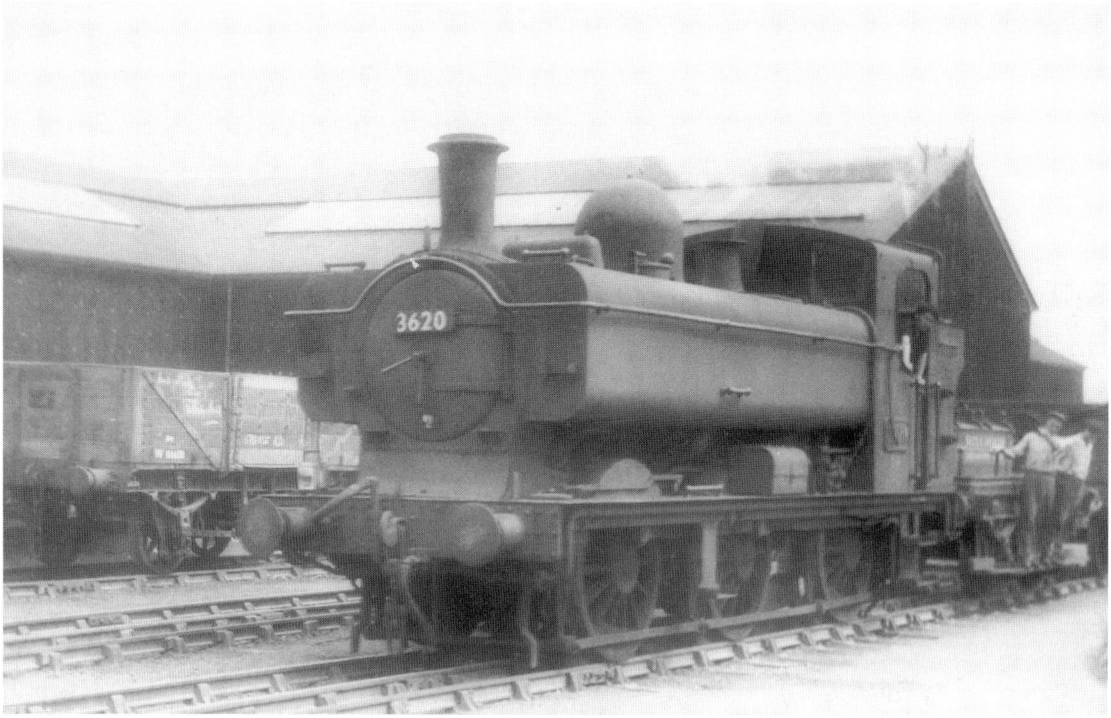

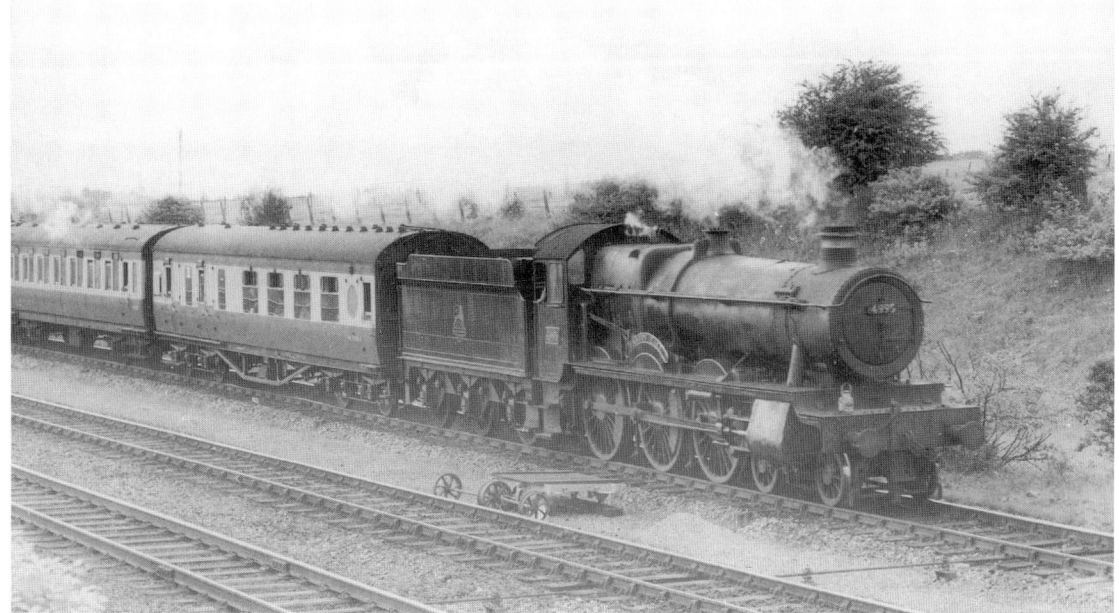

Pannier tank no. 3620 shunting in the chemical works at Hayes.

No. 4995 *Easton Hall* approaching West Drayton.

We are now at a stand in West Drayton, but not for long, just enough time for a quick stretch of the legs, a photograph of a 'Hall' about to leave on the other platform, and back on the train as the guard's whistle sounds. Before the train has picked up speed we are over the branch line to Staines.

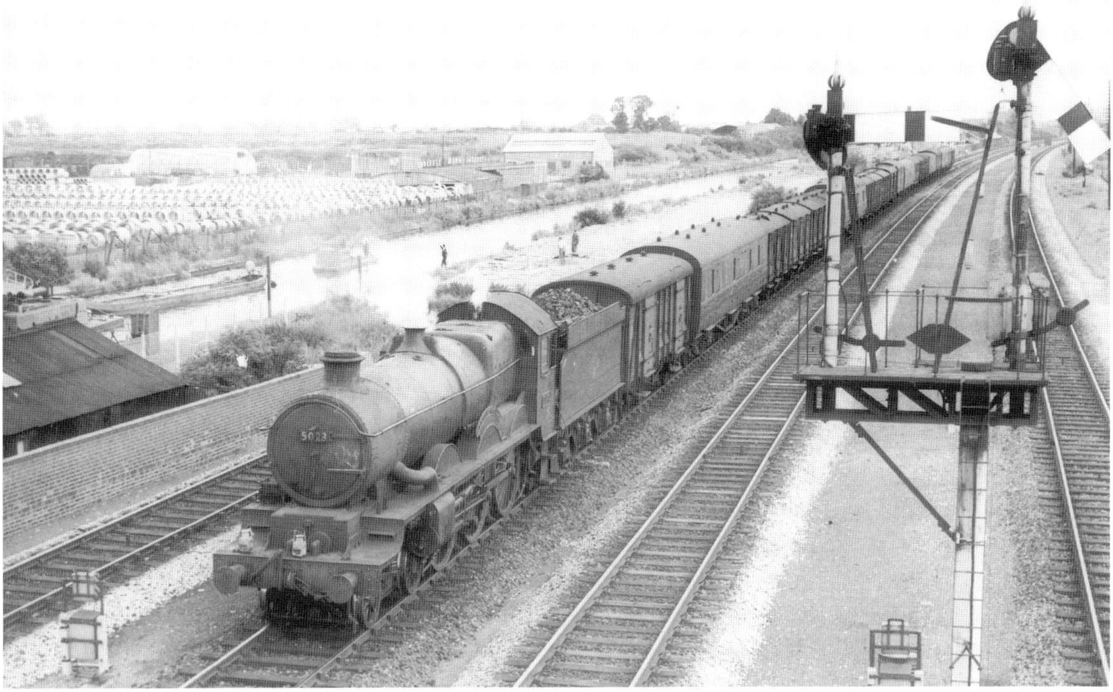

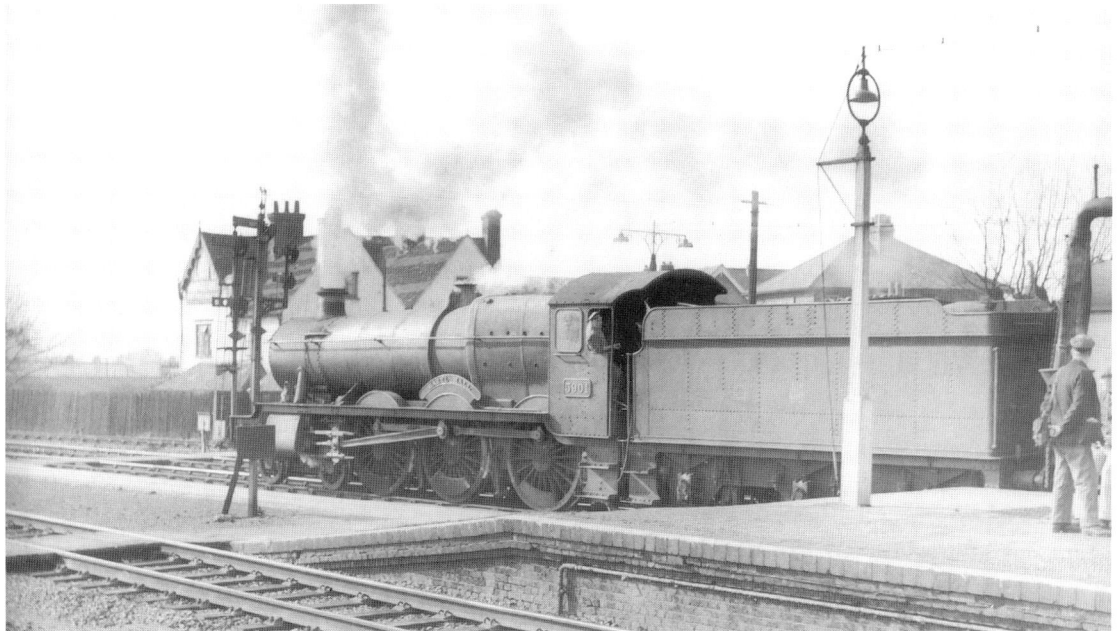

No. 5023 *Brecon Castle* approaching West Drayton with a parcels train.

Leaving Market Drayton is 'Hall' class no. 5901 *Hazel Hall*.

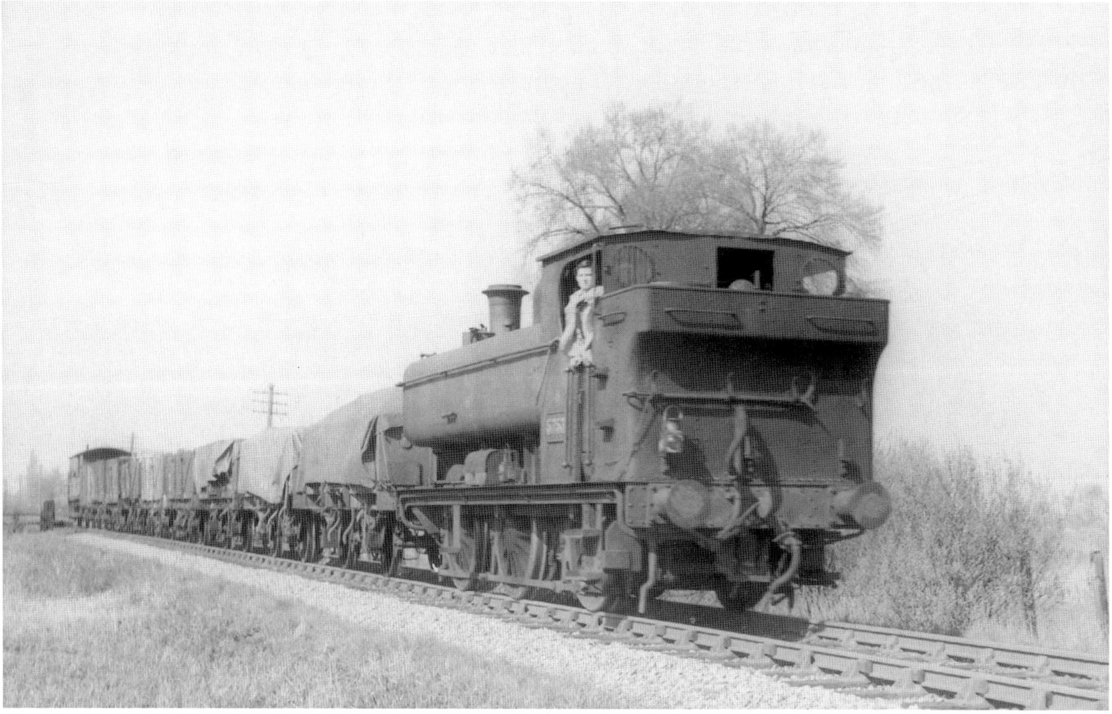

Pannier tank no. 5753 somewhere on the Staines Branch in 1951.

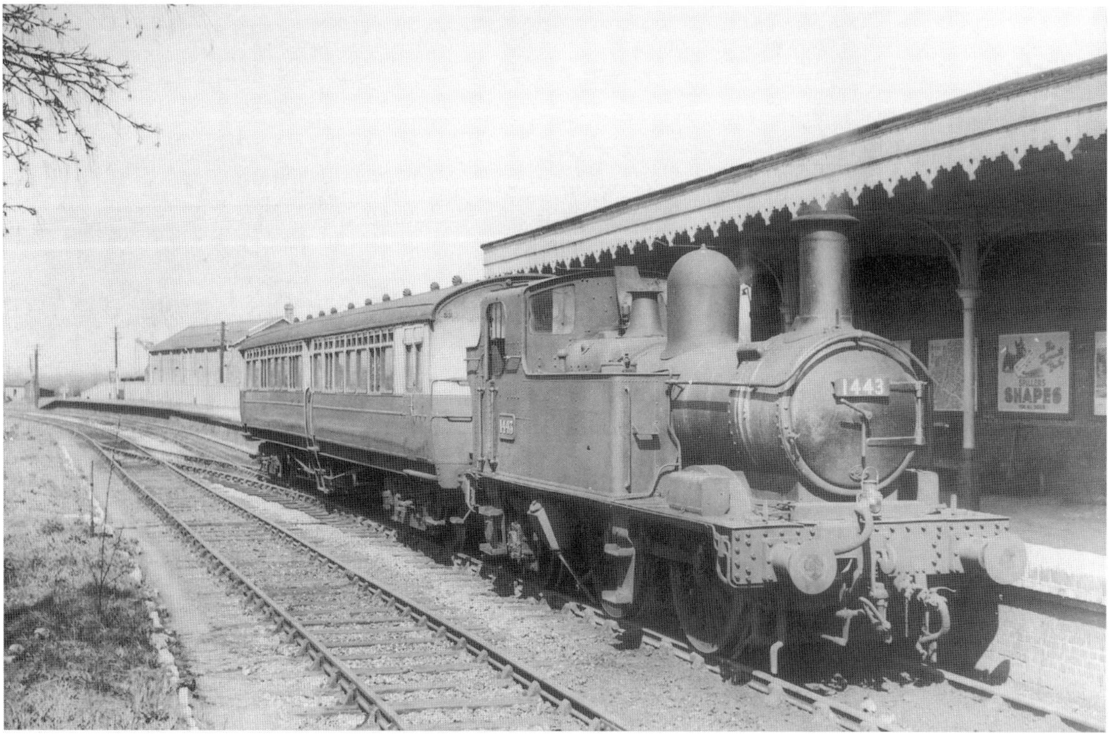

0–4–2T no. 1443, no doubt travelling at a steady pace, has passed through Colnbrook and Runemede and is now simmering quietly in Staines GWR station. The driver and fireman who know the staff well will be enjoying a cup of tea and a chat before heading back to West Drayton.

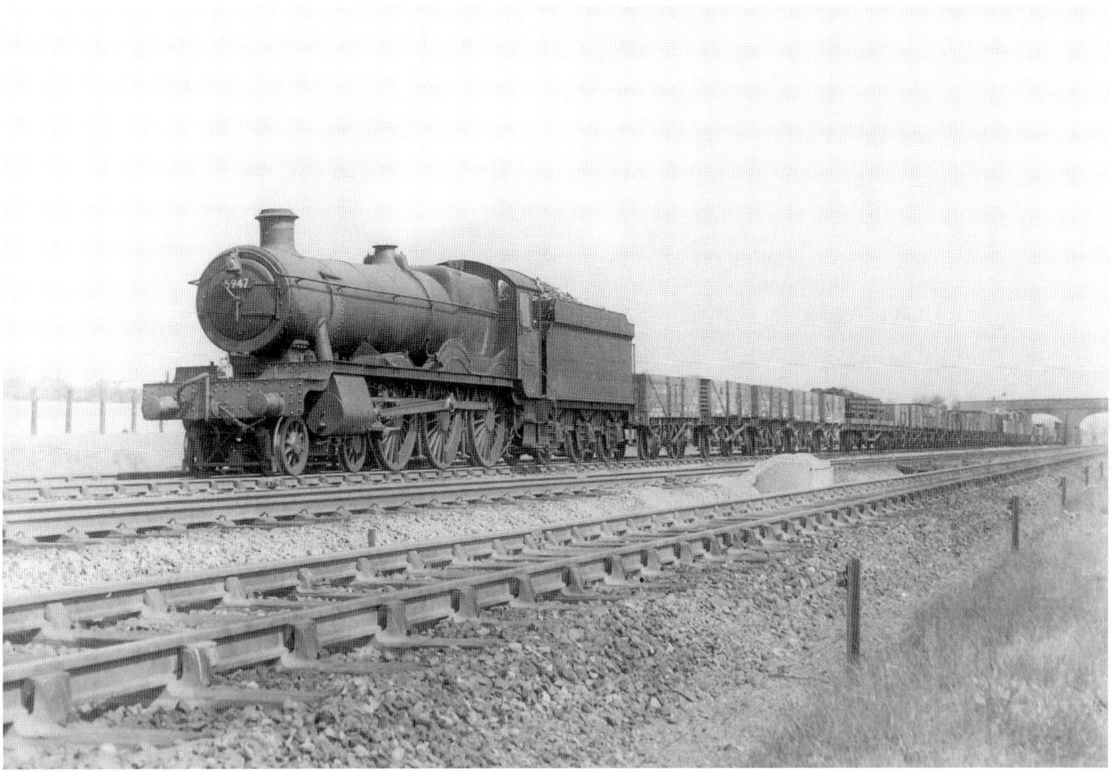

No. 5947 *St Benets Hall* running through Iver with a ballast train in 1954.

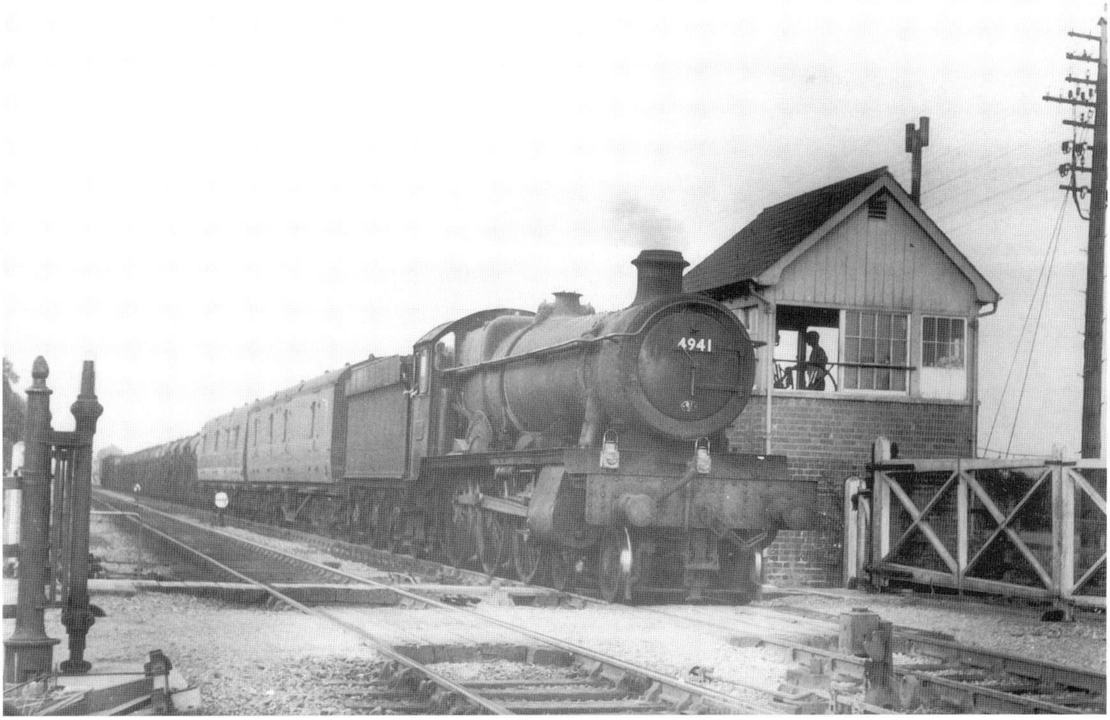

Another 'Hall', this time an earlier one, no. 4941 *Llangedwyn Hall*, carrying a Reading 81D shedplate with a milk train, photographed at Langley Crossing in 1956.

We are now arriving in Slough, very much a commuter centre for those working in London. The rush hour in the mornings saw the station packed with people, and then very quickly a calm would descend and no doubt staff would breathe a sigh of relief and go for well-earned cup of tea. Through Hayes and approaching West Drayton there is a branch to Uxbridge and also Staines.

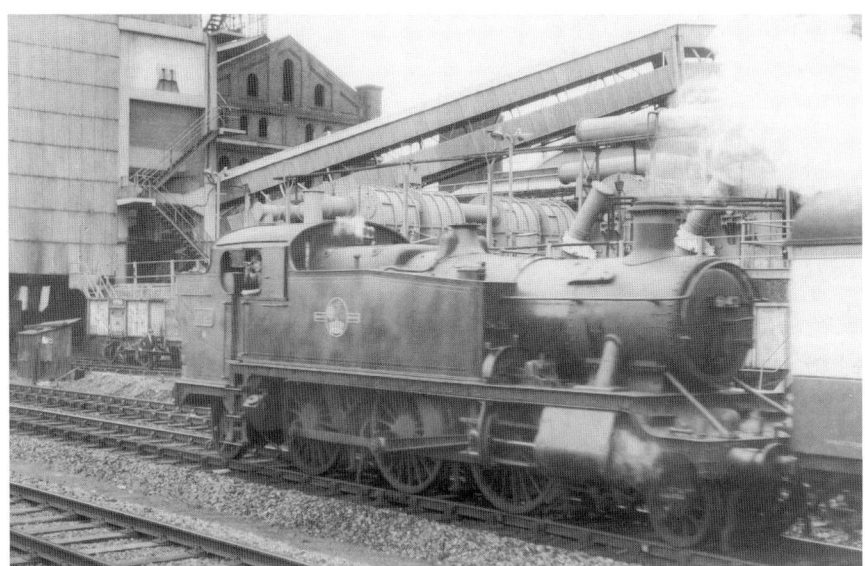

A 2–6–2 prairie tank at Slough in 1958.

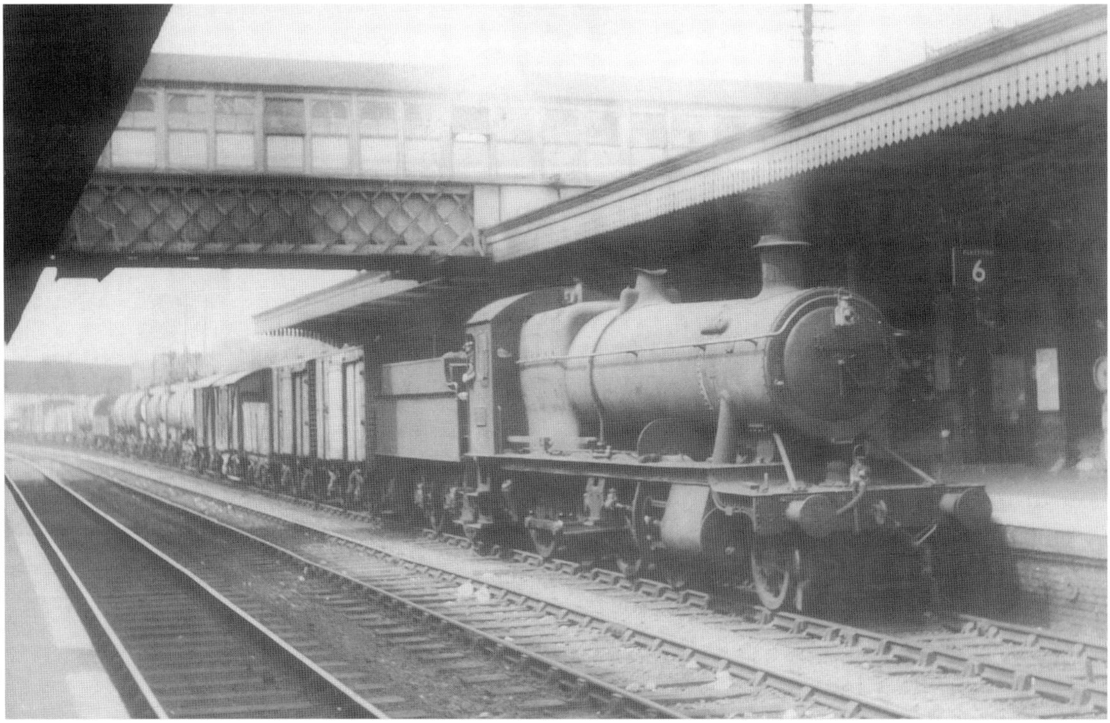

2–8–0 no. 3886 passing through Slough with a mixed freight in 1954.

At Slough we are now in quite an industrialised area, but when the branch to Windsor was opened, and Queen Victoria and Prince Albert travelled this route, it would have been a very different picture. It was a very rural area with probably more cows and sheep than people.

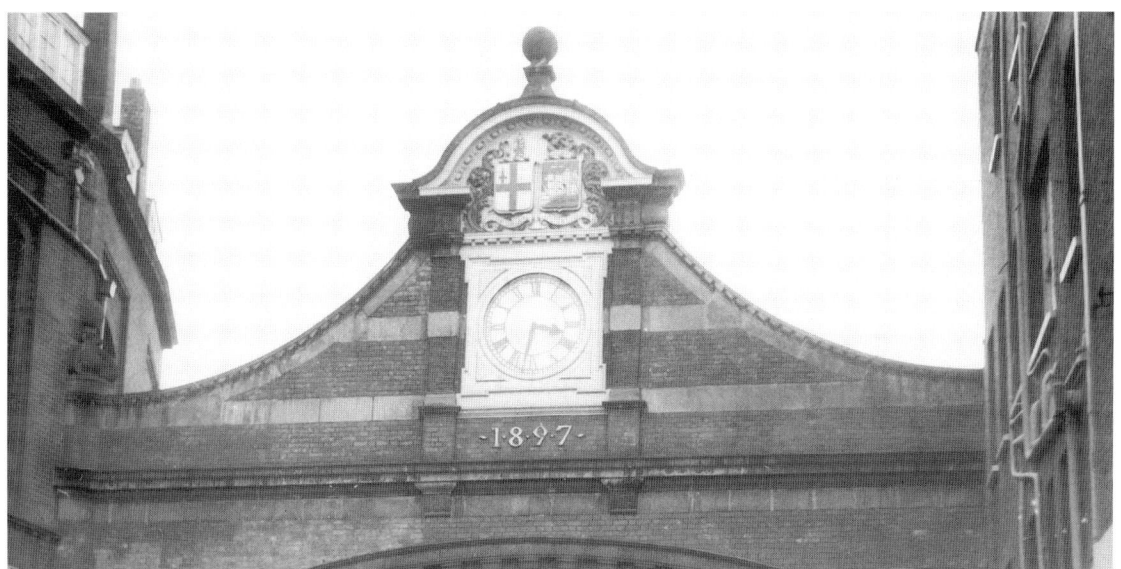

I must admit I am a little confused with these photographs of Windsor. The picture above is of an archway with the GWR coat of arms above it, so I assume this is the Royal station. The date 1897 probably refers to Queen Victoria's Diamond Jubilee. This picture was taken in 1954.

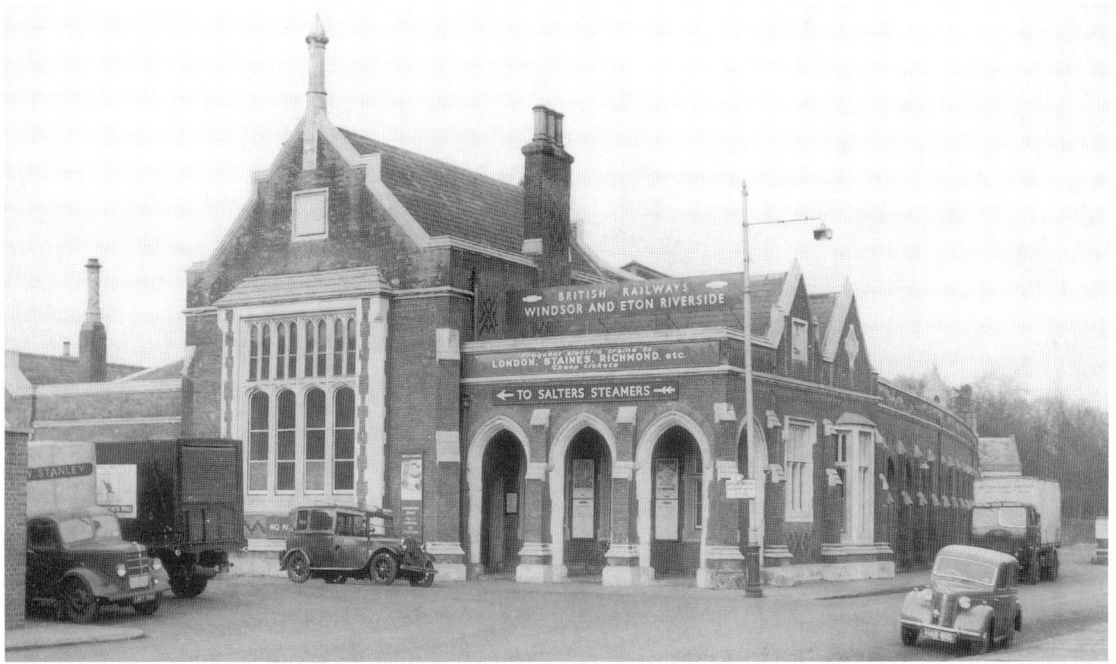

The lower picture is of Windsor and Eton Riverside which was built by the L&SW at about the same time as the GWR station. By the time this picture was taken in 1954, it was of course British Railways.

Off we go again, through Burnham Beeches and Taplow. Here we are travelling at good speed but we shall soon be slowing for Maidenhead. Back in the 1840s when Brunel built the railway bridge over the river, all the experts of the day were incredibly pessimistic. They predicted that it would fall down as the first train crossed it, but here it is, well over a hundred years later still standing, even with the mighty 'Kings' thundering over it at 100 mph!

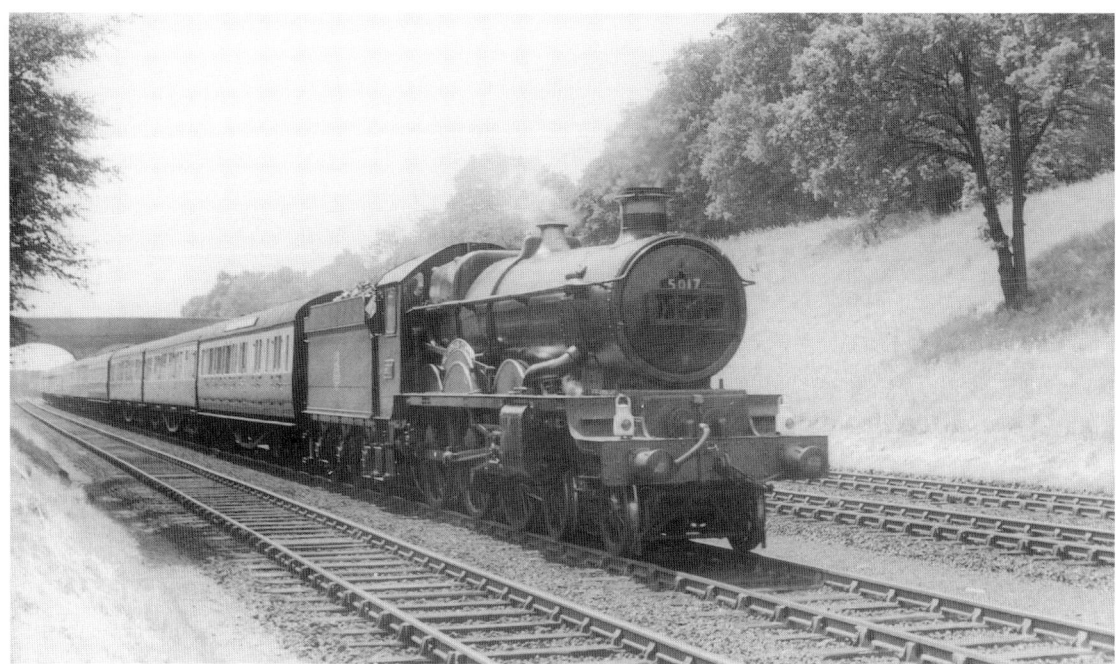

No. 5017 *St Donat's Castle* with an express near Taplow.

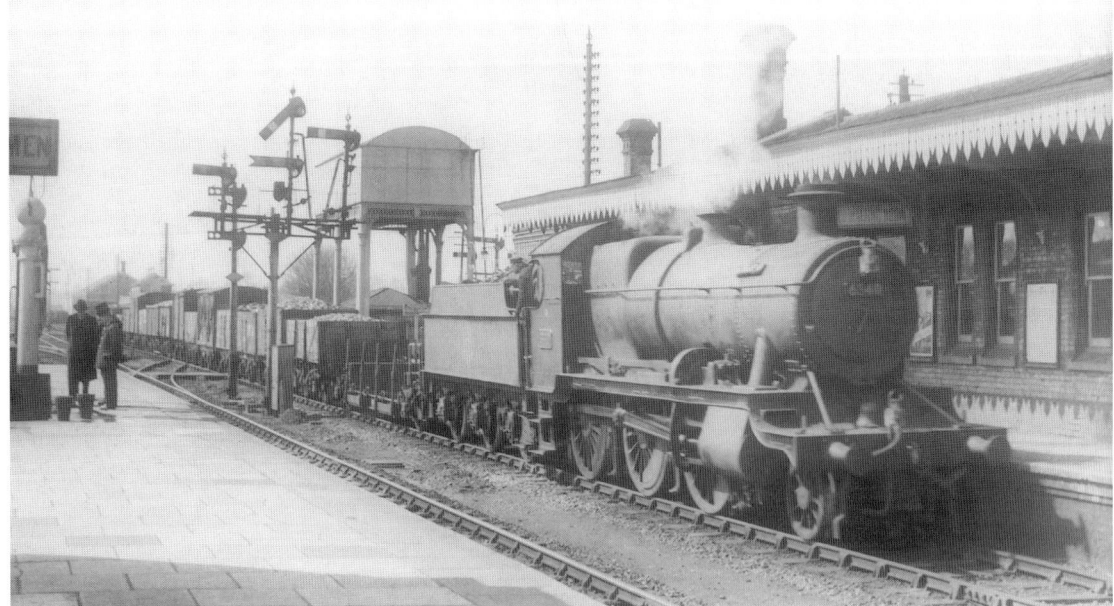

No. 6340 with a mixed freight making a leisurely pace through Maidenhead.

At Maidenhead there was a branch line that made its way back to the Birmingham Line at High Wycombe – we will not go that far – only to Bourne End where there was a short run to Marlow. I believe one of the local trains was known as the 'Marlow Donkey'. Could this be a description of this service – it only went when it felt like it – or was it a friendly service, like a donkey's nature?

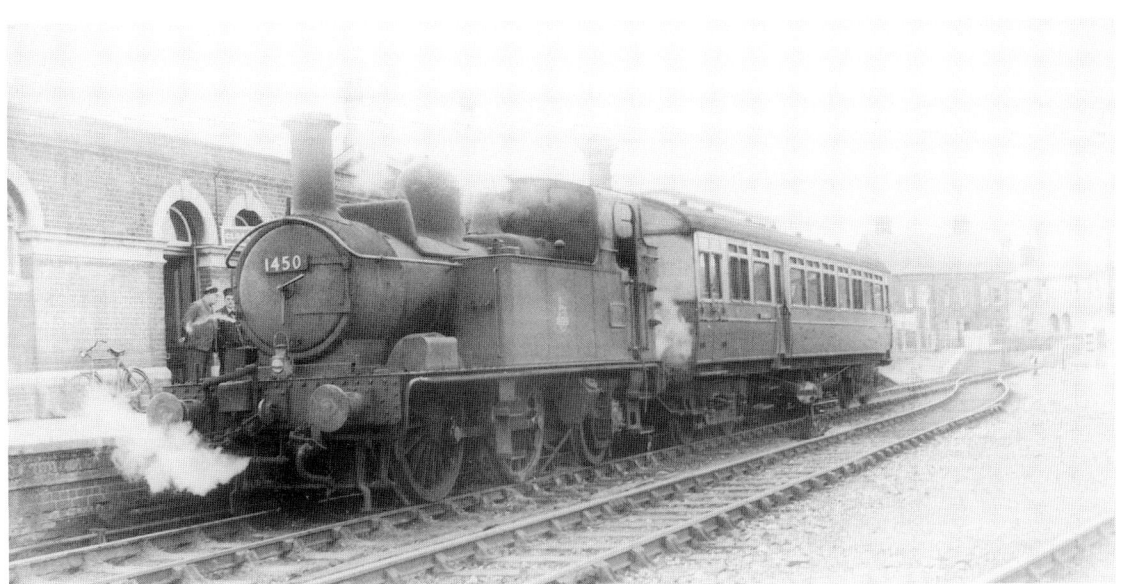

No. 1450 at Bourne End in the early 1950s.

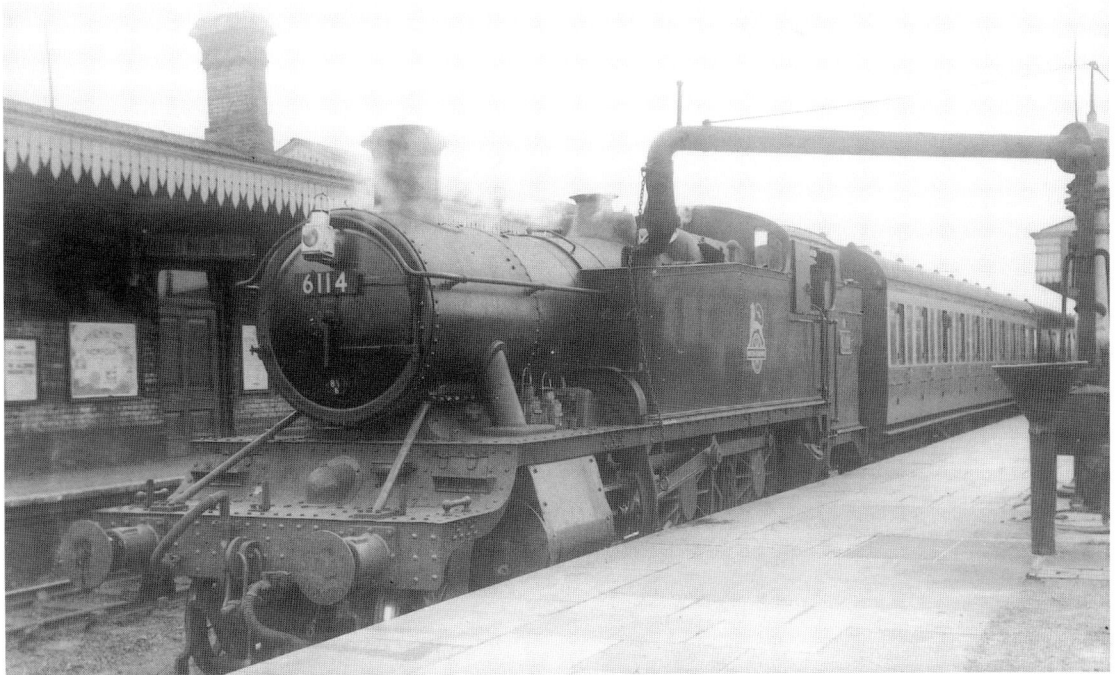

We head back to Maidenhead to continue our journey westward, not by no. 6114 though, which is seen here taking on water heading a local passenger train.

Once again we are on our way – it's now full speed to Reading. Time for a quick sandwich and a hot drink from the Thermos – careful you don't spill it over your note books or films as this is a high-speed part of the journey. From Maidenhead to Twyford is almost dead straight for about 8 miles and then another 5 miles to Reading, so speed will be not far off the 80 mph mark. Get on with your sandwiches as we shall soon be running into Reading, now passing through Sonning cutting, a landmark to the railway enthusiast. On come the brakes and we are at a stand in Reading.

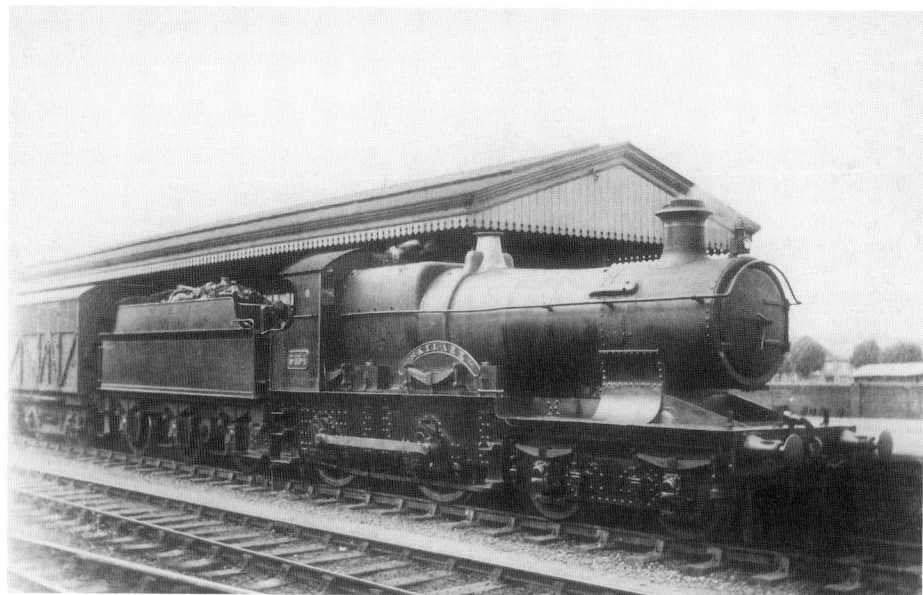

'Bulldog' no. 3454 *Skylark* passing through Reading with a mixed freight.

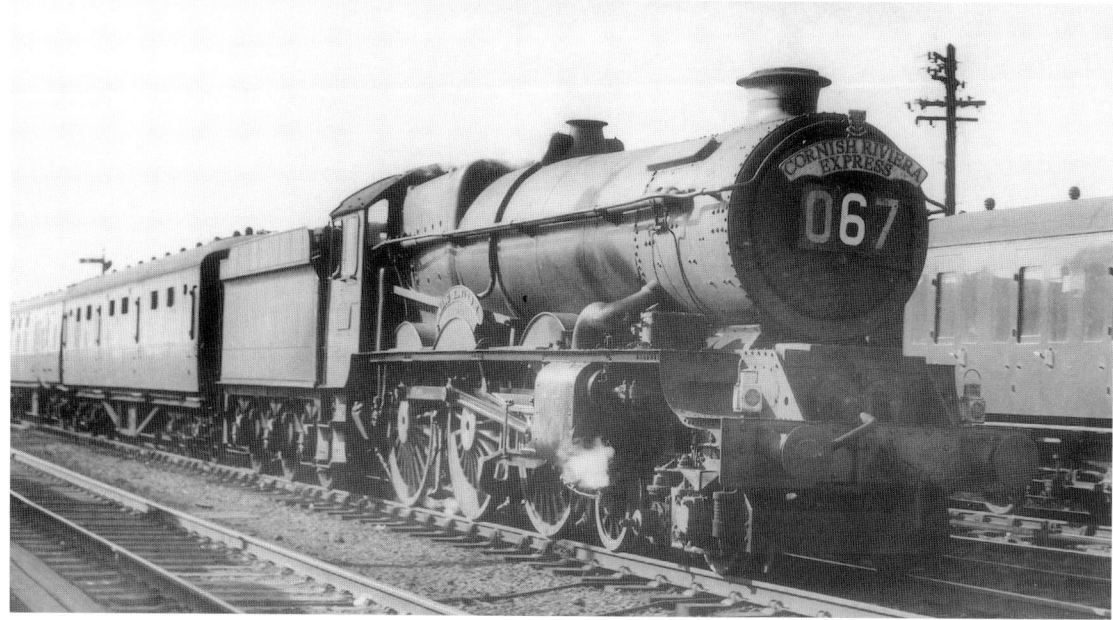

Coming off the West of England Mainline via Westbury, with the 'Cornish Riviera Express' is no. 6024 *King Edward I.*

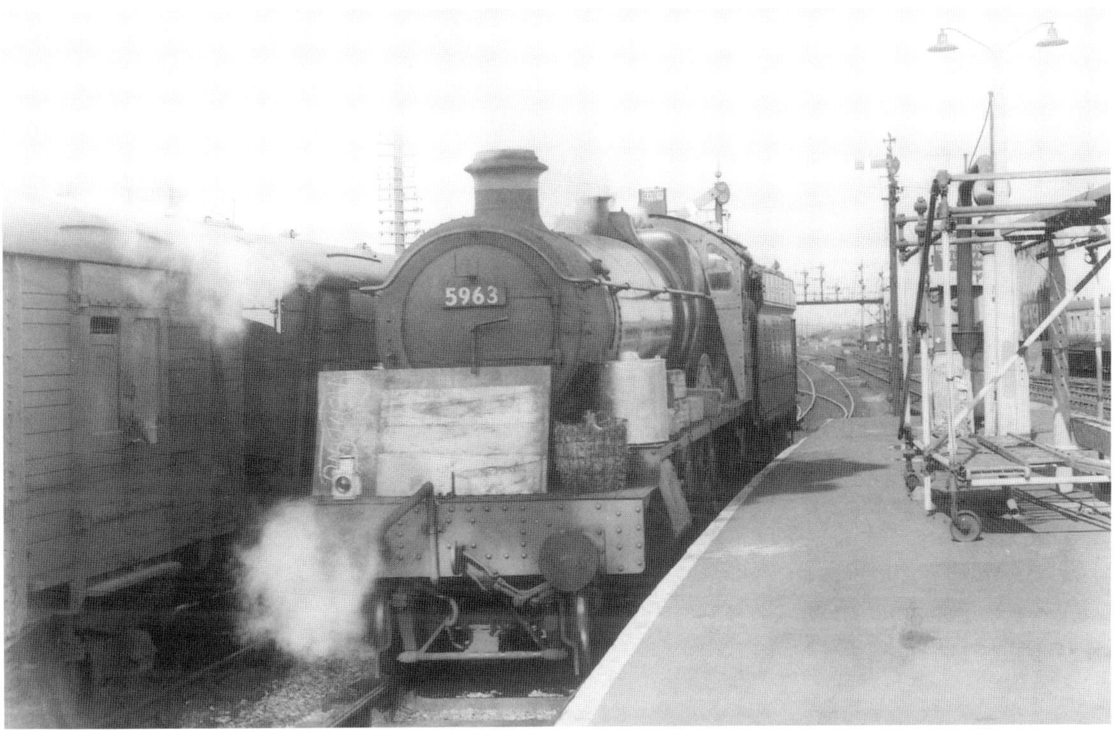

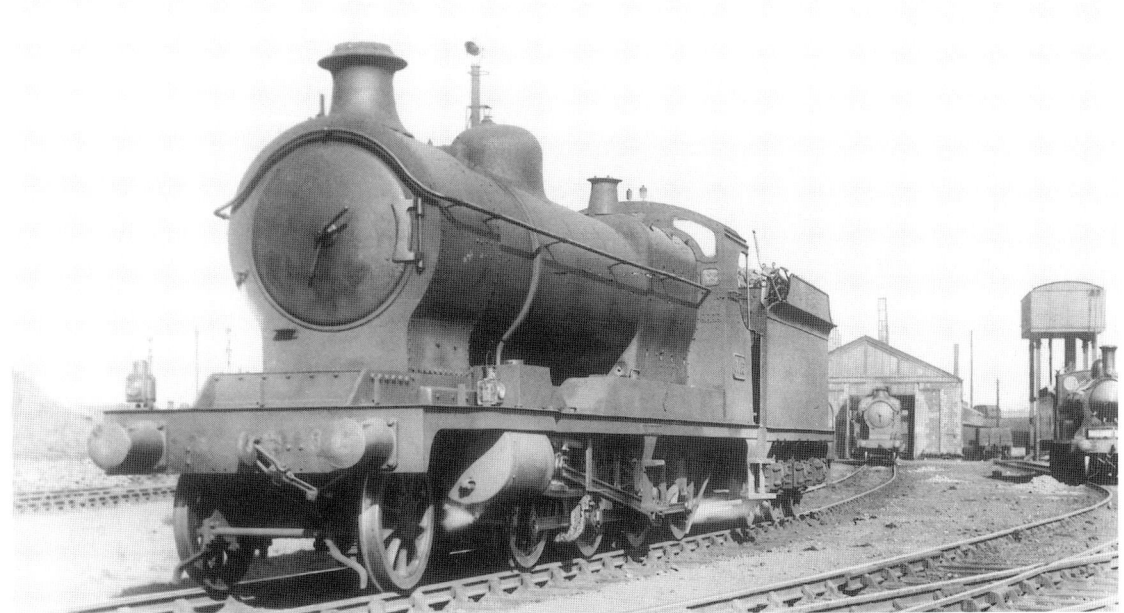

Leaving our coats on our seats in the hope that no one will occupy our compartment, we join the throng on the platform. We shall be here for about 3 minutes. One oddity we spot straight away is 'Hall' class no. 5963 *Wimpole Hall* with its buffer being loaded with stores. The driver told us this was a common event, load and engine that was going on shed with anything that had come in by train addressed to 'stores Reading 81D'.

GWR Rod 305 on Reading shed in 1935.

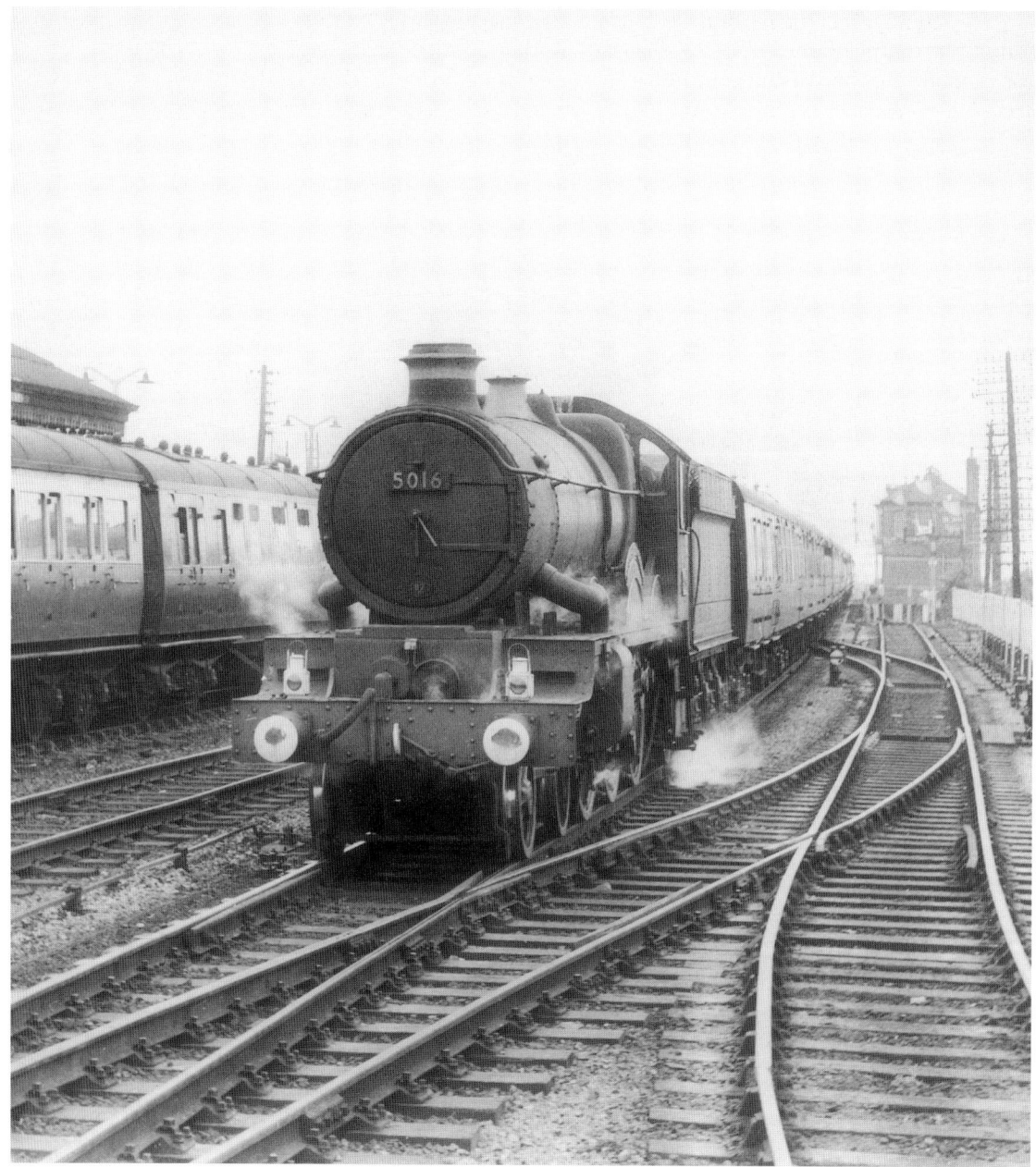

Our train is ready to leave as no. 5016 *Montgomery Castle* roars through carrying an 87E Landore (Swansea) shedplate, 1954. We assume it is on a South Wales Express.

We can now feel the motion of the train again as we leave Reading. If we look out of the windows to the left we may be able to see Southern and Western engines. We are now passing the junction for the Westbury Line, through Reading West, but we keep straight on, heading for Bristol. Very quickly we are through Tilehurst and not long after, Pangbourne. We are now into a real race track on the fast expresses with speeds well over 90 mph.

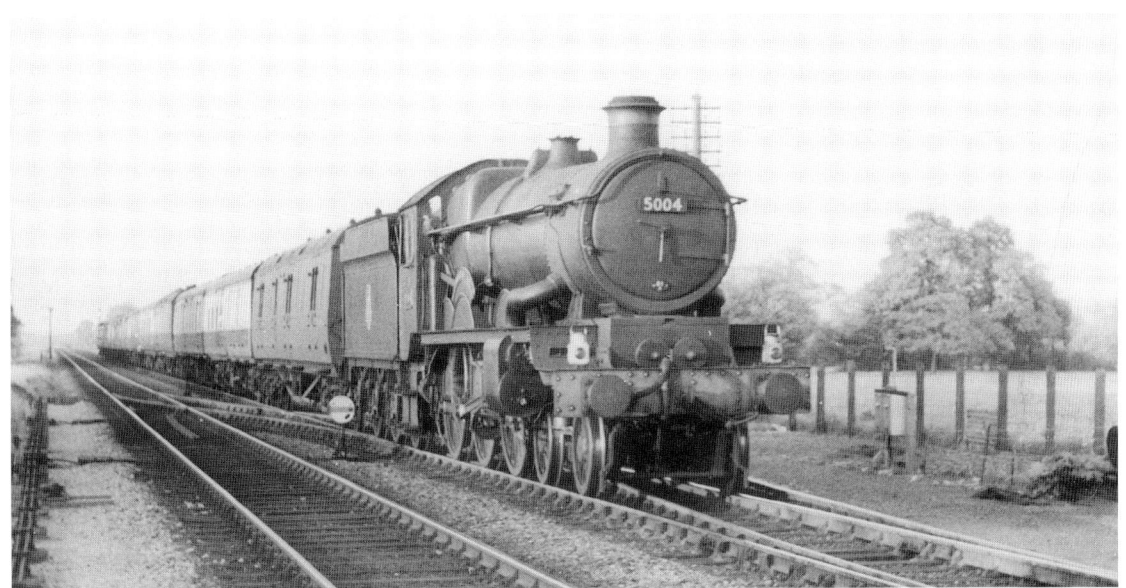

No. 5004 *Llanstephan Castle* near Tilehurst in 1954.

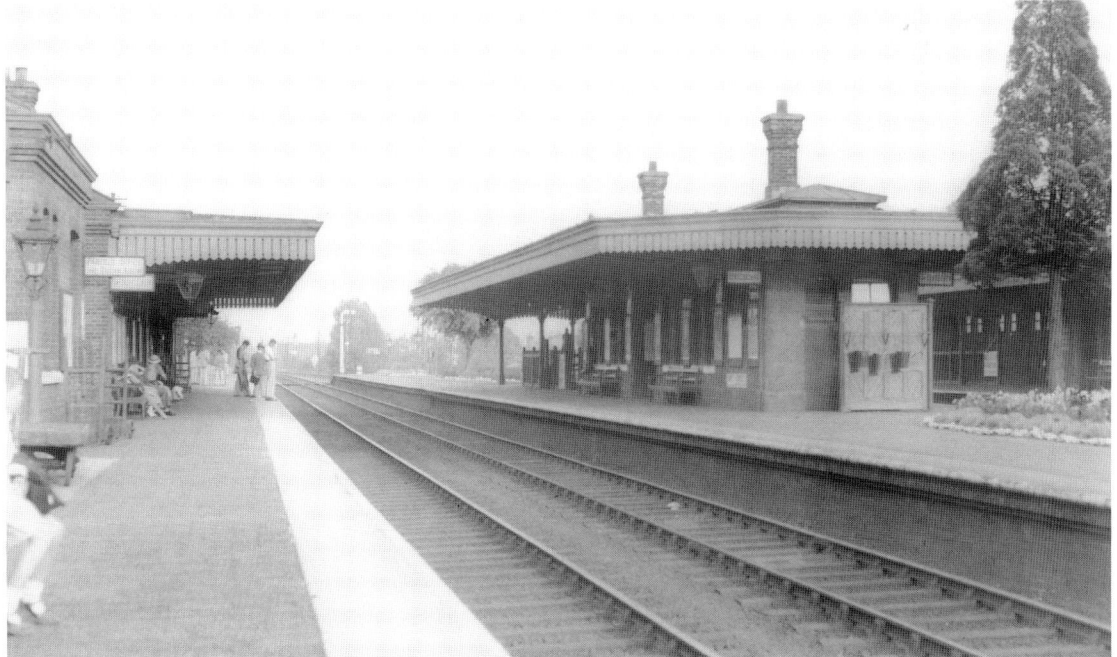

Pangbourne station, 1936. Look at the wide white edge on the platform, warning passengers to stand well back as the trains come through here very fast.

Past Pangbourne the fireman will be preparing to give the engine a drink from Goring Troughs. He will check the tender water indicator to see how much is needed: it may well be 2,000 gallons or so. He will know how long it will take to pick up that much water at any given speed. As soon as the engine is over the trough, he winds the scoop down and starts counting, and at the appropriate moment he will wind the scoop up rapidly. If he miscalculates, he could flood the first carriage, or even worse, if he fails to raise the scoop before the end of the trough he could cause serious damage to the scoop. It has probably taken me longer to write this description than it had taken the fireman to pick up 2,000 gallons.

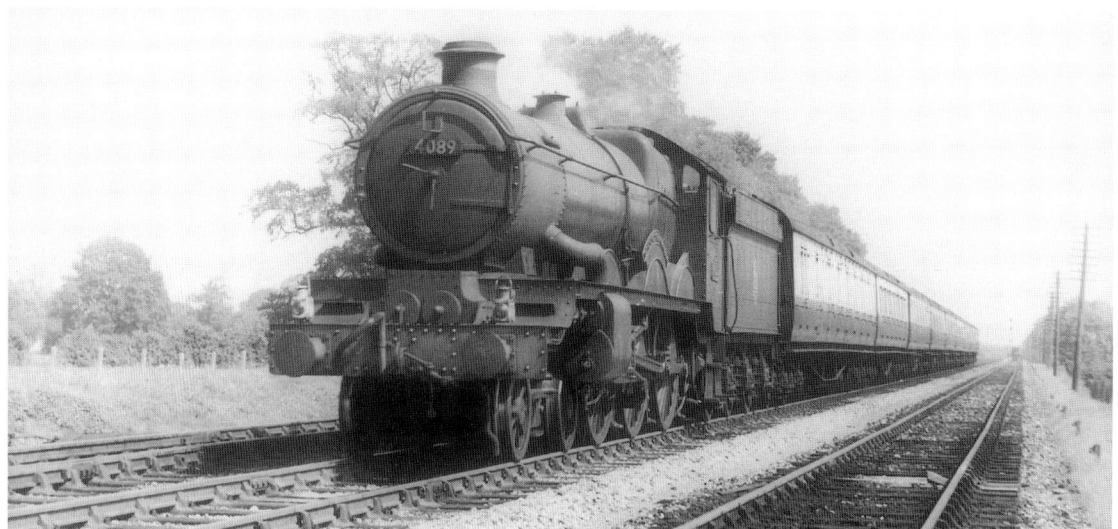

No. 4089 *Donnington Castle* nearing Goring in 1954.

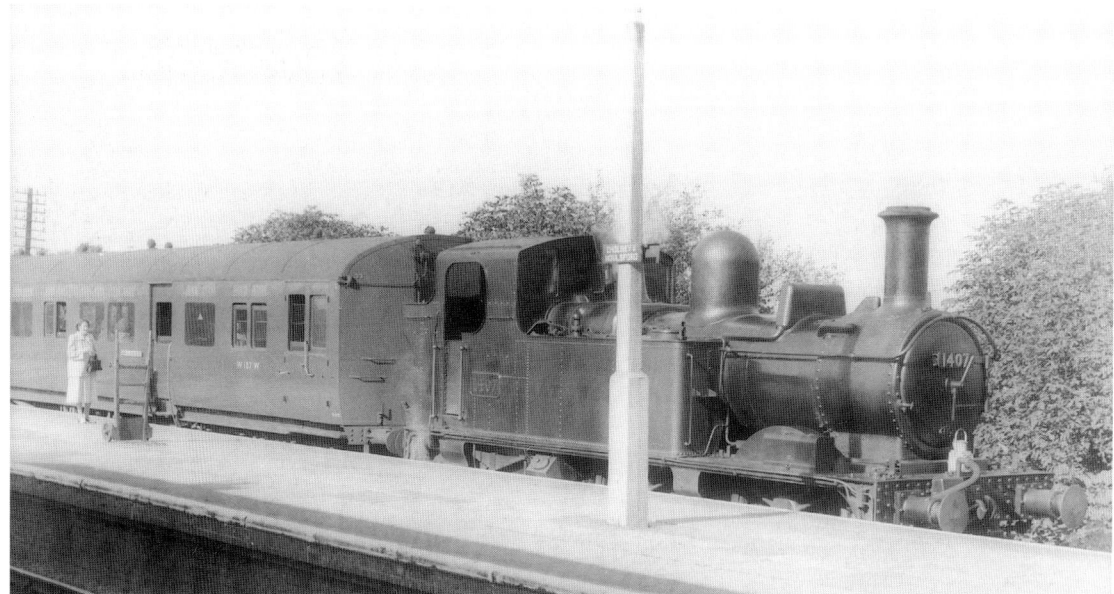

No. 1407 0–4–2T at Cholsey in 1953. It was introduced by Collett in 1932 especially for working branch lines and could be seen all over the GWR system, usually with one or two carriages. It would have been employed working the branch to Wallingford at this time.

Leaving Goring, through Cholsey we are now approaching Didcot. Didcot is a Mecca for railway enthusiasts and we can see the shed as it was in the steam days, full of engines, many under repair and a still-working turntable. On open days there were visiting engines that had arrived on steam specials. We shall be visiting it as a working shed '81E' in the 1950s.

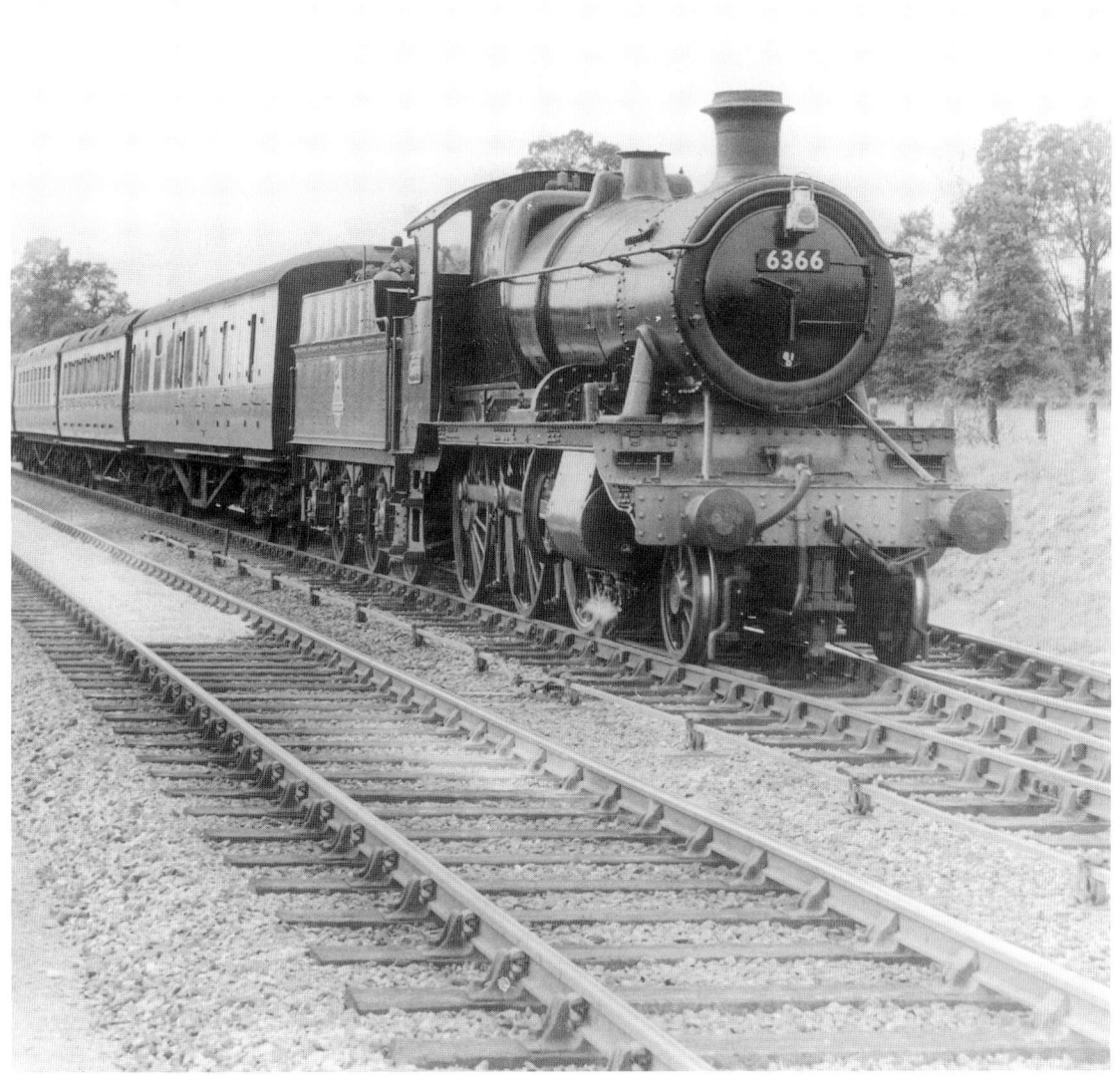

'Mogul' no. 6366 approaching Didcot with a local stopping passenger, 1954.

On come the brakes and passengers start collecting their coats and baggage from the overhead luggage racks. Younger travellers these days will remember nothing but open-plan carriages; they may have visited a rail centre and seen coaches with compartments, but to the older generation, we have memories of what I would call 'real trains' – standing in the corridor with the window open, the smell of steam, and the occasional smut in the eye. Who cares? there was atmosphere! Slide back the door to your compartment, collect your notebooks and camera, as the brakes have done their work and we have come to a stand at Didcot.

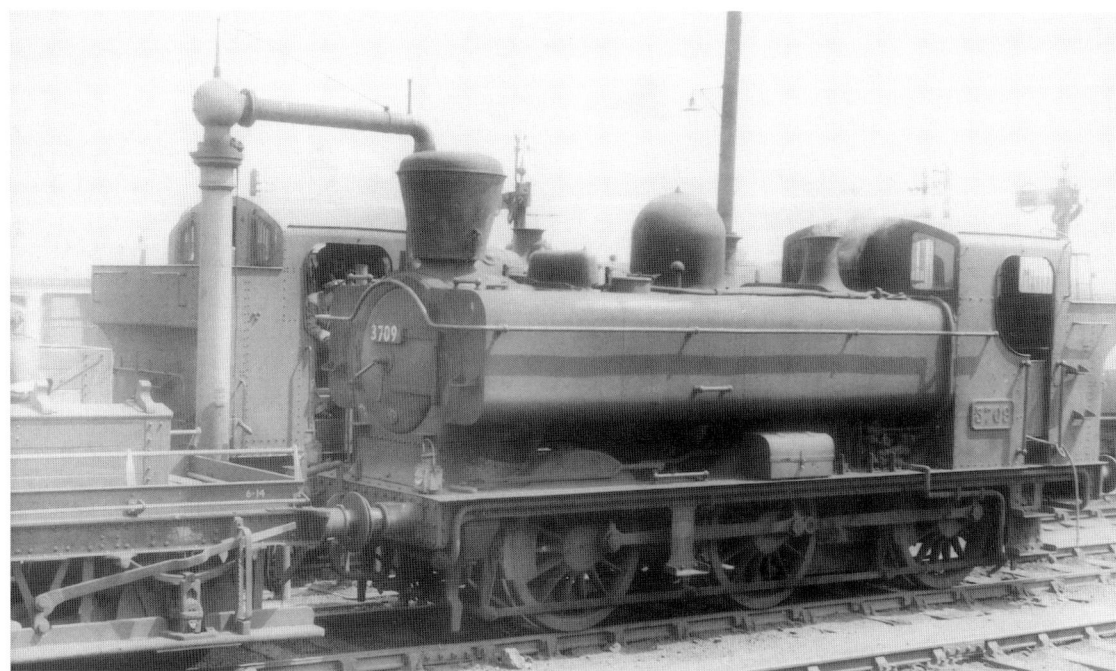

Pannier no. 3709 with spark arrestor chimney for working at the Royal Ordnance Factory where the odd spark from a chimney could cause a big bang, although in this 1955 view it looks as though its taking water through the chimney.

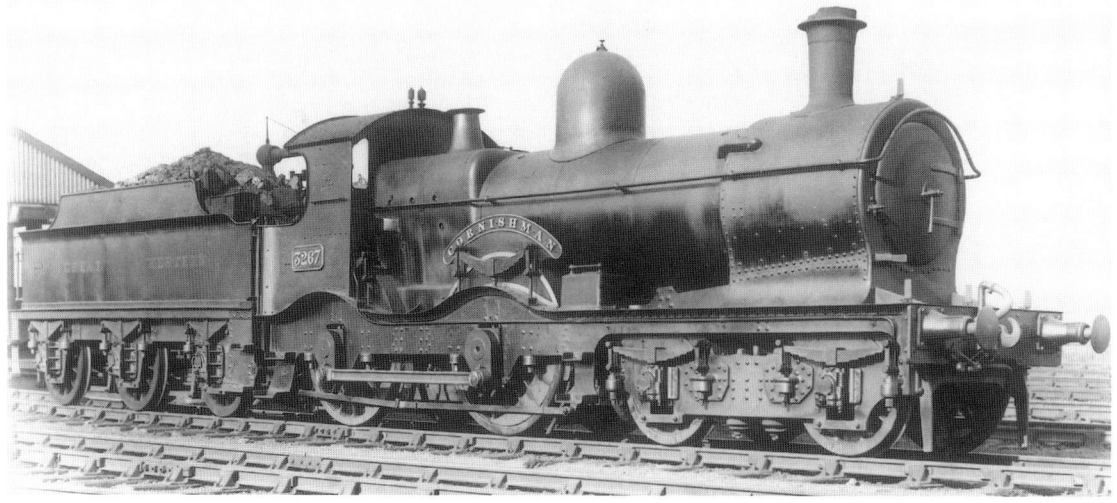

Didcot was home to several 'Dukes' and 'Bulldogs'. Here no. 3267 *Cornishman* awaits its next duty in the 1930s.

Running just past the shed is the main line from Didcot to Oxford through Appleford Culham, and at Radley is the branch to Abingdon. Abingdon Railways opened in 1844, very early in railway days, and joined to the GWR they only had one station, the terminus in Abingdon which was no more than a village at that time. A couple more halts and we are into Oxford.

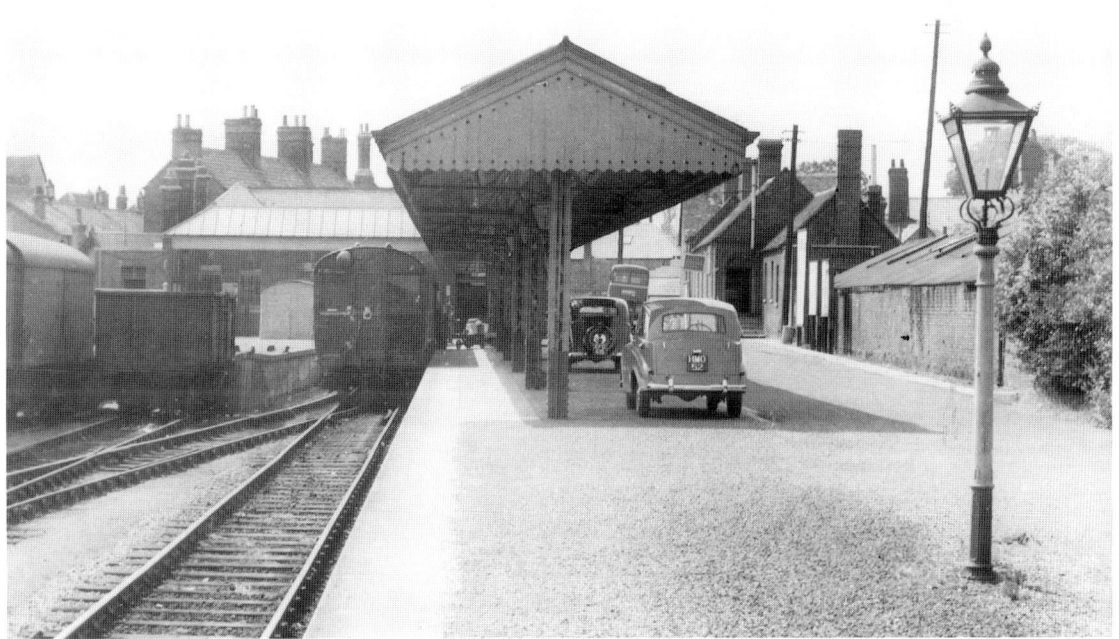

Abingdon terminus in 1953. There seems to be a push-and-pull set in the bay on the left. The whole picture gives a feeling of an unhurried way of life.

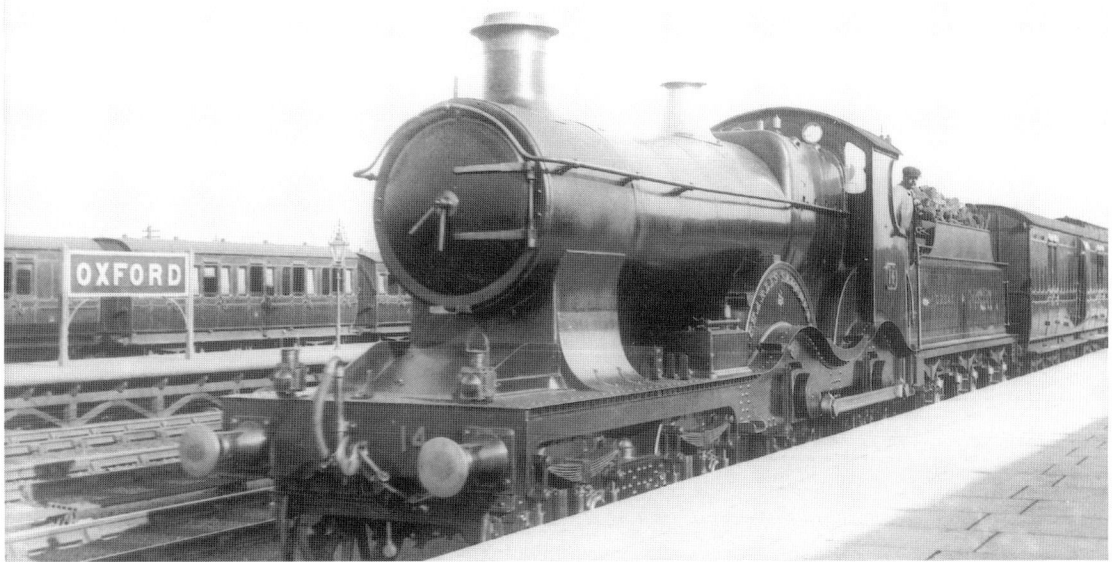

Many years earlier GWR no. 14 *Charles Saunders* started life in 1894 – built by Dean with 7ft wheels. They were fine looking engines. This view was taken in Oxford in about 1904.

Oxford was one of those centres where locos of all regions could be seen and for that reason it was a spotter's paradise. On this journey however, we shall concentrate on the Western.

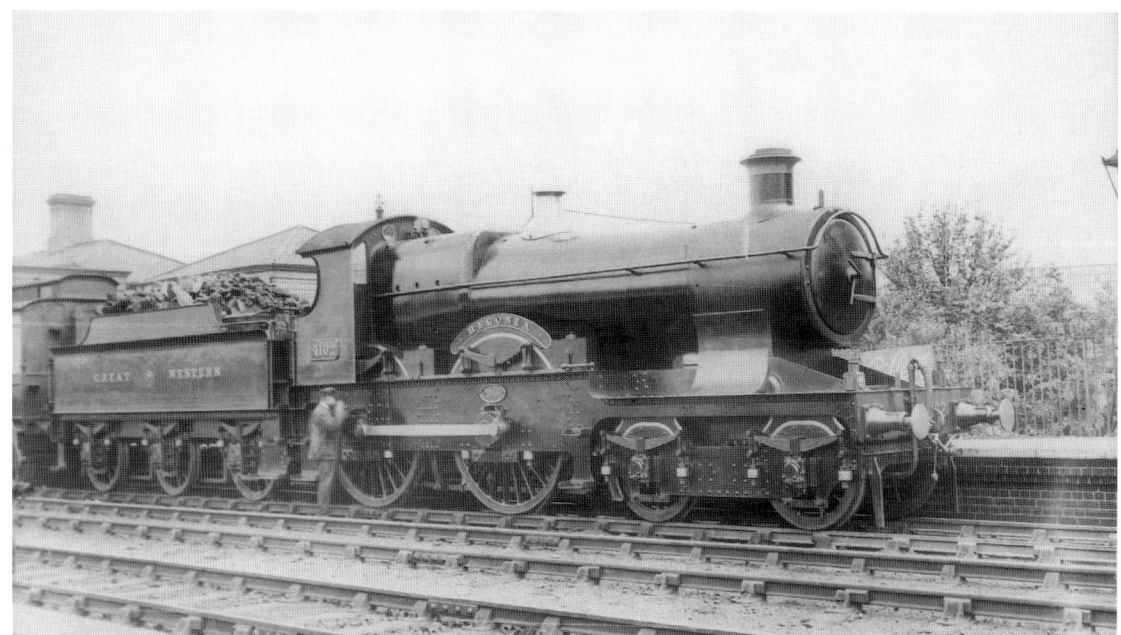

No. 4102 *Begonia*, one of 'Deans Flower' class (built 1908) is seen here about to depart from Oxford, *c.* 1920. It has been said that Churchward was a keen gardener and suggested this new class be named after flowers.

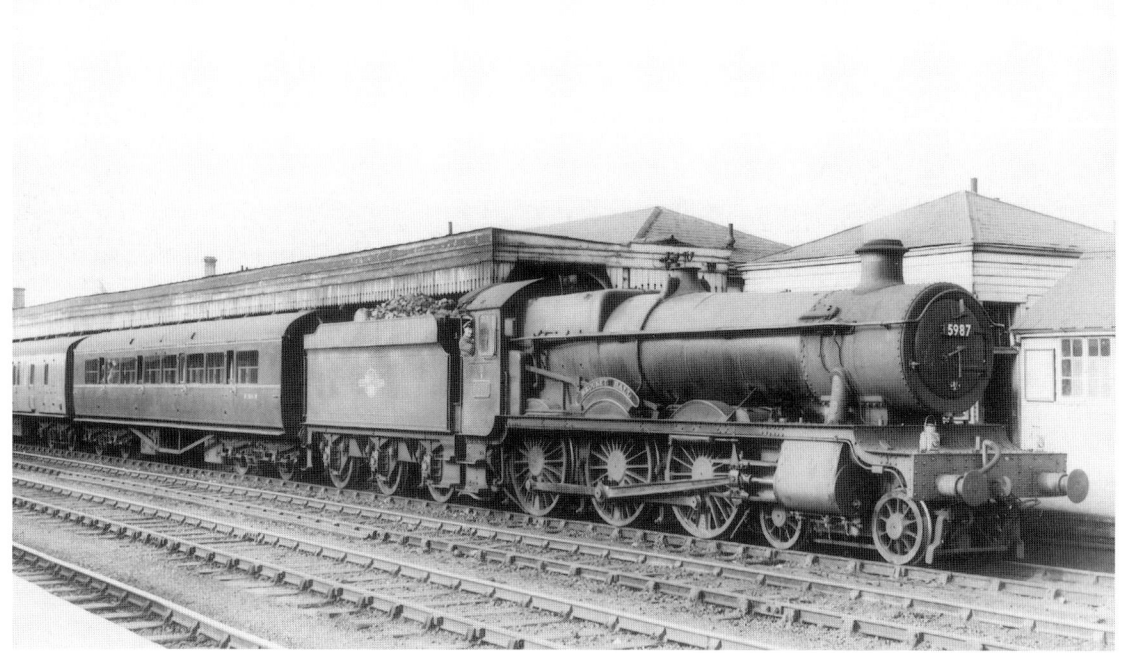

This view of no. 5987 *Brocket Hall* was taken in 1956, many years after the previous view of *Begonia* was taken from almost the same spot.

From Oxford lines diverged to almost any part of the country. We will follow the line to Kingham where there is a junction of the Birmingham–Cheltenham line and the cross-country route to Worcester and Cheltenham. Regrettably we cannot afford the time to explore all the lines in this area, as we have to get back to Didcot.

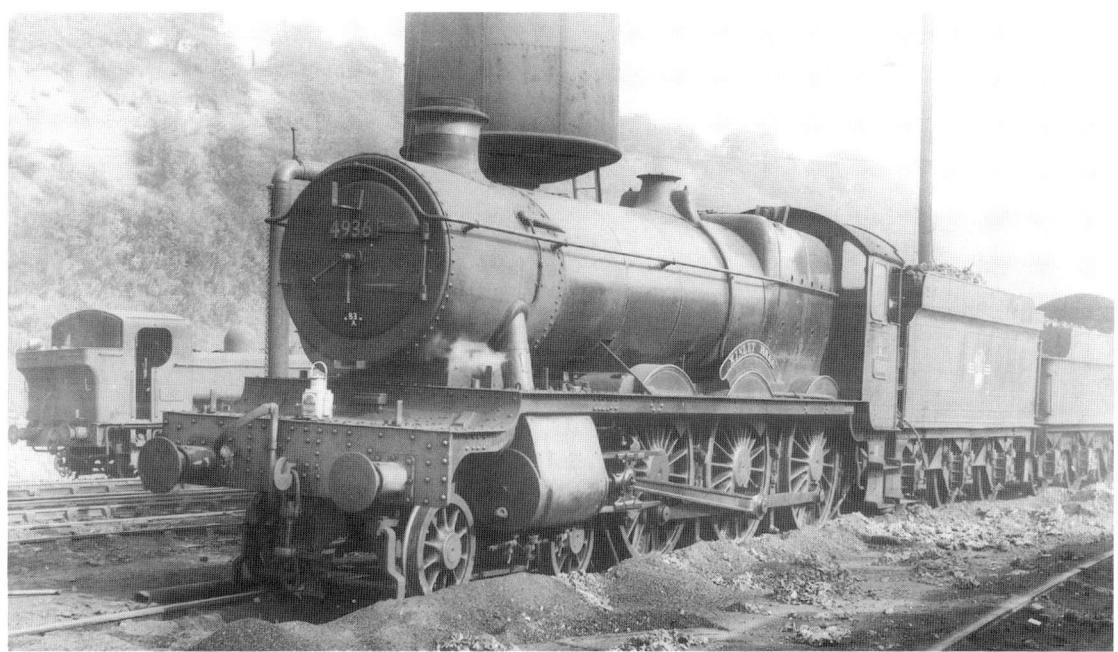

No. 4936 *Kinglet Hall* on Worcester shed in 1960. There is a great view of the shed from the vantage point on top of the cliff in the background.

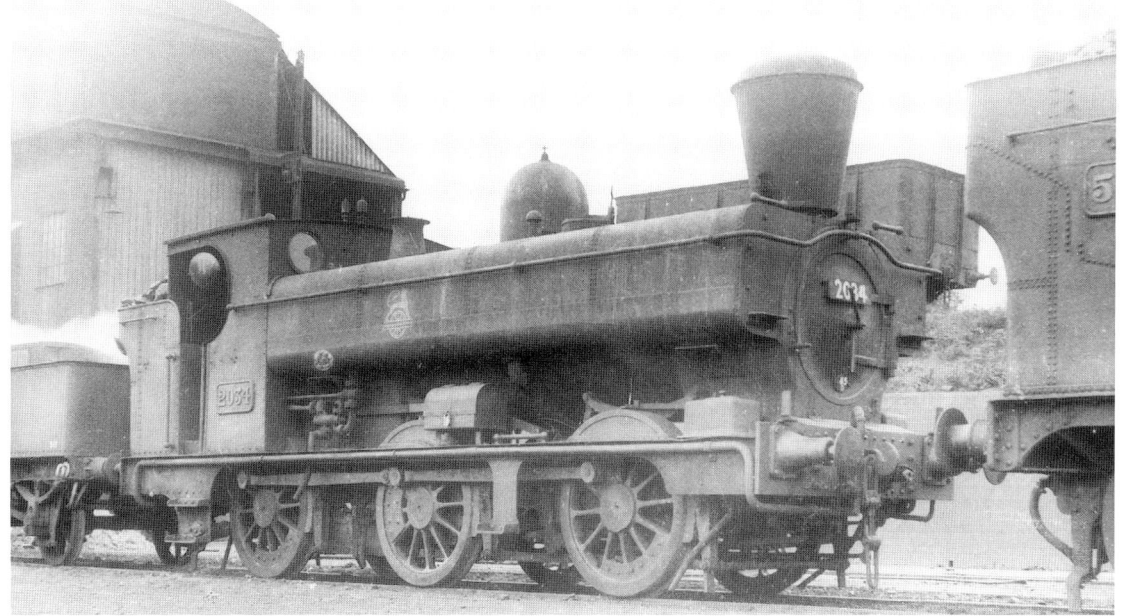

Pannier tank no. 2034 with spark arrestor chimney at Kidderminster, 1953.

The Didcot, Newbury and Southampton Railway was a well-used line from Didcot, and eventually after a meandering journey, arrived at Southampton terminus. During the Second World War much of the line was doubled to enable vast quantities of stores and American servicemen to be taken to the south in preparation for the D-Day invasion. Newbury racecourse had been turned into a huge stores depot, all of which had to be taken to the south coast and then on to France.

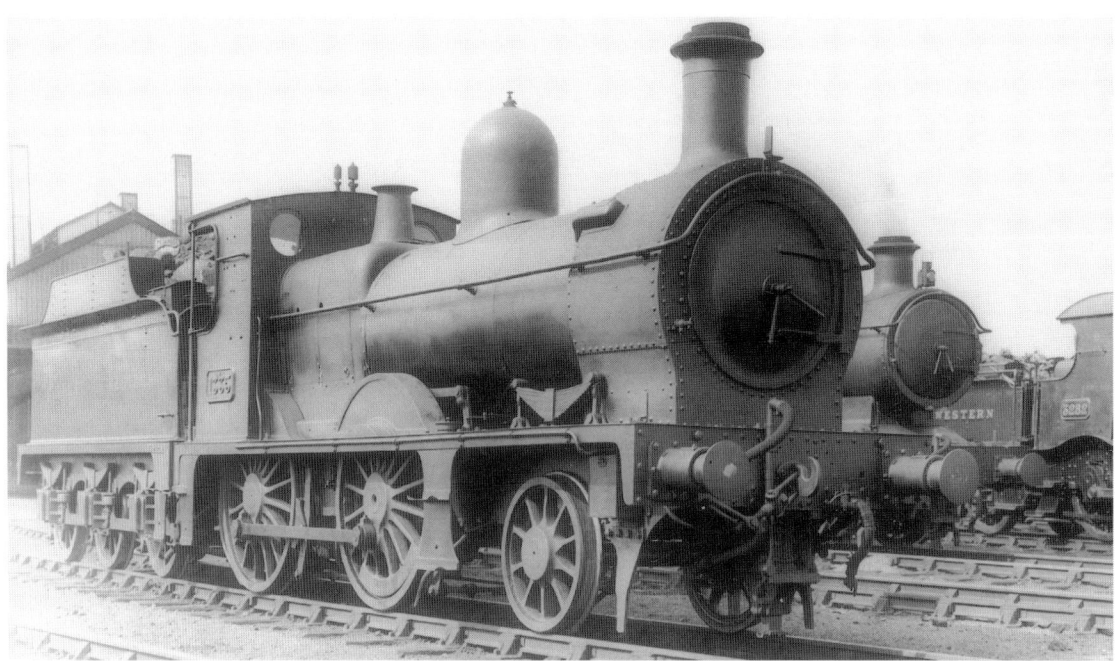

M&SWJR 2–4–0 no. 1335 on Didcot shed, May 1935. Built by Dubs in 1894 it was not withdrawn until the early 1950s. The M&SWJR locos were absorbed by the GWR at the grouping.

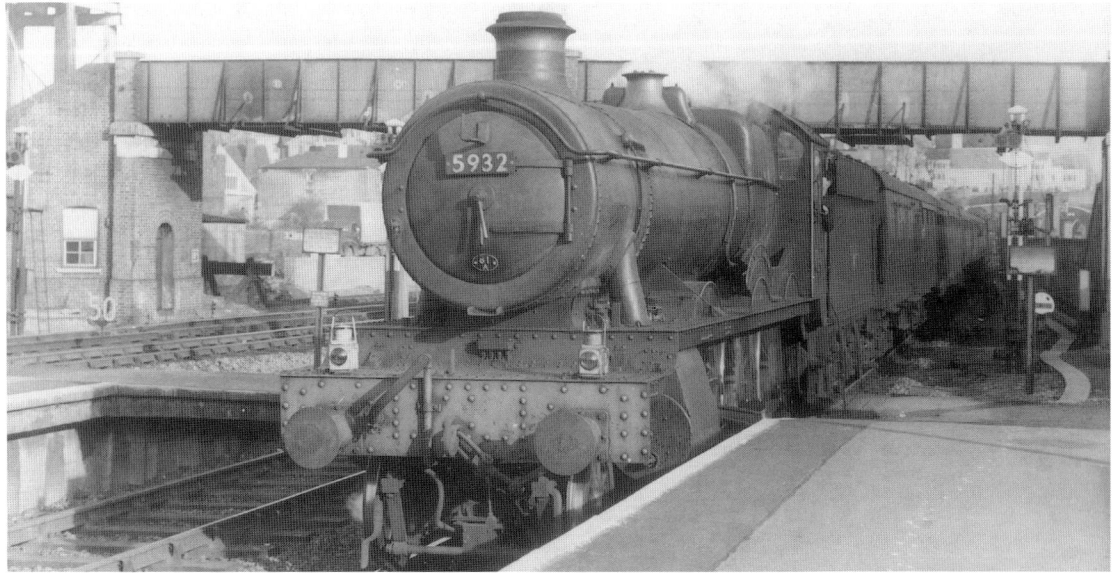

Searching my archive for a photograph at Southampton terminus has proved fruitless. This picture of no. 5932 *Haydon Hall* at Southampton Central in 1961 is the nearest I could muster.

Didcot has been the site of several bad accidents. One in 1955 in foggy weather, involved no. 70026 *Polar Star* hauling a special train from South Wales. It had passed Steventon and was approaching Didcot when it left the rails and rolled down an embankment. Eleven people were killed and nearly one hundred people were injured. Another crash took place in 1964, again on the approach to Didcot station. A train of petrol tankers from Fawley had stopped at signals when another locomotive ran into it. The result was a huge fire so hot that it melted an overbridge.

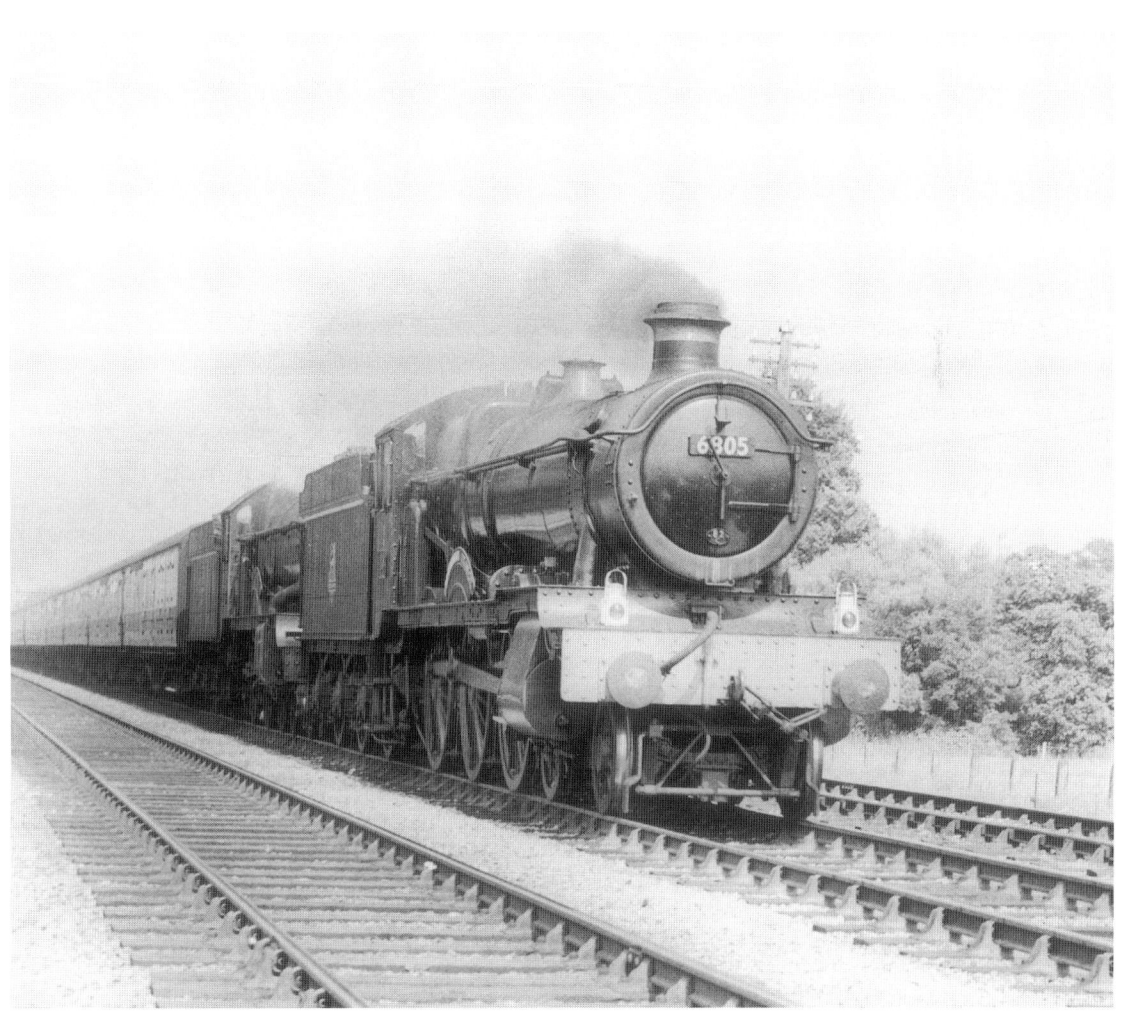

Here we go again, there's the engine whistle, a slight jerk and we are on our way, this time behind 'Grange' class no. 6805 *Broughton Grange*, 1954.

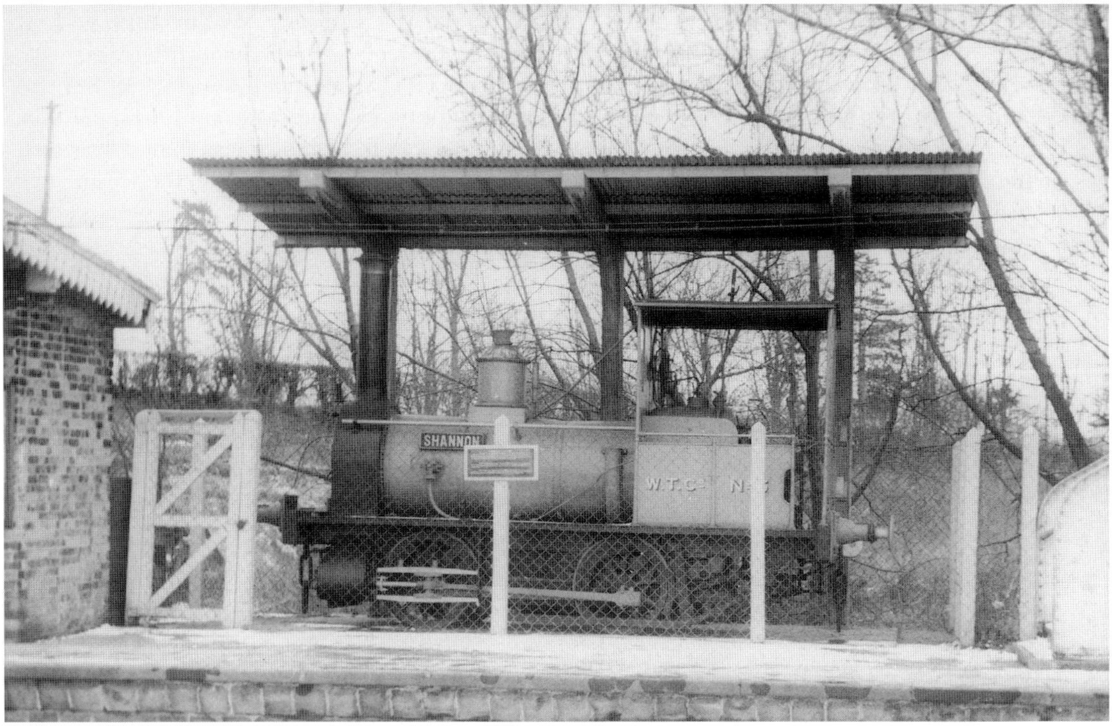

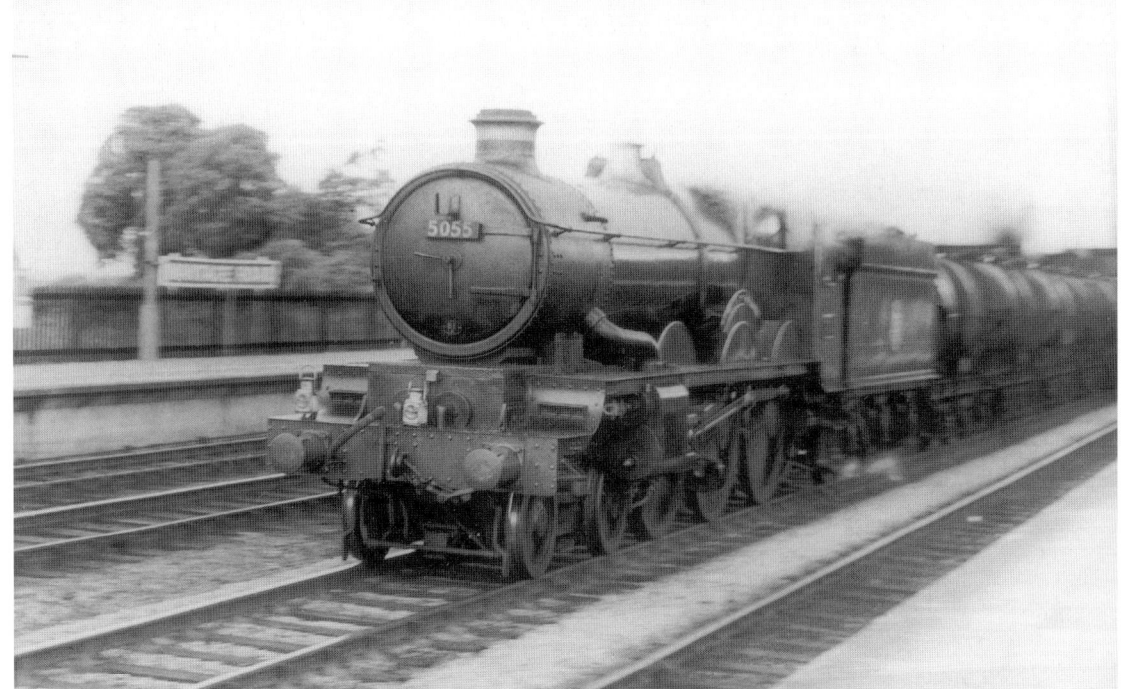

We are travelling at a fair speed now through Steventon and approaching Wantage Road. On the platform at Wantage Road is Wantage Tramway No. 5 *Shannon*. This locomotive was built in 1857 and when the tramway was closed in 1946 it was restored by Swindon and placed on the platform at Wantage, under partial cover. It is one of the oldest locos in the world still in working order.

'Castle' no. 5055 *Earl of Eldon* travelling very fast at Wantage Road with a milk train in 1954.

Now through Wantage, next comes Uffington with a branch to Faringdon. We are still travelling fast. Speeds of 90 mph are frequent on this stretch of track. We are now approaching Shrivenham, site of a bad accident in 1936 involving no. 6007 *King William III* and a freight train. The 'King' was at the head of a mail train from Penzance and a freight train had broken its couplings and was still in the path of the express. In the early hours of the morning the driver saw the trucks in his path, the brakes were slammed on, but he had no chance of stopping in time. The 'King' came off the tracks and onto its side; wooden carriages were smashed and two people were killed and many passengers were injured. The driver was regrettably badly scalded and died in hospital. The track was closed for several days.

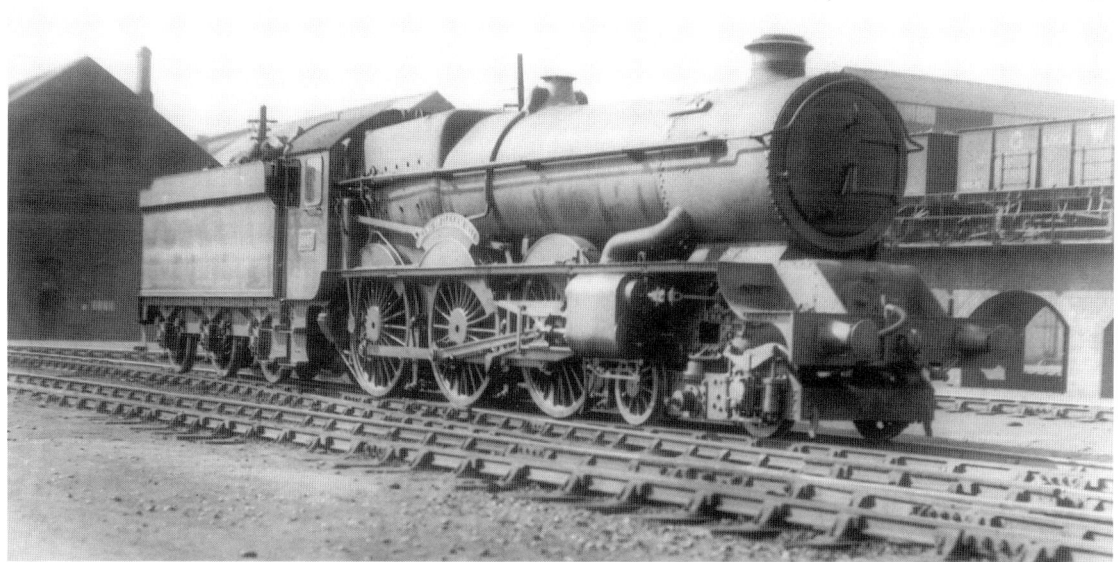

No. 6007 *King William III*, at Old Oak Common in 1935, shortly before its accident.

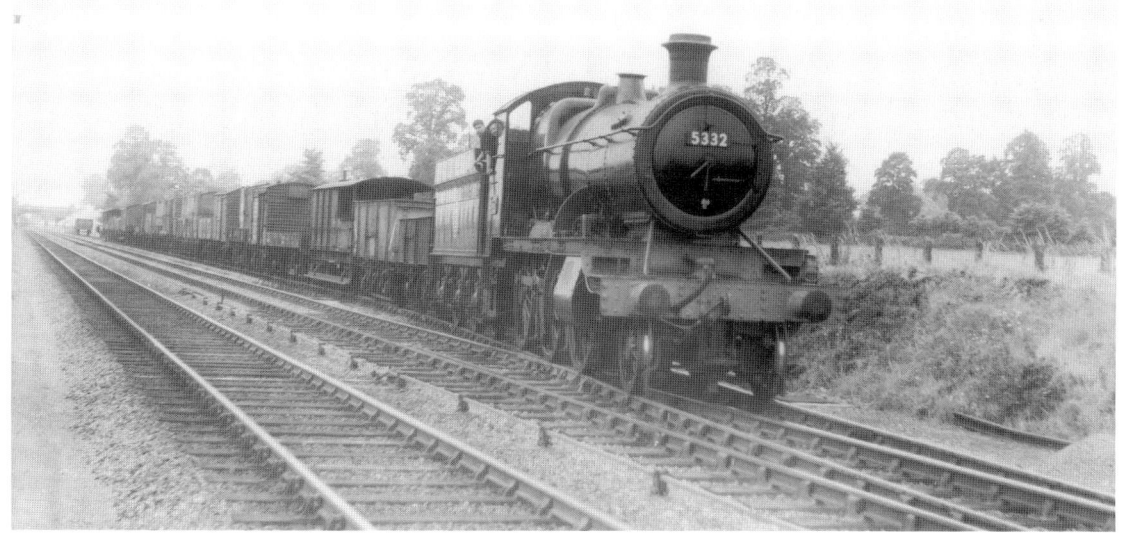

No. 5332 at head of a freight near Shrivenham, 1955.

We are now slowing and about to stop at Swindon, a Mecca for all GWR/WR enthusiasts.
On go the brakes and we come to a halt. Doors fly open and many enthusiasts make a dash for
the works entrance. As many will remember, the works held a regular Wednesday afternoon
opening at around 2 p.m. I can remember as a young man the queues that accumulated to go in.
The excitement, the expectation, everyone speculating about what might be seen, would there
be any 'Kings' on the works?, would there be any 'Bulldogs' on the dump?, as they were in their
final days when I first went on a works visit.

The queue starts to move, notebooks come out, a few of us have cameras (this is a long time
before cameras were obligatory for enthusiasts). Probably not more than one in a hundred had a
camera and the majority of these would have been a Box Brownie. My camera was a Selfix
Ensign which was a very good camera for the day. Final checks and into the tunnel that leads
under the main lines and comes up outside the works.

After more than fifty years the route we took is rather blurred in my mind, but I know I took a
lot of pictures and walked a fair distance. Unfortunately all my notebooks for this period were
thrown out during a spring clean by my mother, so I cannot give a detailed account of what
locos were there.

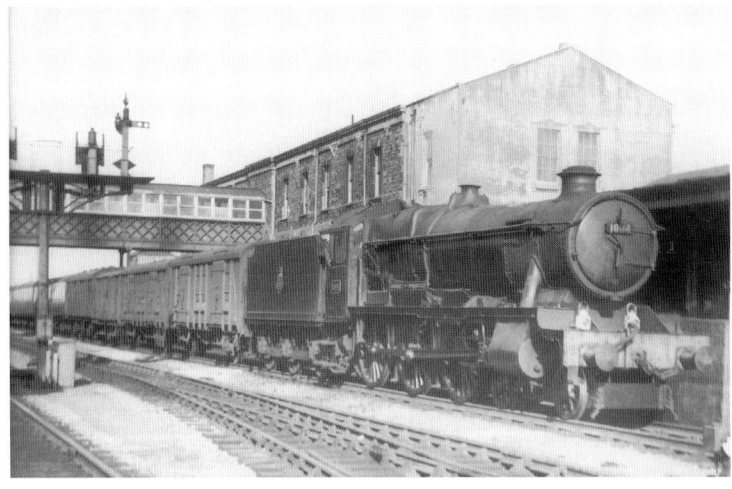

No. 1004 *County of Somerset*
arriving at Swindon in the early
1950s.

Near where the long
tunnel comes up in the
works are three crane
locos. No. 1299,
originally a South Devon
Railway loco, built in
1878, is seen here when it
became a GWR engine. It
was fitted with a crane in
the early 1880s, spent
many years in the works
and was eventually
scrapped early in the
1930s. To the left is no. 18
Steropes, built in 1901 by
Dean, and on the right,
Hercules, built twenty
years later. Both were
withdrawn in 1936.

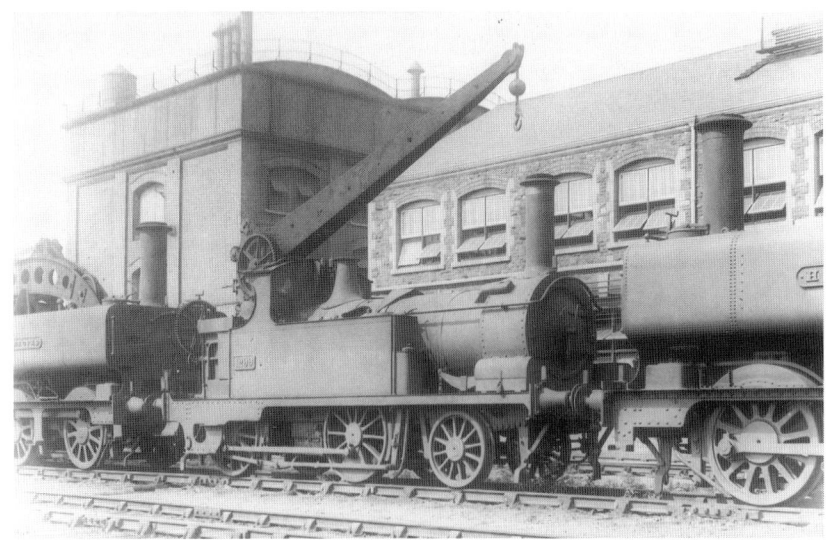

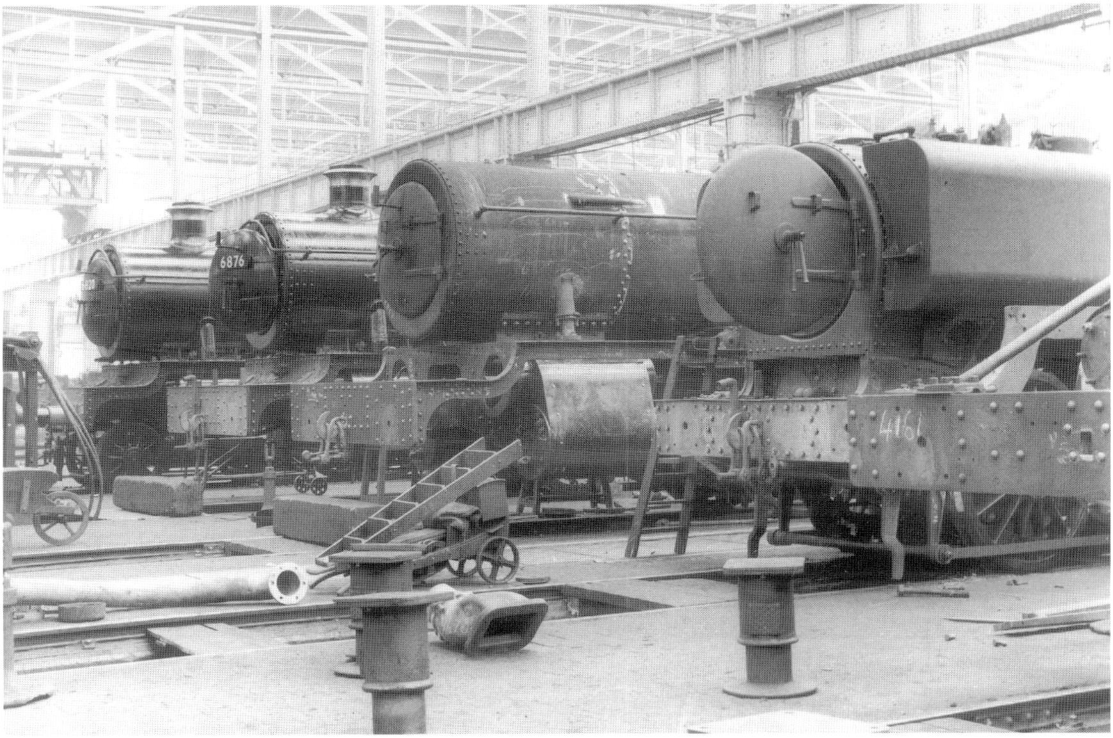

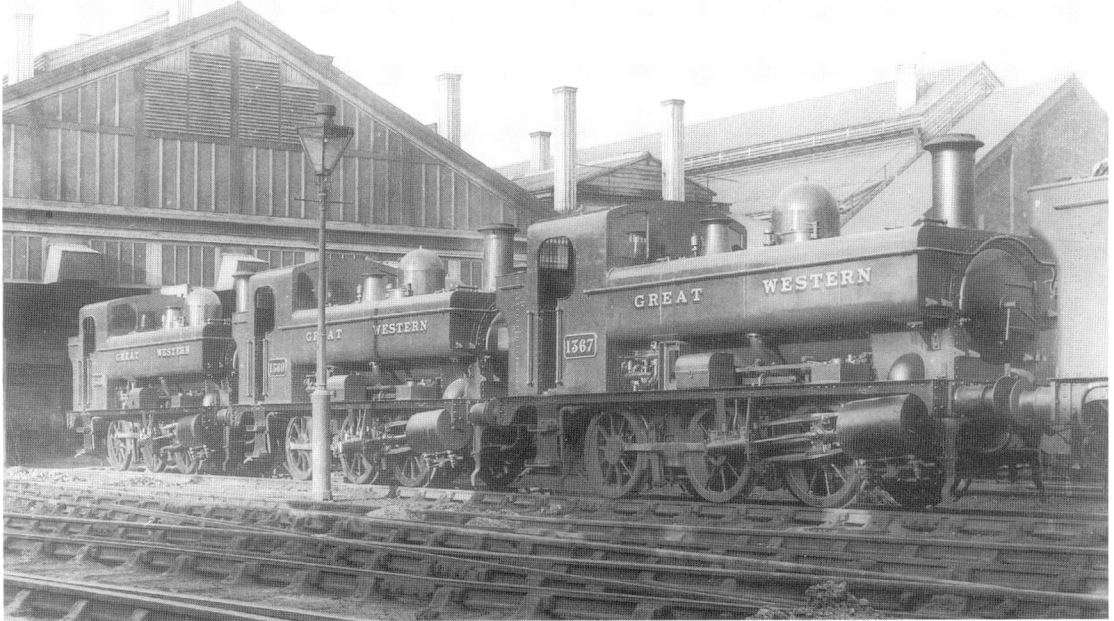

A view inside the main works. Here we see no. 6820 *Kingstone Grange* and no. 6876 *Kingsland Grange*. With the aid of a magnifying glass the number 6833 can just be made out over the steam pipe on the third. The fourth engine has no number on the loco, but there is a pipe of some sort. The rectangular one in front of the step-ladder has no. 9675 on it, and the buffer beam of no. 4161 just creeps into the picture on the right. The upside-down buffers were used by the workmen during their lunch break.

This view in Swindon shed 82C must be fairly unusual as there were only six of this class of engine built, and to be able to capture three (nos 1368, 1369,and 1367) in ex-works condition was very lucky. These engines saw service in many areas and towards the end of their lives could be seen in Weymouth and Wadebridge.

At Swindon heading westward, the main line for Gloucester diverges northwards just outside Swindon main line station, so a quick trip to Gloucester will be of interest before we head for Bristol once more. Round the curve we go, passing very close to the works through Purton, Ashton Keynes and Kemble (known to aircraft enthusiasts as a one-time large RAF base and home to the Red Arrows). Also at Kemble there is a branch to the Cotswold town of Tetbury, and another for the Roman town of Cirencester.

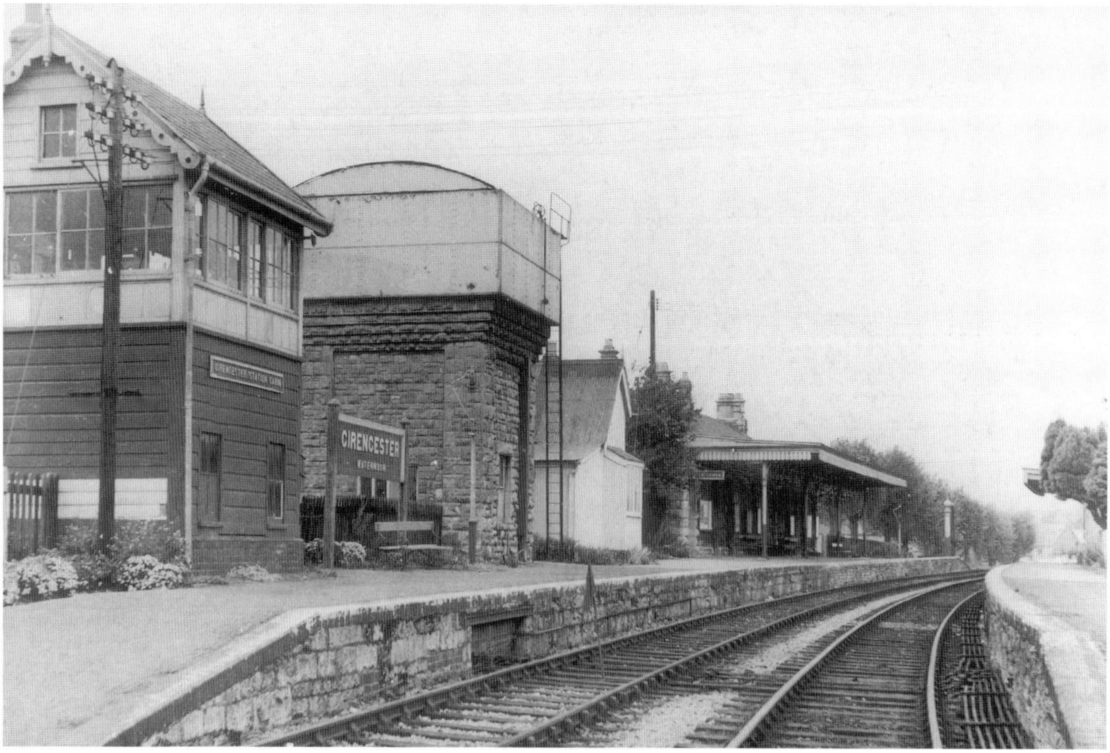

Cirencester, a lovely Cotswold town, has its station is rather spoiled by a huge water tower which dominates the scene.

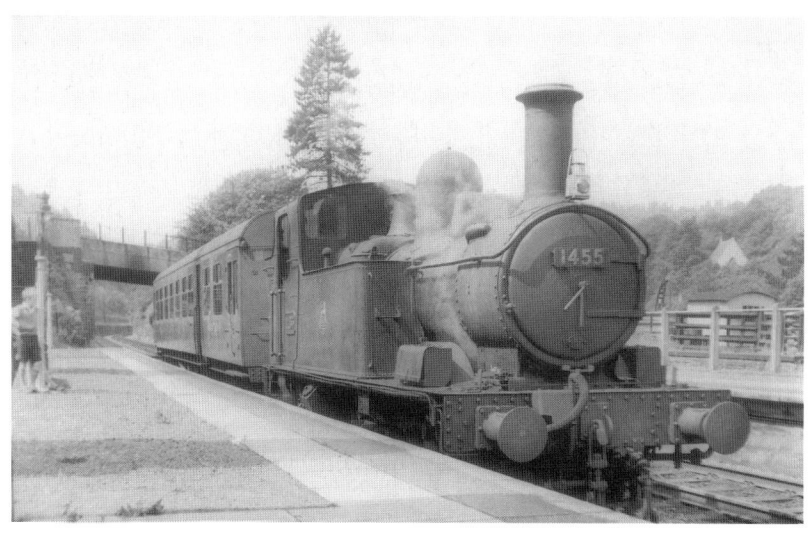

0–4–2T no. 1455 takes a leisurely rest at Chalford in the 1950s.

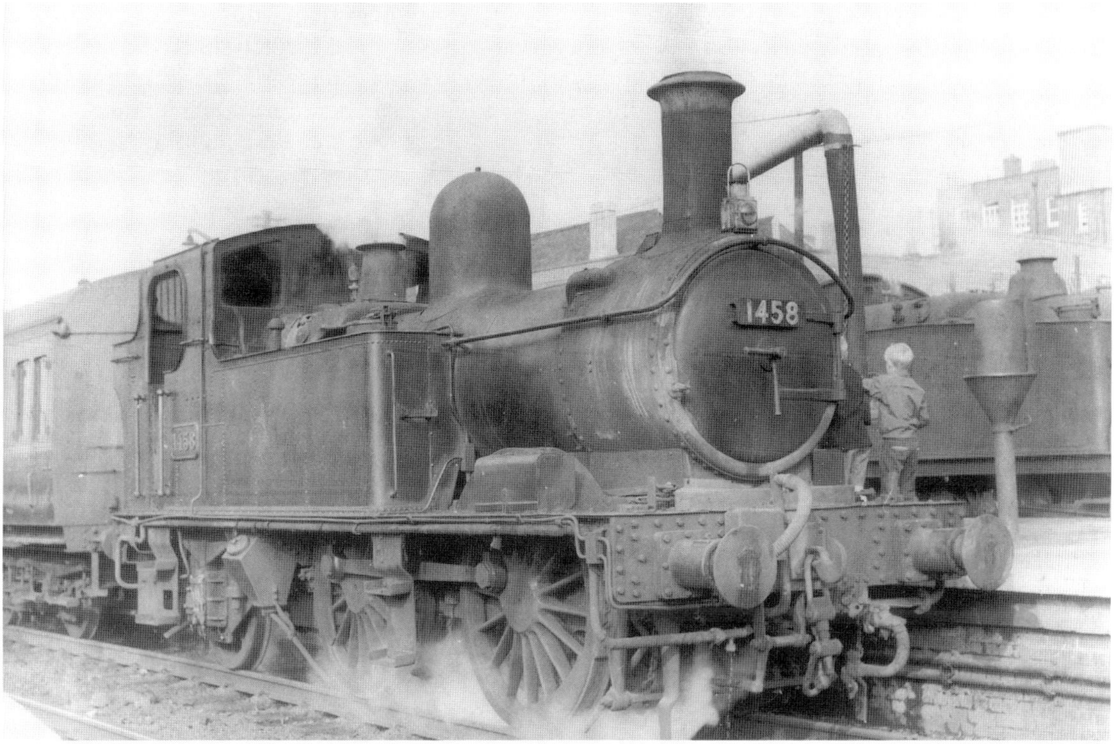

The 0–4–2T of the 14xx class seemed to be the most popular locos to work in the Cotswolds. Here no. 1458 is photographed in Stroud in the 1950s.

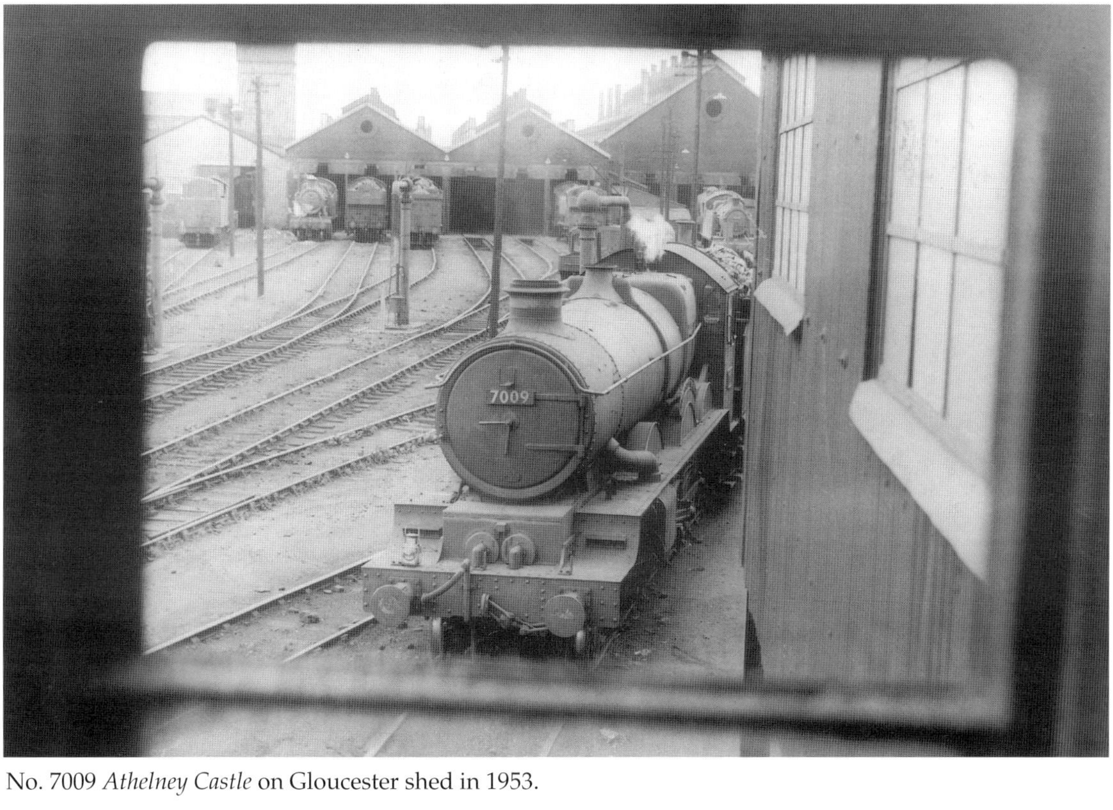

No. 7009 *Athelney Castle* on Gloucester shed in 1953.

We have to make our return journey to Swindon after our quick visit to Gloucester, out through Tramway Junction, through the Cotswolds, and into Swindon. The M&SWJR made its leisurely way down through the Cotswolds via Andoversford, Cirencester and Cricklade and ran into Swindon Town station. After Swindon it continued to Marlborough and Savernake.

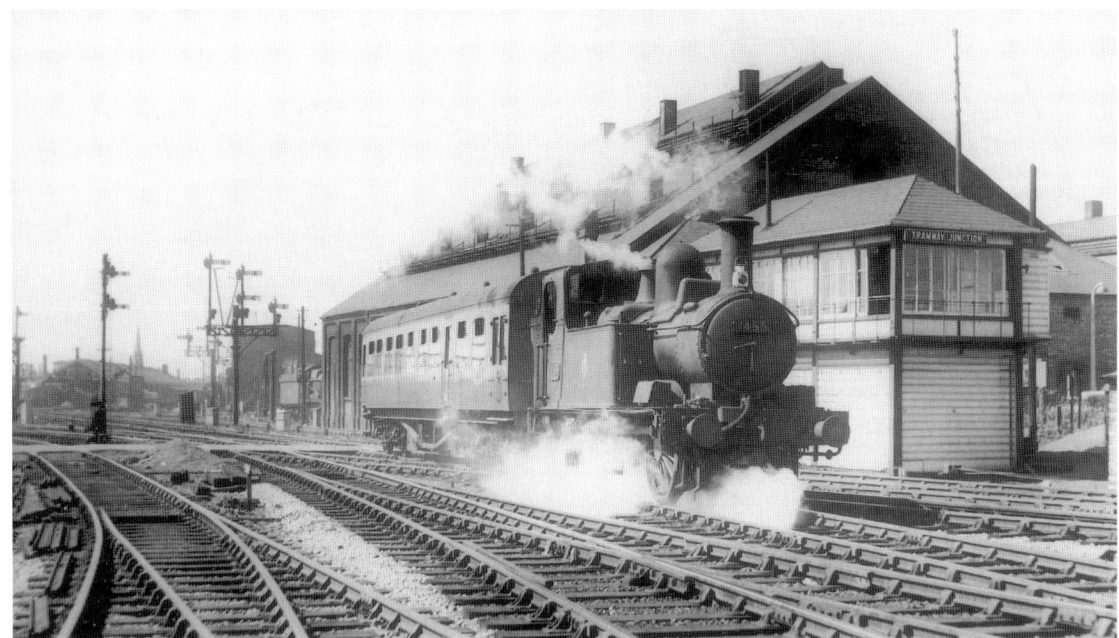

Leaving Gloucester is 0–4–2T no. 1455 with a one-coach train making its way to the Cotswolds, 1953.

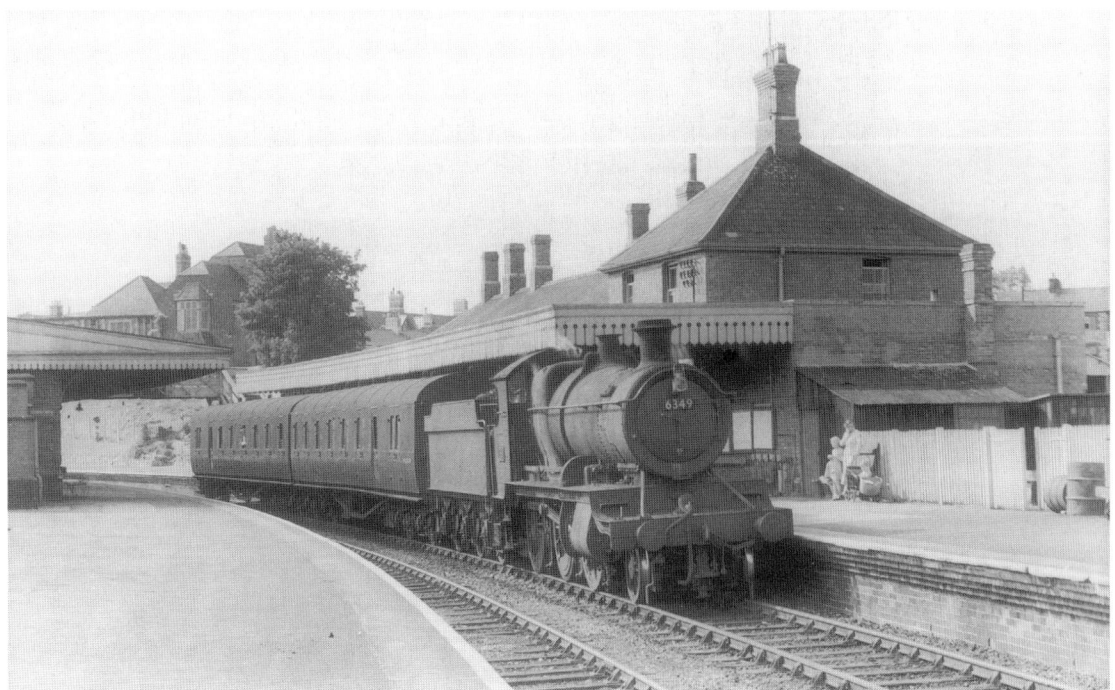

'Mogul' no. 6349 arrives at Swindon Town in 1953.

Many years later as a professional photographer, at the time when most of Swindon Works was being demolished, I was asked to take a series of photographs which I undertook with a certain sadness. One of the buildings which was going to be taken down was a huge galvanised shed. I was told it was a stores shed but I have never been able to find out if this was a fact. I was also told it was one of the first of its type to be built. It was being donated to the West Somerset Railway, and I was asked to photograph all the joints and how it all fitted together; in other words, what went where so that it could be re-erected on the Minehead Line.

I found it quite thought-provoking as I went about my task. There were also adjoining buildings with obvious broad-gauge entrances. I was all alone in these buildings and in my imagination I was back in the 1840 and '50s, listening to the sounds and conujuring up images of Gooch's engines rumbling in and out.

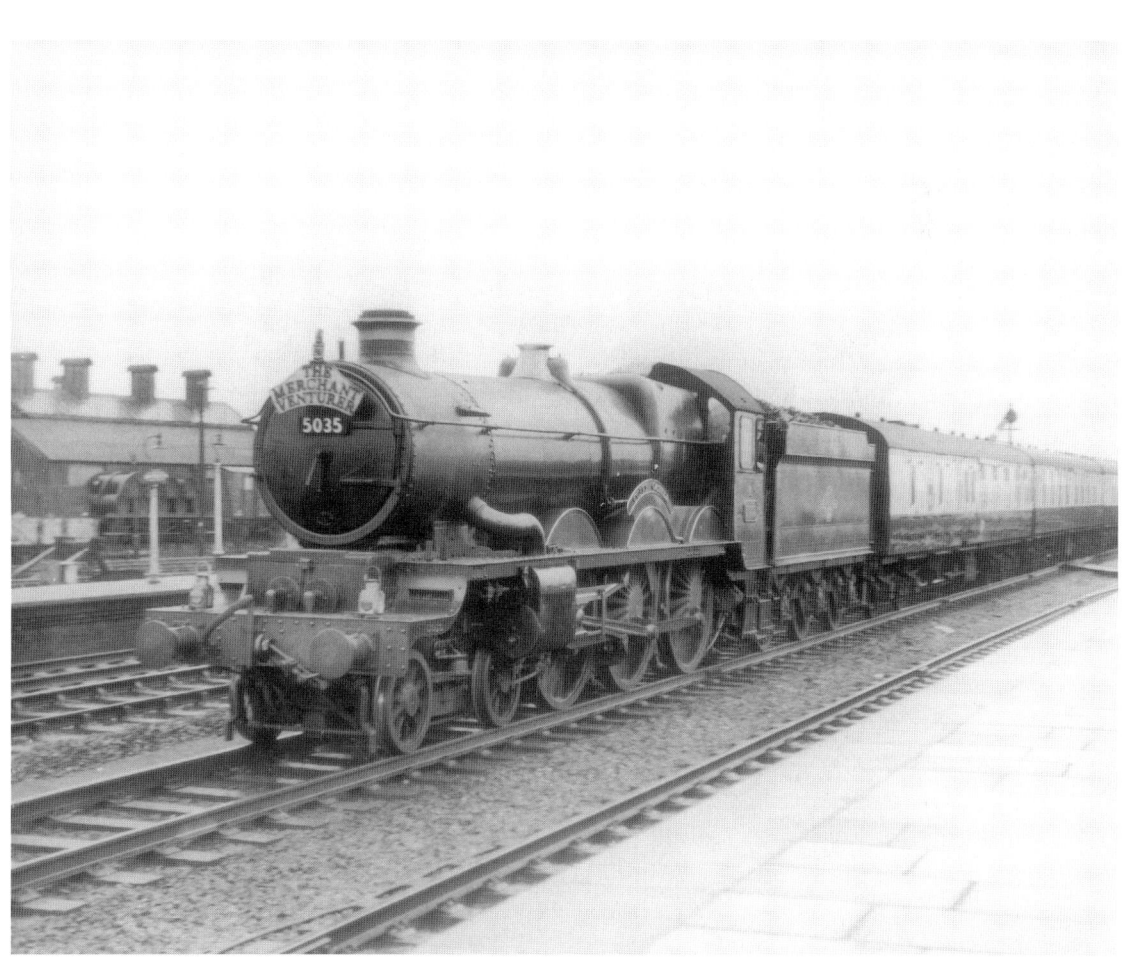

No. 5035 *Coity Castle* roars through Swindon on the centre road on its way to Bristol and Weston-super-Mare with 'The Merchant Venturer'.

We keep up a lively pace after leaving Swindon, then we feel the brakes come on and the knowledgeable ones among us will say 'Ah, this is Wootton Bassett coming up, we are going onto the Badminton Line'. Sure enough there is a squealing as our train swings onto this line, which was built after the Severn Tunnel had been opened. Time was wasted by trains having to go through Bath and Bristol and then back out of Bristol to go through the tunnel, but the route through Badminton saved many miles and much time.

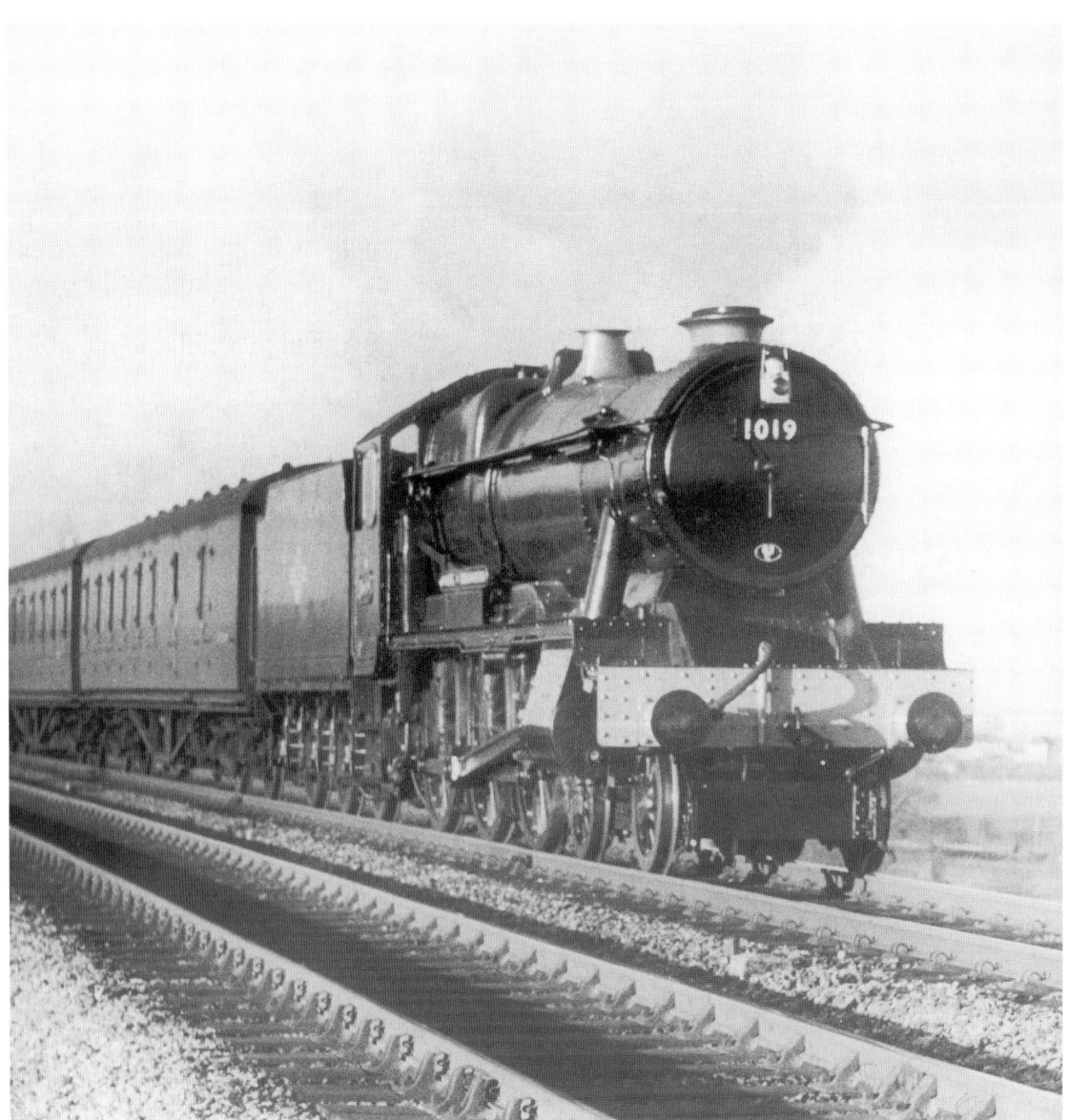

No. 1019 *County of Merioneth* in immaculate condition near Wootton Bassett on a stopping train, 1958. It was obviously new out of works and was running-in.

Named expresses which passed Wootton Bassett included 'The Red Dragon' (Paddington–Carmarthen), 'The Bristolian' (Paddington–Bristol), 'The Merchant Venturer' (Paddington–Weston-super-Mare), 'The Pembroke Coast Express' (Paddington–Pembroke Dock), 'The South Wales Pullman' (Paddington–Swansea) and 'The Capitals United Express' (Paddington–Cardiff).

We are picking up speed again and we shall pass through a number of locations well known to enthusiasts through the recordings of such authors as O.S. Nock. First comes Little Somerford and Hullavington, then we are into Badminton. Nearly all the stations on this line are similar in appearance, having been built by the same contractor and architect when the line was finished in 1903.

Badminton itself was a little different because there was a royal connection. The Duke of Beaufort who owned the land would only agree to a sale if he was granted the right to stop trains for himself and his family (and of course any royal visitors he had). This right was granted, and at the station there was a much more regal waiting room.

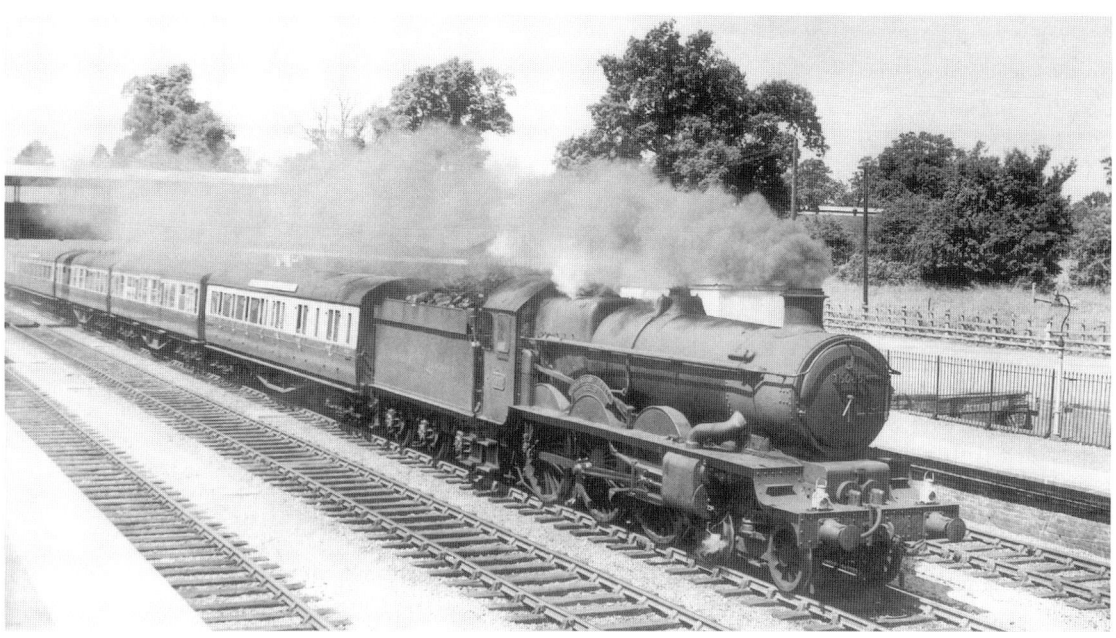

No. 5085 *Evesham Abbey* on the fast through line at Badminton, June 1949.

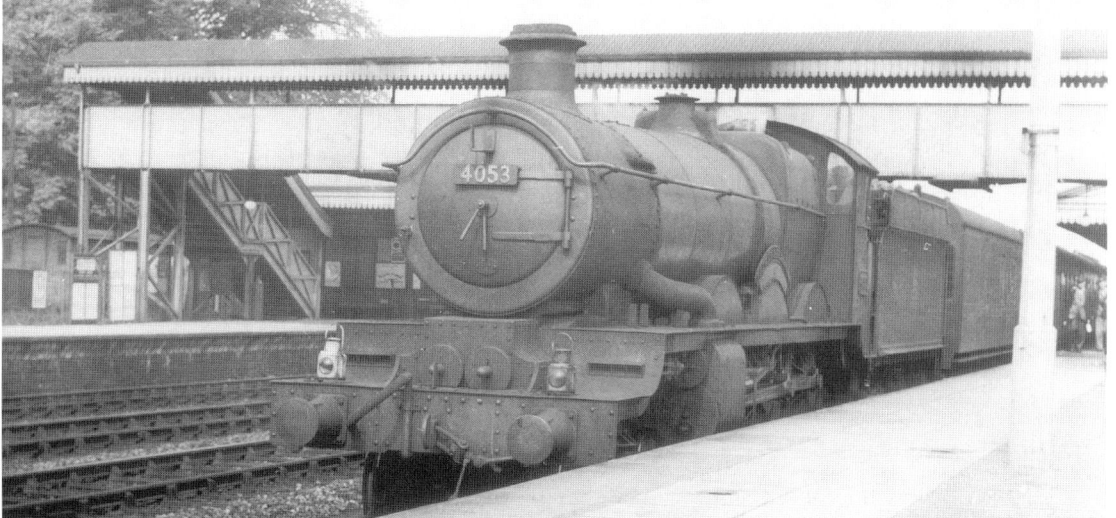

No. 4053 *Princess Alexandra* about to depart from Badminton, 1951. I wonder if the duke was on board?

On the move again, shortly after leaving Badminton, we plunge into the darkness of Chipping Sodbury Tunnel. About 2½ miles long, this tunnel has suffered from flooding on occasions following severe weather. We emerge into a blaze of sunlight, still travelling at good speed, through Chipping Sodbury station. We will shortly be passing over the main Midland line into Bristol at Westerleigh. Next comes Coalpit Heath, an appropriate name in view of all the coal mines in the area. Now we are crossing the eleven arches of Winterbourne Viaduct, through Winterbourne station which is just at the end of the viaduct and we are now running into Stoke Gifford which will be the end of our diversion from the main line at Wootton Bassett.

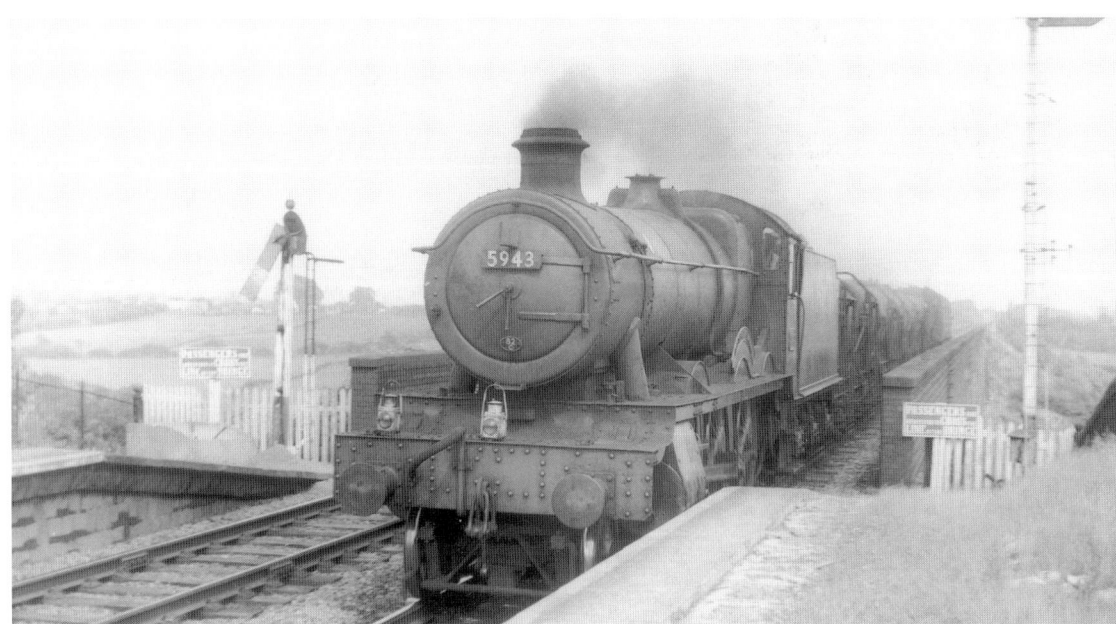

No. 5943 *Elmdon Hall* coming off Winterborne Viaduct with a milk train, 1959.

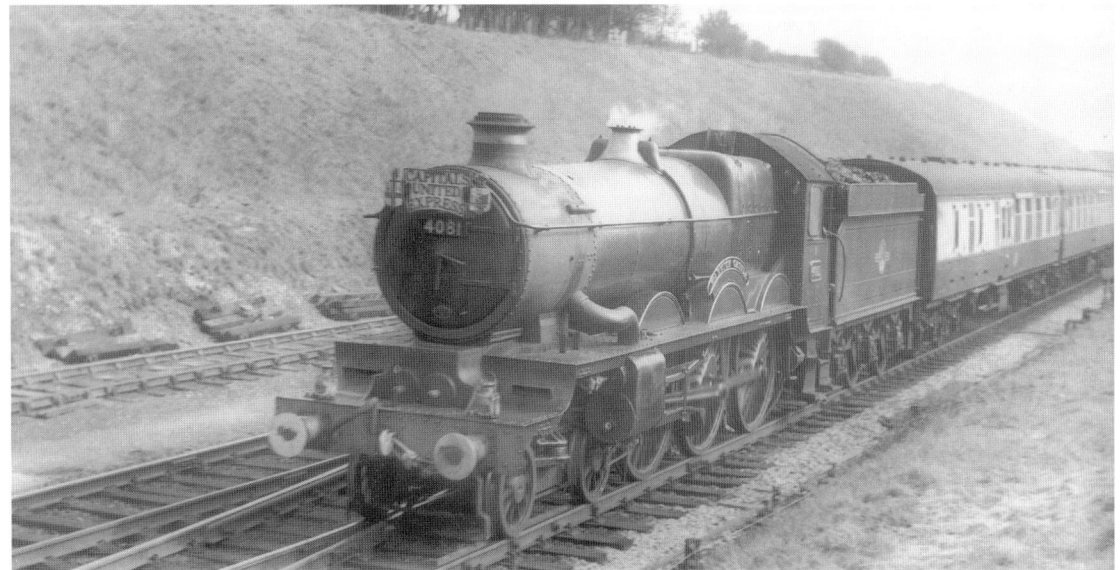

No. 4081 *Warwick Castle* with 'The Capitals United Express' running into Stoke Gifford, 1959.

'The Bristolian' was introduced in 1935 to celebrate the centenary of the GWR. It was scheduled to cover the 118 miles to Paddington in not much over one and a half hours. It had its own set of coaches, including a buffet coach and bar, and was a very popular train. The first locos diagrammed to work it were 'Kings', but 'Castles' soon took over.

In April 1958 it performed its record run. The engine involved was no. 7018 *Drysllwyn Castle*, which touched over 100mph in places. It arrived in Paddington 93 minutes and 50 seconds after leaving Bristol.

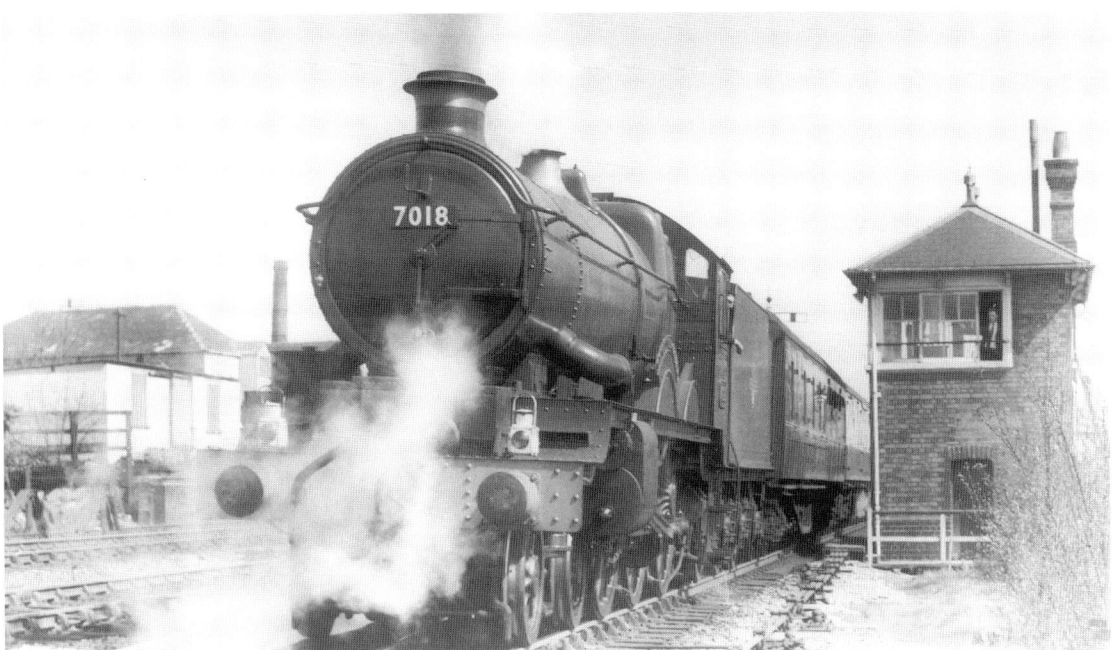

No. 7018 *Drysllwyn Castle*, 1958.

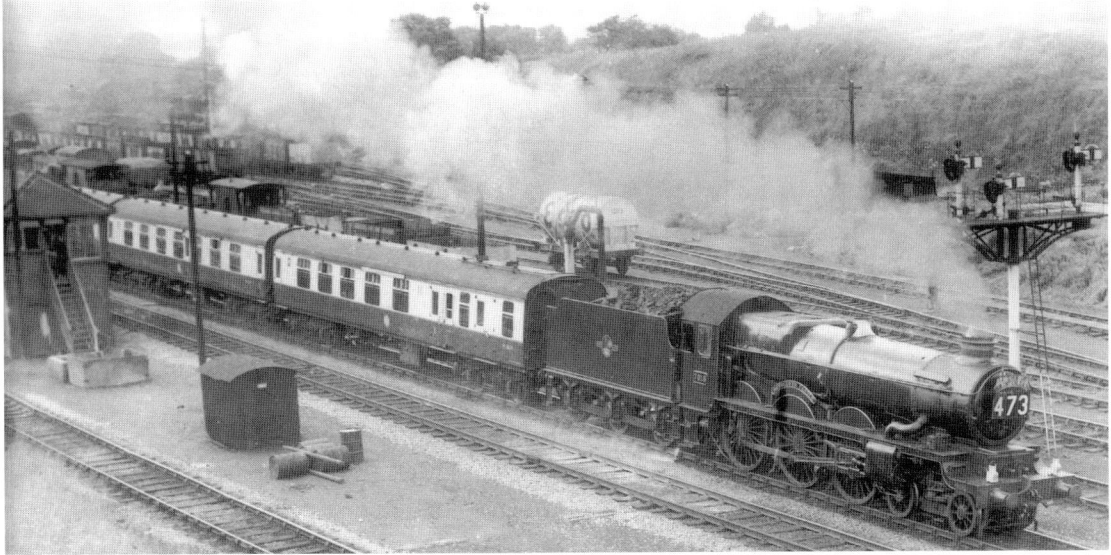

'The Bristolian' picking up speed through Stoke Gifford, now the site of Bristol Parkway. This picture of no. 7018 *Drysllwyn Castle* was taken a few days after its 1958 record run.

We have enjoyed a pleasant diversion, having seen 'The Bristolian' at speed, but we must keep heading westwards. We are now nearing Dauntsey where there is a branch to Malmesbury, a pretty market town. The branch line passes under the Badminton Line near Little Somerford. Once through Dauntsey our next stop is Chippenham. There are usually a couple of engines on the right-hand side at the approach to Chippenham, so once again we drop the window down and get ready with the camera.

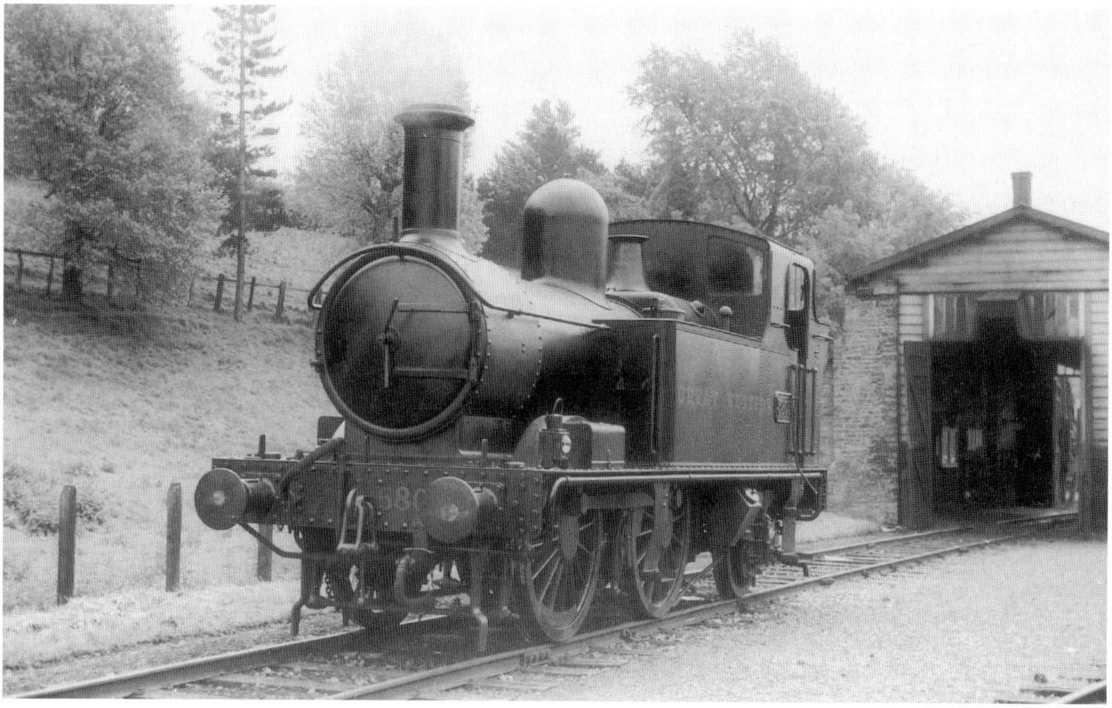

GWR no. 5805 at rest at Malmesbury shed. Not many sheds have such a rural setting as we see in this photograph, taken in 1935.

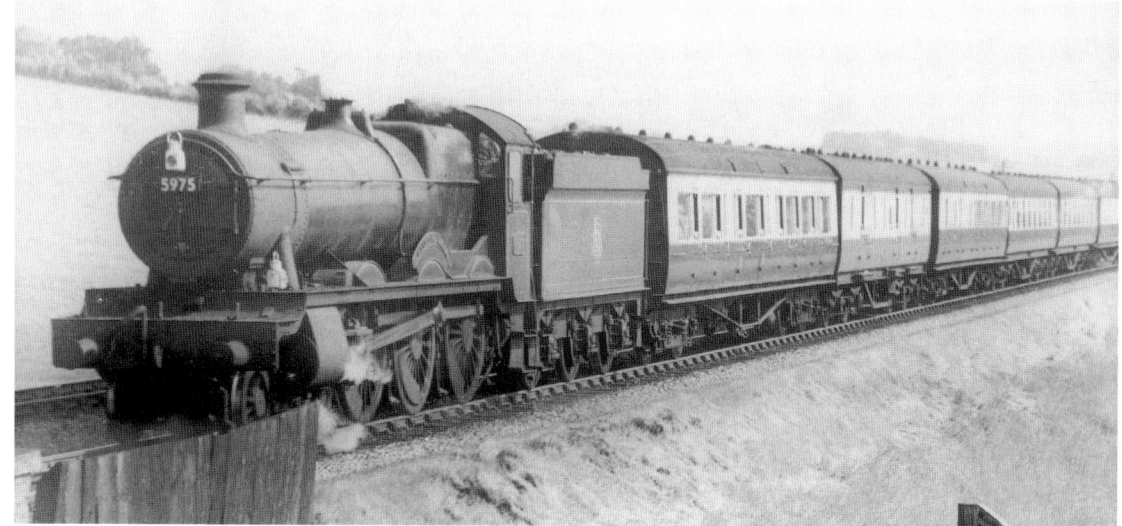

We are leaving Dauntsey behind no. 5975 *Winslow Hall* on its way to Chippenham, 1956.

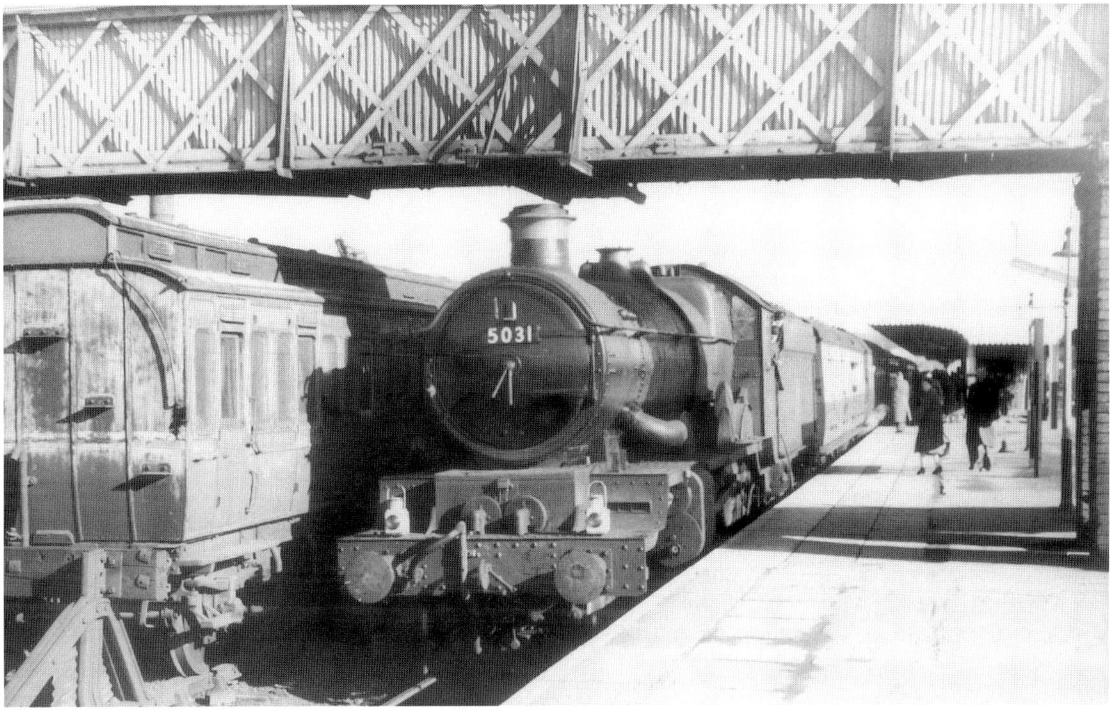

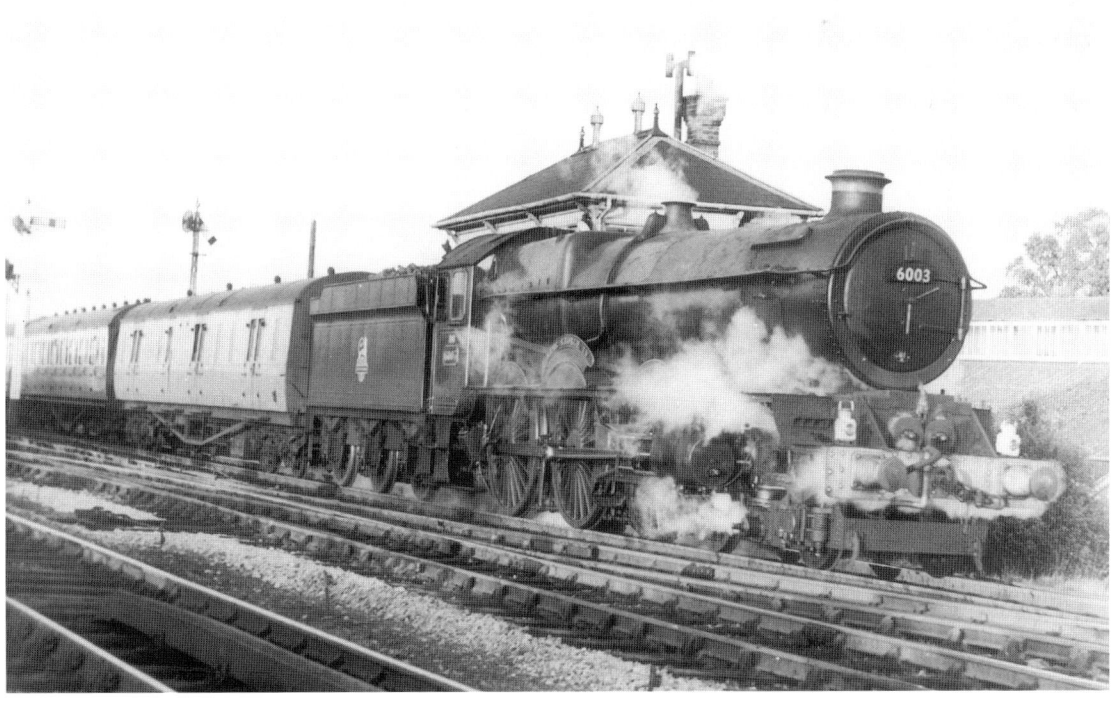

Out of our train at Chippenham, camera at the ready, we only have a couple of minutes so we must get a quick photograph of our train with no. 5031 *Totnes Castle* at the front. On the central line against the buffer stop is an early GWR clerestory coach in a very dilapidated condition. It may have been in use as a workmen's coach.

Leaving Chippenham and making its way to Bristol is no. 6003 *King George IV* in 1955.

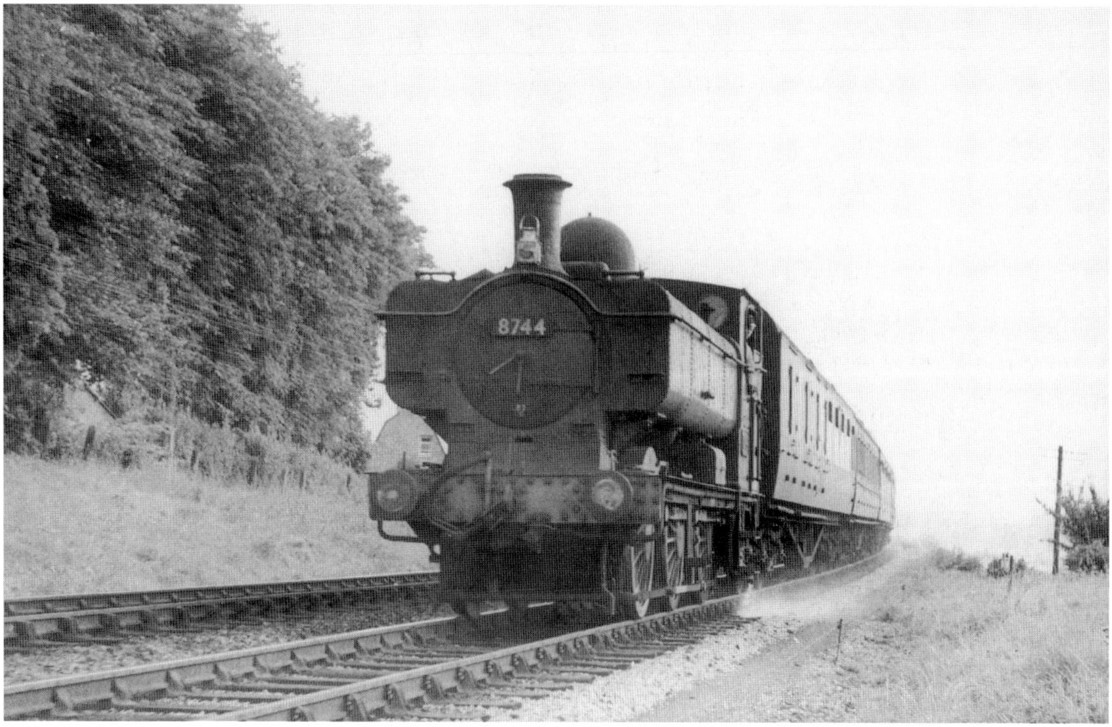

From Chippenham there is a short branch line to Calne. Here pannier no. 8744 will shortly be leaving the main line at the east of Chippenham to go onto the single line to Calne, 1956.

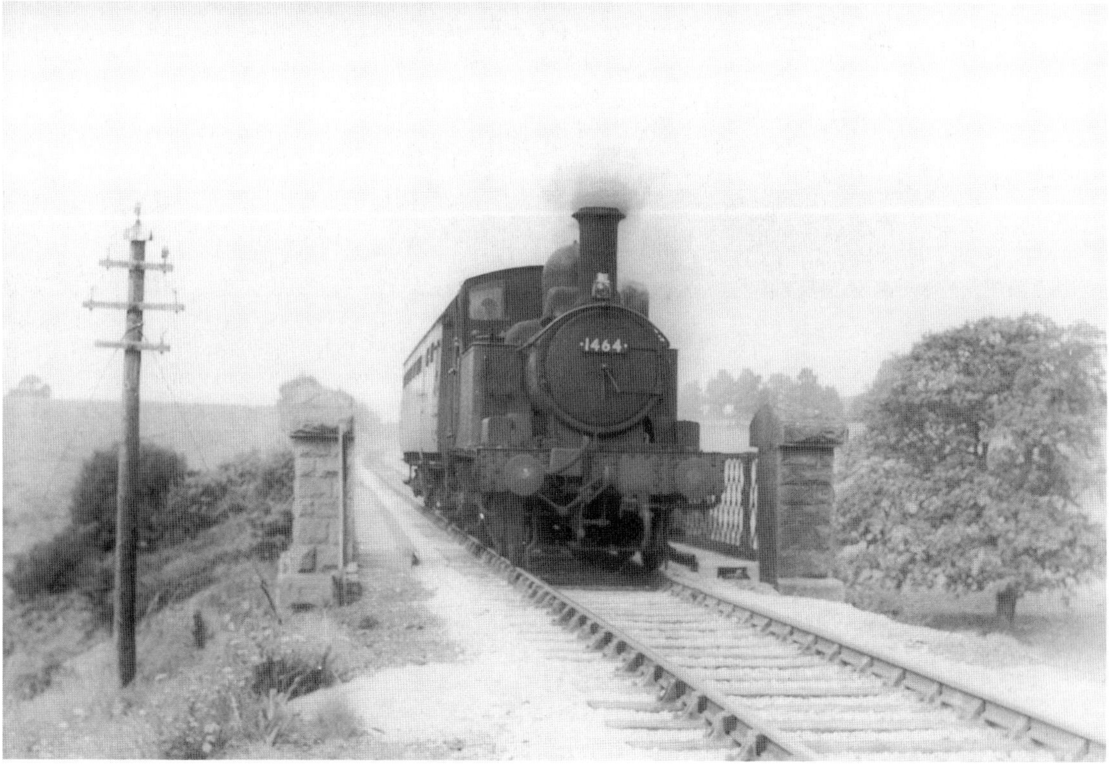

On the branch to Calne ia an ever popular 0–4–2T. This is no. 1464 in 1955.

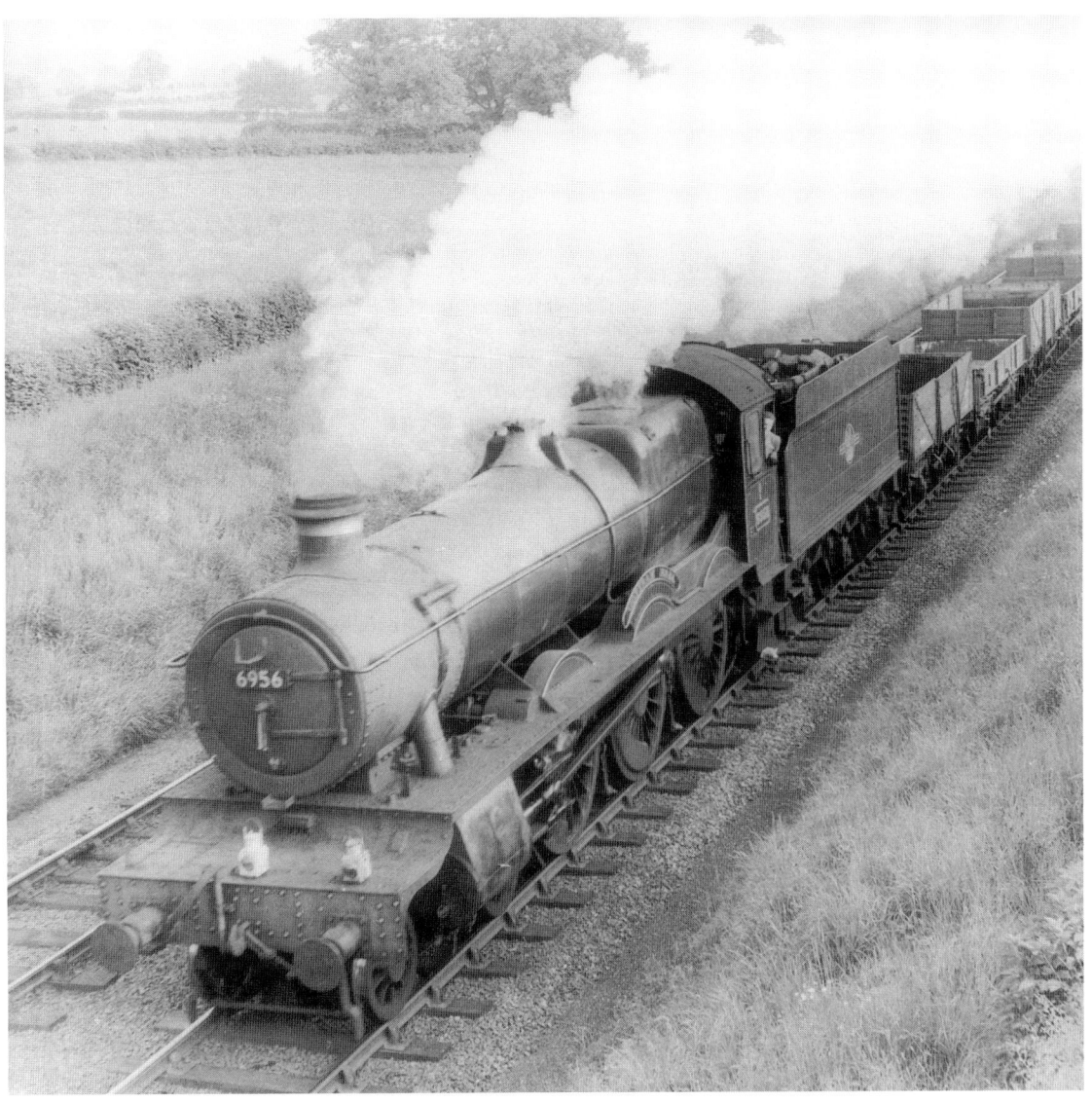

We are now back on our train, picking up speed nicely. There will not be time for any more sandwiches or coffee as we shall shortly be passing Thingley Junction – perhaps a further opportunity to spot another train, so it's back to the window on the off-chance. Here no. 6956 *Mottram Hall* is near Thingley, 1959.

We are now at a fair speed in a cutting, but suddenly the daylight has gone and with a roar we have entered the famous Box Tunnel. The construction was started in 1836 and completed in 1841. Between 1,000 and 4,000 men were employed at various times and more than a hundred lost their lives. These men had to break through solid rock using hundreds of tons of explosives and clearing the rock by pick and shovel. It is 1¾ miles long and descends at 1:100. We shall be through in less than two minutes. I wonder how many passengers thought of the hardships those men suffered so that we could speed to our destinations?

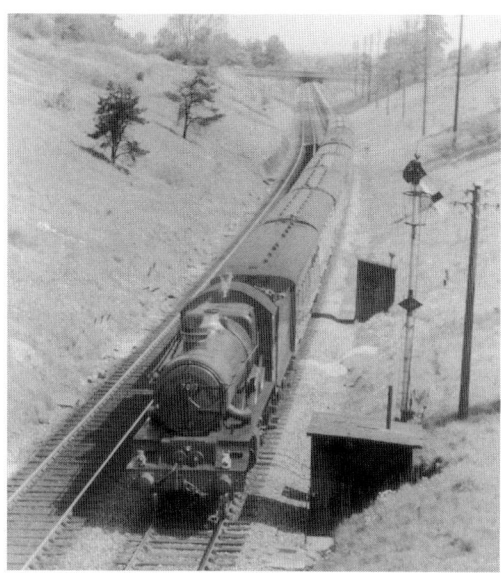

Left: No. 7017 *G.J. Churchward* approaching Box Tunnel in 1955.

Below: No. 6936 *Breccles Hall* near Bathampton in 1957.

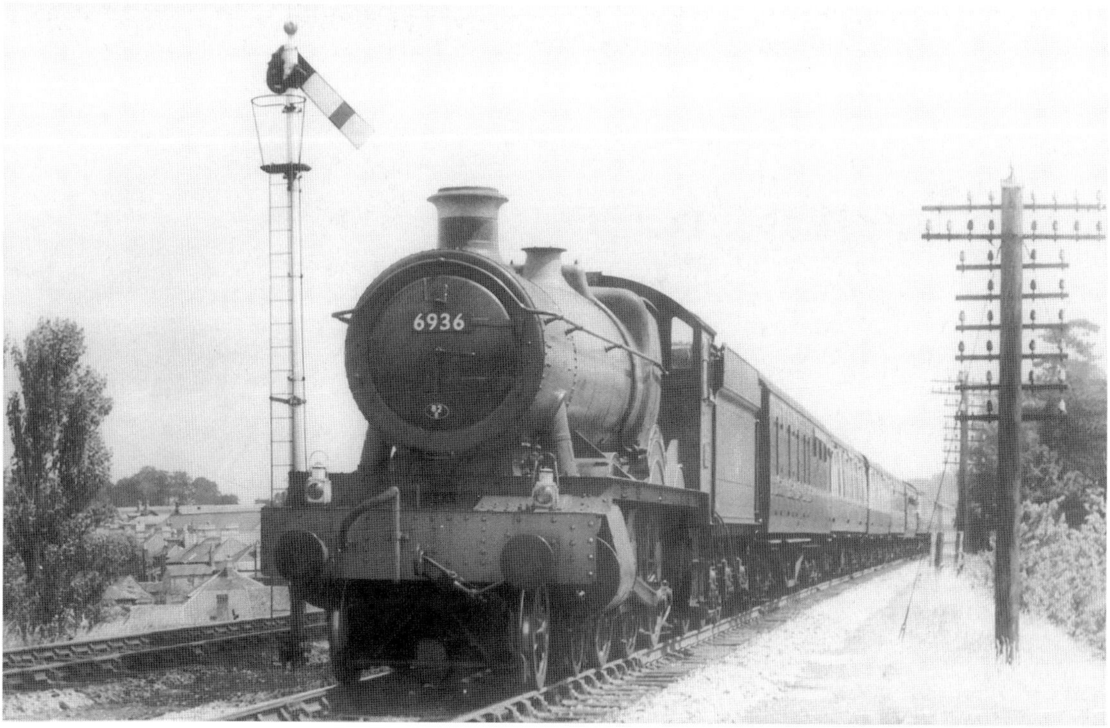

At Bathampton there is a junction from the main line into Bath which goes to Westbury, and this is the line we shall travel on for a quick visit to Weymouth. On our journey we will pass through Limpley Stoke, from where a branch ran to Camerton – it was this line which was made famous by the film *The Titfield Thunderbolt*. On we go to Bradford on Avon, into Trowbridge and then Westbury. Further down the West of England Mainline to Castle Cary, then Yeovil, Dorchester and various other stations. One of the stations we encounter just before we run into Weymouth always sticks in my mind – Upway Wishing Well Halt.

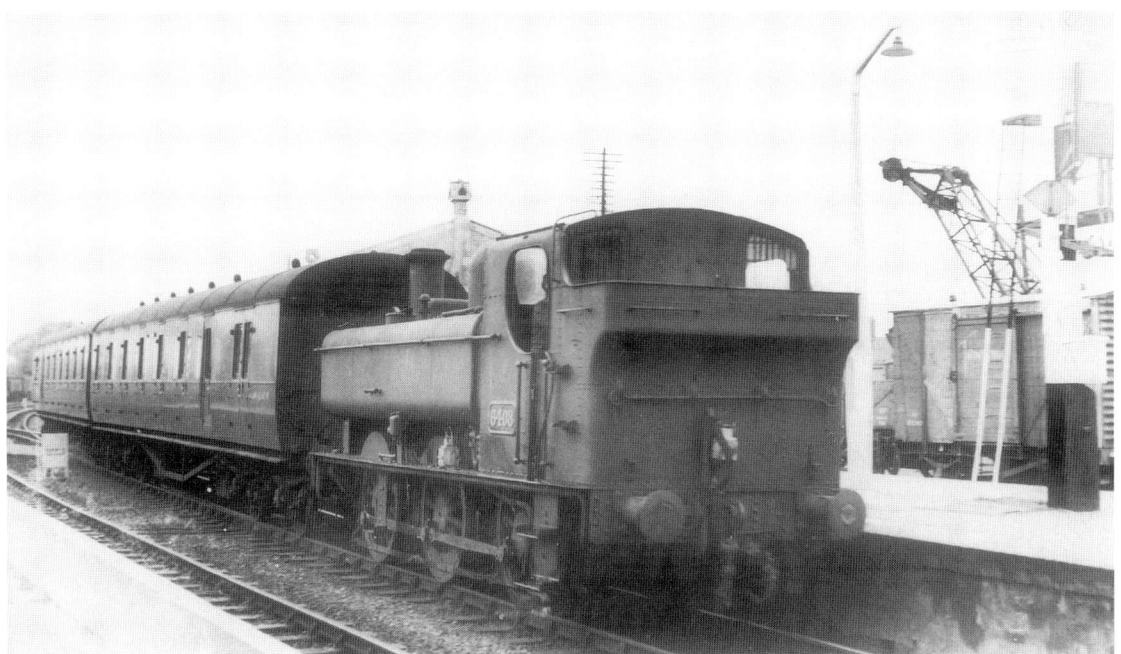

Pannier no. 6408 running into Trowbridge with a stopping train, 1959.

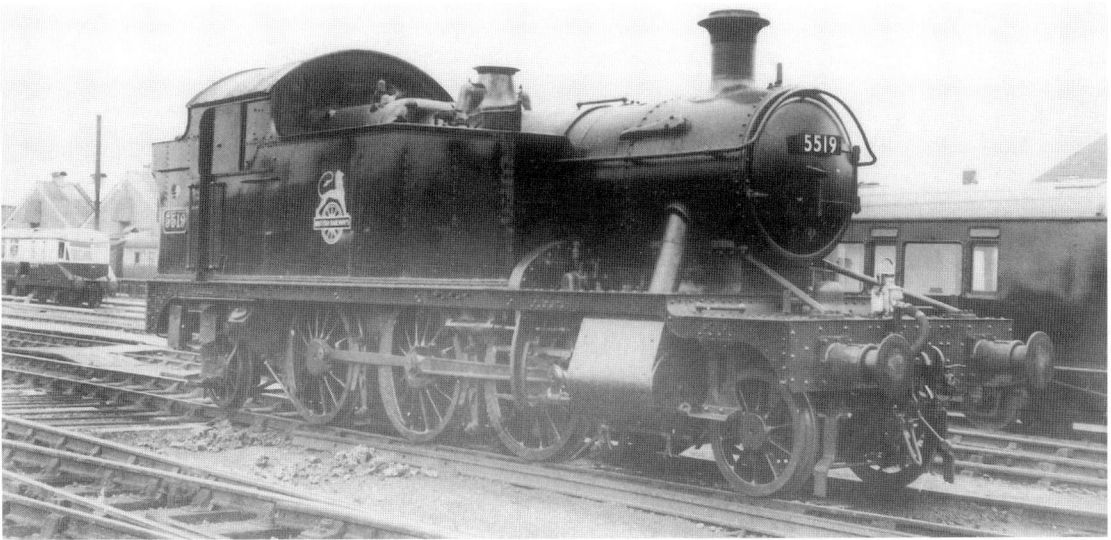

Prairie tank no. 5519 2–6–2T carrying a light engine code at Westbury, 1953. Perhaps it is going to work light engine back to its home shed. It is carrying an 83B shedplate denoting Taunton.

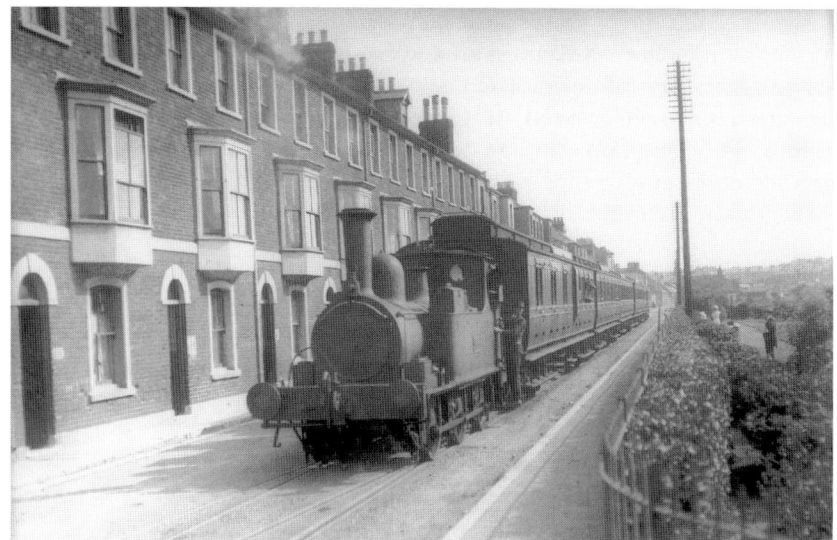

GWR no. 1376 on the quayside at Weymouth in the early 1900s.

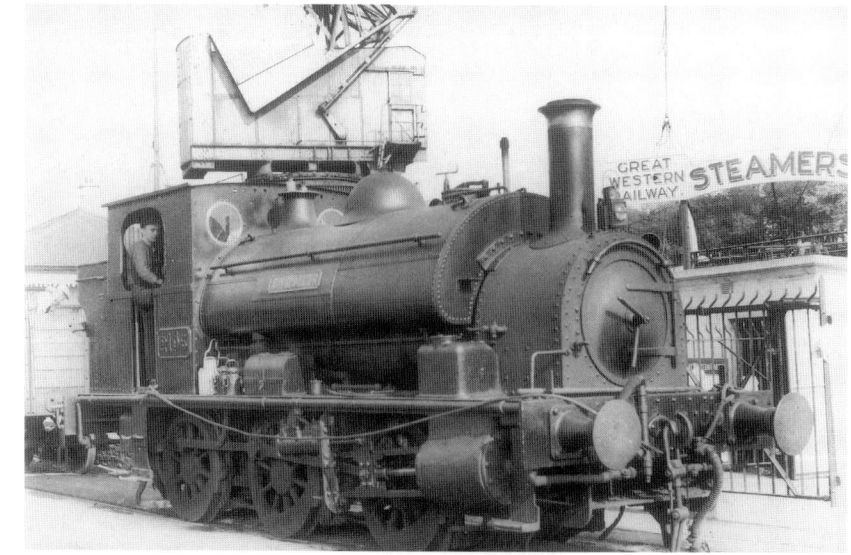

A later view of ex-Burry Port and Gwendraeth Valley Railway loco no. 2195 *Cwm Mawr* on the quayside in the 1930s. By this time it was under GWR ownership.

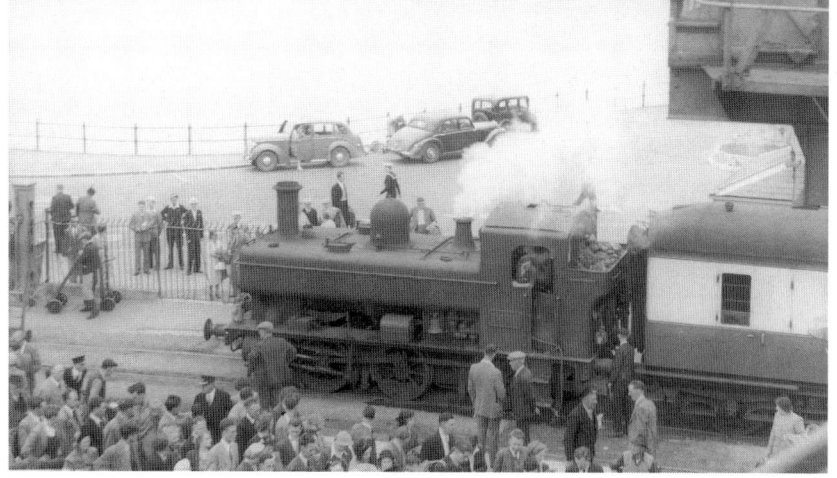

Later still, this time in 1953, pannier tank no. 1370, one of the few with outside cylinders, is obviously arriving with empty stock judging by the crowds waiting on the quayside.

We have no time to paddle in the sea, so it's back to Bathampton and into Bath Spa. We go through Sydney Gardens which is a lovely area near the centre of Bath. This garden was the result of spoil that was dug out of a slight hillside and arranged in mounds. Of course in the 150 years or so since it was opened, it has matured and is now a lovely spot, made even better by ornamental balustrading, separating people from the railway and lovely wrought iron bridges crossing the line. Well done Mr Brunel!

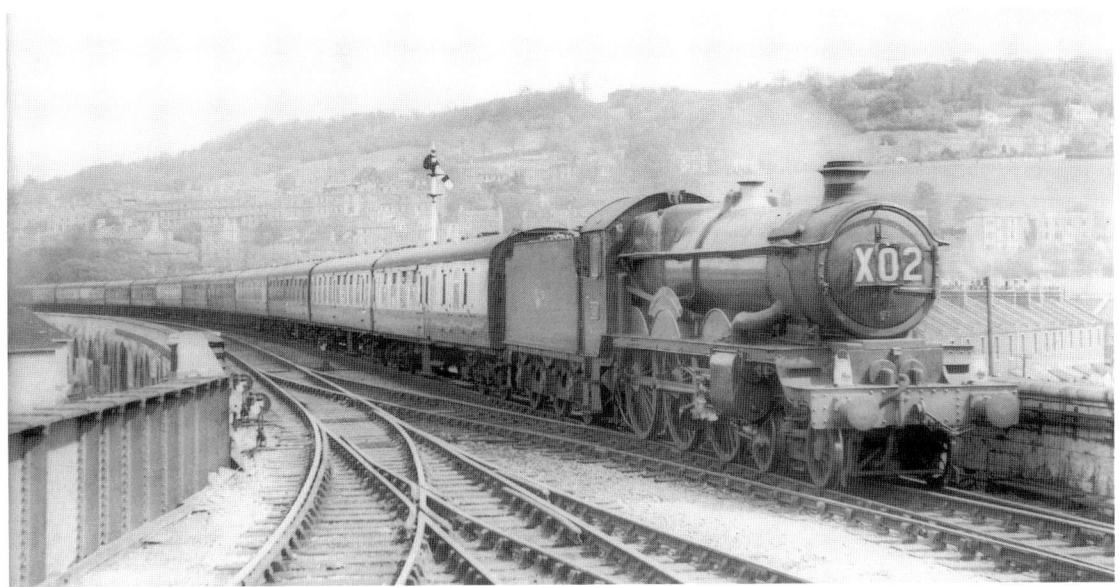

No. 7020 *Gloucester Castle* arriving at Bath Spa in 1959.

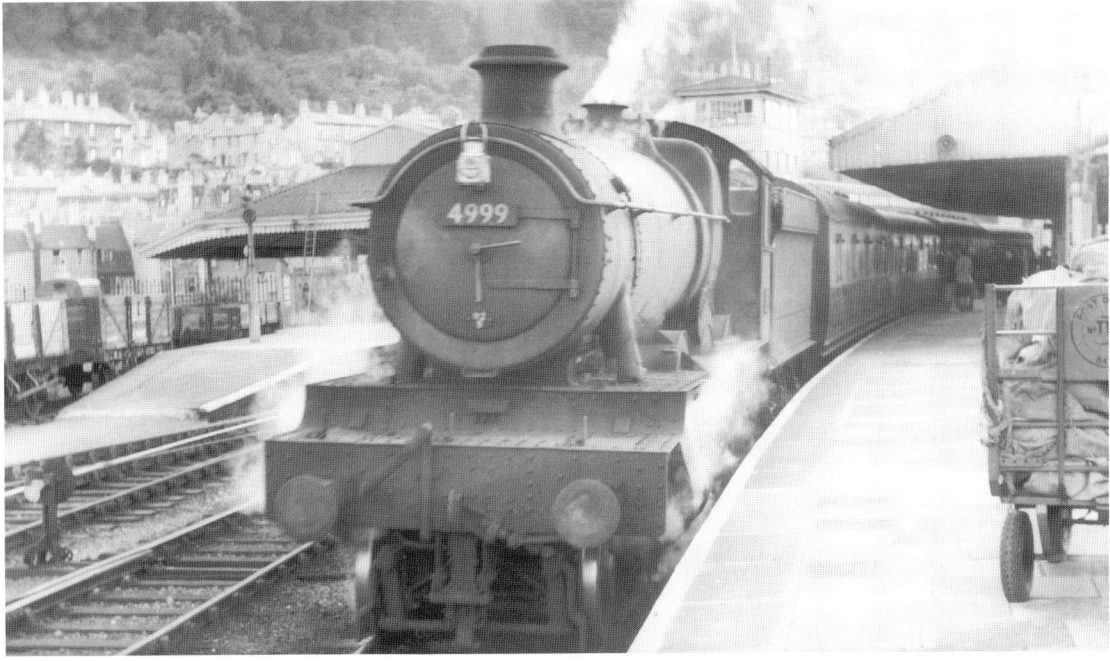

No. 4999 *Gopsal Hall* about to depart Bath Spa with a stopping train through Westbury, either to Portsmouth or Weymouth, 1958.

Off come the brakes, that little movement backwards, as the buffer springs expand, then the gentle pull of a typical Great Western start. No spinning of wheels and columns of smoke, just a very efficient start. A sharp bark at the chimney and once again we are picking up speed on our last few miles to Bristol, through Saltford then Keynsham. Just before Keynsham station is a short spur into Fry's Chocolate Factory, and then we are riding on an embankment that runs alongside a main road very straight for about 1½ miles. I have travelled this road hundreds of times and always in my imagination I see Gooch's *Great Bear* and many others. If I could have one wish I would go back in time to this spot in the early part of the 1900s. We are now running through a short tunnel at St Anne's, and now into Bristol Temple Meads. This will be a quick visit to Bristol as we have to be on our way to Shrewsbury and Wales. We shall have more time in Bristol on our return from Wales.

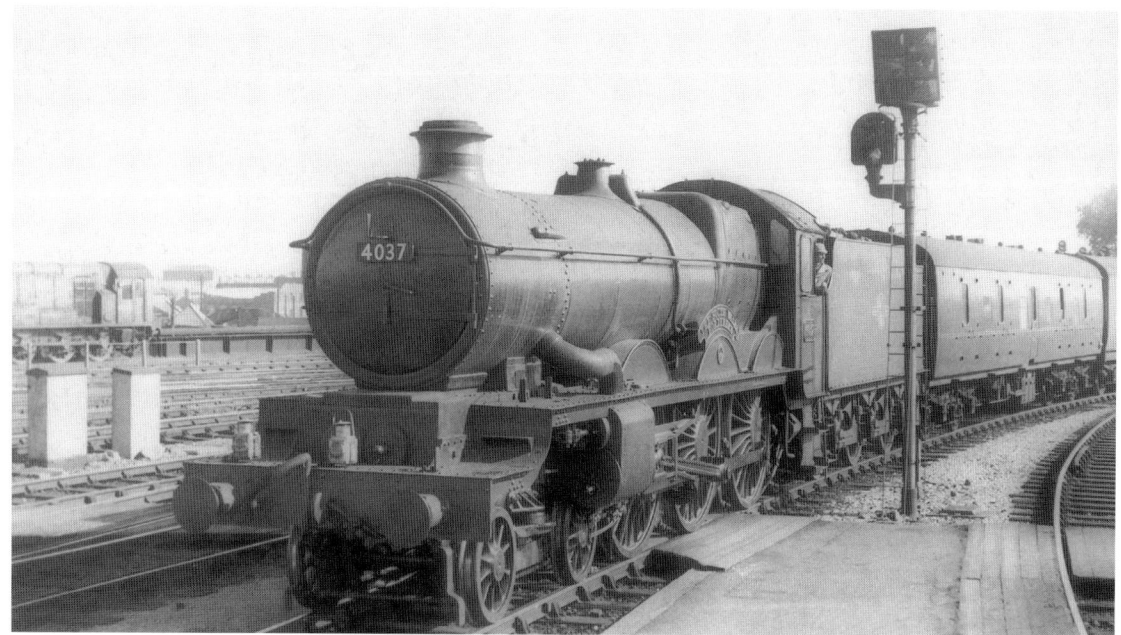

'Castle' class no. 4037 *The South Wales Borderers* runs into Temple Meads, 1959.

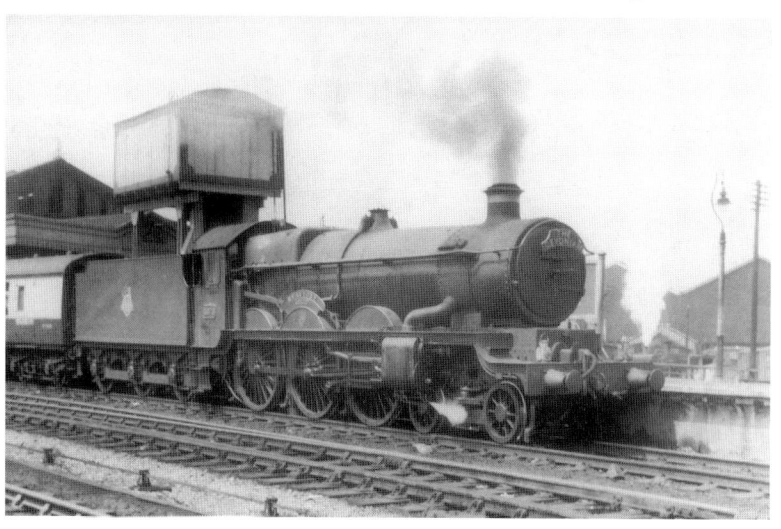

Another 'Castle', no. 5078 *Beaufort*, 1954. A recent arrival at Temple Meads it will hand over its train 'The Devonian' to an LMS 'Jubilee' for the journey northwards.

We are now on our way again, this time northwards out of Bristol, Stapleton Road, and then Ashley Down Bank. At the Bristol United Press Offices, where I worked as a photographer, I met a lovely young lady. After a couple of months we started to date, and then I was taken home to meet her parents. What a delightful surprise – the main line out of Bristol ran at the bottom of their garden. The garden had a perfect view of all four lines, the two far ones were Up and Down to the Badminton Line and also trains for Gloucester and the north, the two nearer lines were for the Severn Tunnel to South Wales and Shrewsbury.

That young lady swore it was the railway at the bottom of the garden that induced me to ask her out, but would I have married her, and still be married to her forty-five years later on the strength of that? Mind you, I did spend many hours at the bottom of that garden. . . .

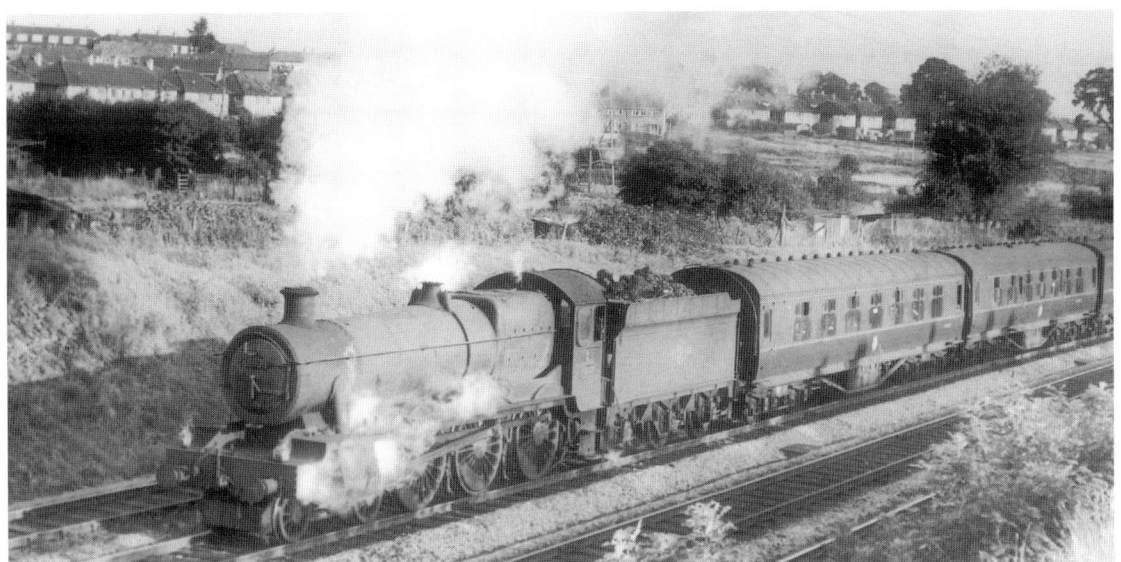

No. 6997 *Bryn-Ivor Hall* near Horfield station (at the bottom of that garden).

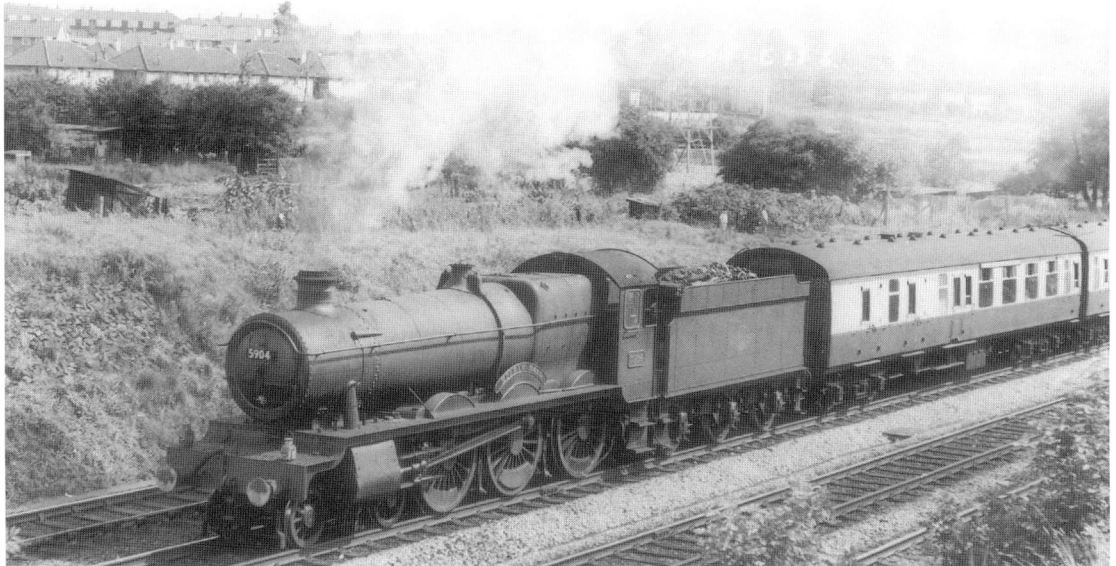

No. 5904 *Kelham Hall* from the same vantage point, 1960.

Another favourite spot of mine is Patchway, on the outskirts of Bristol. The track is the same today, but the backdrop is horrendous. In the top view there is a waste disposal unit right in the background and the lower picture is even worse with a bus and coach repair yard spoiling the view. Down Patchway Bank, through Pilning and we are approaching the Severn Tunnel.

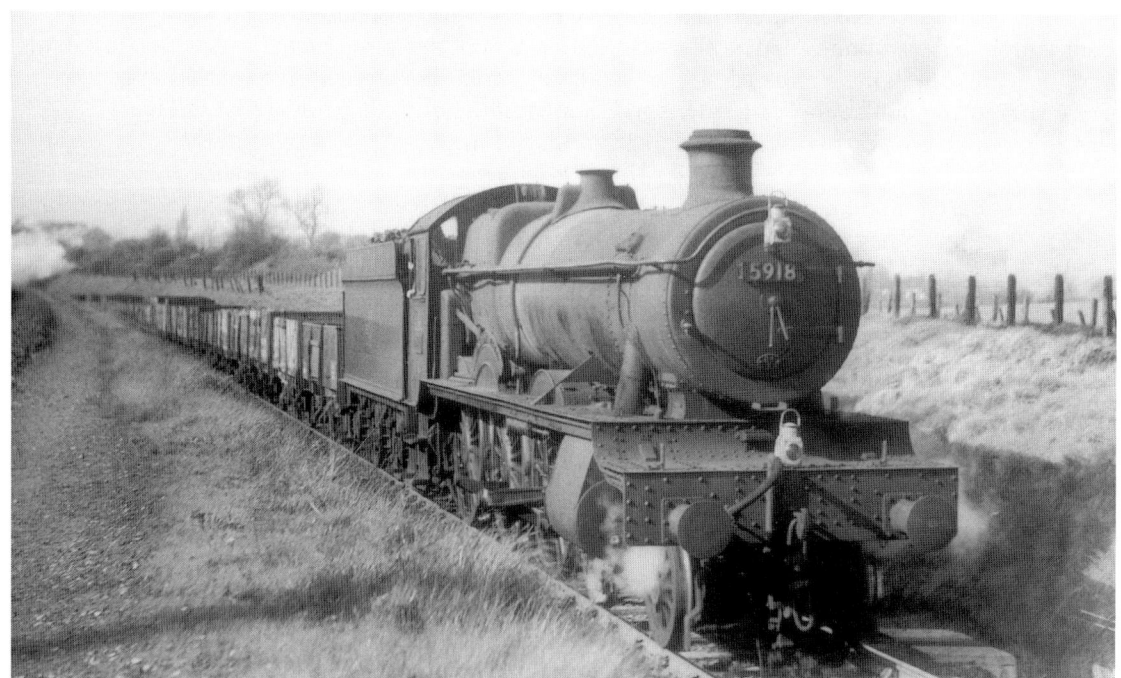

No. 5918 *Walton Hall*, with a coal train, probably for Didcot or Acton, near the top of Patchway Bank.

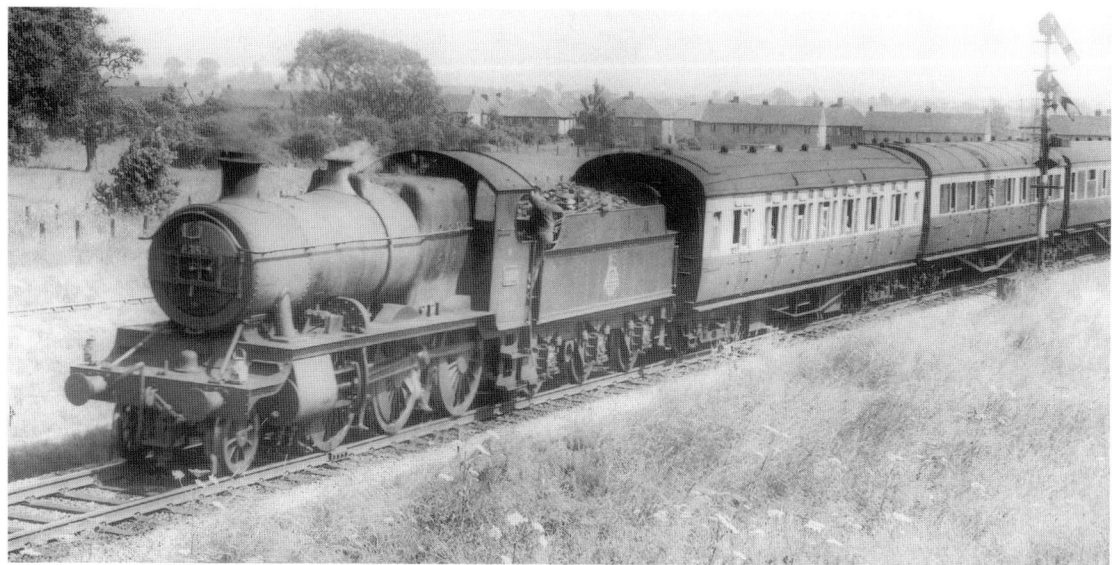

No. 6352 with a Bristol–Newport train just having left Patchway station, 1958. The train will go through Patchway Tunnel shortly, and give passengers a taste of what to expect when they go through 'the big one' – the 4 miles of the Severn Tunnel.

During my career as a professional photographer I undertook many assignments for British Railways, and in 1986 I was asked to take a series of photographs inside the Severn Tunnel for a presentation they were doing to commemorate the centenary of the opening in 1886. I had to meet a BR manager at the Bristol end of the tunnel at 11 p.m. one Saturday in February, when the tunnel was closed to traffic until 6 a.m. the following morning. It was early in the year, pitch black and freezing. We had to walk nearly a mile to the worksite.

We walked by the light of a torch and occasional wall lighting. The constant sound of dripping water and trying to balance on wet sleepers kept bringing Arnold Ridley's *Ghost Train* to mind! Eventually the sound of machines and voices started to echo around the walls, and we arrived at a scene of blazing lights, dust, and men working with incredible skill and speed. Track was being lifted by a crane-mounted vehicle on the Up line, which was part of a train headed by a class 47.

The crew accommodation was essential, as the men had to work incredibly hard to meet the 6 a.m. deadline. They kept changing over so that work was continuous – removing old track, putting in new ballast, laying new track and completing the welding – all checked and ready for the first trains in the morning.

I am not sure of my figures, but I seem to remember they laid 600yds of track. I was well looked after with tea – enough to wash the dust down my throat. It was time to make the long trek back to the car with the sounds of machines and voices fading. I had only been taking photographs but by the time I arrived home I was worn out. How the real workmen felt I can only imagine.

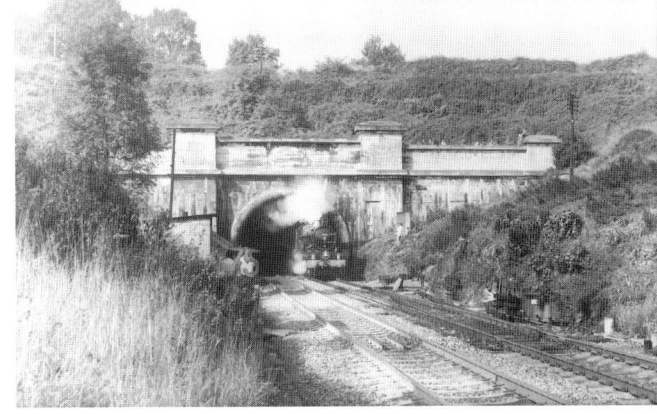

Right: The Bristol end of the Severn Tunnel.

Below: Track being lifted by cranes mounted on rail vehicles.

Below, right: Using a blow torch on the rails.

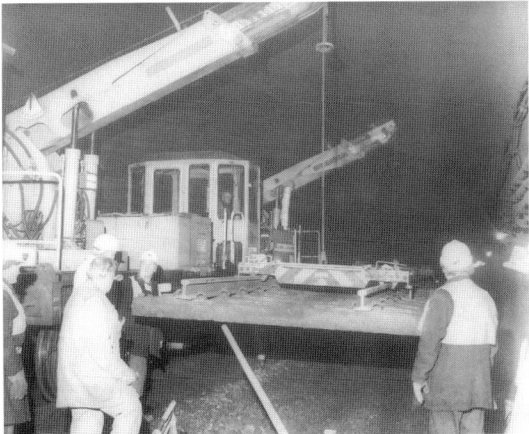

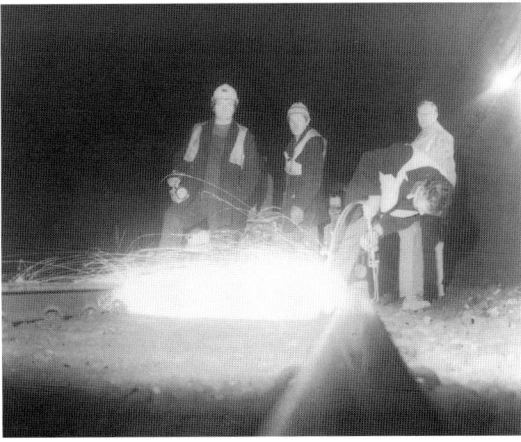

Through the Severn Tunnel we shall have to change trains, this time at Severn Tunnel Junction, as I want to make a short trip into the Wye Valley – a lovely part of the country. First we pass under the Severn Bridge, not, I hasten to add, the watery part, but the road part that leads to the suspended road over the Severn. Then comes Chepstow, which has another of Brunel's tubular suspension bridges which carries our train over the Wye. Shortly after Chepstow we branch from the main line, and we are now on the Wye Valley Line, through Tintern, St Briavels and into Monmouth Troy.

There are many branches that penetrate the Forest of Dean to such places as Coleford and Parkend. Many were small stations, but many were mere halts, with just a platform and a small shed for some protection for passengers. At Monmouth we could potentially catch a train that would take us back to the main Newport–Shrewsbury line, but we shall going to Symonds Yat and Ross. We will then make our way back to Severn Tunnel Junction via Grange Court, where we join the main Gloucester–Newport line through Blakeney and past the site of the old Severn Bridge that sadly was knocked down by a barge on a foggy night. Now come Lydney, Chepstow and into Severn Tunnel Junction, to the sounds of clanking trucks as there is a huge freight yard here.

Right: Chepstow Bridge.

Below: No. 4074 *Caldicot Castle* approaching Chepstow station. In the background is Brunel's bridge over the River Wye.

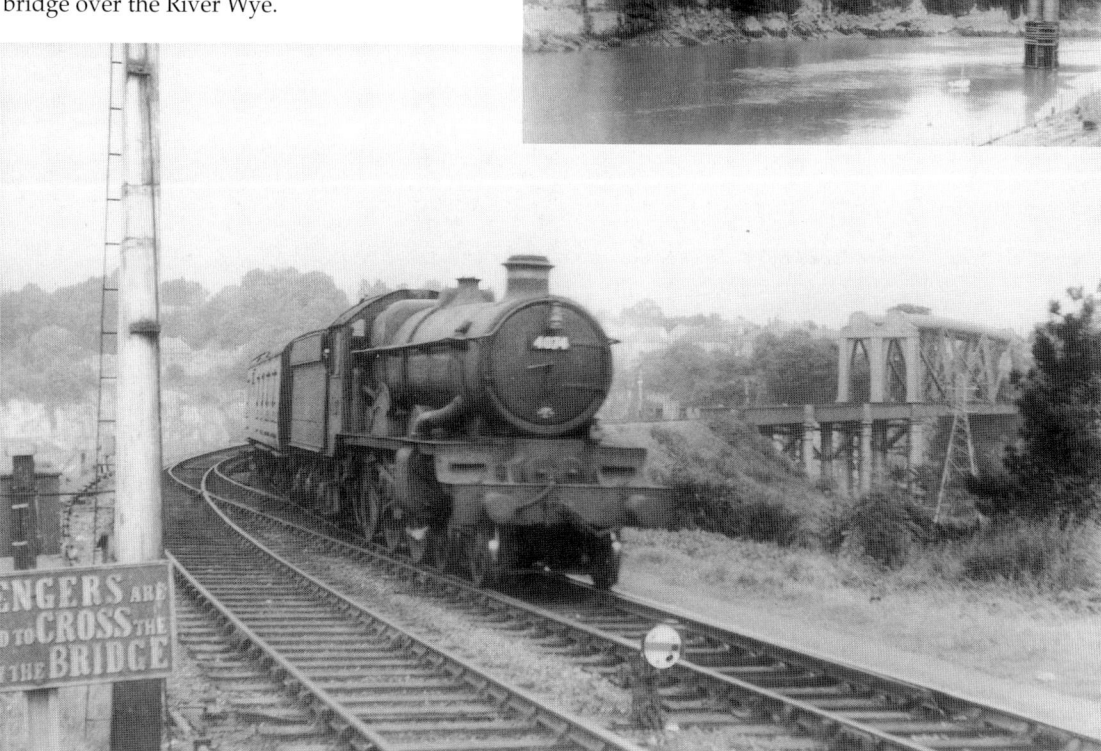

The most popular loco for operating on rural branch lines was the 0–4–2T. This is no. 1456 at Monmouth Troy. The sight of the driver and fireman relaxing on the platform seat suggests an unhurried way of life that we would all appreciate.

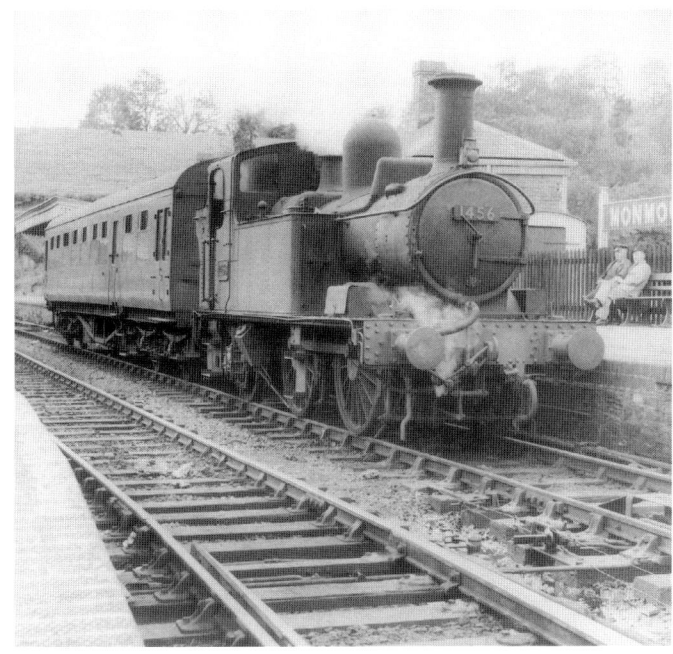

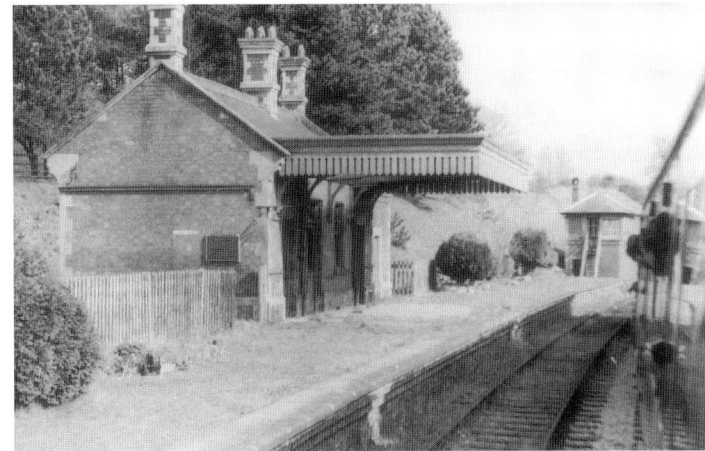

On the line from Monmouth to the Shrewsbury Line is Raglan, a typical country station, not far from Raglan Castle. The loco, no. 5008, was named after the castle.

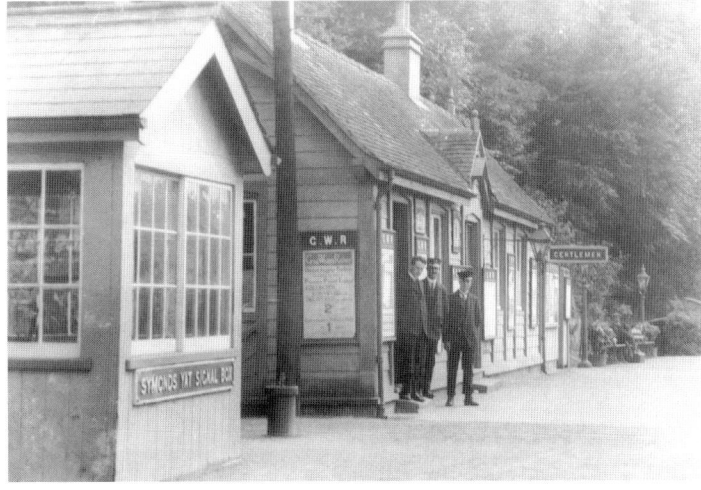

We are making our way to Ross and at Symonds Yat and we run alongside the River Wye for a short distance. This photograph was taken in the late 1920s.

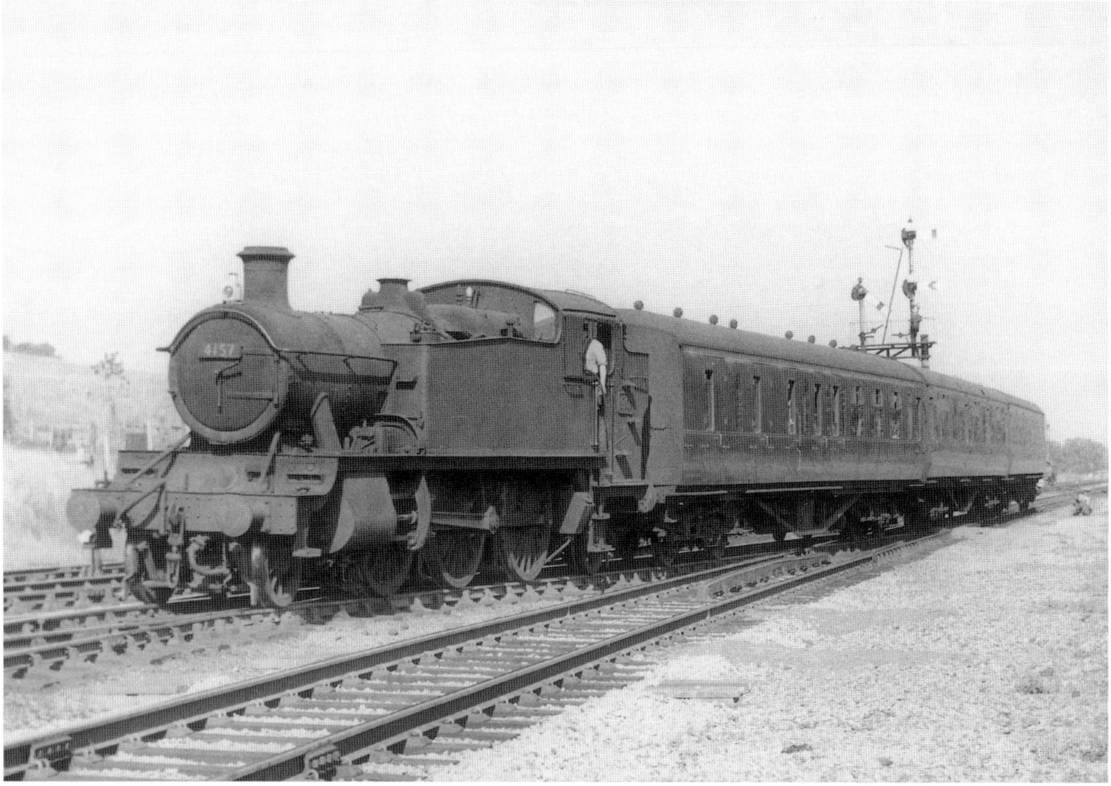

No. 4157 at Grange Court Junction, 1955, from where we shall make our way back to Chepstow.

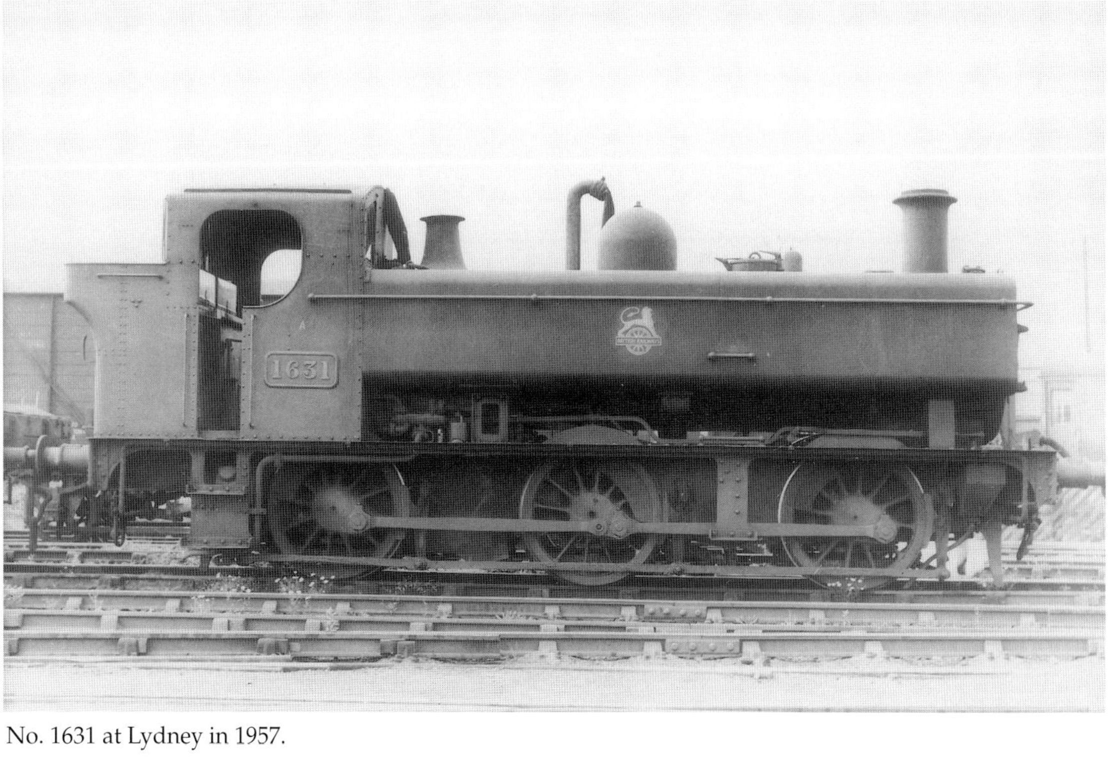

No. 1631 at Lydney in 1957.

Through Lydney, Chepstow and into Severn Tunnel Junction, we are just in time to catch a train from the west that will take us to Shrewsbury. Brakes off and we are away, heading towards Newport. We won't go into the town itself, but will take the Maindy Curve and head for Pontypool Road, through Caerleon and Llantarnam.

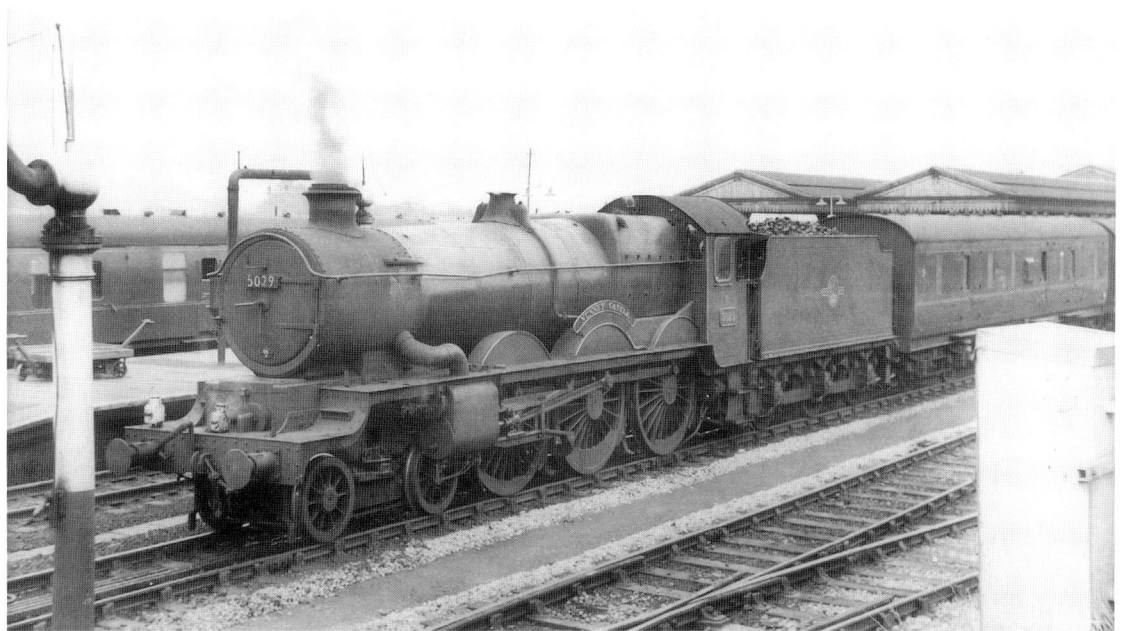

Another locomotive that is still with us today, no. 5029 *Nunney Castle*, about to leave Pontypool Road in 1961.

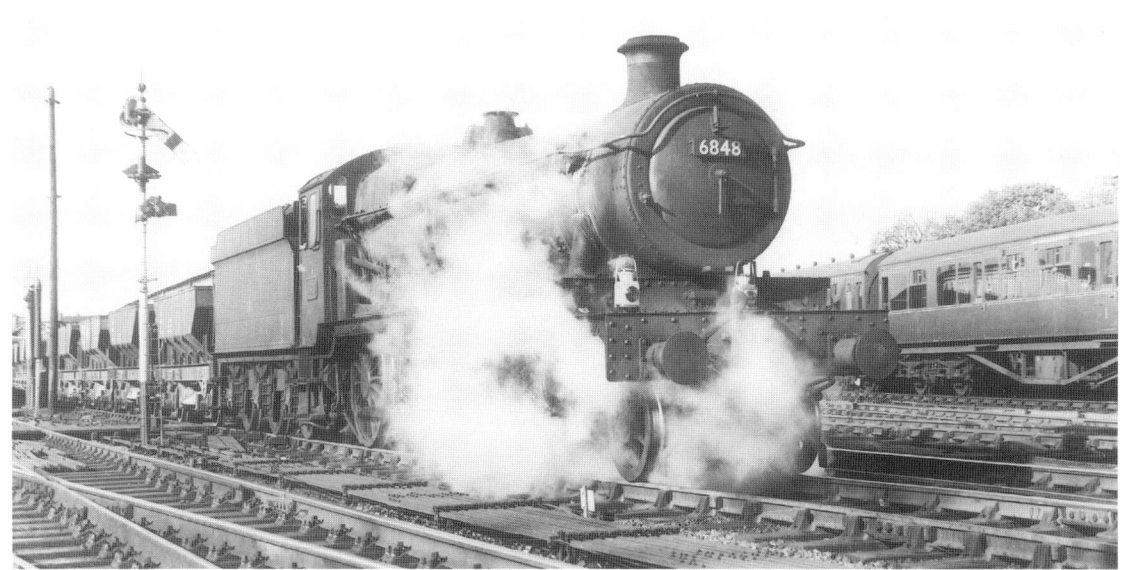

No. 6848 *Toddington Grange* with a coal train will soon be leaving Pontypool Road behind, 1959.

We leave Pontypool Road and make for Abergavenny. Just after Pontypool Road we pass a junction to the right, this is the line we talked about earlier when we were at Monmouth Troy. We may see a Midland 0–8–0 in this area and there is a junction that belonged to the LNWR before the grouping. We are now storming up Llanviangel Bank, and it won't be long before we run into Hereford, so get the camera ready – there is usually a lot of activity here.

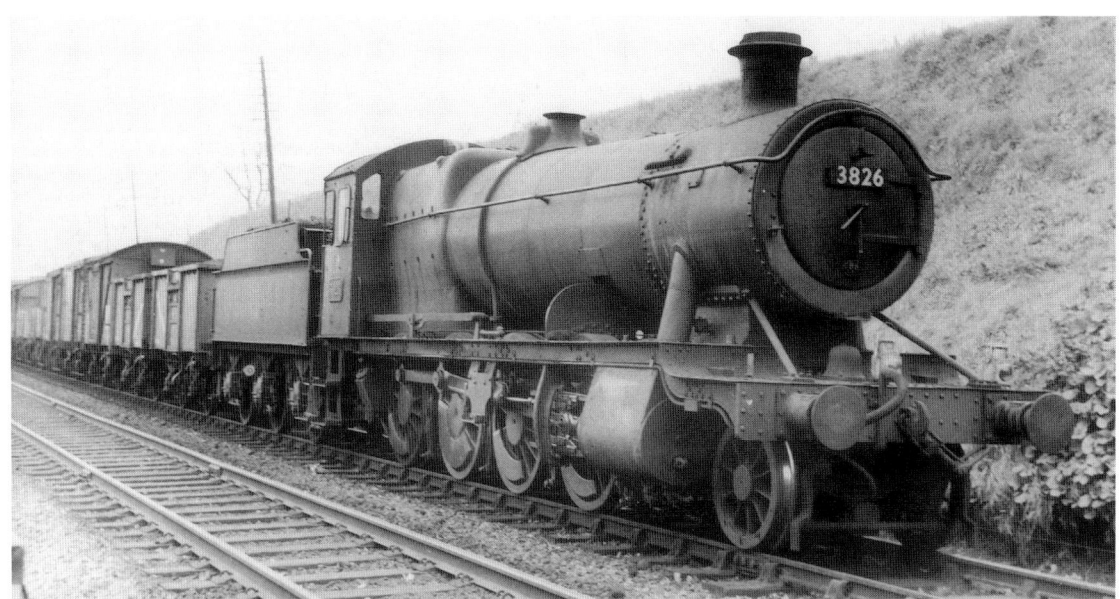

No. 3826 with a freight train near Abergavenny. It is carrying a light engine headcode which suggests the fireman has not done his job properly.

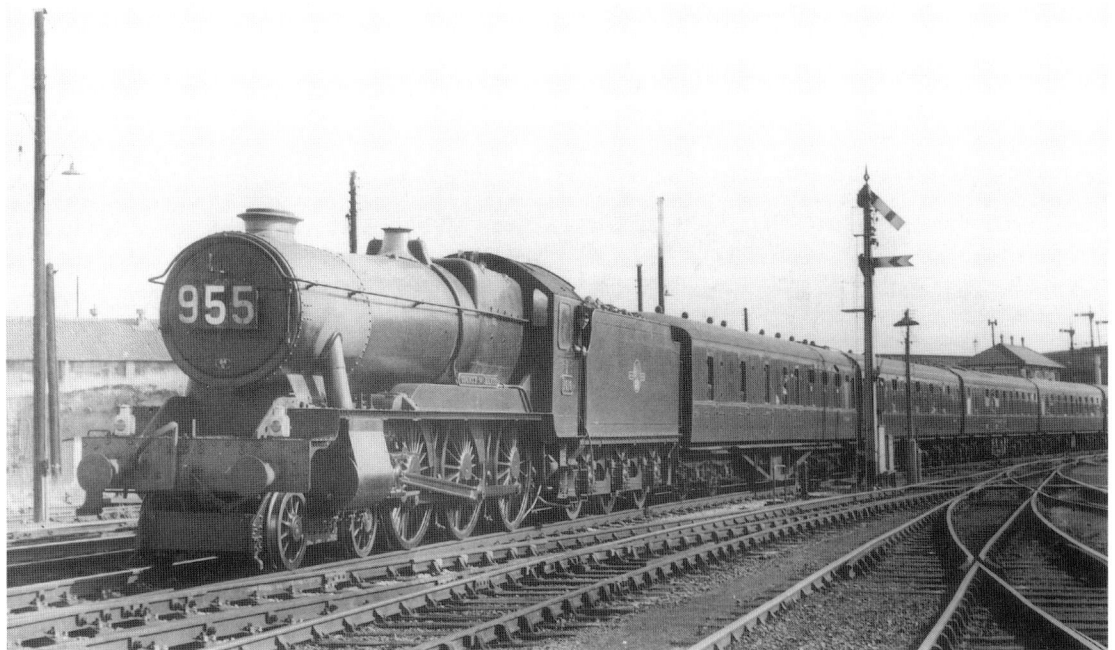

No. 1016 *County of Hants* running into Hereford, 1959.

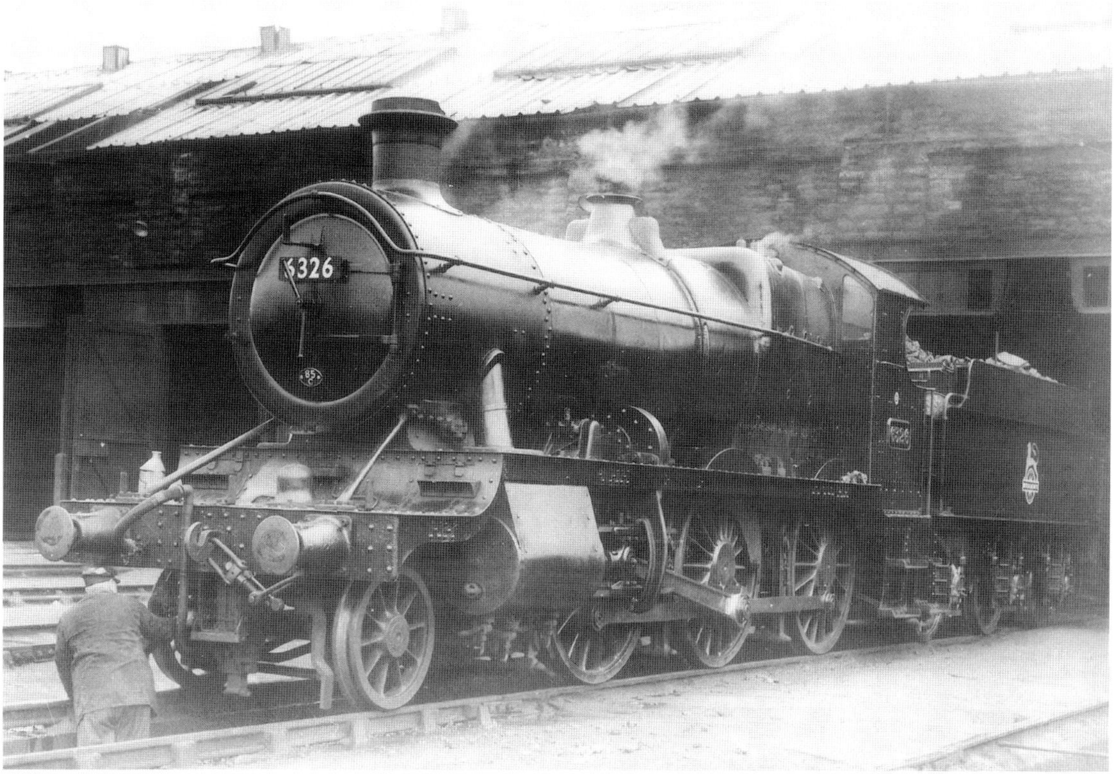

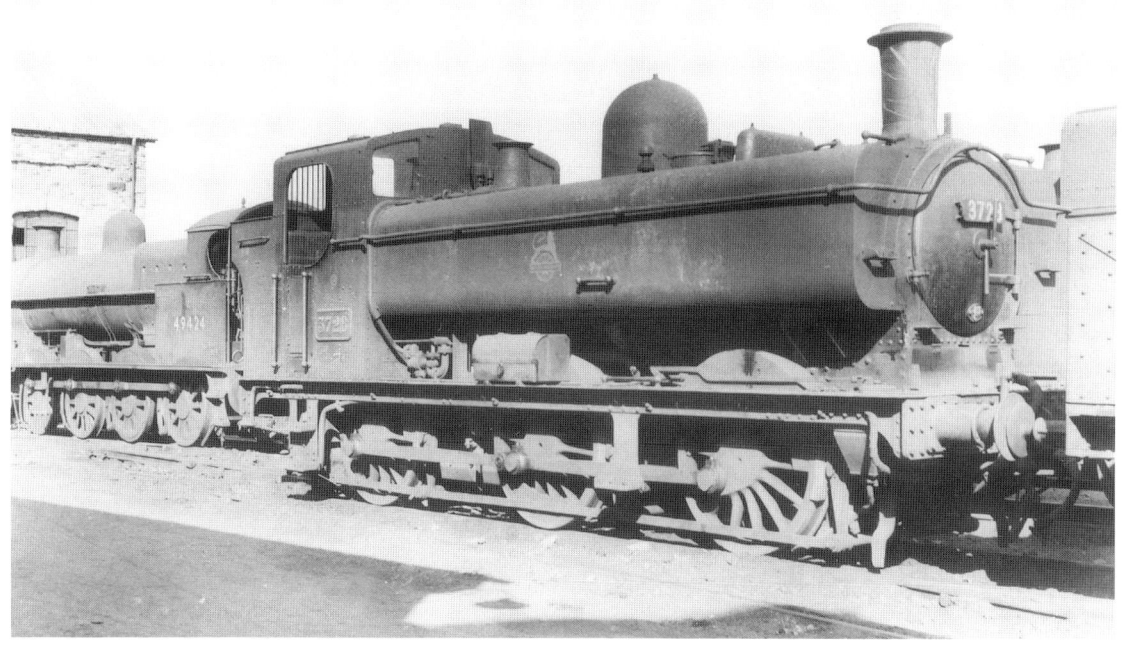

Out of the carriage we run to the end of the platform to capture a photograph of our train engine. Now we will make a hurried visit to shed 85C; years ago we would have seen 'Bulldogs' and 'Saints' but no luck today. A 2–6–0 'Mogul' no. 6326 cleaned and ready for duty, a little grimier pannier no. 3728 does not look quite so ready for duty. Both photographs were taken in 1954.

Rush back to the station (Barrscourt) and once again our coats left on our seats have done their job, and we still have the compartment to ourselves. We are comparing notes as our train starts to pull up the incline out of the station, the general topic seemed to be disappointment that there wasn't much on Hereford shed. Shortly after leaving Hereford, there is a branch to Great Malvern and Worcester.

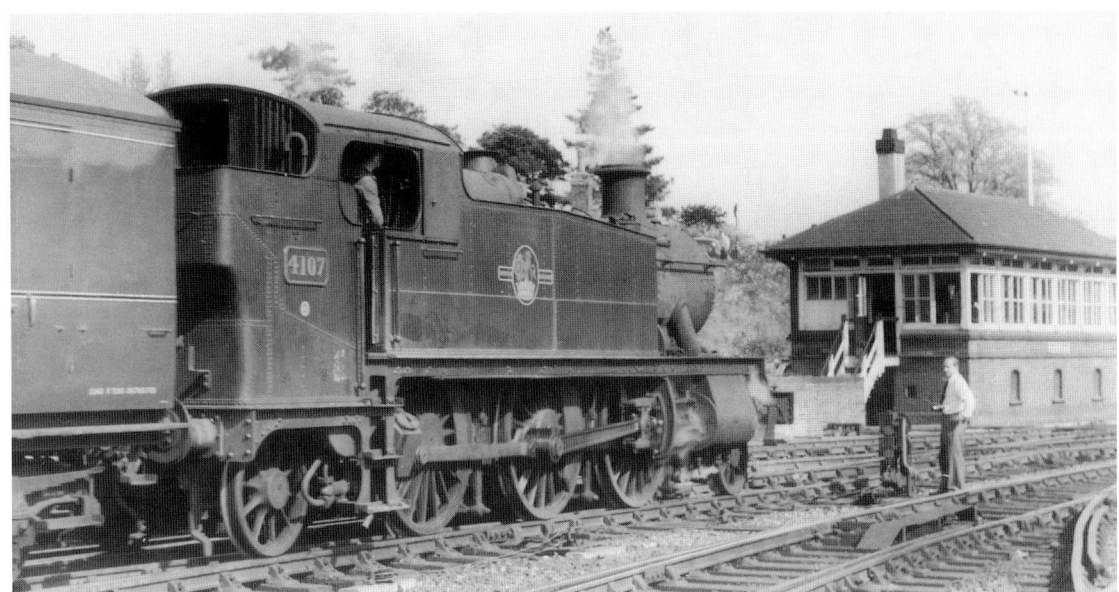

Prairie tank 4107, heads South, out of Hereford in 1960.

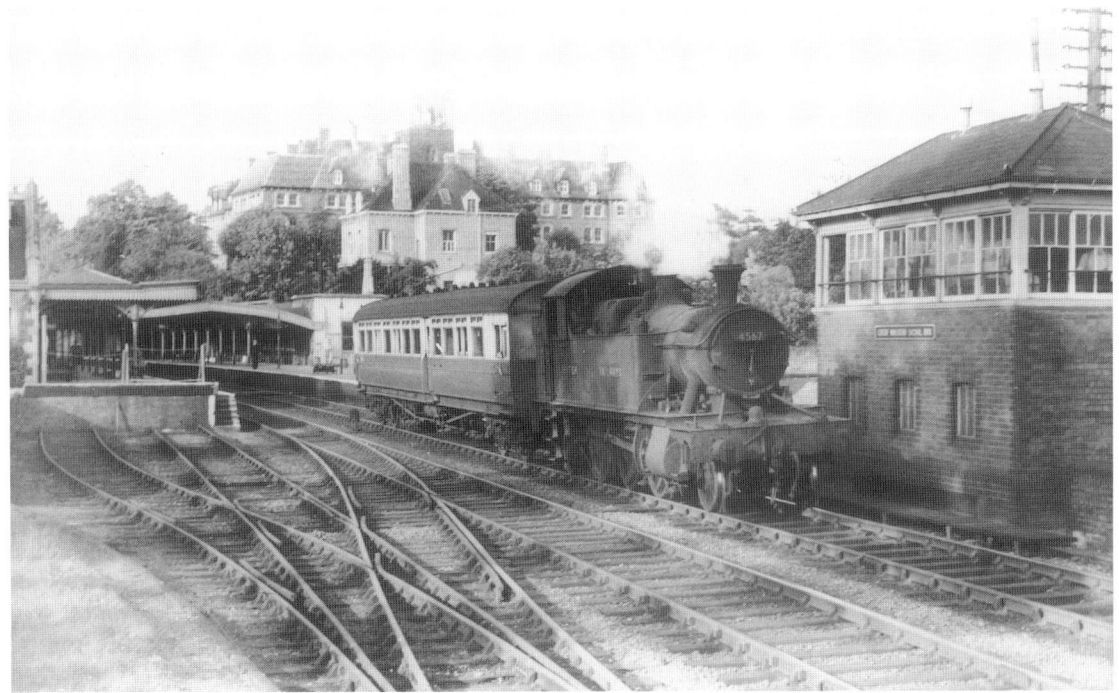

No. 4567 leaving Great Malvern in 1949.

Onwards we go through Moreton-on-Lugg and Dinmore Tunnel to Leominster, and with the whistle sounding, we roar through Woofferton Junction and then on to Ludlow. We have passed a number of branch lines on our way to Shrewsbury, but we don't have the time to explore them.

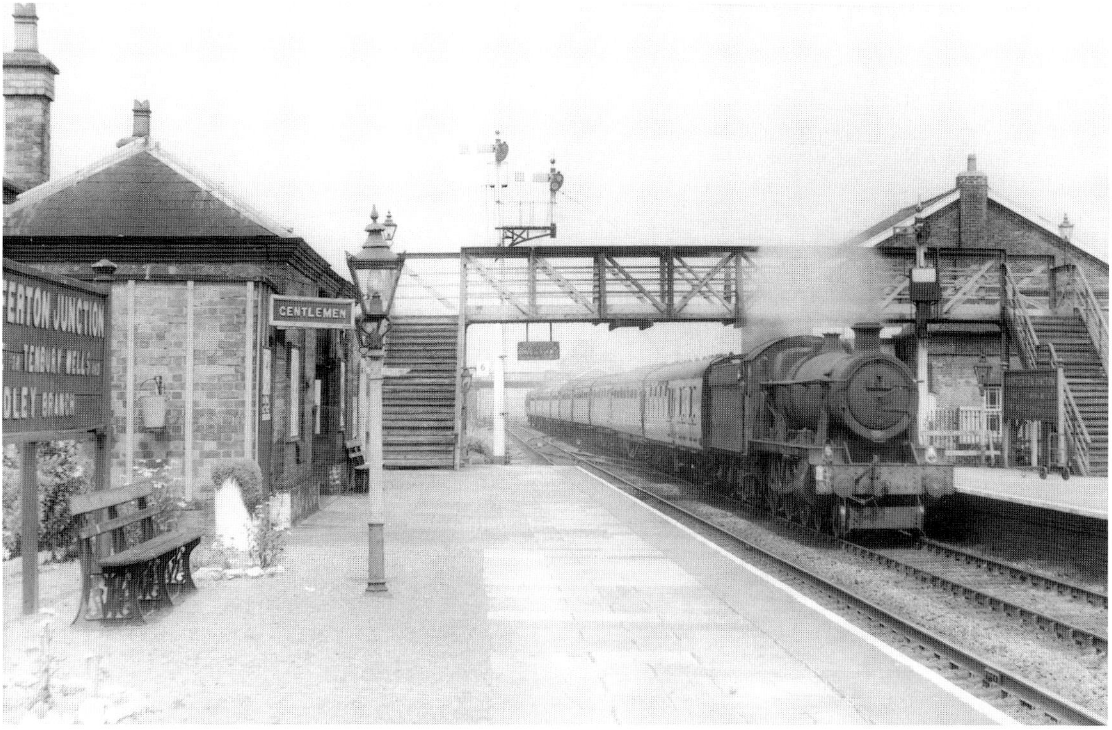

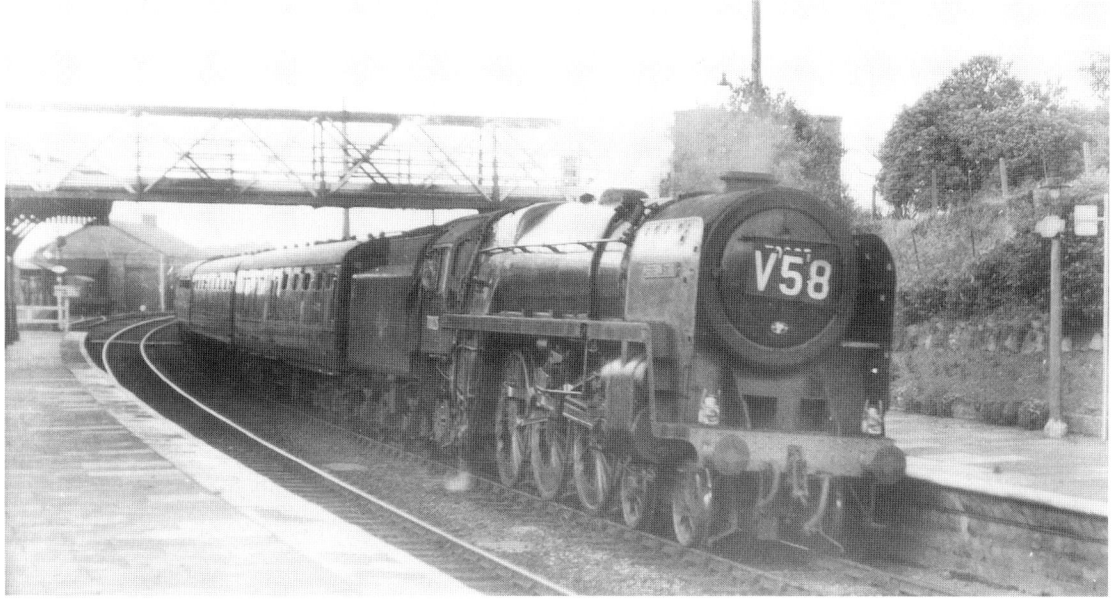

No. 7913 *Little Wyrley Hall* on its way through Woofferton Junction in 1955.

'Britannia' no. 70025 *Western Star* in dull weather, 1958. With its twin-tone whistle blowing it is working hard through Ludlow.

Now we are at Craven Arms and we have just passed the LNWT junction that heads through Central Wales, through Llandrindod Wells, and Builth Wells. Just after Craven Arms is the branch to Bishops Castle, and shortly after, the line branches right to Much Wenlock and back towards Birmingham, but our train keeps up a steady pace towards Shrewsbury.

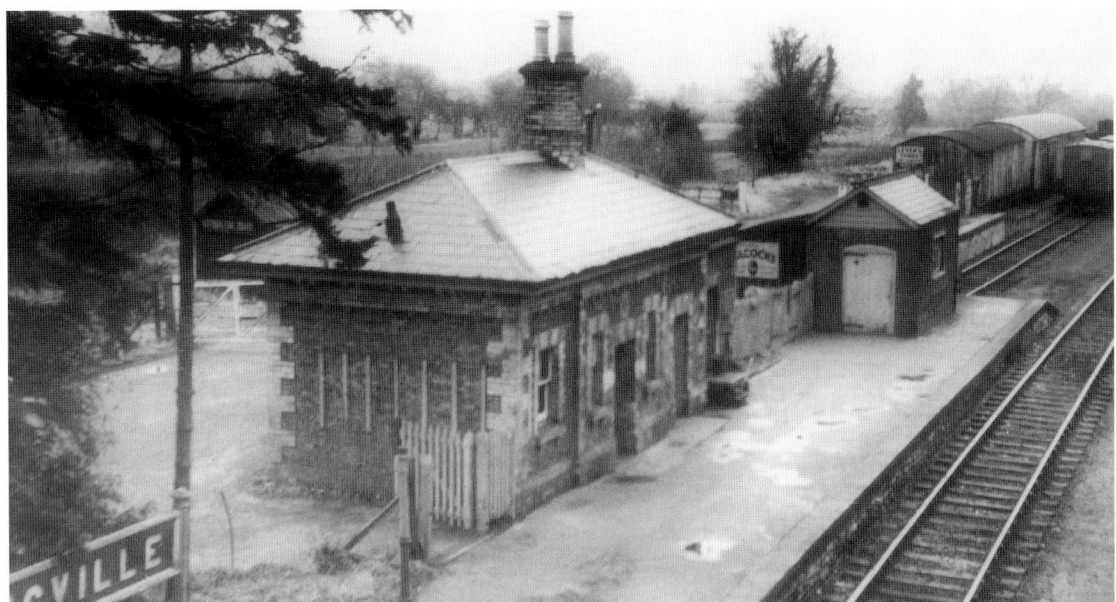

Longville station on a damp day in 1954. This station is on the Birmingham Line that we passed just after Craven Arms.

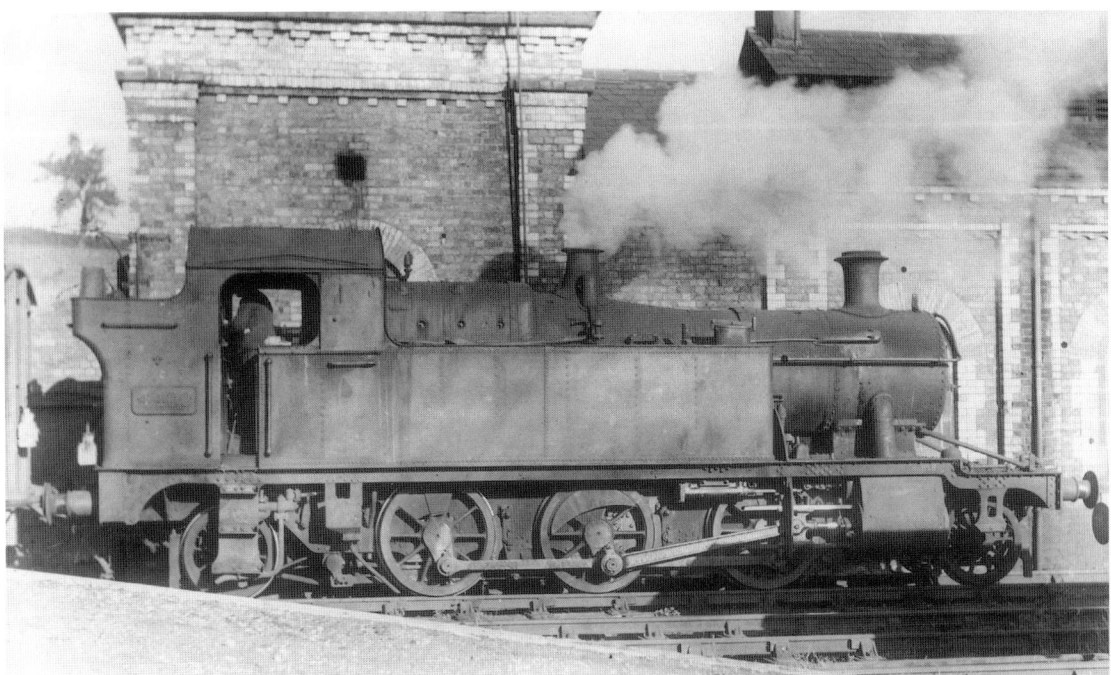

No. 4400 preparing to leave Much Wenlock station.

There is a lot of activity in our compartment now as we approach Shrewsbury. As we come into the station we see one of the biggest signal-boxes in the country. We pass the Cambrian Line from Wolverhampton on the right, so there are always several locos waiting to go on shed or into the station. Shrewsbury was also a run-in line for Crewe, giving enthusiasts the chance to see spotless Duchesses, Royal Scots, etc. I was tempted to include some of the streamlined Duchesses I have in my collection at Shrewsbury, but as the title is *Western Steam Journey*, they had to go back into the archive.

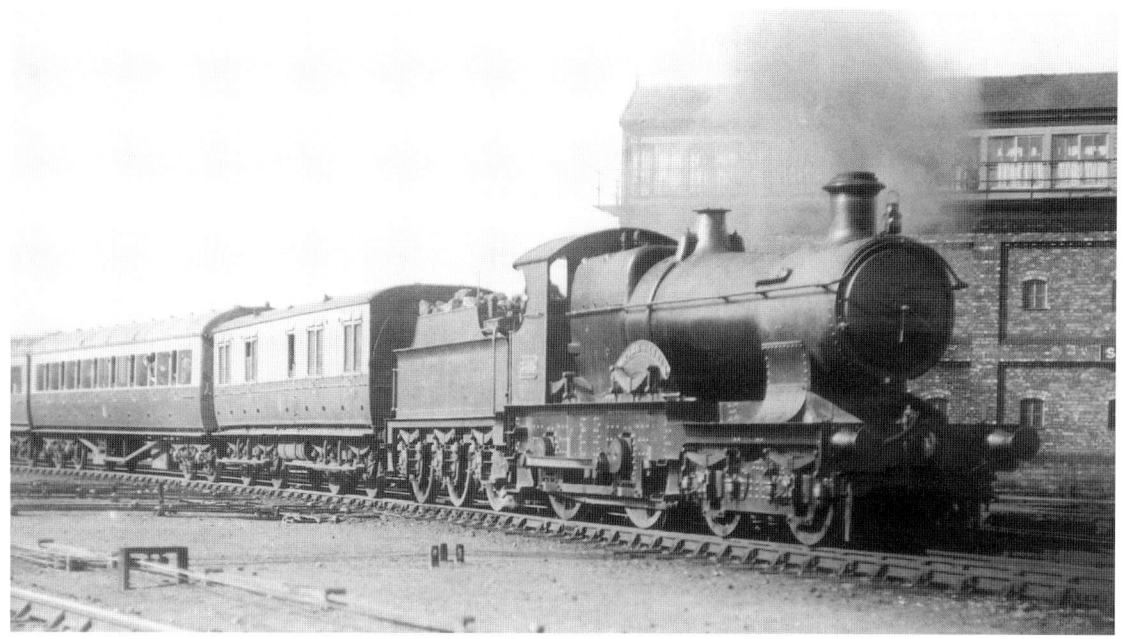

A pre-war view at Shrewsbury of 'Bulldog' no. 3405 *Empire of India*, coming into the town from Wolverhampton. In the background is Shrewsbury's huge signal-box.

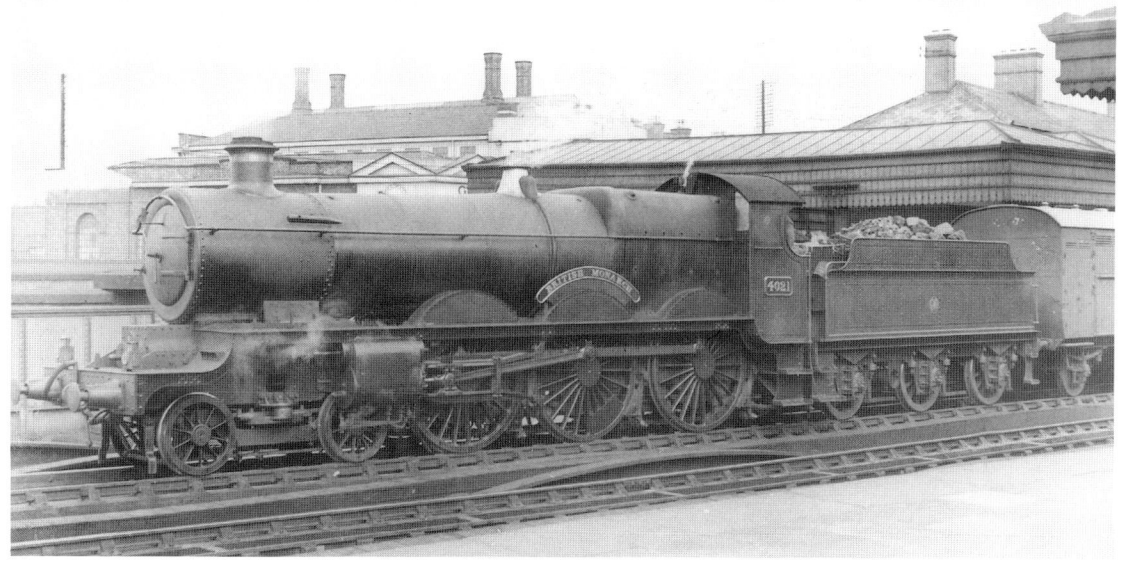

Another pre-war Shrewsbury view of 'Star' class 4–6–0 no. 4021 *British Monarch*.

We have time between trains to visit Shrewsbury shed. The GWR and LMS sheds are very close together. Part of the GWR shed looks like a big house. I presume these are the administrative offices, as Shrewsbury is a very busy railway centre.

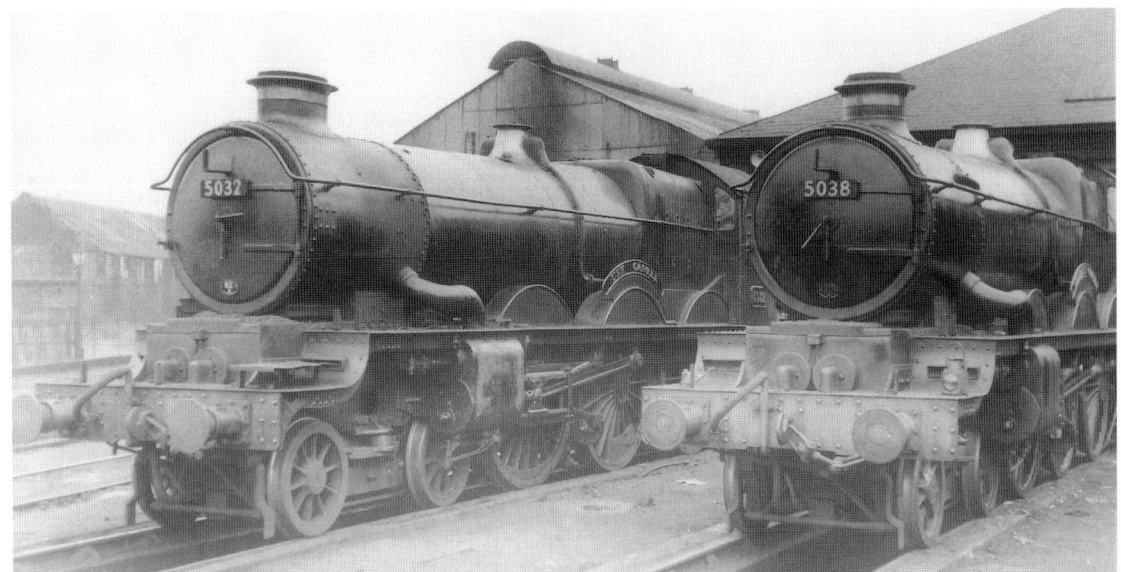

On arrival at Shrewsbury shed our small group could not get the cameras working fast enough. This view is of two 'Castles' – no. 5032 *Usk Castle* and no. 5038 *Morlais Castle*. What more could a railway enthusiast ask for?

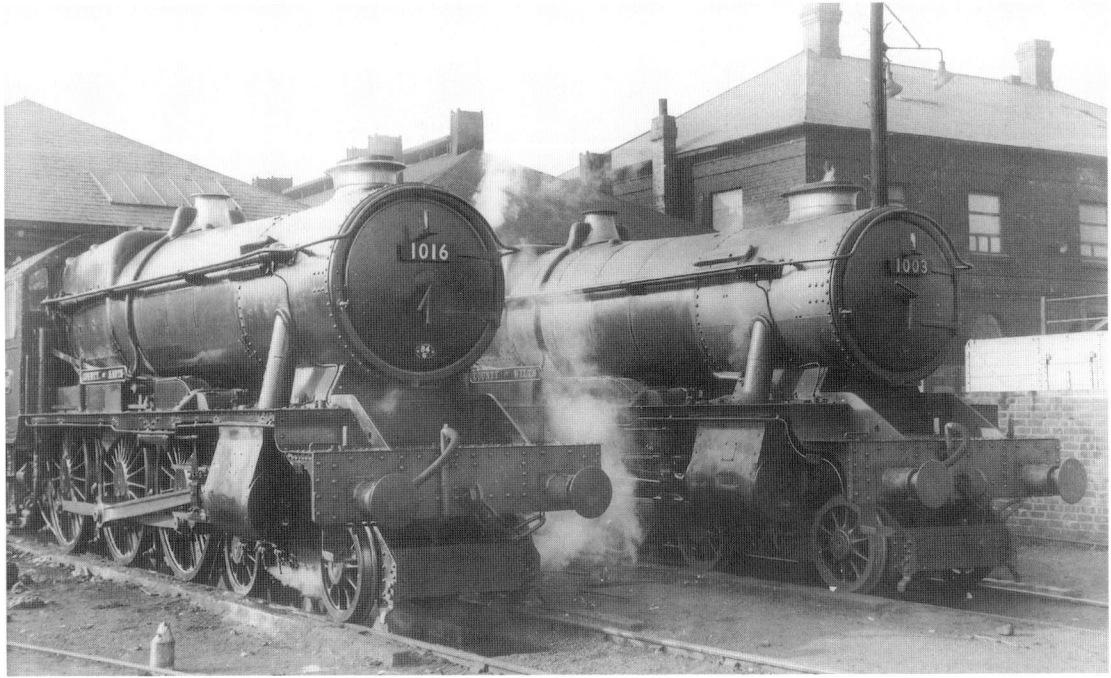

This is what more a railway enthusiast could wish for: two 'County' class locos posed perfectly, side by side – no. 1016 *County of Hants* and no. 1003 *County of Wilts*.

We are now all back in our compartment, a bit breathless, but the adrenalin is flowing and everyone is talking at once about what was seen on shed. We are so busy talking that we didn't hear the guard's whistle, so it took us all by surprise when we started moving. On this part of our journey we shall be heading as far north as the GWR reached – to Birkenhead.

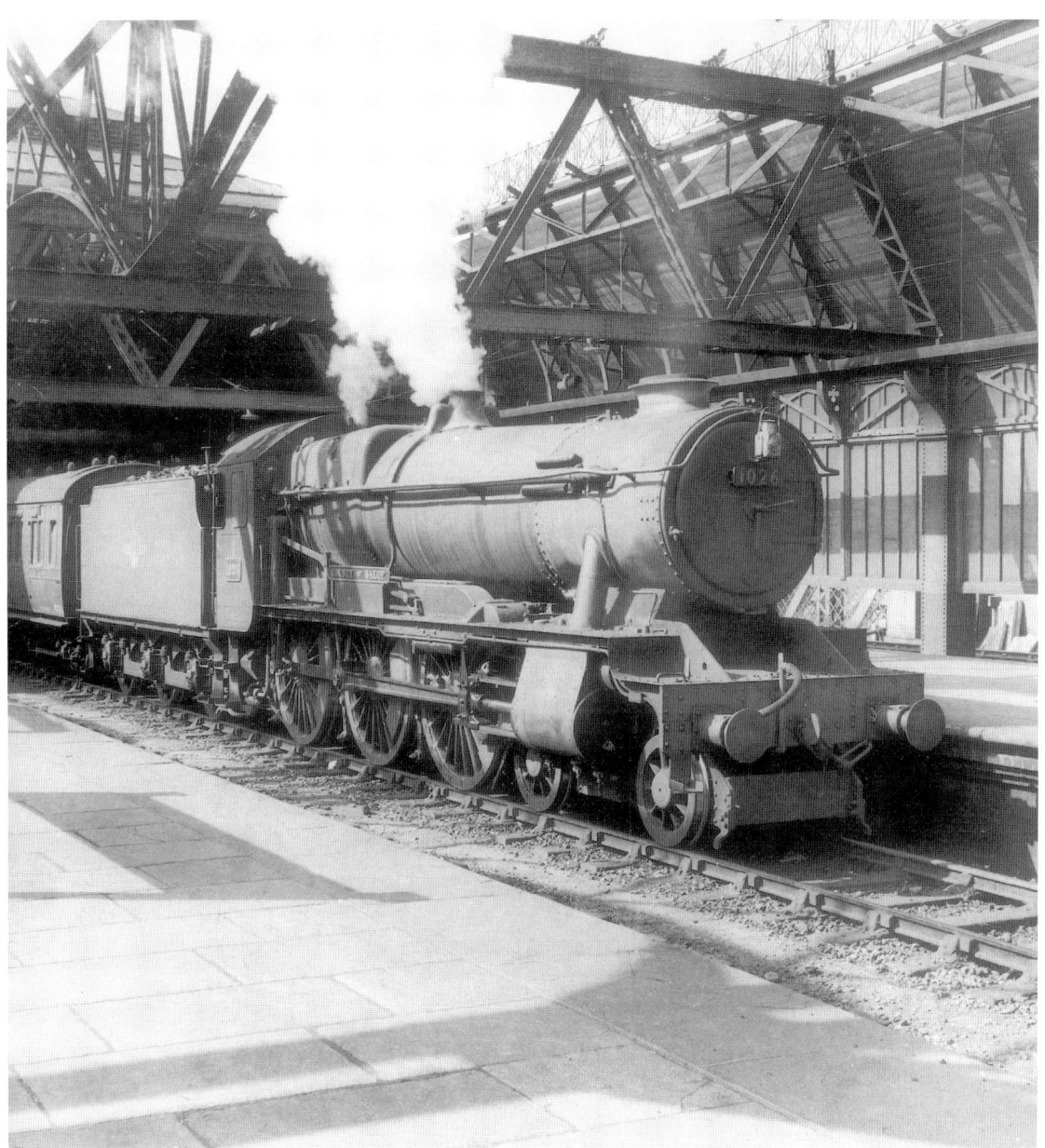

A very appropriate loco to photograph in Shrewsbury was no. 1026 *County of Salop*, blowing its whistle and ready to depart, 1959.

None of us seem to know about this part of the journey, so a map is produced. Gobowen seems to be the next fairly big station. According to the map it is not far from Oswestry, which I read somewhere was the headquarters of the Cambrian Railway. This, of course, was taken over by the GWR many moons ago. Then it is on to Wrexham and then, one of the group spots a name he is familiar with, Gresford. Apparently he has seen photographs of 'Castles' pounding up a steep bank.

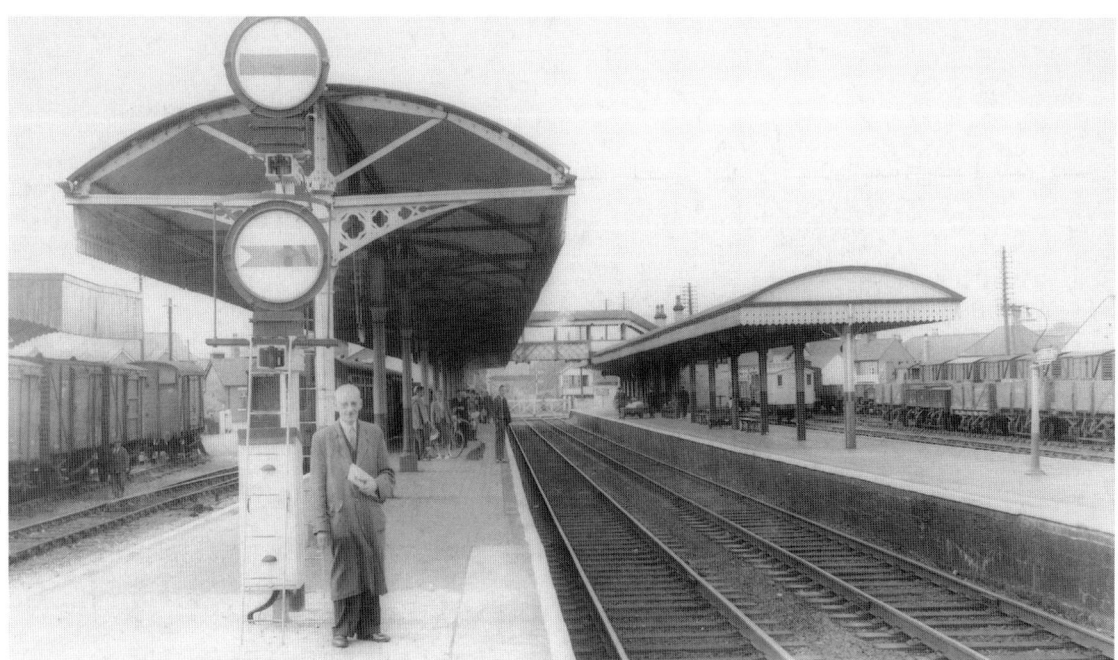

Gobowen station on the GWR main line to the north. I wonder if the old gentleman is related to the photographer, or is he a member of the public that we have all come across – one of those who stands just where they spoil the picture.

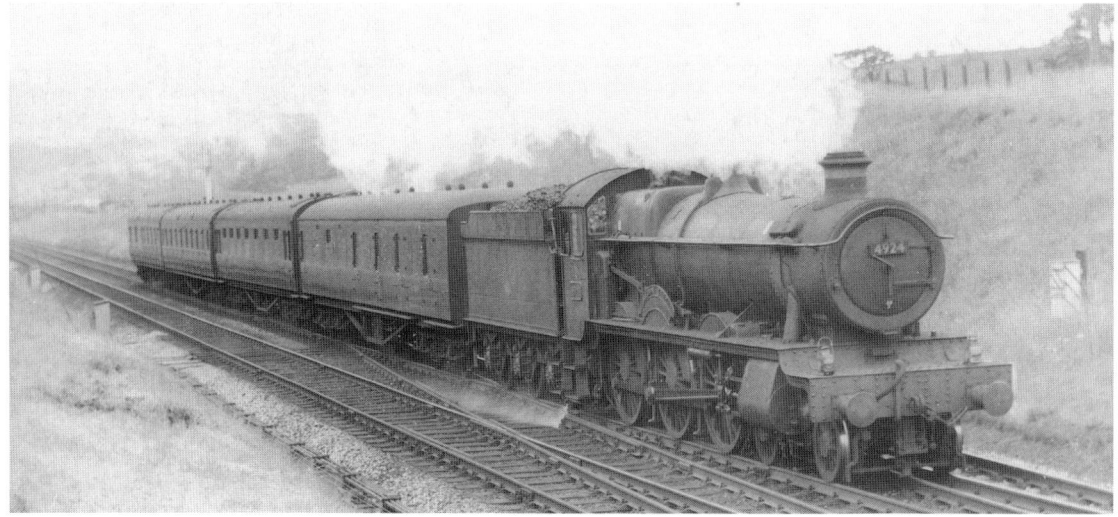

No. 4924 *Eydon Hall* near Ruabon, 1958. There are many junctions in this area, so I will not try to guess excatly where it can be.

There are masses of lines going in all directions in this area. I could spend the rest of the book trying to sort out which goes where, but I shall stick to Wrexham, Chester and Birkenhead, part of our journey. It is quite a long stretch between Shrewsbury and Birkenhead and my archive is not well served in this part of the country.

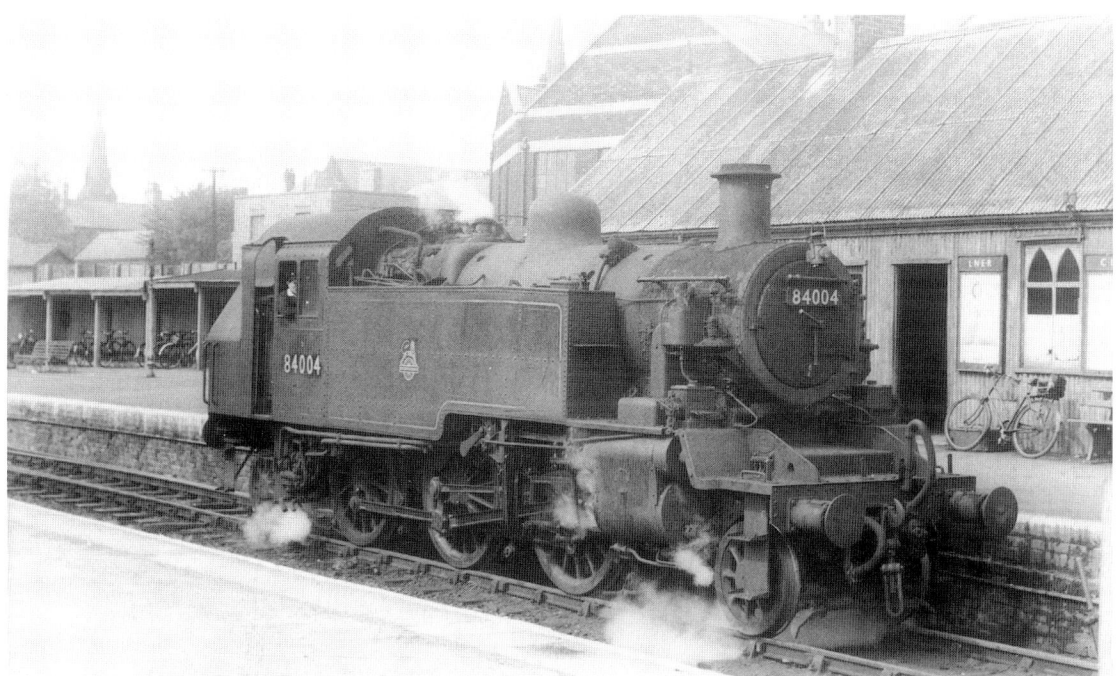

The only photograph I could find in Wrexham shows British Railways Standard no. 84004, 1955.

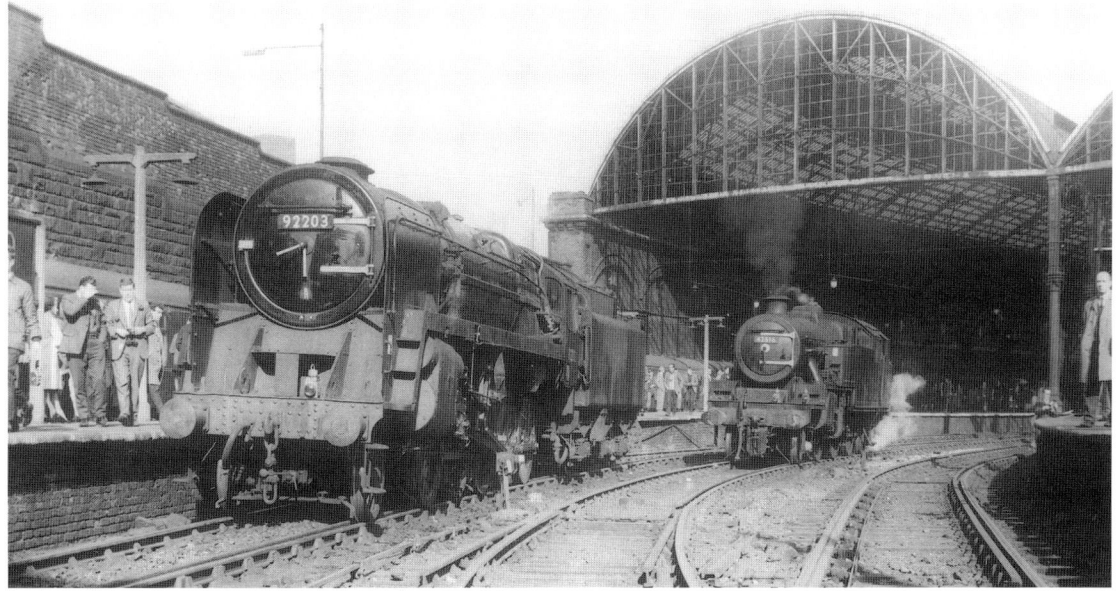

Another British Rail design, the popular and efficient 2–10–0. This is no. 92203 in Birkenhead, saved by David Shepherd and named *Black Prince*.

When we reach Gobowen on the way back, we can change trains and go through to Oswestry. As I have already mentioned it is the headquarters of the Cambrian Railway, and there are many names on this route that are well known to enthusiasts, inlcuding Welshpool, home of 'The Earl' and 'The Countess'. We managed to get some more refreshments at Gobowen, so now is the time to stoke up our energies with the good old British Rail sandwich and bottle of pop. Talk once again comes round to what we will see, 'Manors', 90xx Dukedogs, and before we realise it, we are nearing another name well known in railway history, Abermule.

In January 1921, owing to a series of mistakes by station staff, there was a terrible head-on collision in which fifteen people were killed, including a director of the Cambrian Railway. We are now well on our way to Machynlleth. We will have a short stop there, but there will not be enough time to get out, so we shall have to hang out of the window to see we hope, the 90xx and yes, there are a couple there. Now we have but a short journey to Dovey Junction, where the line branches to Aberystwyth in the south, and north to Pwllheli.

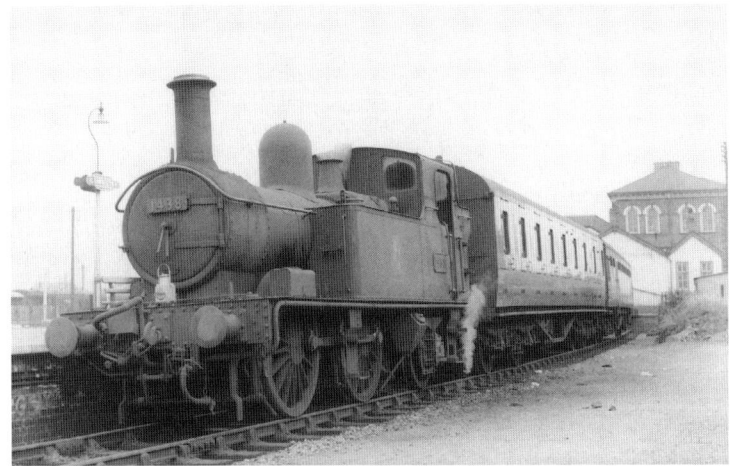

The ever-popular 0–4–2T, this time no. 1438 waiting to leave Oswestry, 1955.

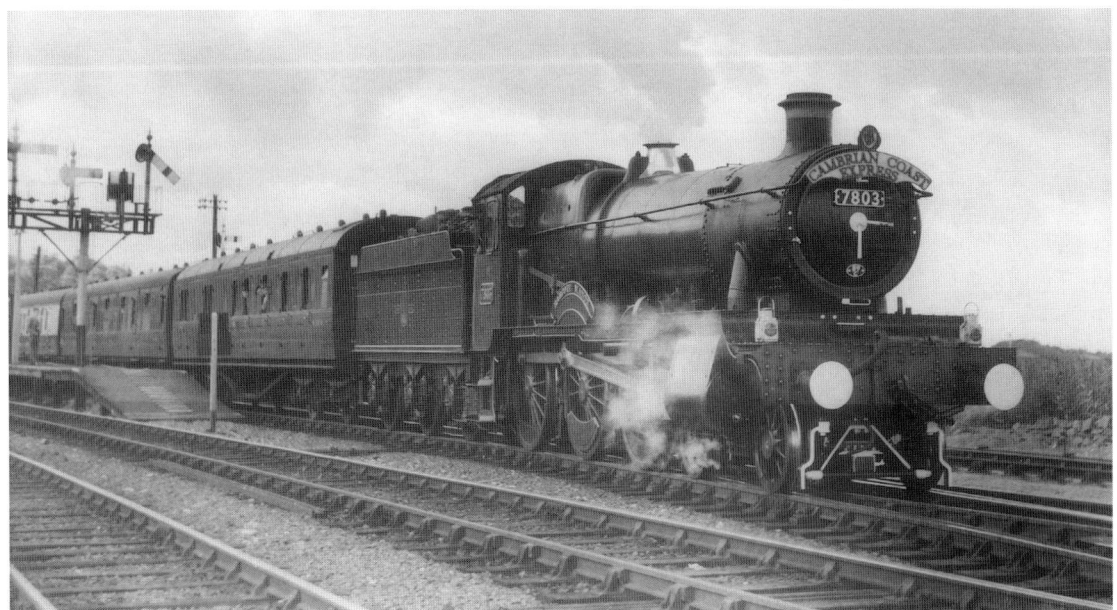

No. 7803 *Barcote Manor* pulling out of Dovey Junction, with the 'Cambrian Coast Express', 1959.

Great excitement at Dovey Junction – our train has arrived with a 90xx. First we are going to Pwllheli which is to the north. Through Aberdovey, the train stops at Towyn to allow passengers to alight to enjoy a trip on the Talyllyn Narrow Gauge Railway. Off again to Barmouth, we cross the estuary on what looks like a flimsy structure, but has been in place for a great many years. Our train is performing well and we are now at Harlech. On we go, and another stop for narrow-gauge enthusiasts – Portmadoc – for the Ffestiniog Line, on through Criccieth and then Afon Wen, where the LMS goes off to the right to the North Wales Line and Holyhead. Finally we run into Pwllheli.

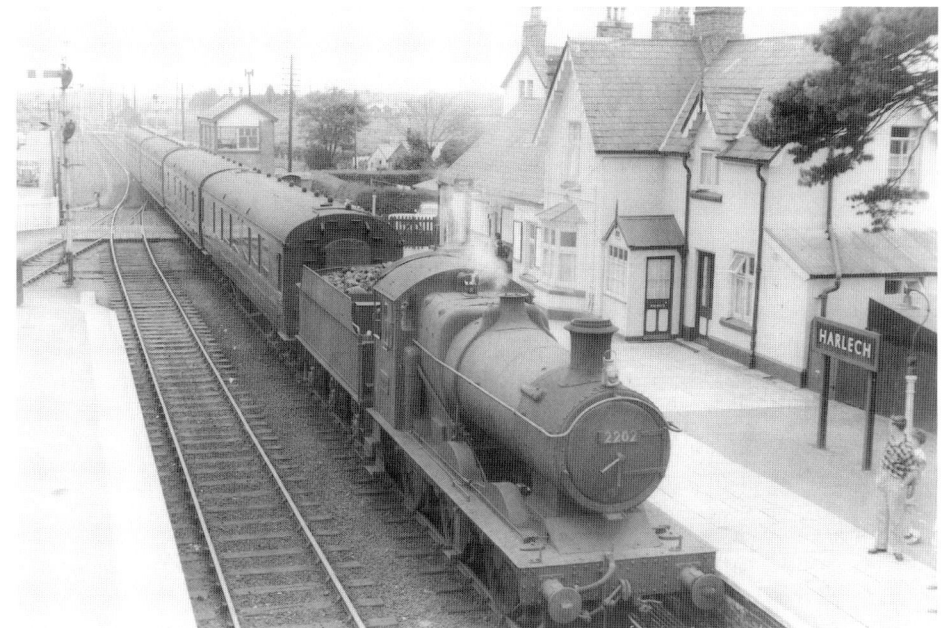

0–6–0 no. 2202 picking up passengers at Harlech, 1956.

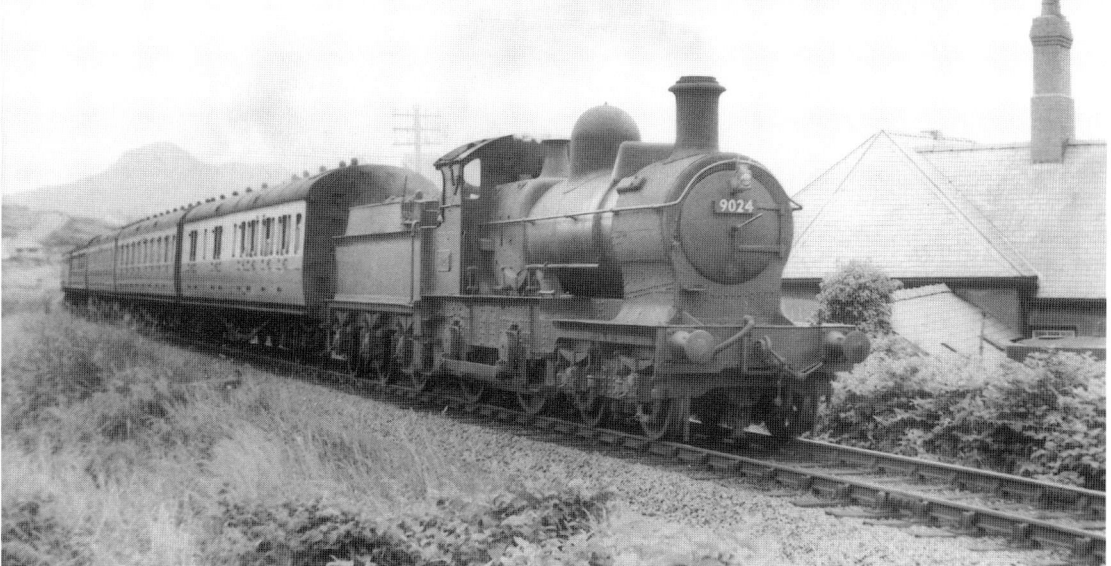

'Dukedog' no. 9024 at Criccieth. These engines were called 'Dukedogs' because they were built with the boilers from 'Dukes' and the frames from 'Bulldogs', 1954.

Back now to Dovey Junction to go south to Aberystwyth, but not so far as the Pwllheli route and this time we have a 'Manor' taking us south. We stop at Borth for a few minutes, then pass through a couple more stations, and we arrive at Aberywsyth. We get a few pictures in the station and then we have just a few stops to see the 'Vale of Rheidol' engines.

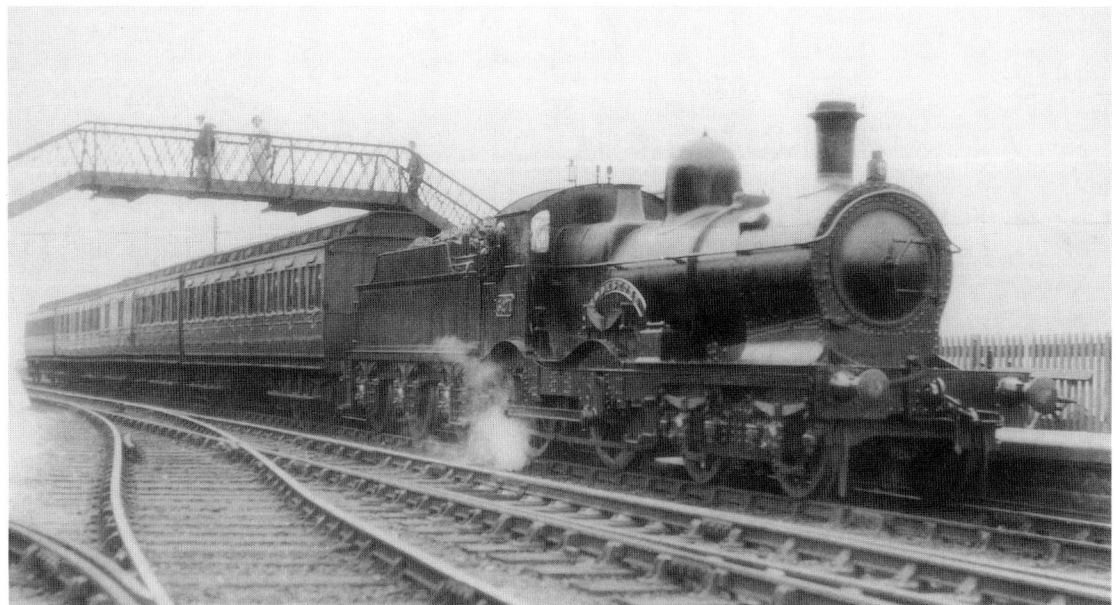

'Duke' no. 3271 *Eddystone* at Borth in 1930.

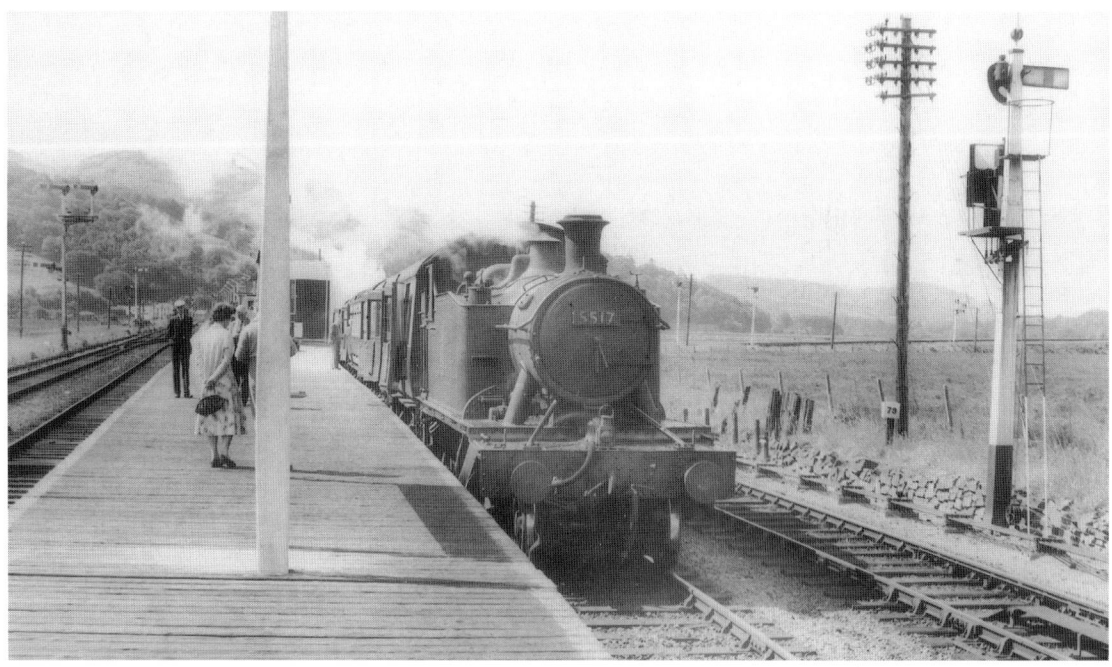

No. 5517 at Dovey Junction on a lovely summer's day. This can be a very different picture on a wild winter's day!

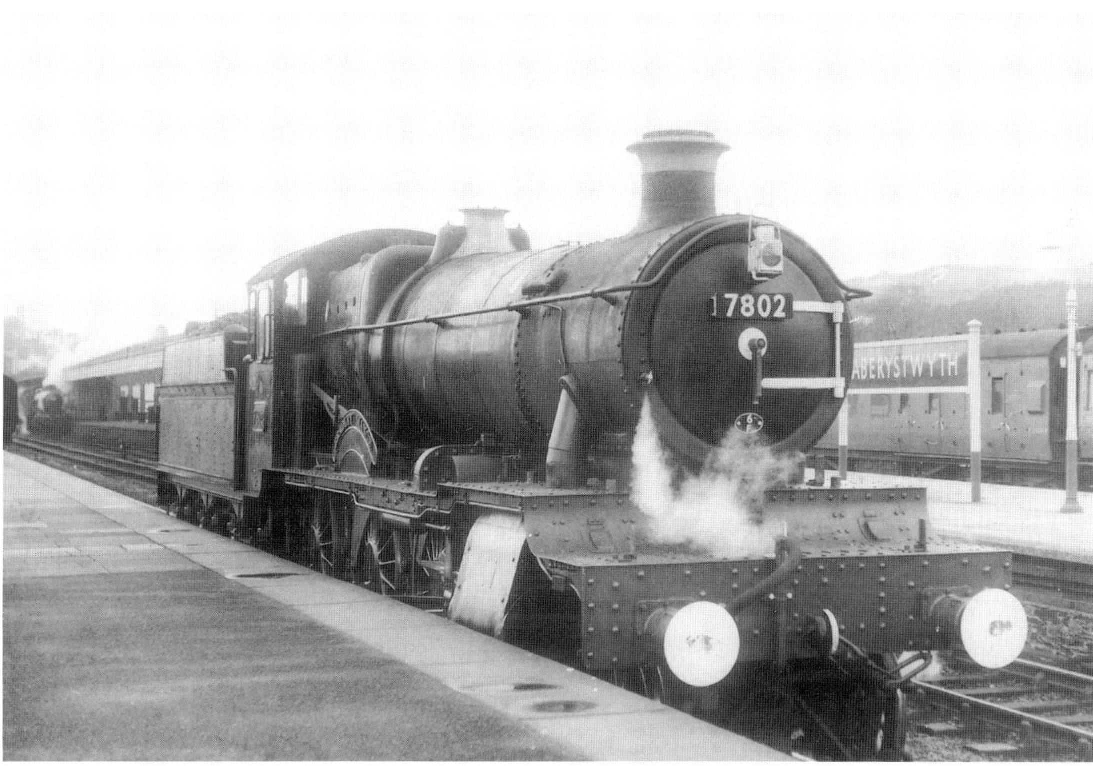

No. 7802 *Bradley Manor* backing down onto carriages which it will take to Shrewsbury.

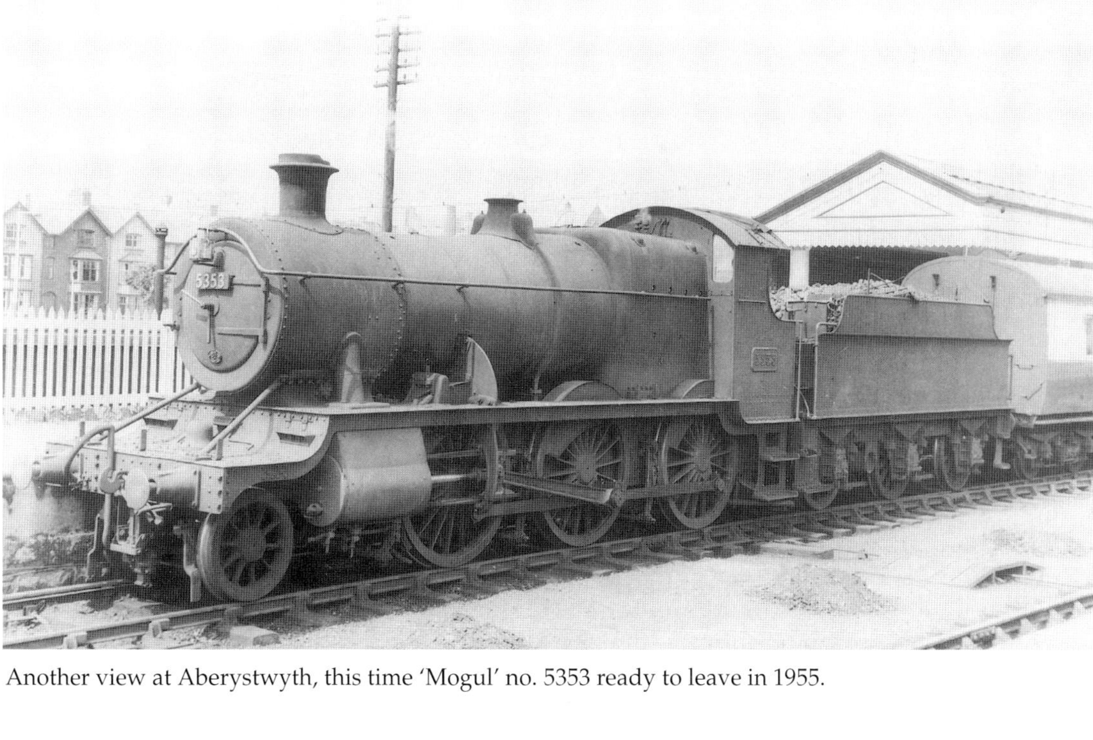

Another view at Aberystwyth, this time 'Mogul' no. 5353 ready to leave in 1955.

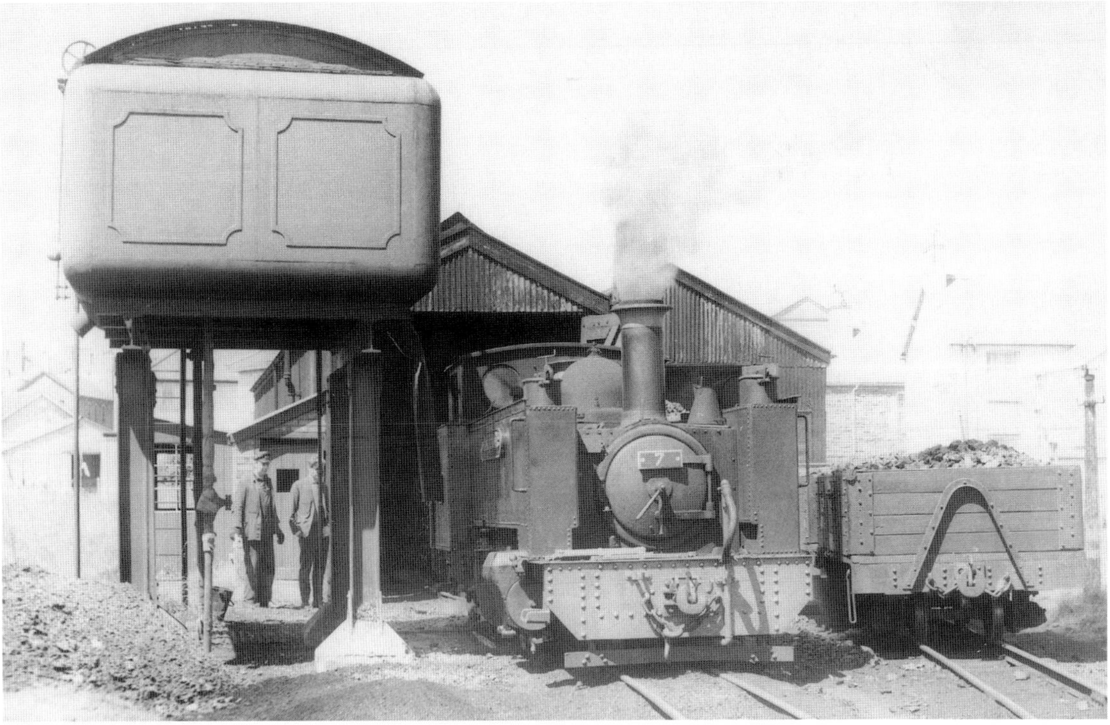

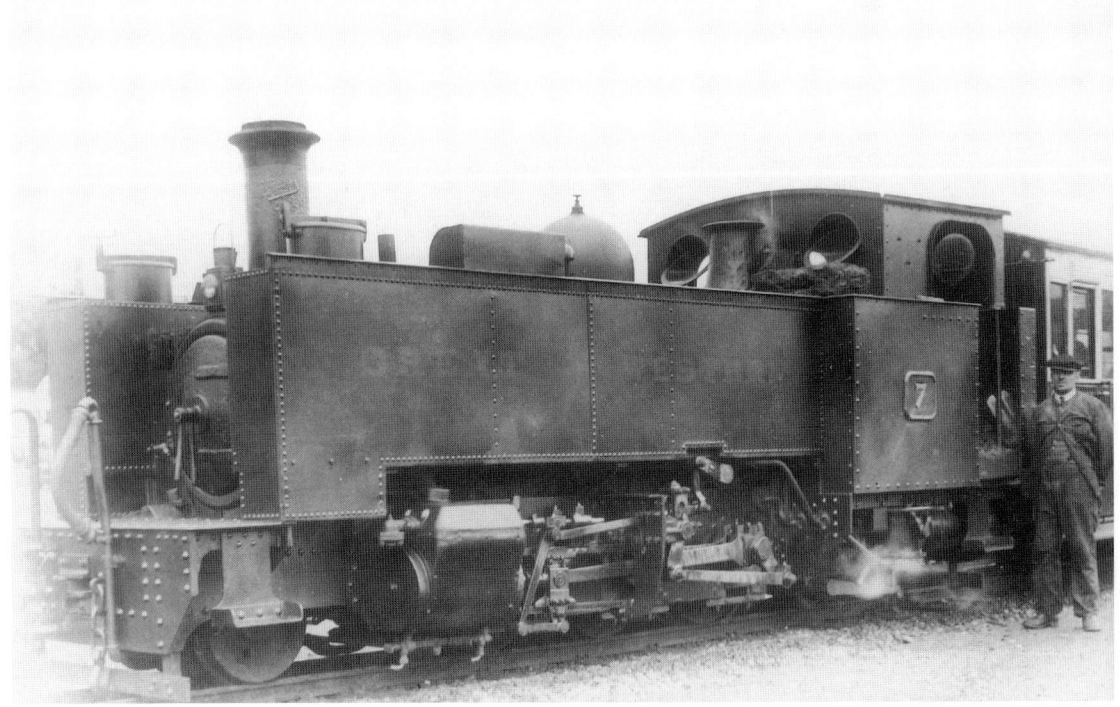

'Vale of Rheidol', no. 7 *Owain Glyndwr* being prepared at the small Vale of Rheidol shed at Aberystwyth, 1956.

A pre-war view of no. 7 before its name was restored. This view was taken in the station before setting out for Devil's Bridge.

It is a pity there was not time to take a Vale of Rheidol train to Devil's Bridge, but we must get back to our train and head south. Apart from lovely scenery there is not much for the railway enthusiast to see on the stretch of line southwards. The Vale of Rheidol was originally owned by the Cambrian Railway, but it was absorbed by the GWR at the grouping in 1923. There were three engines in the Cambrian stock, but only one has survived – no. 9 – which was built in 1902. Nos 7 and 8 of today's Vale of Rheidol were built in 1923–4 by the GWR. We have been travelling south for quite some time and our train is now approaching Whitland and things will start to get lively soon. We shall see locos in all directions, and hopefully the low number engines that were absorbed by the GWR at the grouping.

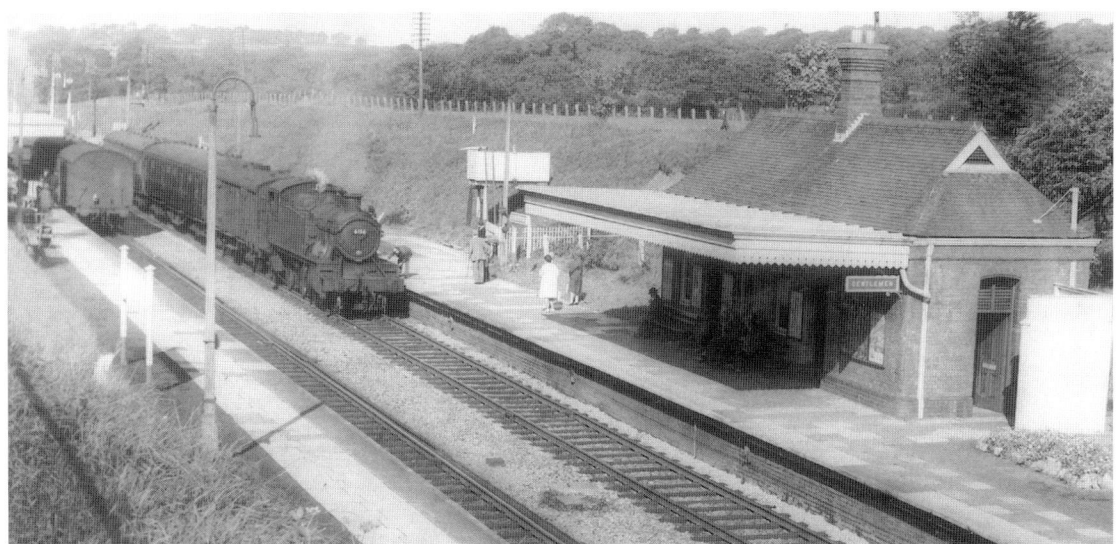

Clarbeston Road on the Whitland–Fishguard line with loco no. 6116 drawing into the station, 1954.

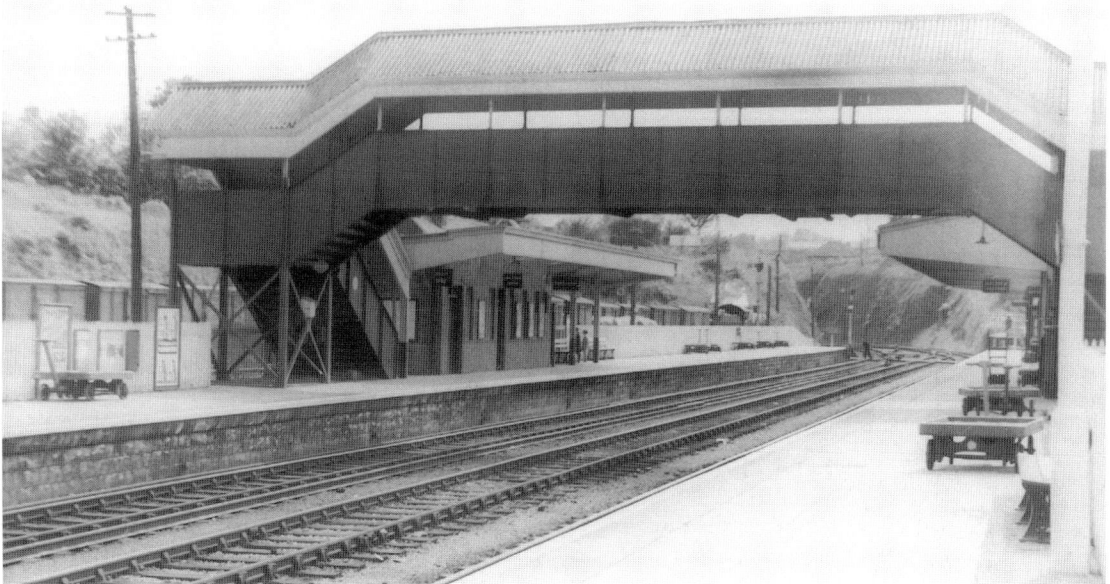

Haverfordwest is a busy station on the line from Clarbeston Road to Neyland and the oil terminals at Milford Haven, seen here in 1954.

Onwards we go and we are getting nearer to those low number engines. Through Carmarthen, heading for Kidwelly, we run alongside the River Towy for quite a distance. Next comes Kidwelly, the furthest west that the Burry Port and Gwendraeth Valleys Railway ventured. We shall soon be passing through Burry Port itself. Time once more to get the camera at the ready as Llanelli is nearly upon us.

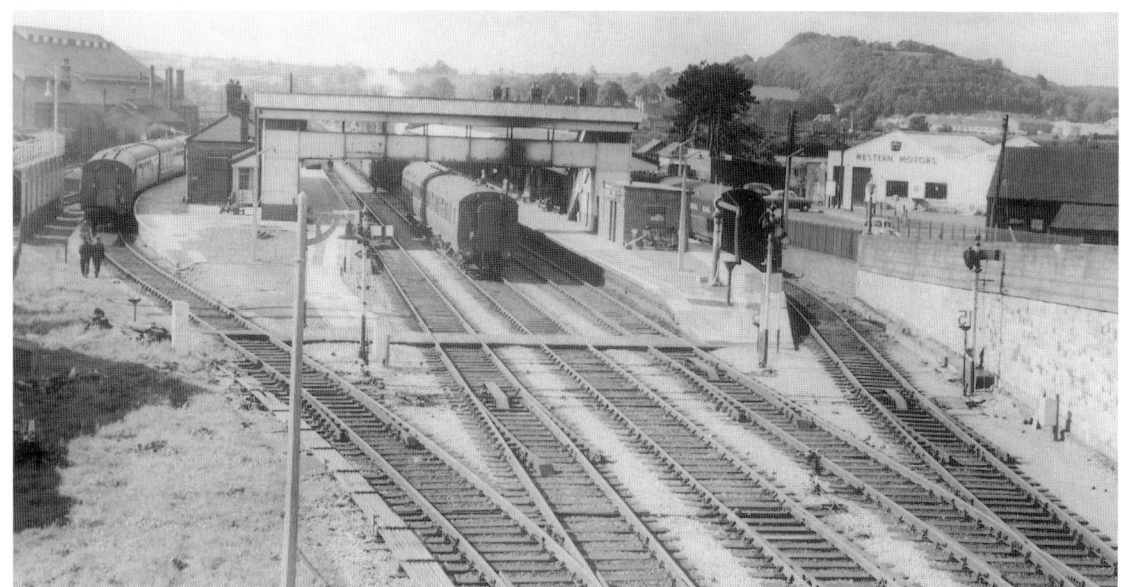

A general view of Carmarthen station in 1954.

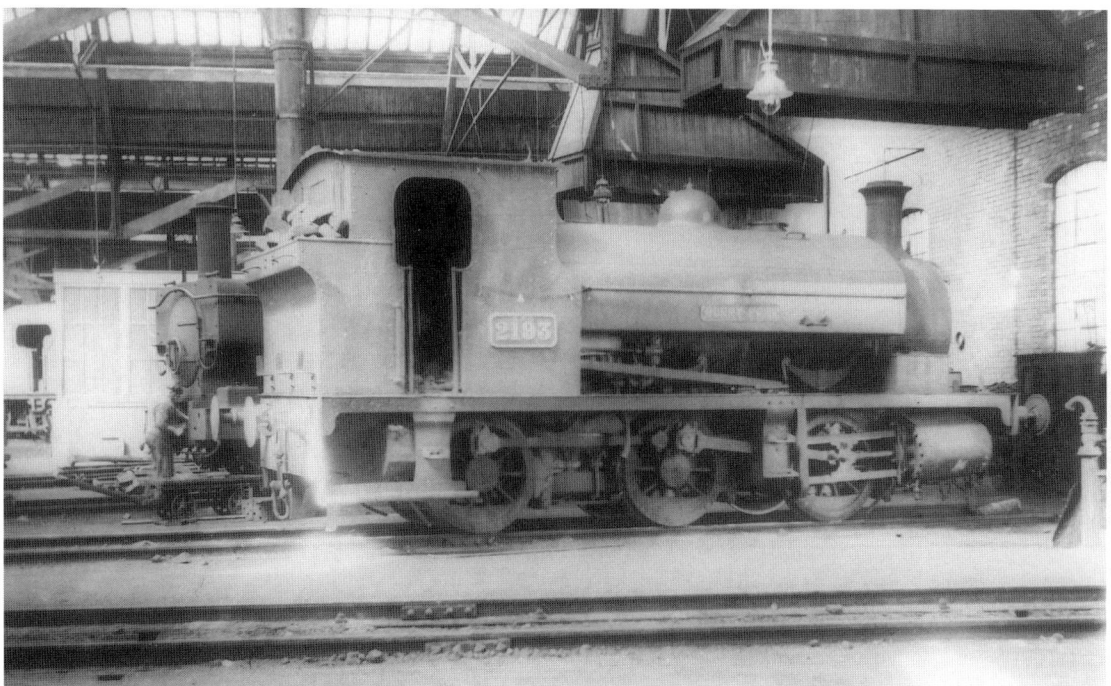

No. 2193 Burry Port inside Llanelli shed in 1952.

From Llanelli we shall pass many junctions and branches that lead off to collieries. We are now passing through Gowerton and after a short distance we had better get the window down and be ready with the camera as we will be approaching Landore, the first main line shed we have seen since Shrewsbury. Landore was well known for keeping their 'Castle' class engines spotlessly clean and you always knew a Landore engine from a distance by its polished buffers, or in some instances they were painted white.

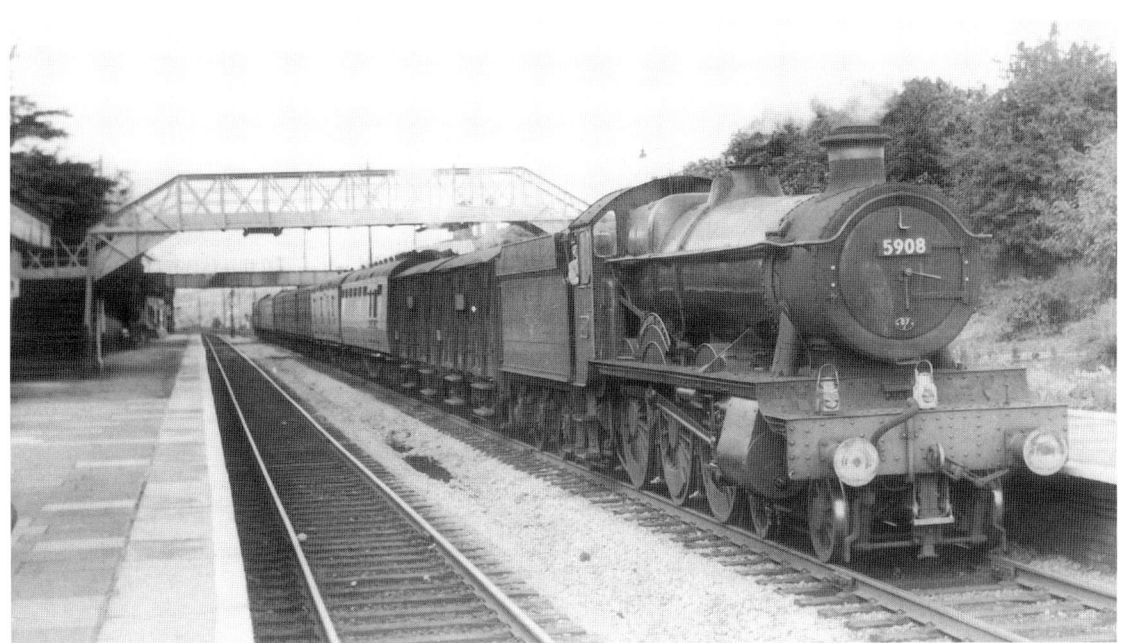

No. 5908 *Moreton Hall* with a parcels train running through Gowerton.

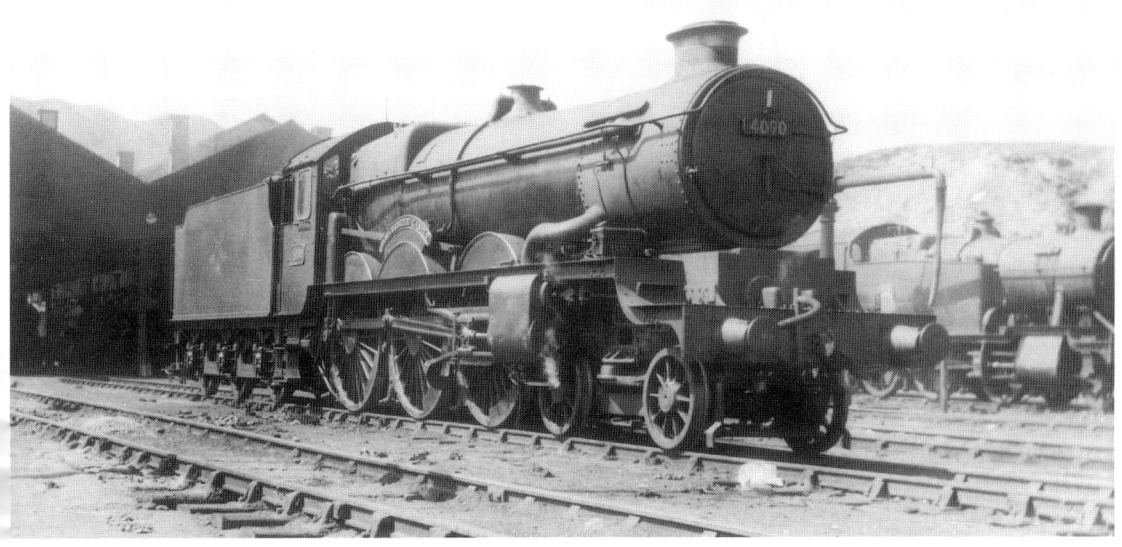

No. 4090 *Dorchester Castle* on Landore shed, 1959.

From Landore into Swansea is only a short distance. There are many lines and branches with lots of locos shunting, passing or waiting in sidings. Record books are busy and cameras are clicking when we come to a squealing halt at the station. We shall make time to visit Swansea East Dock and Danygraig 87C home of the 11xx locos (0–4–0T) which were especially used for working the docks area.

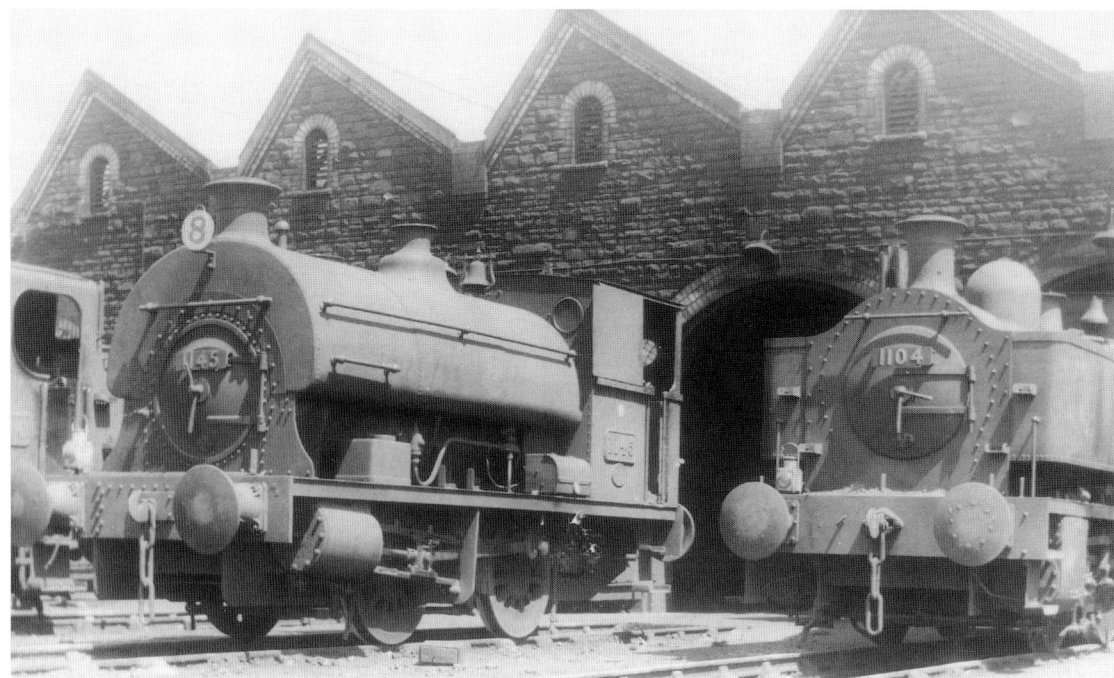

Nos 1145 and 1104 on Danygraig shed in Swansea. These locos were used almost exclusively in the docks.

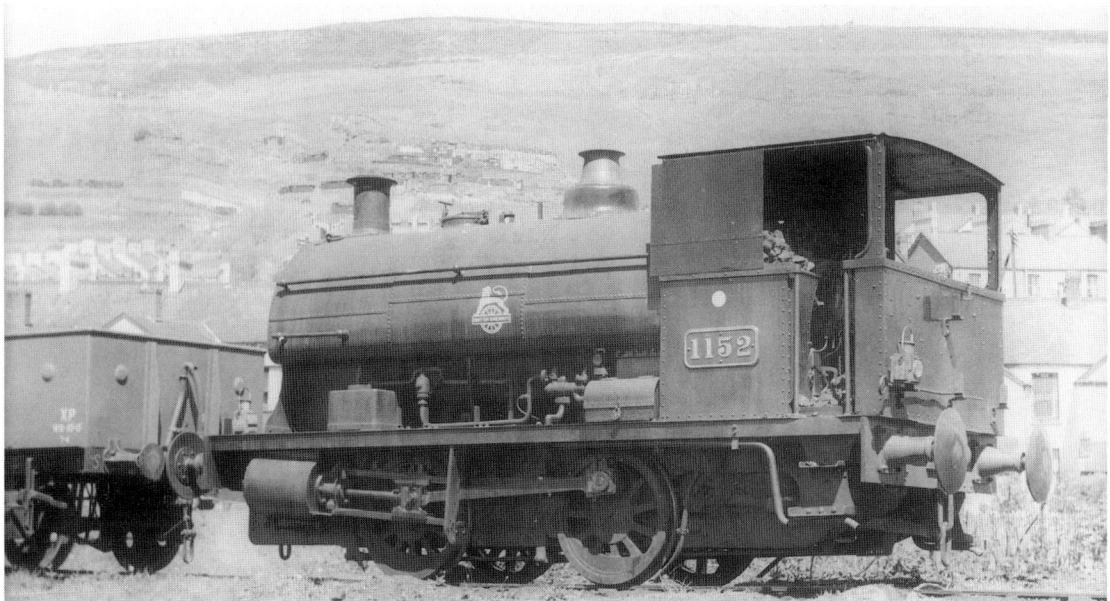

0–4–0T no. 1152 working in Swansea East Dock, 1956.

Swansea High Street came into being in 1850 and serves a large area. In the early days it served industry, coal mines and the docks, but after the Second World War rail traffic increased with the growing popularity of tourist destinations like the Gower Coast, the Mumbles and the lovely Pembrokeshire Coast. This was fortunate for Swansea because by the 1950s industry and coalfields were in decline. There goes the guard's whistle and with the familiar gentle jolt we are off again.

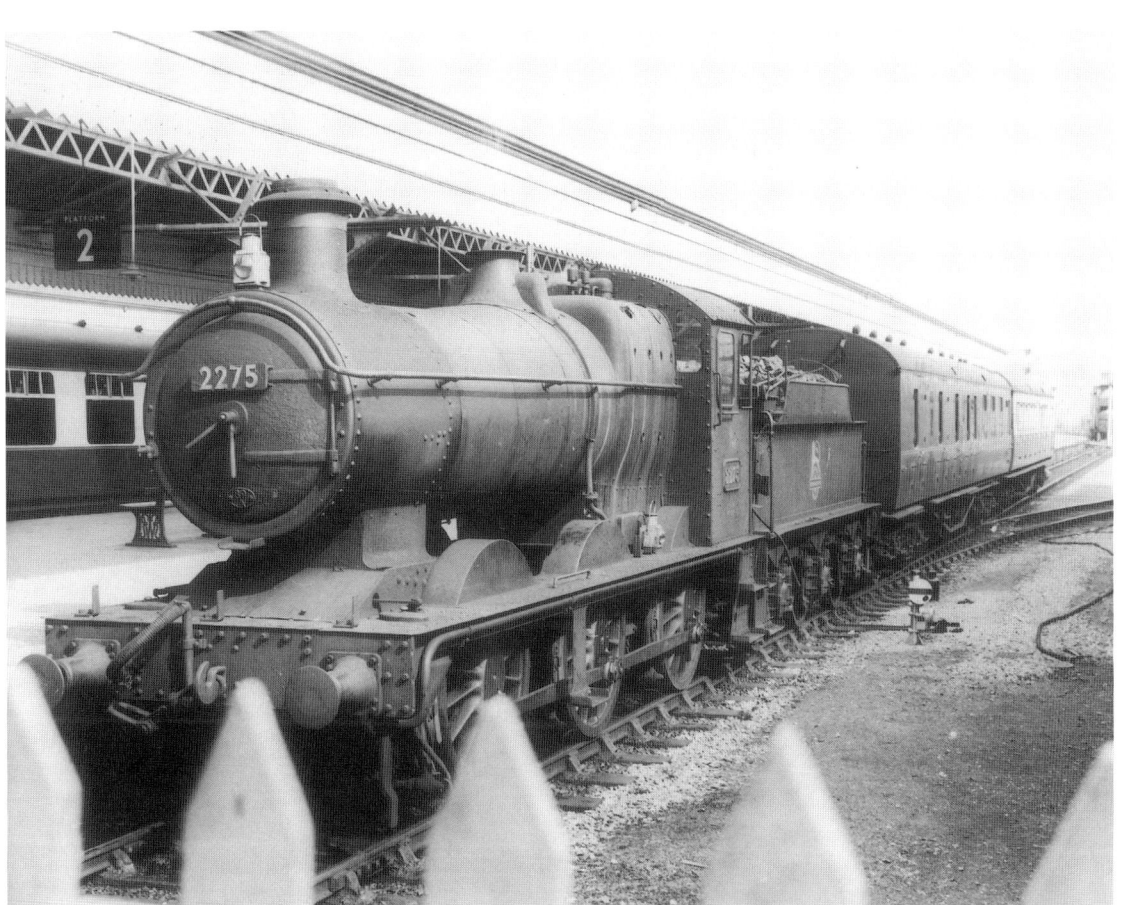

0–6–0 no. 2275 with a local stopping train in Swansea High Street, 1954.

We will not get much rest from now on, as there are sidings and coal trains around every curve. Now we are heading into Neath. I wish we could explore all the lines in the area, but if we do that, this journey will not get beyond Cardiff, and we certainly want to get to the end of our journey in Penzance. After Neath we run through another dock area, Port Talbot. On past the large steel works at Margam, we head towards Bridgend. At Bridgend we go onto the line to Barry which has a large compliment of low number engines we'd all like to see. On go the brakes at Barry, the carriage doors open and we are on the platform, moving at a fast rate for the sheds.

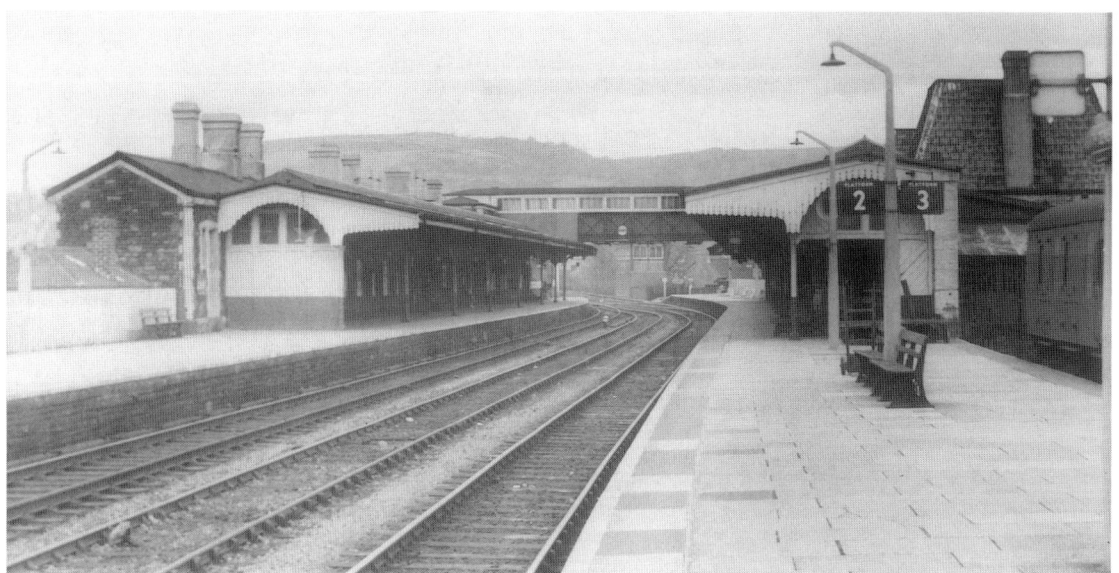

Neath General station in 1957.

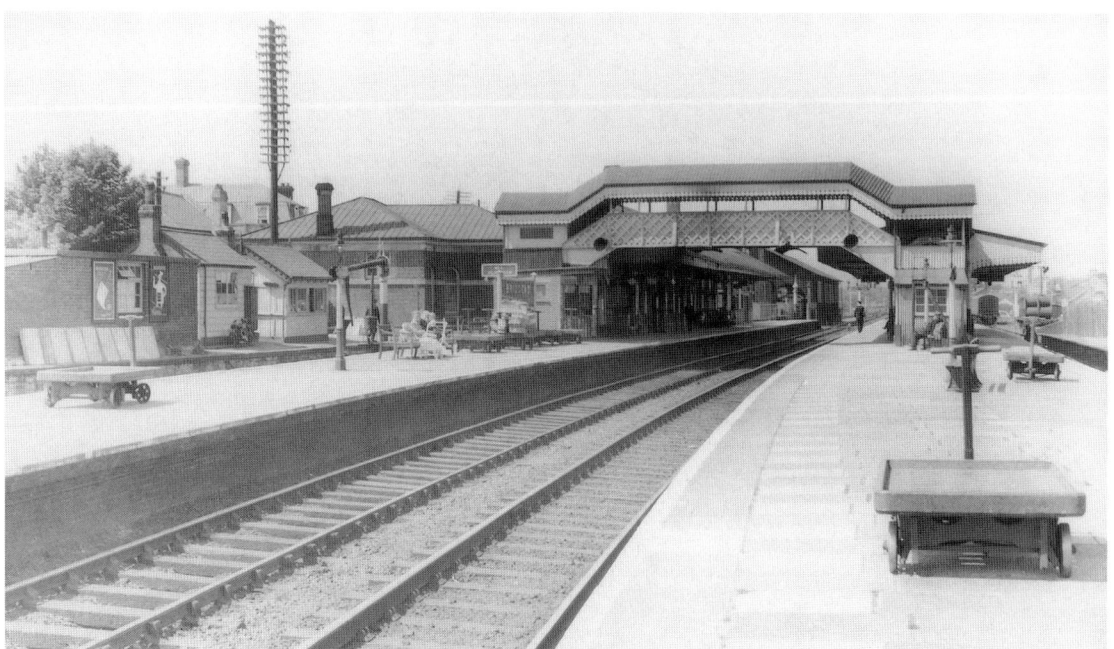

Bridgend Junction for the direct line to Cardiff and the Barry Line.

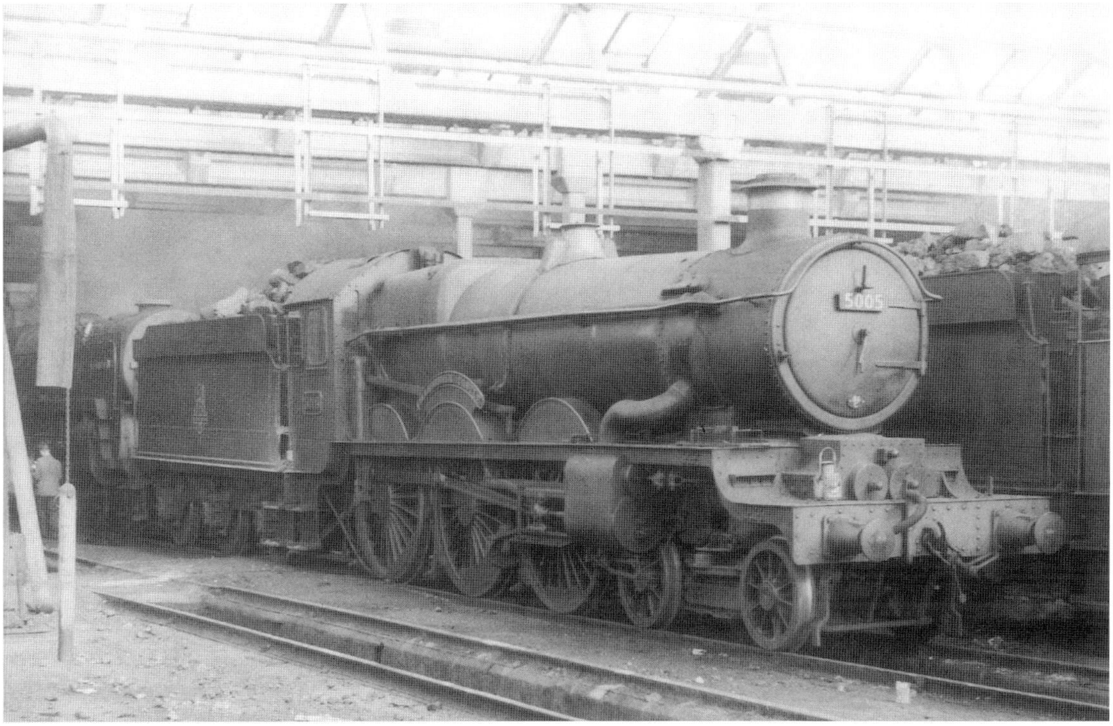

No. 5005 *Manorbier Castle* on Barry shed in 1954. This was one of the two locos that the GWR experimented with streamlining. It was a disaster. It was as if someone (rumoured to be Collett) had tried to make the engine look as ugly as possible. The experiment didn't last long.

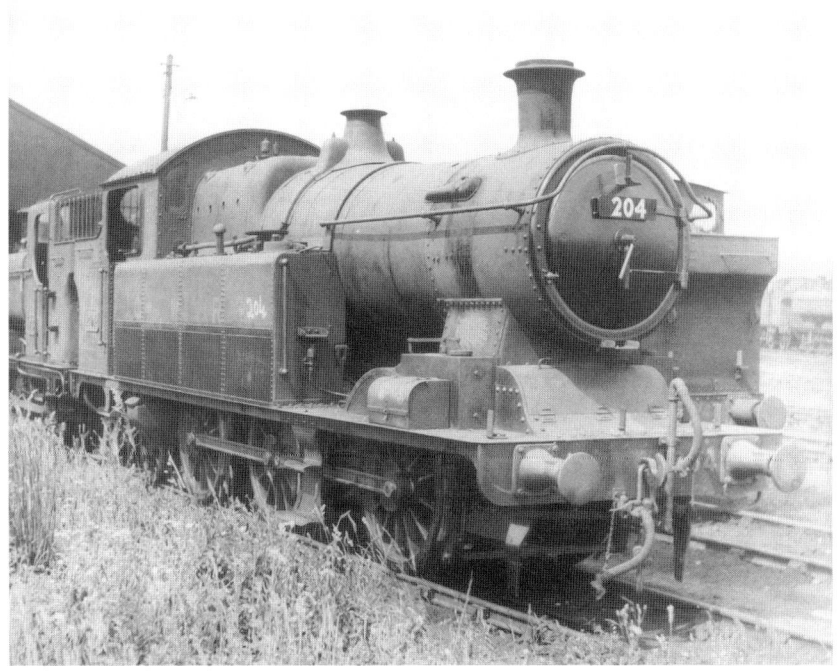

No. 204 was one of the many low numbers on Barry shed. This was originally a Taff Vale engine.

On the move again, we have only a short distance to cover until we arrive at Cardiff – a Mecca for any Western enthusiast, as so many lines converge on the Welsh capital.

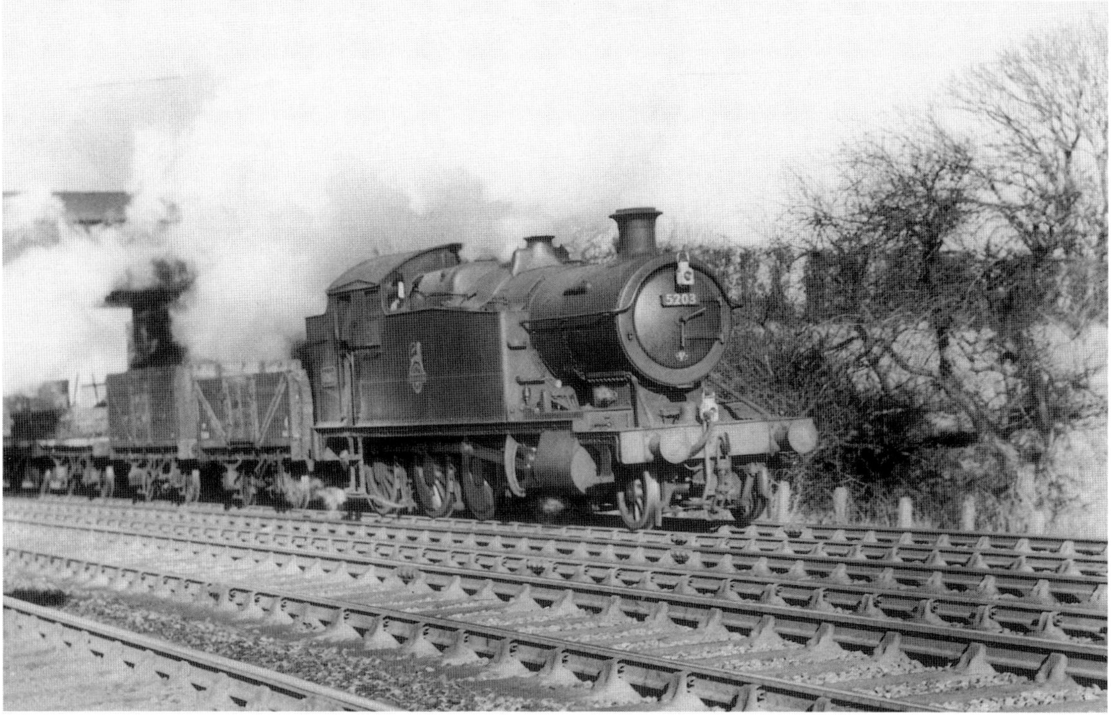

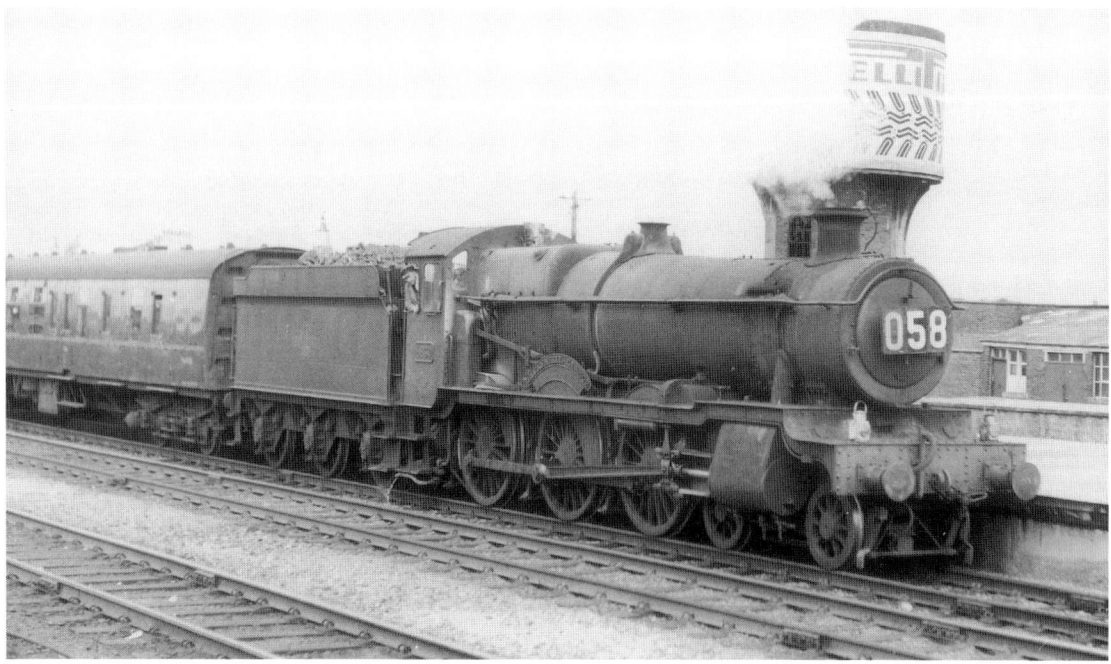

No. 5203 nearing Cardiff in 1955.

No. 6830 *Buckenhill Grange* arrives at Cardiff, with the well known landmark in the background, 1960.

We are pulling into Cardiff General and there seem to be coal trains rolling through in all directions. The Taff Vale and the Rhymney Railways used Queen Street station. There is a huge dock system, and I am sorry to say we will only be able to see a small selection of locos that are here today. There are three sheds in Cardiff; Canton 86C which was the main line shed with 'Castles', 'Halls' and earlier 'Saints' and 'Stars'; 88A Cathays for coal and freight; and also 88B East Dock.

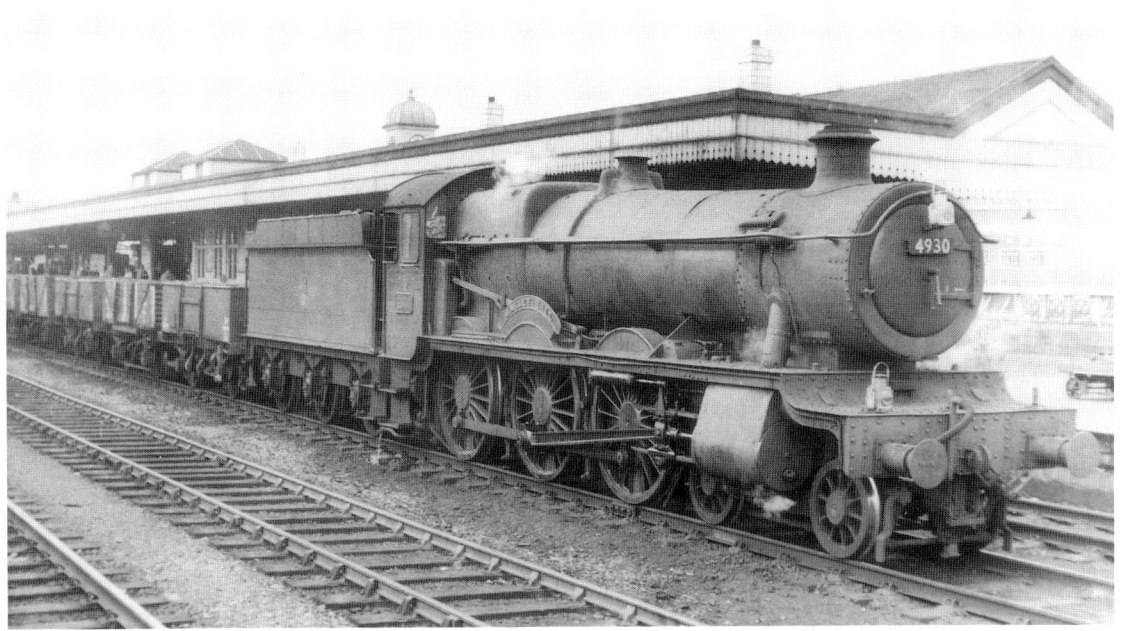

No. 4930 *Hagley Hall* passing through Cardiff General with a ballast train in 1958.

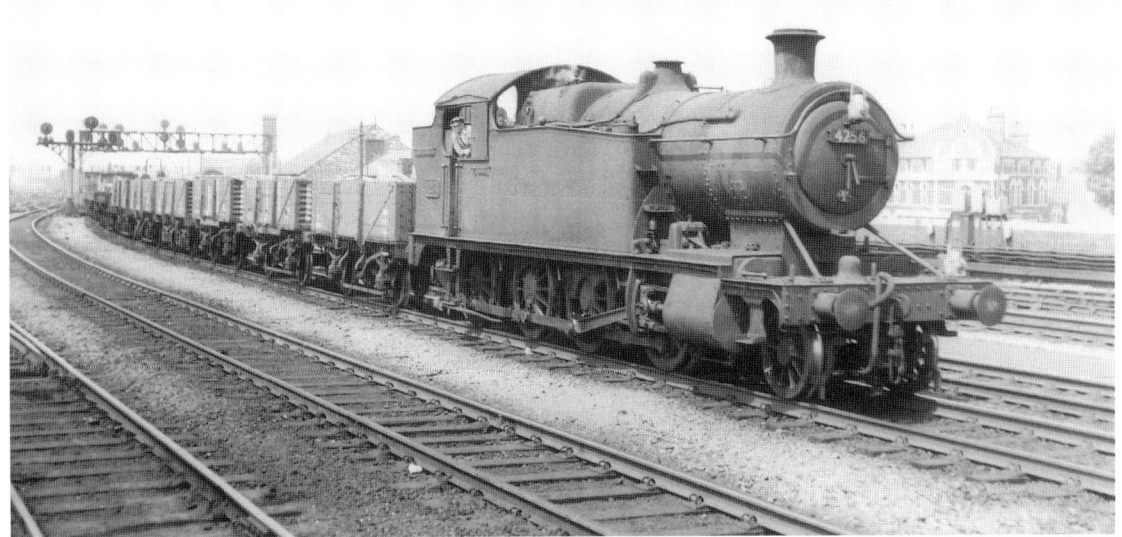

No. 4256 heads another freight train through Cardiff, 1958.

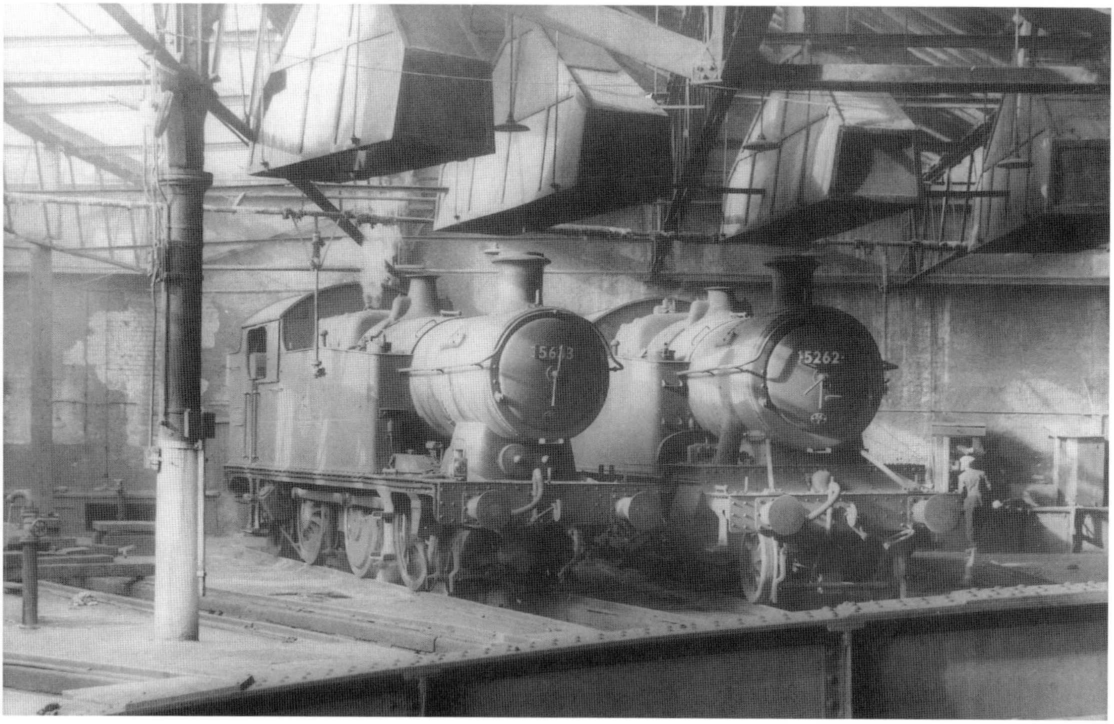

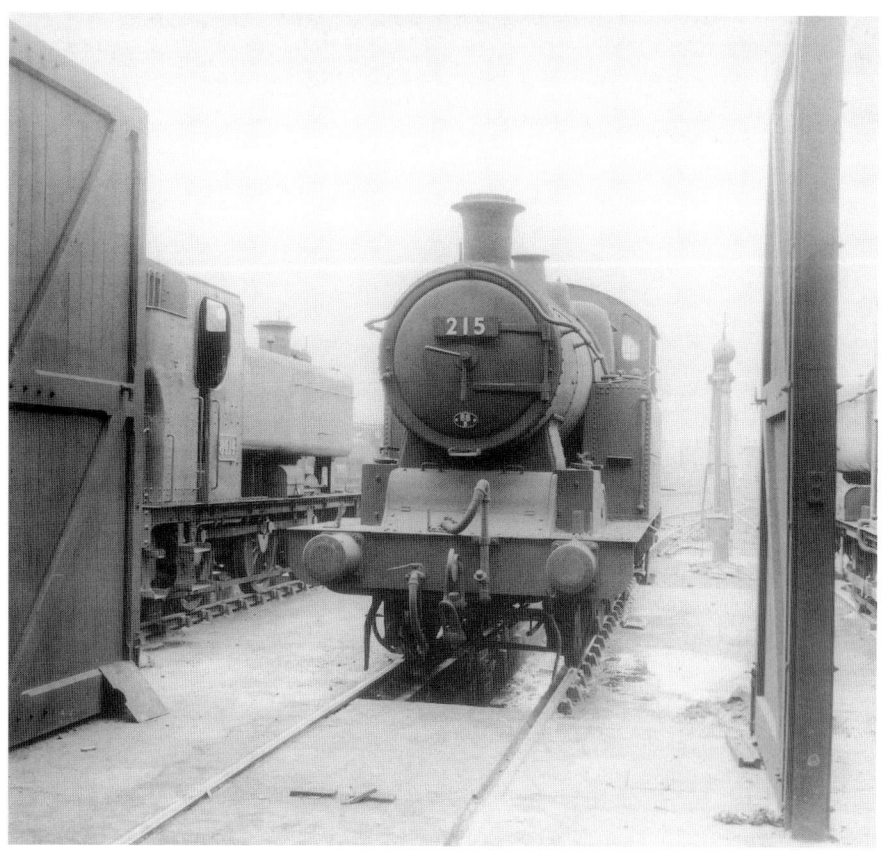

No. 5633 on Canton shed. Keeping it company is heavy freight 2–8–0T no. 5262.

Cardiff East Dock is the setting for this picture of no. 215 of ex-Taff Vale in 1955. No. 8414 is its companion.

Back in our carriage, we regret that we were unable to visit Caerphilly. The Rhymney Railways works, up in the valleys, opened in 1901 and the original works were in Cardiff, but as the railway grew, they needed to expand the Cardiff site but found it impossible, so Caerphilly was chosen instead. The works closed in the 1960s with the advent of the diesels, particularly the DMUs, which took over all passenger work in the valleys. To most steam enthusiasts Caerphilly will be remembered for the heavy freight and low numbered locos. Caerphilly, in the last few years, did repair the odd 'Castle' and 'Hall'.

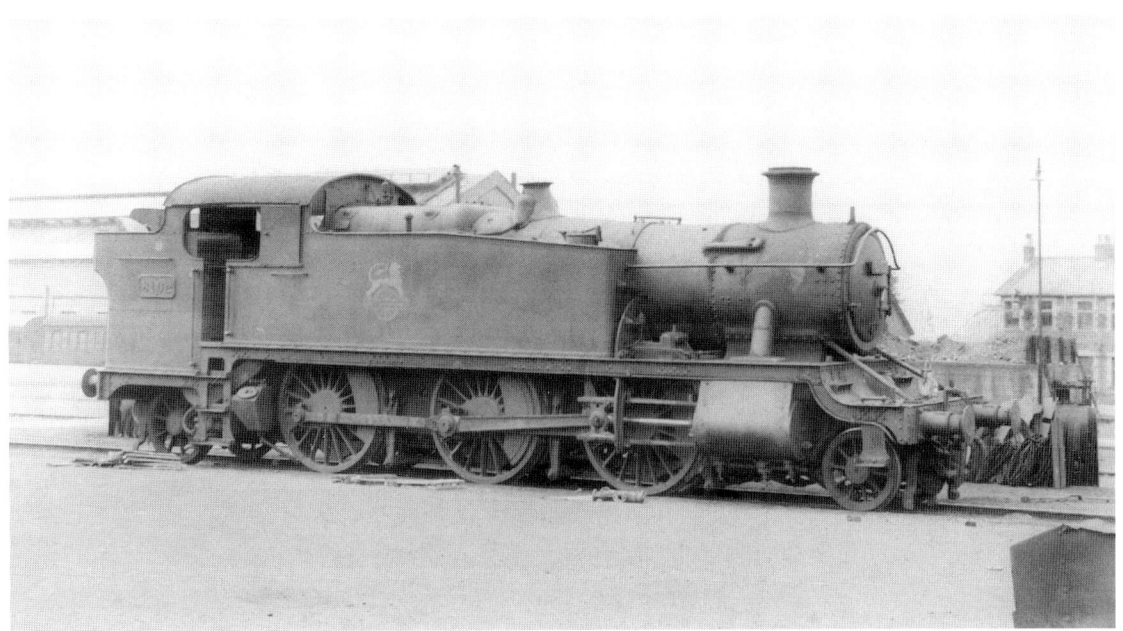

No. 8102 at the Caerphilly works in 1954.

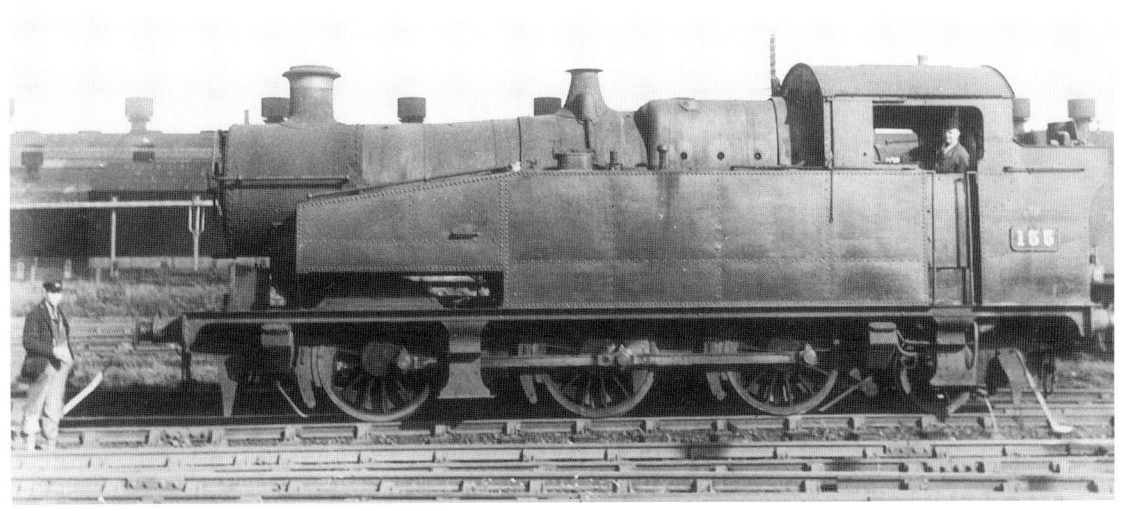

No. 155 ex-Cardiff Railways 0–6–2T, as rebuilt by the GWR in 1928 with a GWR taper boiler, October 1949.

On our way again the next stop is Newport – a very busy station. It is a major route into South Wales, and the town also has a large dock system. We will not leave the train as it only stops for a couple of minutes. Platform occupation is kept at a minimum, as it is such a busy station.

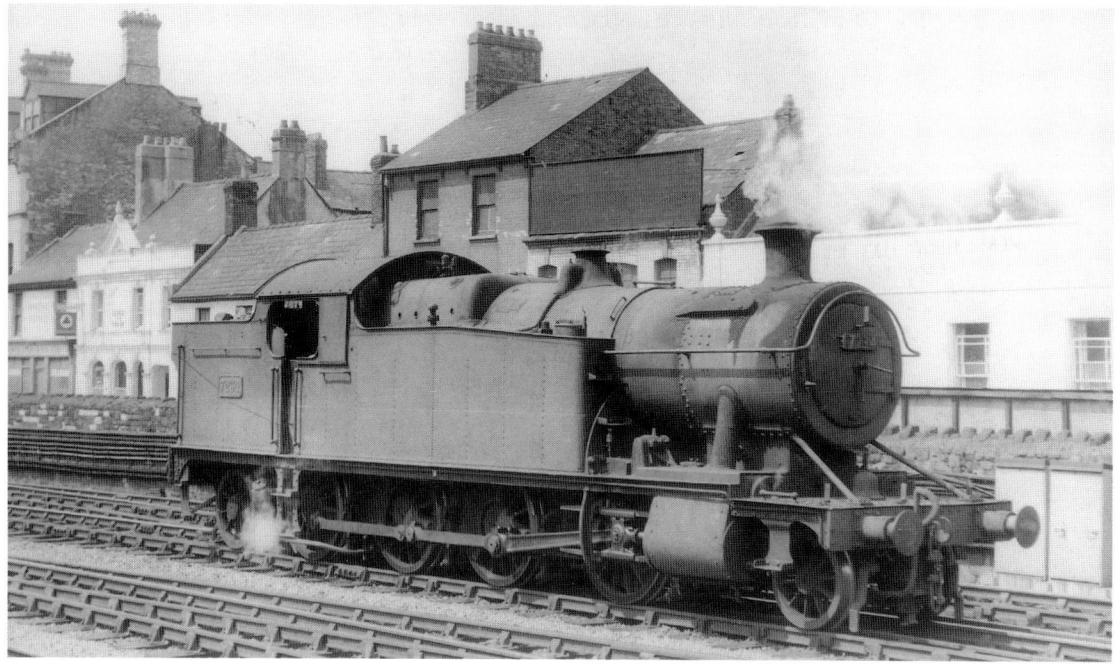

Heavy freight 2–8–2T no. 7234 running light back through Newport station, 1962.

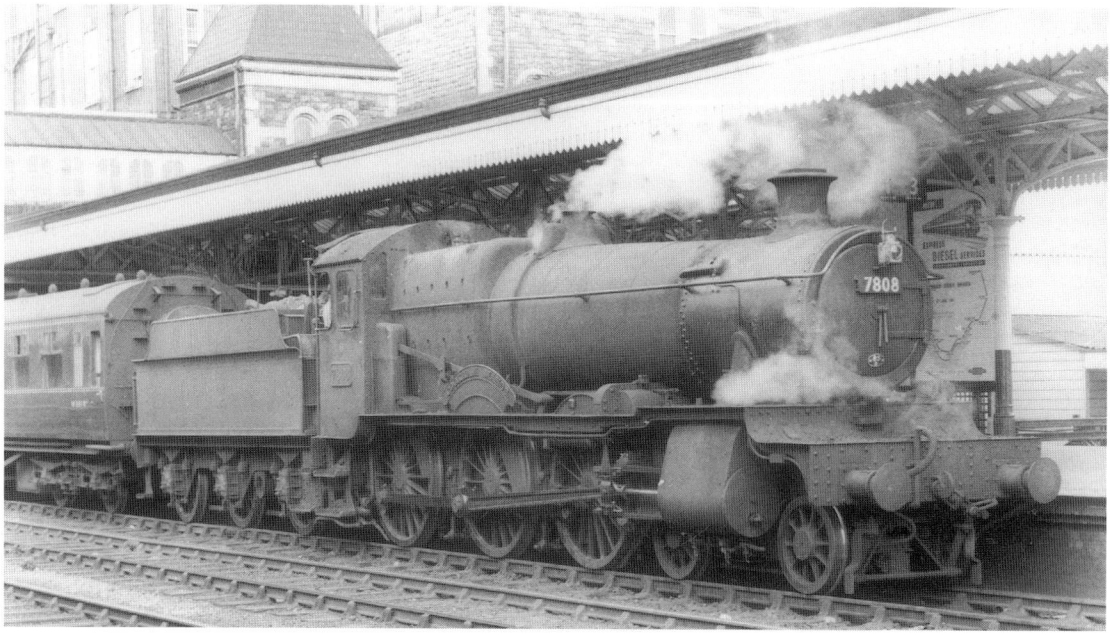

No. 7808 *Cookham Manor* carrying an 85A Worcester shedplate. It has probably brought a stopping all stations train from Worcester, and is shown at rest in Newport.

That lovely western bark from the chimney echoes back from the walls of Newport Castle, which is located close to the railway. As we cross the bridge over the River Usk, only a hundred yards or so from the station around the Maindy Curve, there is now a fairly straight and fast track to the Severn Tunnel. Enginemen like to keep the speed up on the way down. As a passenger, you feel the speed rising and speeds of 90 mph have been recorded. We then noticeably level out and the long climb starts. From now on the line rises almost continually until it tops the incline at Badminton. The gradient varies between 1:68 and 1:300. The distance from the bottom of the tunnel to the top is approximately 18 miles. At Patchway the line divides to the left onto Badminton, and the right to Bristol, which is where we are heading.

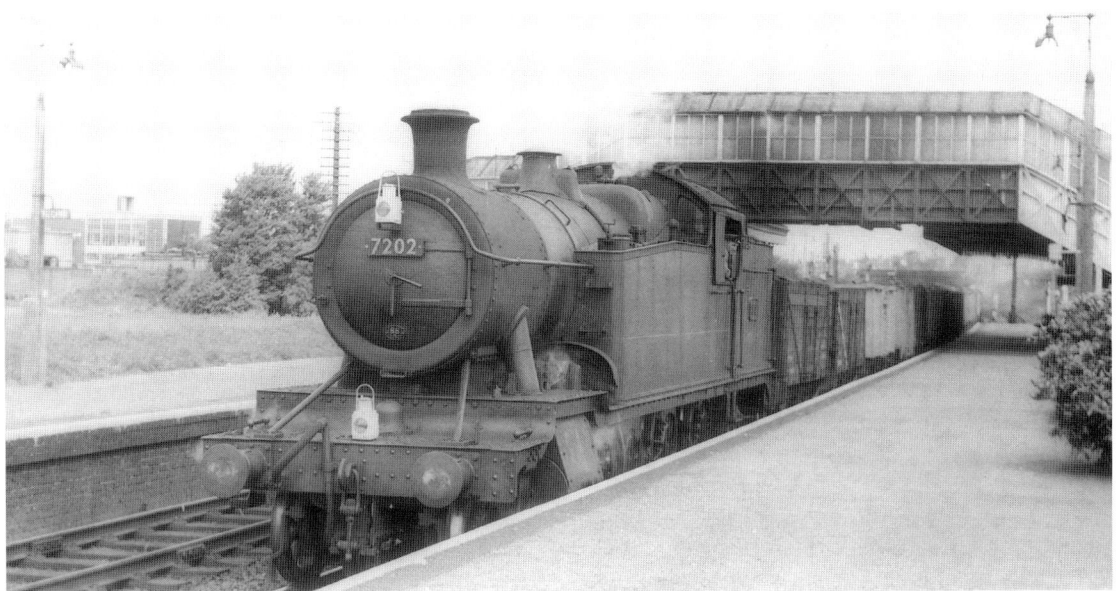

No. 7202 tops the bank at Patchway.

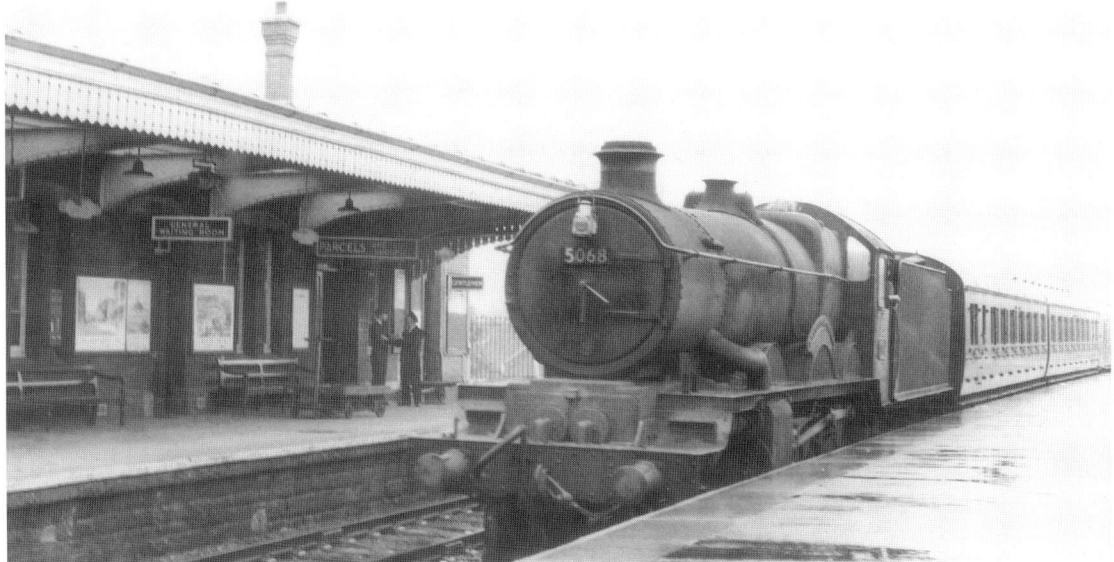

No. 5068 *Beverston Castle* passing Stapleton Road, Bristol.

A quick run down Ashley Down Bank, through Stapleton Road, under the Midland Bridge that carries the LMS line out of Bristol and we are now through Lawrence Hill and running into Bristol Temple Meads.

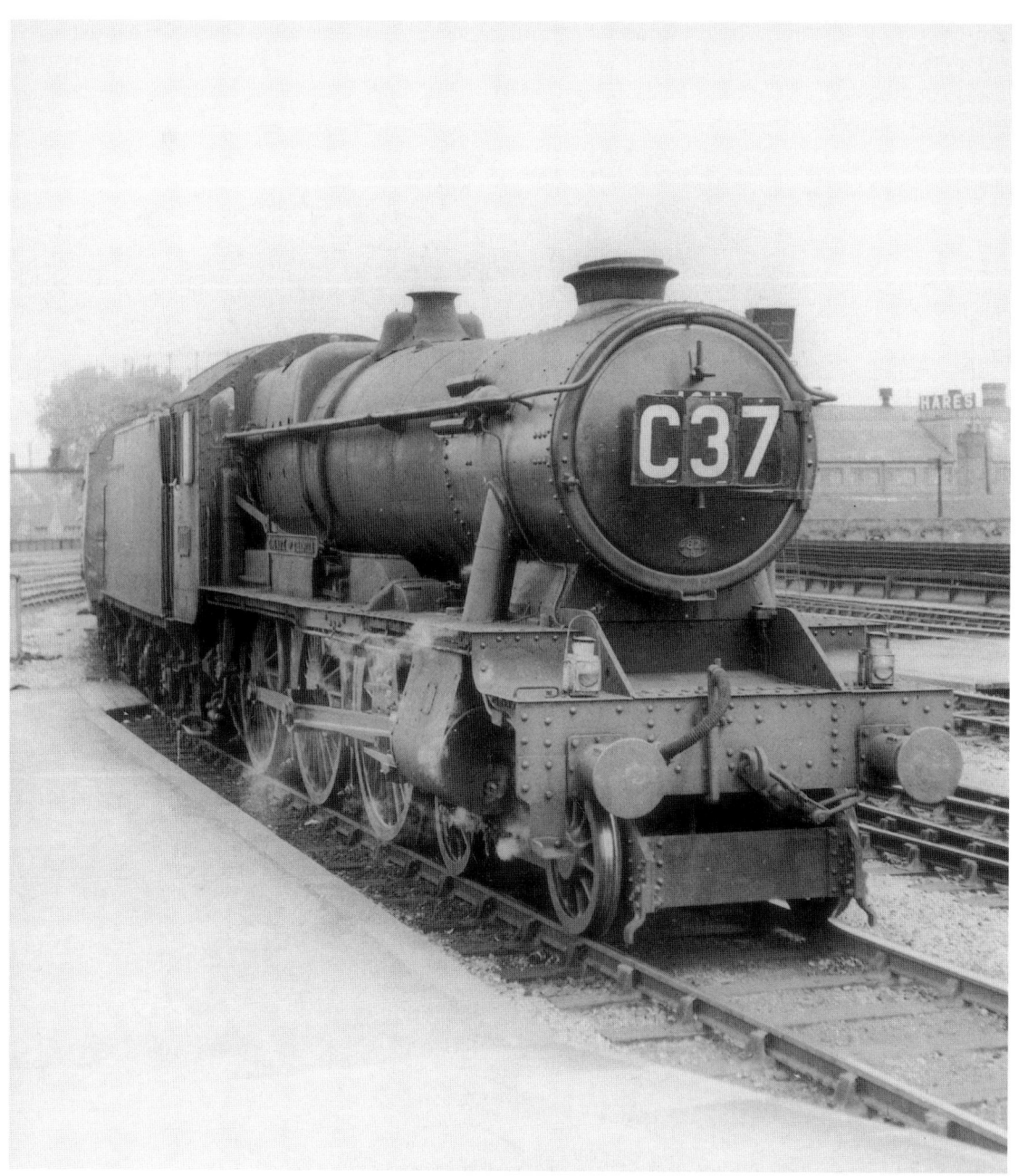

No. 1011 *County of Chester* pulls into Temple Meads in 1959.

We shall soon be on our way to Penzance, but we do, however, have the time to look around Temple Meads. Bath Road shed 82A is just off the end of platforms 3 and 4. Bristol has many 'Castles' and other named classes and it has had a couple of 'Kings' shedded here, but this class is mainly 'just visiting'. The other Bristol shed, 82B, chiefly dealt with freight engines. The cameras have once again been busy, as have the record books, but the guard is blowing his whistle, so it's back on board and off we go on the last leg of our journey.

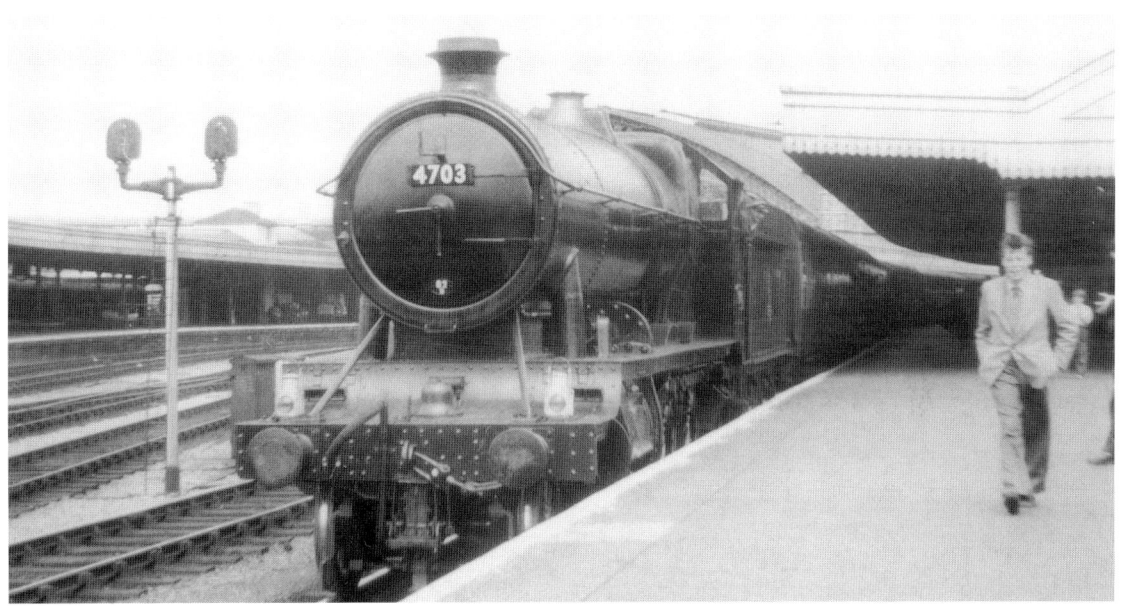

No. 4703, one of Churchwards' massive 2–8–0s, was quite capable of hauling express passenger trains, although they were originally introduced for fast freight services. It is seen here heading a train to the West Country from Temple Meads in 1955.

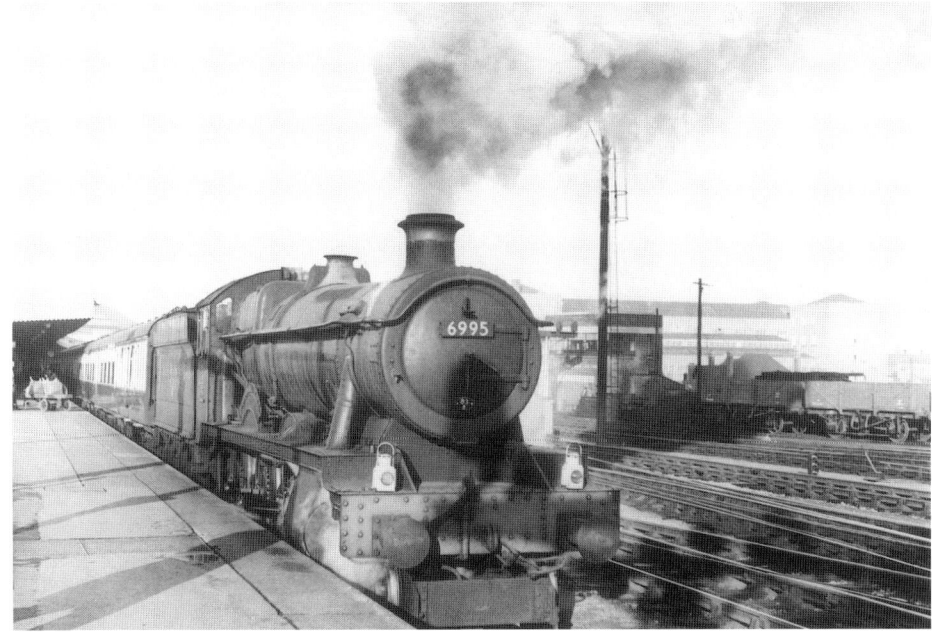

Another express for the West Country, headed by no. 6995 *Benthall Hall* in 1959.

Through Bedminster Parson Street and we are on the way to Bedminster Junction. The Portishead Line leaves the main line here, through Ashton Gate platform, especially built to deposit thousands of football fans at Bristol City's football ground. Shortly we shall be passing under the famous Clifton Suspension Bridge – a credit to Brunel – but sadly not finished until after his death. We finish this short journey in Portishead which was also the end of the journey for the Weston, Clevedon and Portishead Railway which closed in 1940.

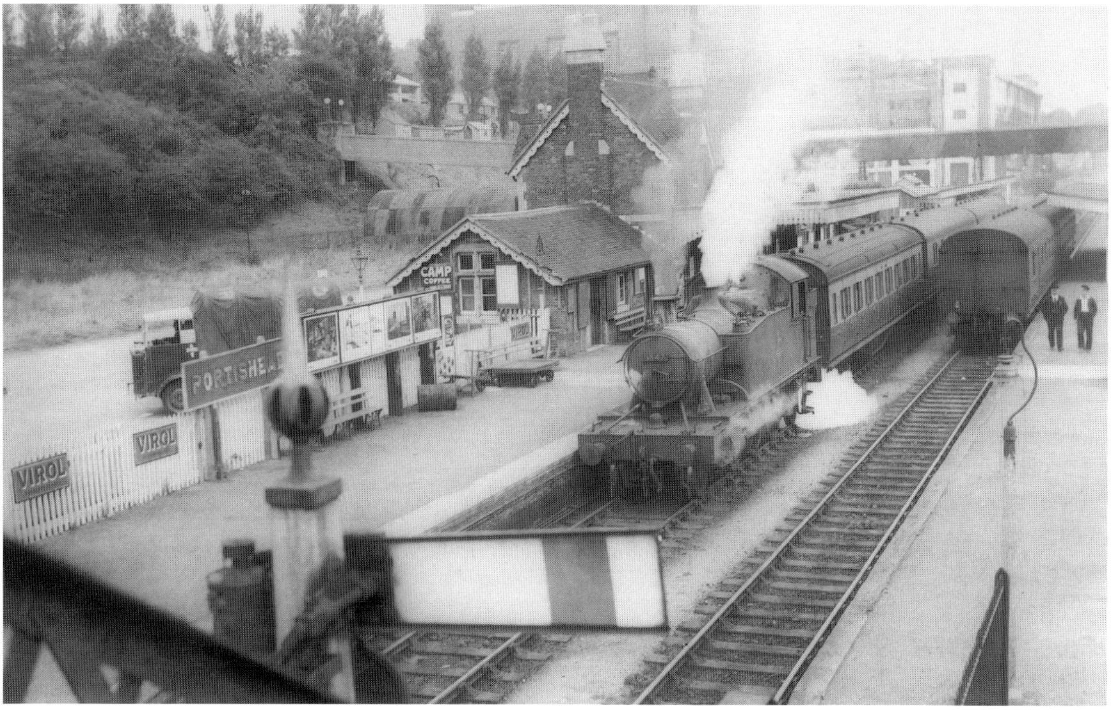

Prairie tank no. 5547 at rest in Portishead station in 1950.

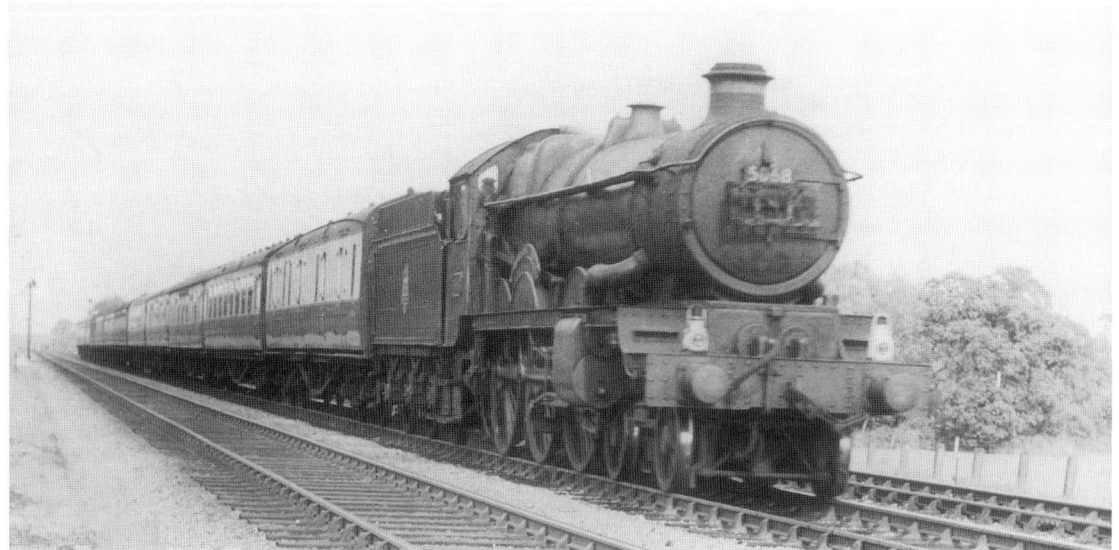

No. 5068 *Beverston Castle* near Nailsea in 1954.

We are passing Yatton now and there is a small sub-shed we must look out for on the right. On our left is the branch line to Cheddar, known locally as the Strawberry Line, a name well deserved as the area produces the best strawberries in the country.

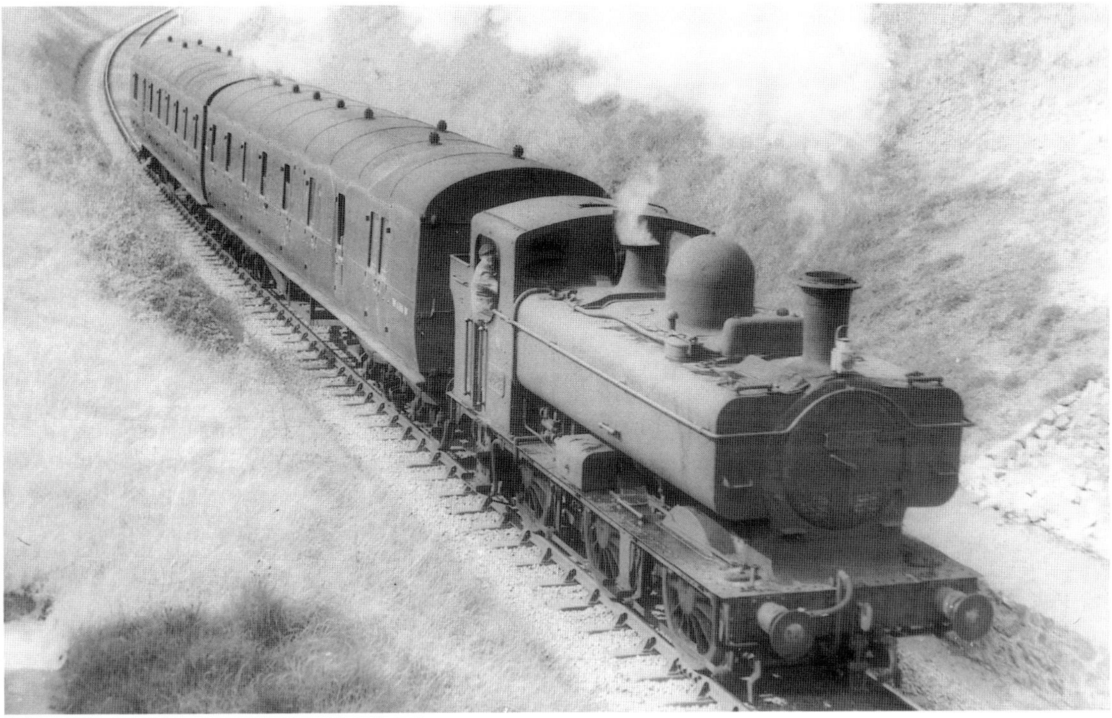

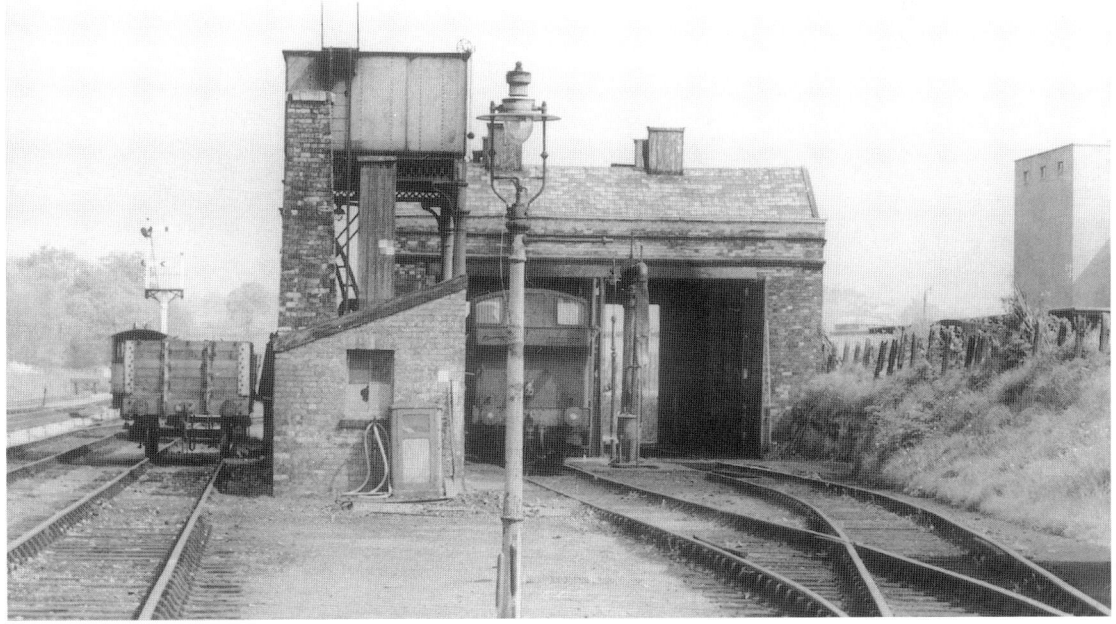

Pannier tank no. 9623 on the Strawberry Line near Cheddar in the 1950s.

Wells GW shed with a pannier tank awaiting its next duty in 1952.

We are still travelling at good speed, but soon the brakes go on and we slow for the junction that will take us off the main line and into Weston-super-Mare. Had this been a hundred years ago, we would have still been on the main line as the line avoiding Weston-super-Mare was not built until the turn of the century. We come to a halt at the station and a multitude of holidaymakers in happy mood leave the train, no doubt in a hurry to get on the beach and have a paddle. What a pity we cannot join them, but our railway journey comes first, and we return to join the main West of England Line at Uphill.

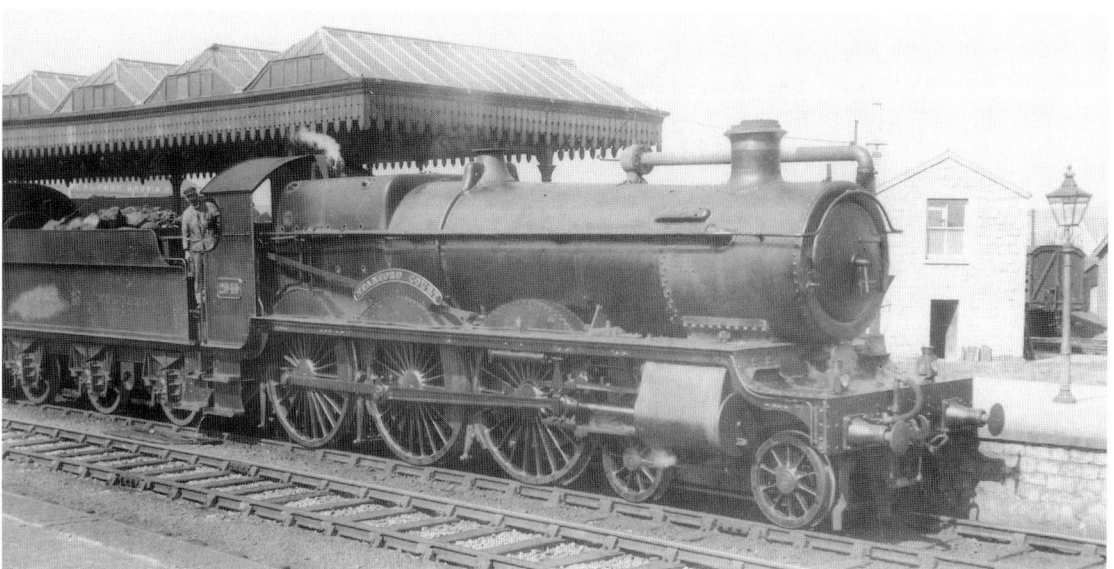

No. 2940 *Stanford Court* about to leave Weston-super-Mare, no doubt with holidaymakers making their way home.

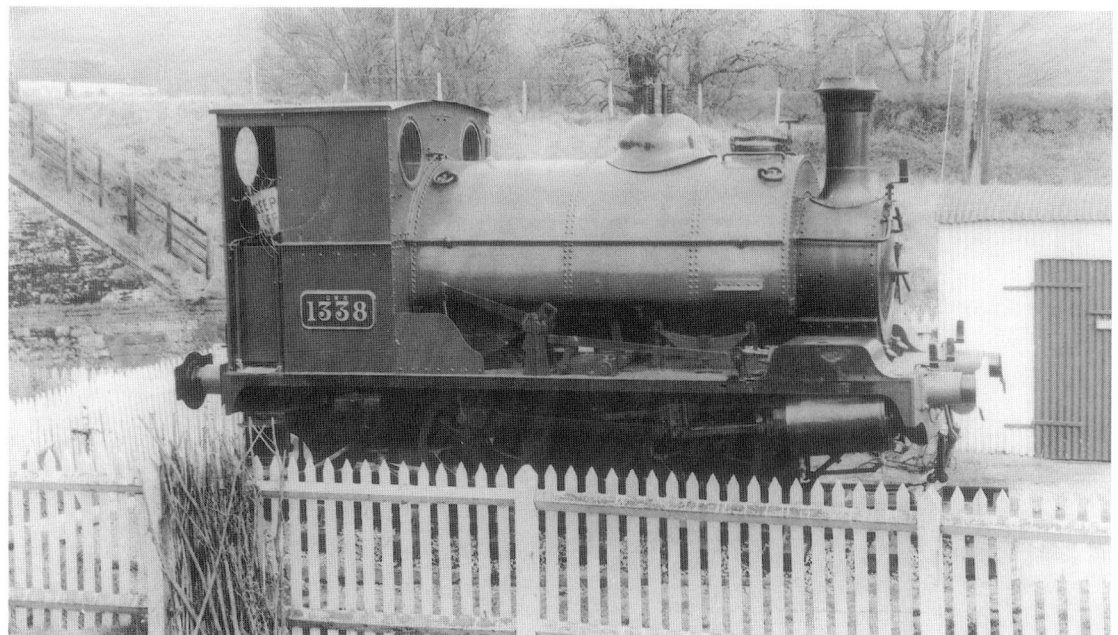

Cardiff Railways no. 1338, an 0–4–0ST for dock shunting. It spent several years preserved on Uphill station.

With a squeal of flanges, we are back on the main line heading for Highbridge. As we go into the station we shall cross over the Somerset and Dorset Railway line that has a terminus at Burnham-on-Sea. If we look out of the left-hand window, we shall see the Somerset and Dorset station which is adjacent to the GWR station and also a number of buildings which were the main works of the Somerset and Dorset Joint Railway. Be quick though – if you are not fast enough, you will miss the view, as we are doing about 70 mph on a straight line through to Bridgwater.

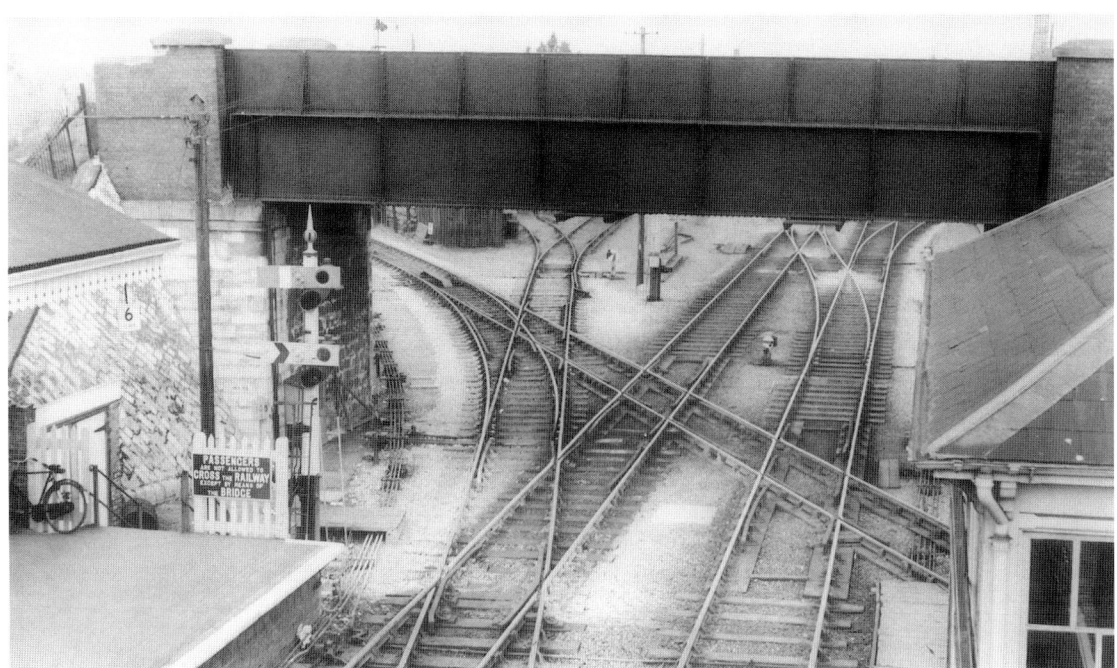

Highbridge station showing the S&DJR crossover to Burnham-on-Sea on the left, 1953.

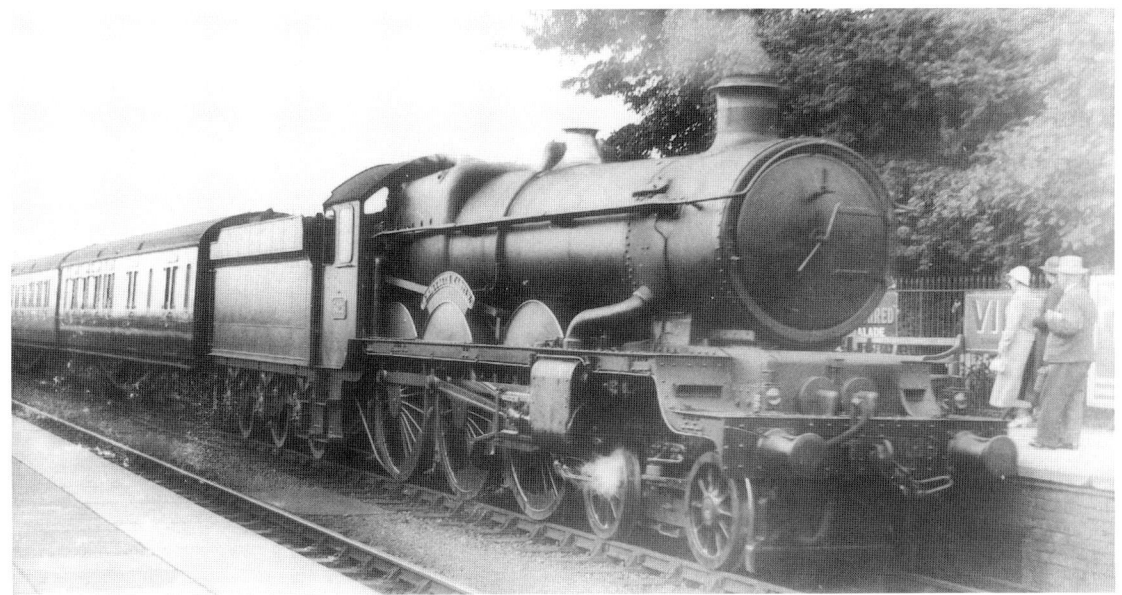

No. 5026 *Criccieth Castle* slowing to pick up passengers at Highbridge in the 1930s.

There will not be much for us to see at our next stop, Bridgwater. There is a small dock but it is not in sight of the station. So we will stay in our seats, and perhaps take some refreshment before we come to Cogload Junction where the line from Reading to Taunton will join us.

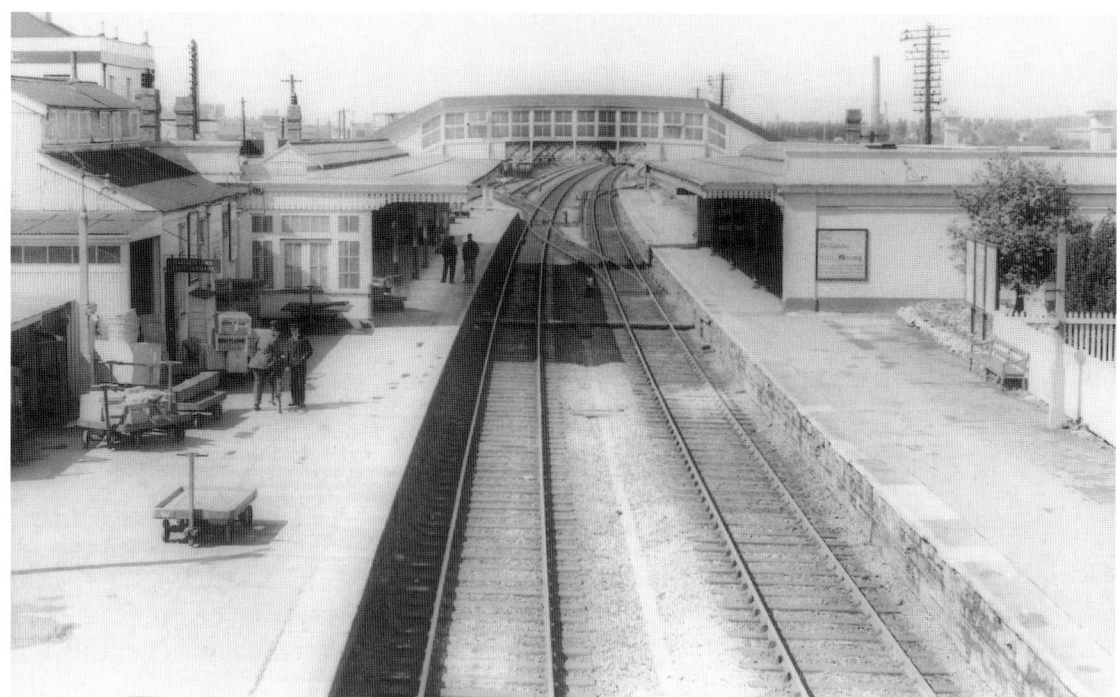

Bridgwater station on a quiet summer's day in 1955.

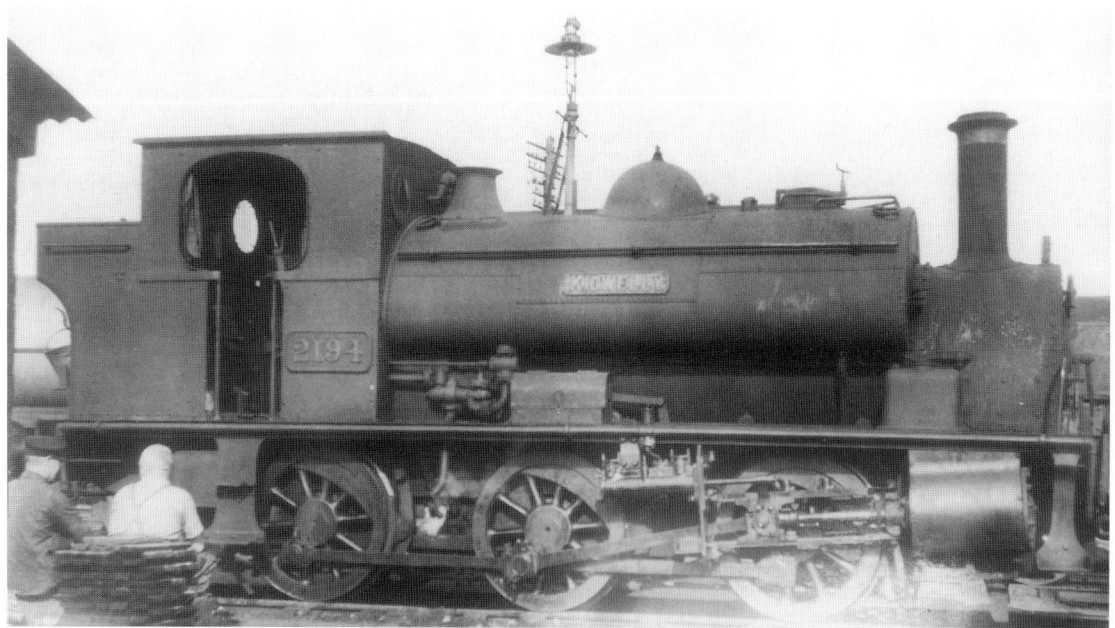

Ex-Burry Port and Gwendraeth Railway no. 2194 *Kidwelly* shunting at Bridgwater Dock, 1947. The driver and fireman are relaxing, so perhaps it is lunchtime.

Leaving Bridgwater, one of our companions who came from the London area, tells us about the route from Reading to the west by way of Westbury, and that we shall be meeting this line at Cogload. In the August holiday season this was the junction that caused huge losses of time, and trains could be backed up for miles. As if to make the point, the brakes have come on and we come to a halt at signals at Cogload Junction. Our companion continues his story about the Reading main line to the west.

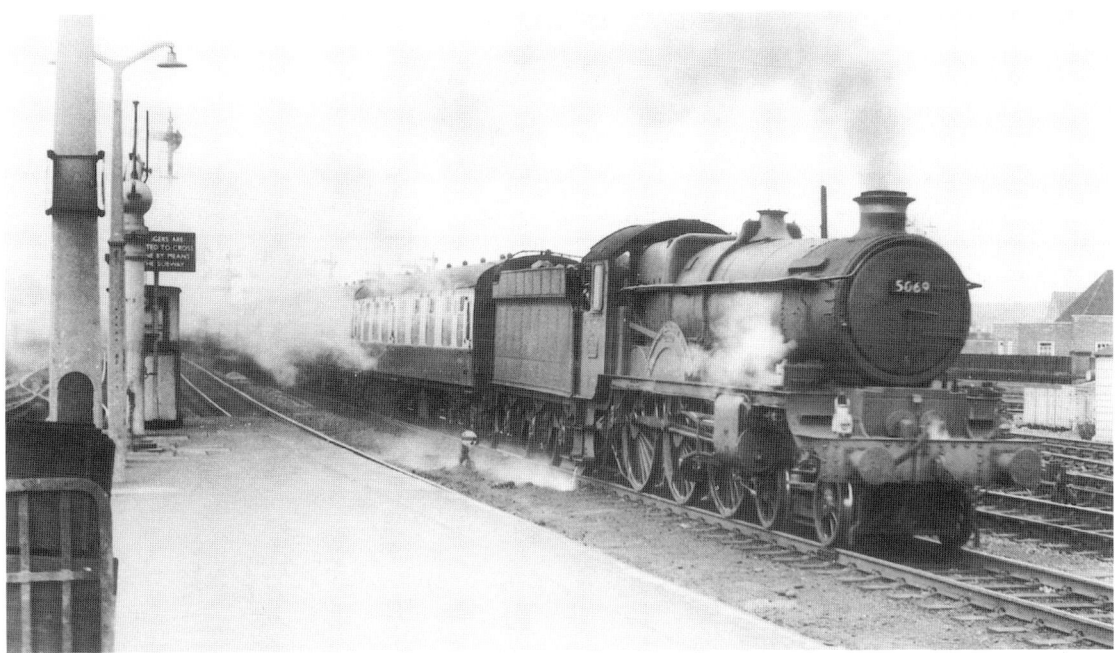

No. 5069 *Isambard Kingdom Brunel* comes off the West of England Mainline and into Reading in 1959.

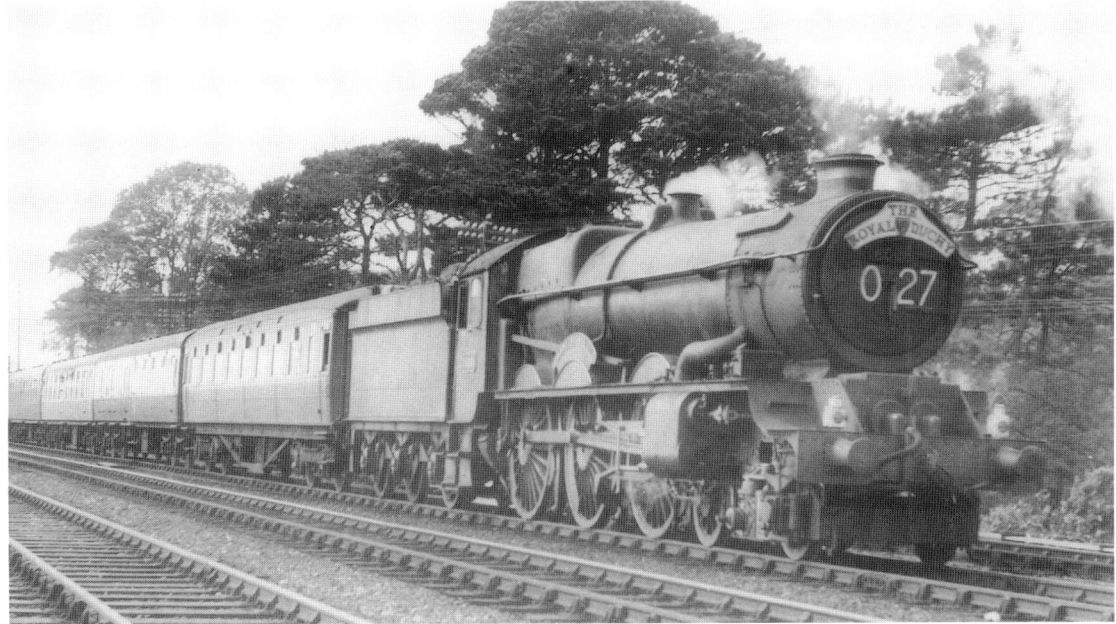

No. 6008 *King James II* near Reading West, with 'The Royal Duchy'.

We are told that after leaving Reading General, the train leaves the Bristol line and heads through Reading West, a favourite haunt of that well-known photographer Maurice Early. Another popular point on this line is Aldermaston. We pass through Thatcham and then comes our first stop, Newbury.

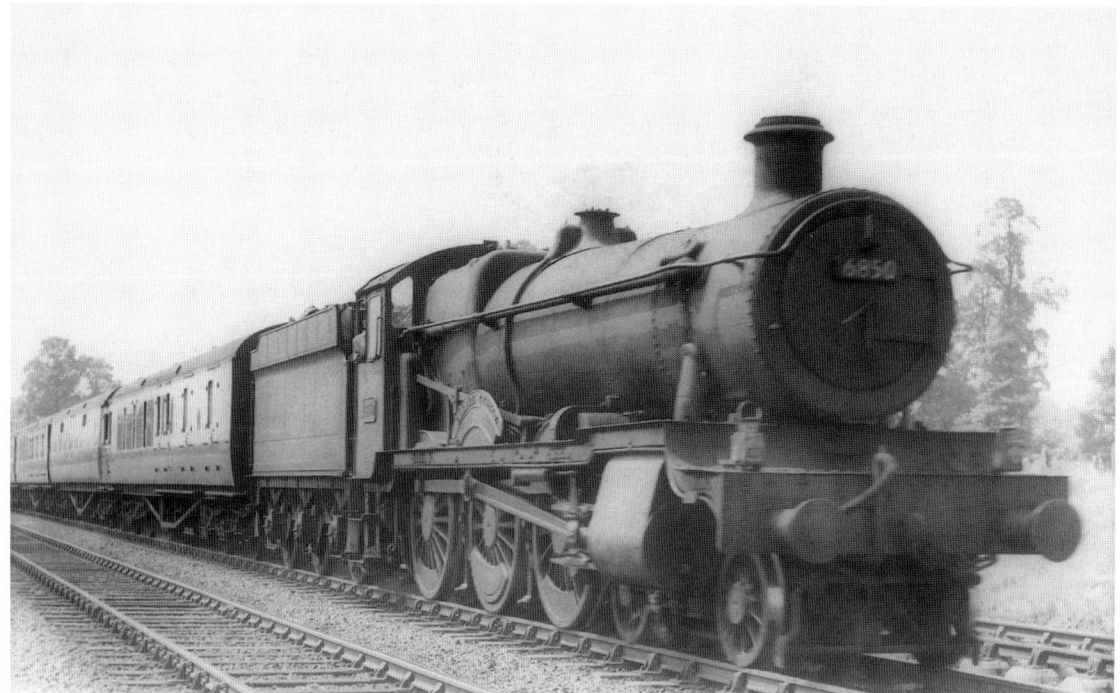

No. 6850 *Cleeve Grange* near Aldermaston in 1954.

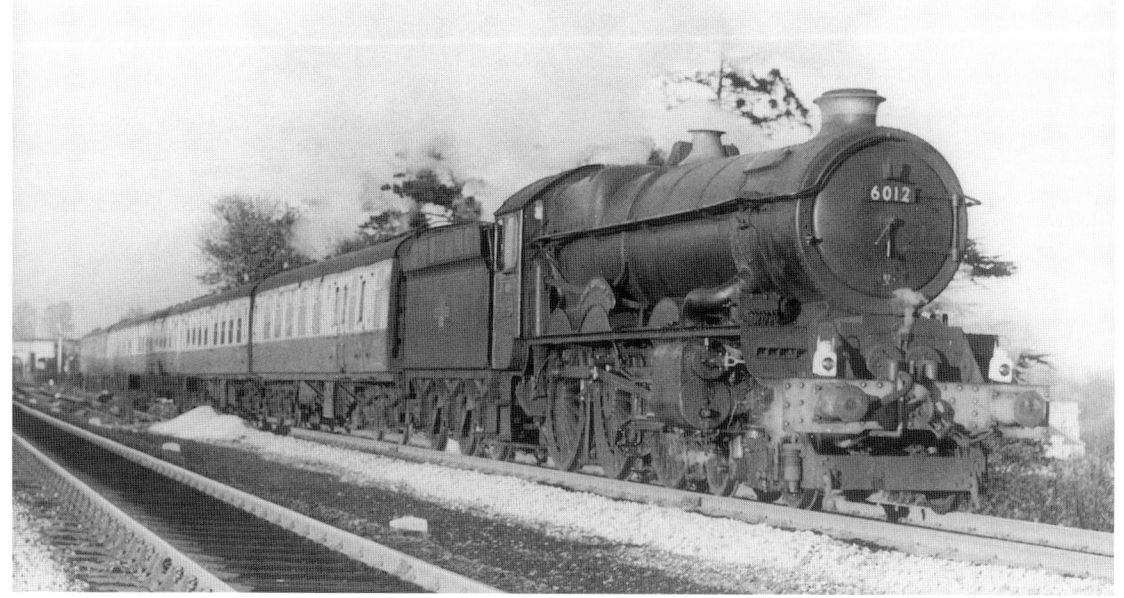

No. 6010 *King Edward VI* was a regular loco on this route to the West Country in 1959.

At Newbury we are told there is a branch line to Lambourne. No doubt many horses were carried on this line, as the Berkshire Downs are renowned for its many racing stables.

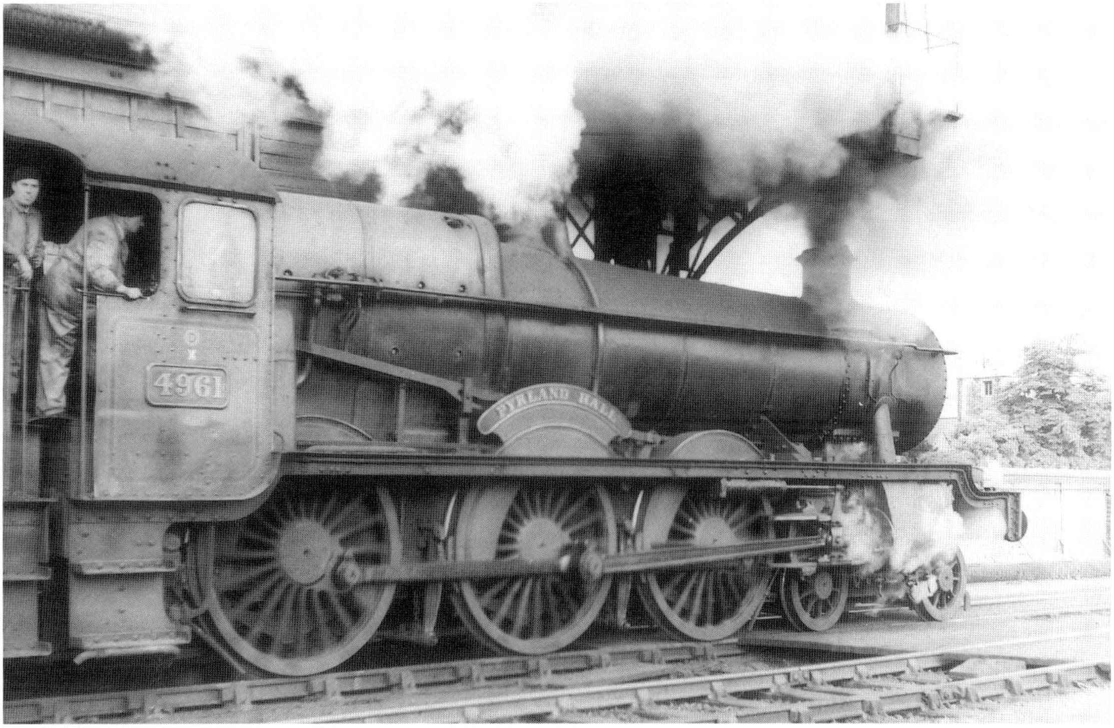

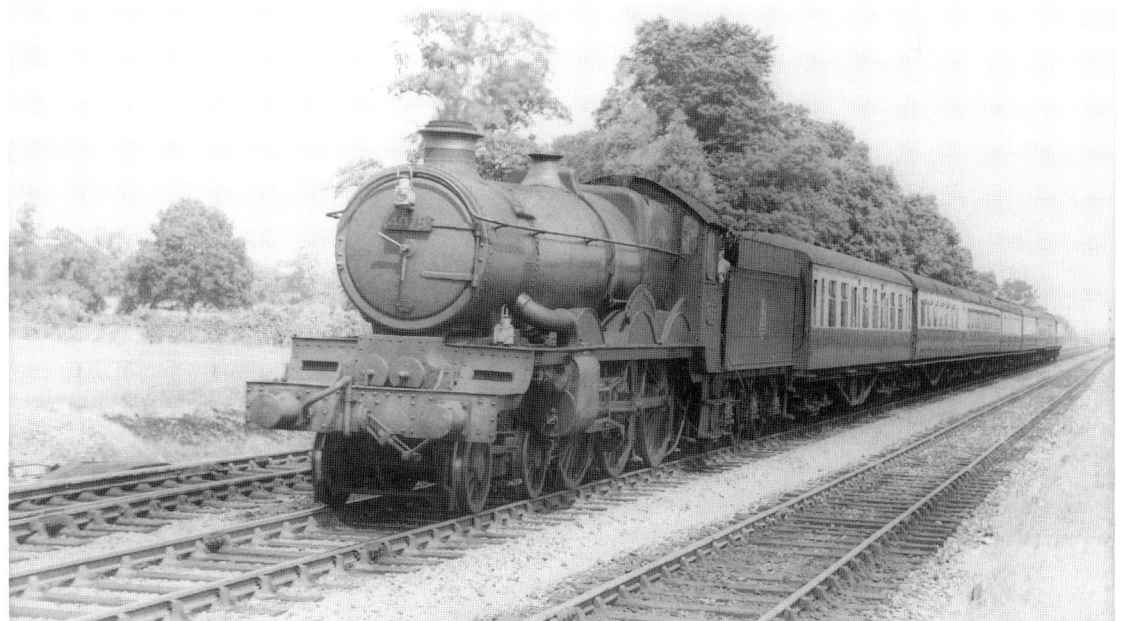

No. 4961 *Pyrland Hall* leaving Newbury in 1956.

No. 4075 *Cardiff Castle* en route to Hungerford in 1954.

After Hungerford it is a fairly fast run to Savernake, where the MSWJ Line to Swindon can be seen. It will not be long before we are at Westbury.

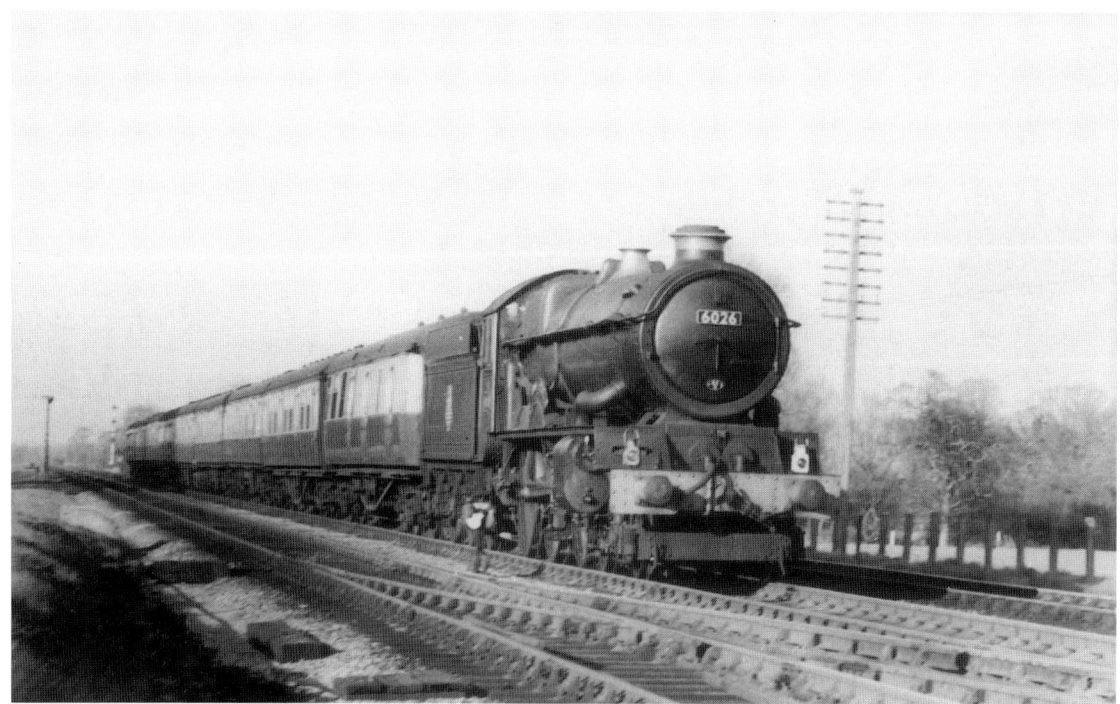

No. 6026 *King John* with a Laira shedplate near Savernake in 1954.

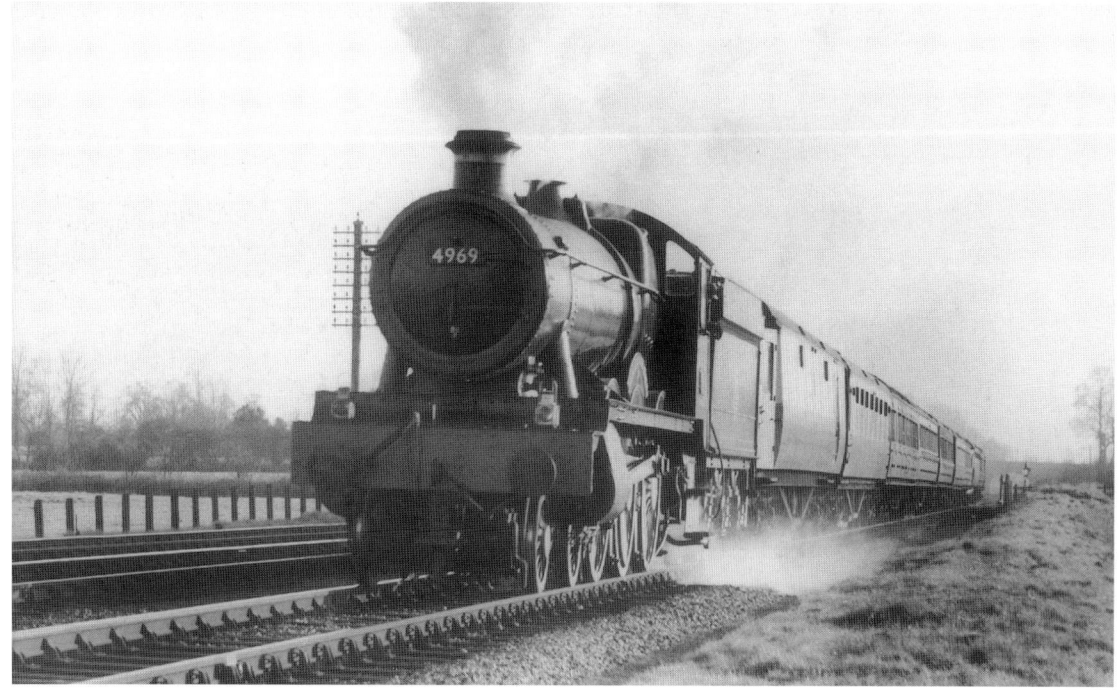

No. 4969 *Shugborough Hall* near Westbury in 1954.

At Westbury all trains had to go into Westbury station, losing time for non-stop expresses. It was decided therefore, in the early part of the 1900s, to build a bypass from Heywood Road Junction to Fairwood Junction, which saved a great deal of time.

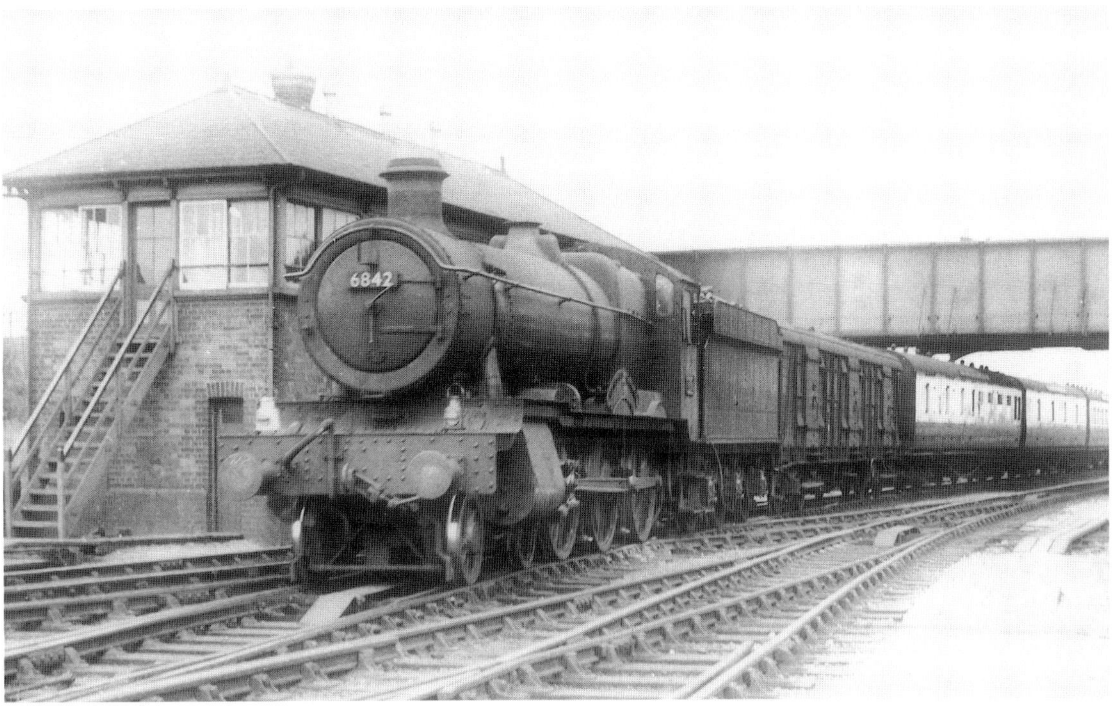

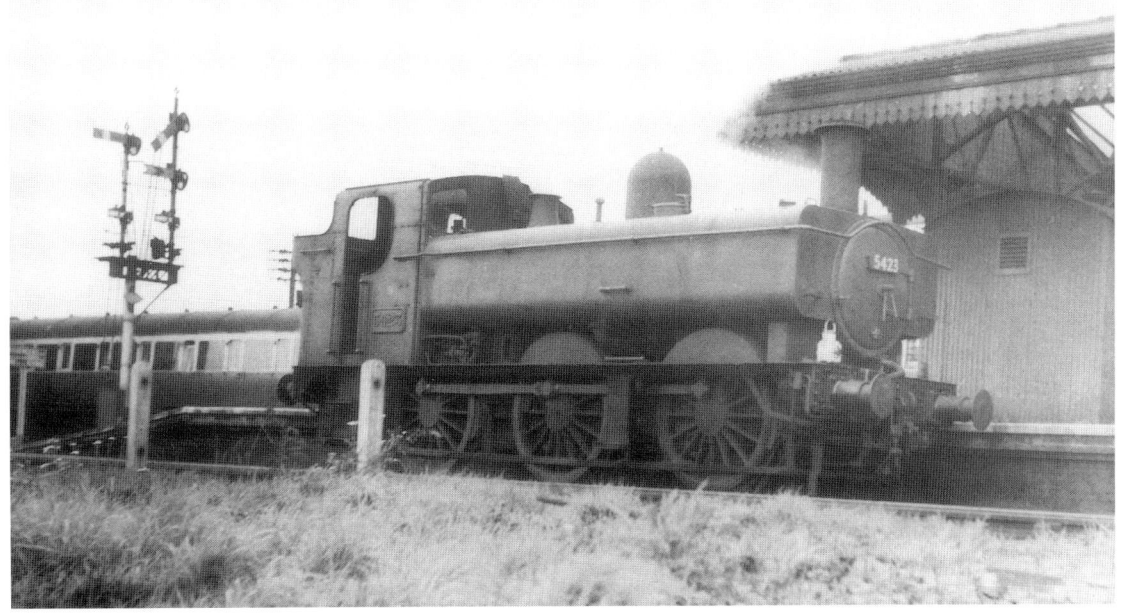

No. 6842 *Nunhold Grange* arriving in Westbury with a Portsmouth train from Cardiff, 1959. This will take the route through Dilton Marsh and Salisbury.

No. 5423, a station pilot at Westbury.

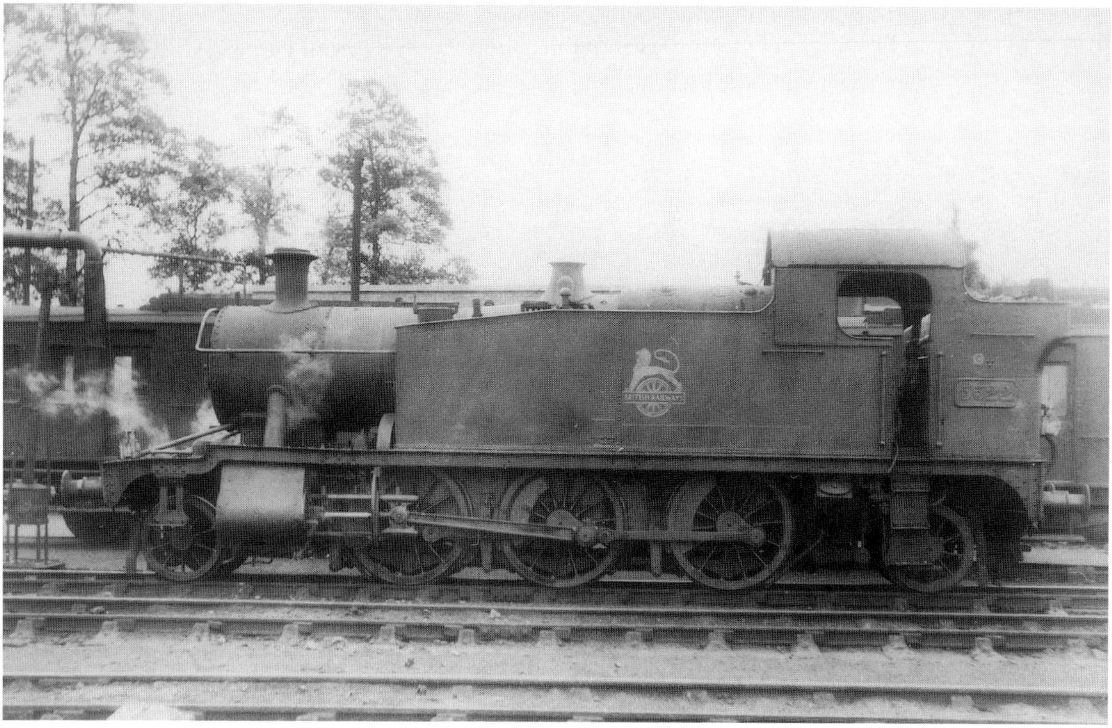

Prairie tank no. 5522 at Westbury in 1953.

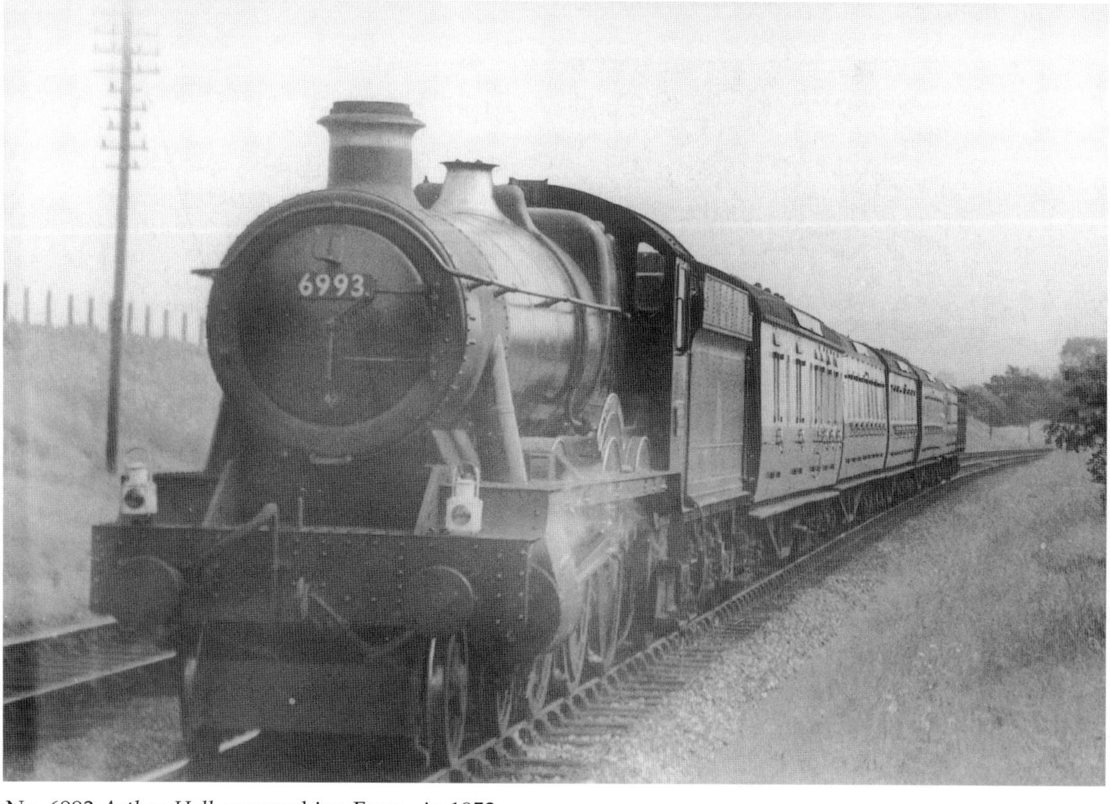

No. 6993 *Arthog Hall* approaching Frome in 1953.

Not far from Westbury is Frome, which still has its original Brunel station with an overall roof. Frome also has a short cut-off route, enabling non-stop working to be maintained.

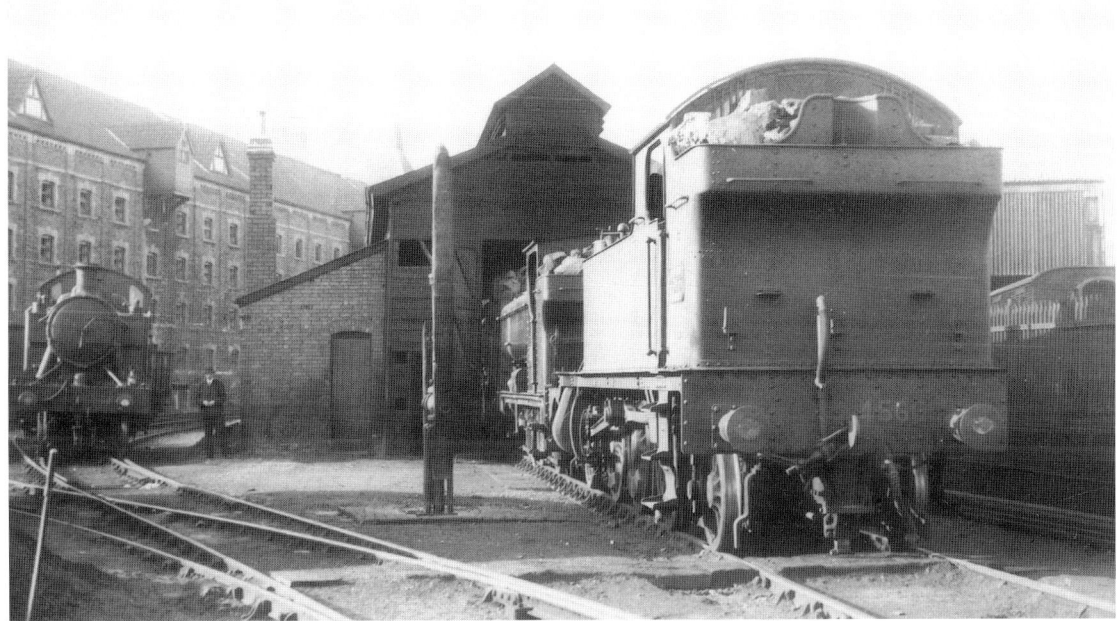

The small shed at Frome in 1935.

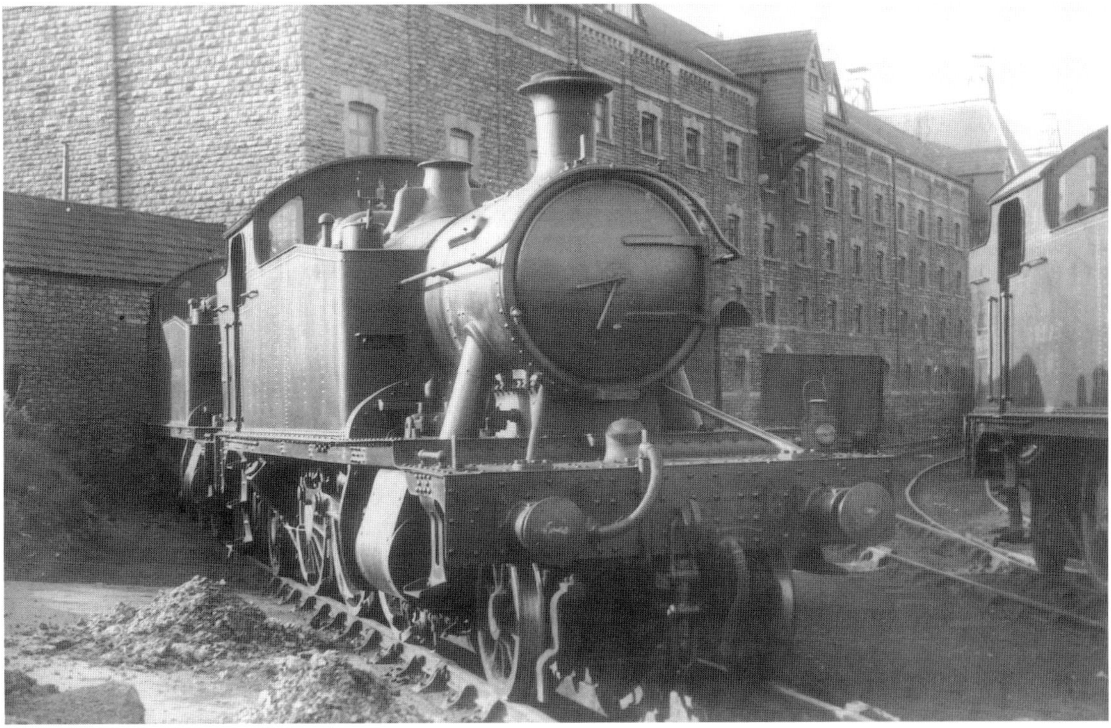

GWR no. 5556, one of the tank engines on Frome shed in 1935.

After Frome comes the junction at Witham that leads back to Bristol. On this line is Cranmore, where there is a huge stone quarry at which the heavy 2–8–0 locos bring long stone trains on to the main line, and head to many parts of the country. The West of England trains head on through Castle Cary, where there is a junction for Yeovil, Langport and finally Cogload Junction where we are waiting. Our signal comes off and we head into Taunton.

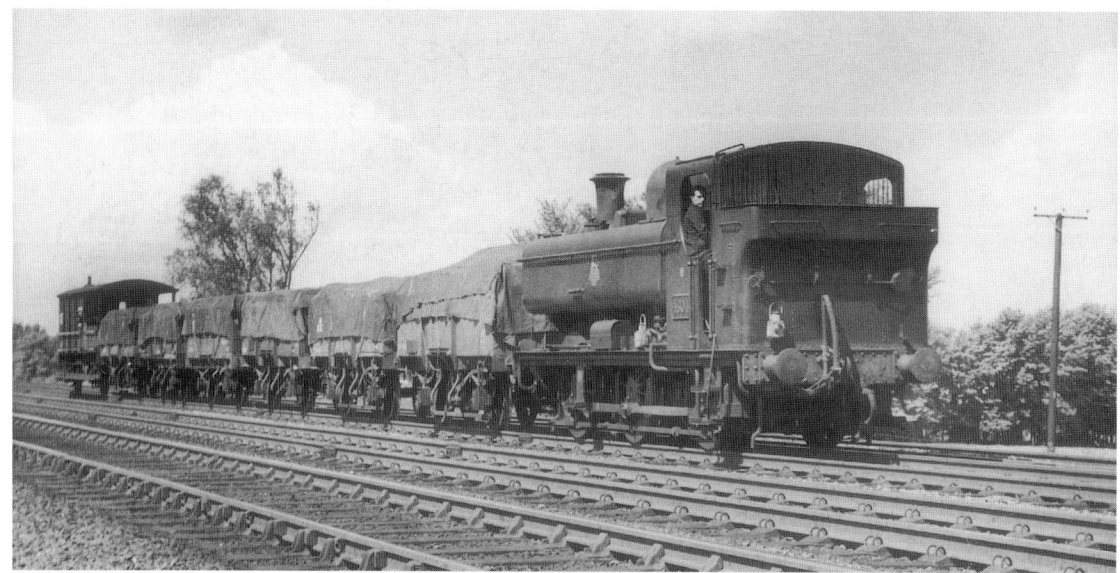

Pannier tank no. 4604 nearing Cogload in 1952. Some of the named expresses which passed Cogload Junction included 'The Cornish Riviera Express' (Paddington–Penzance), 'The Torbay Express' (Paddington–Kingswear), 'The Royal Duchy' (Paddington–Penzance), 'The Mayflower' (Paddington–Plymouth), 'The Cornishman' (Wolverhampton–Penzance) and 'The Devonian' (Bradford–Paignton).

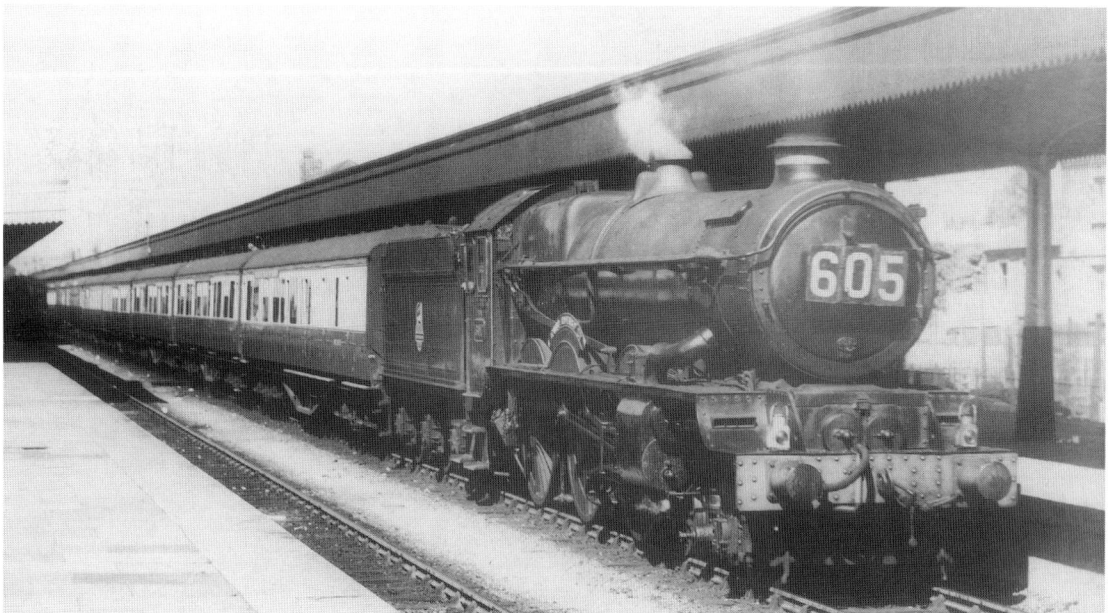

No. 6017 *King Edward IV* at rest in Taunton station in 1952.

Having followed an express from London into Taunton, we will have time for a quick visit to the shed. It will not take long as the shed is near the station, so once again cameras at the ready, we are on the platform.

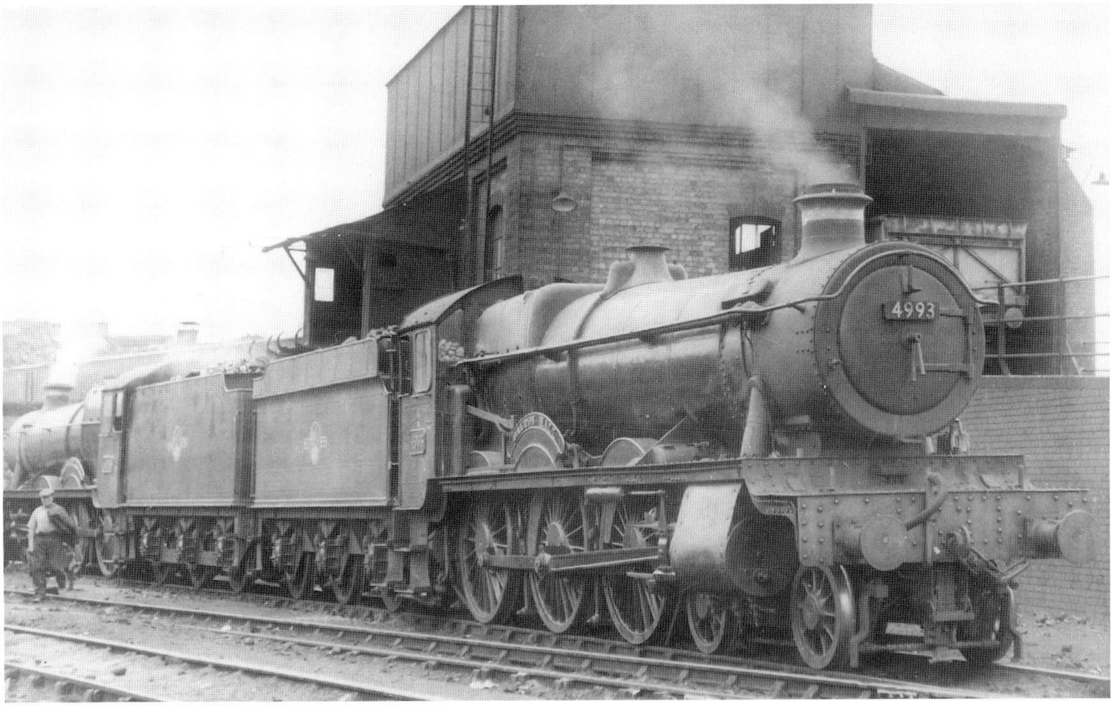

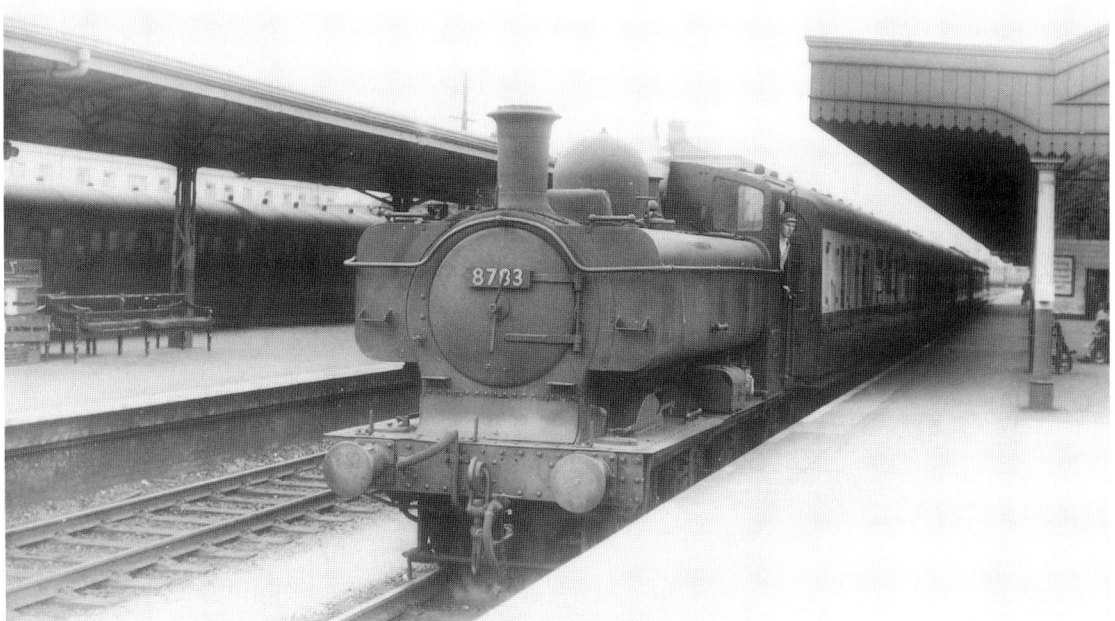

No. 4993 *Dalton Hall* has just had its tender filled with coal in preparation for its next duty in 1959.

No. 8783, a station pilot, 1959. I was surprised that it still had GWR on the left-hand pannier.

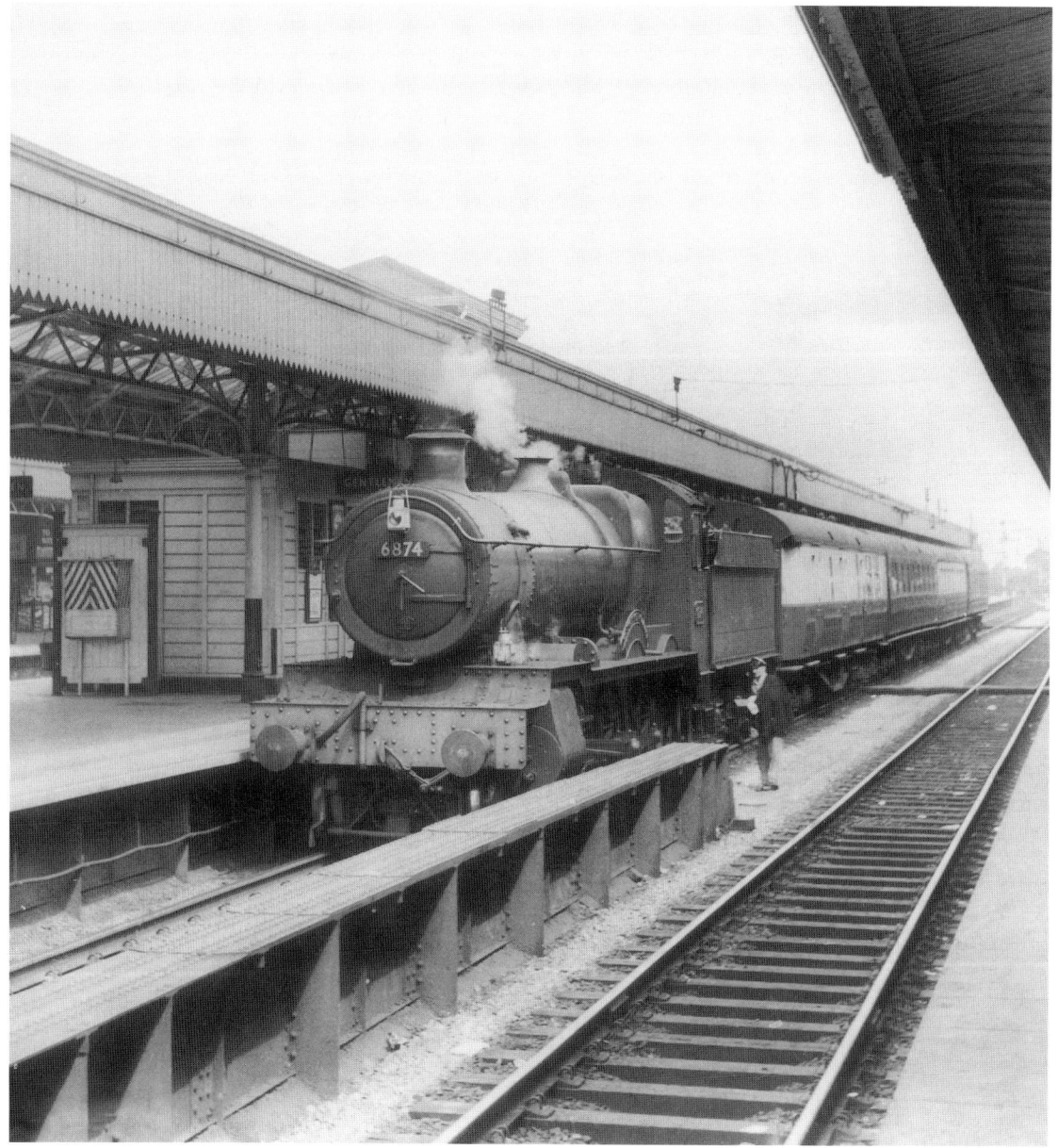

We had better get back to our train, as it will be leaving very soon. However, there is just time for a picture of no. 6874 *Haughton Grange*, just arrived with a local stopping train.

From Taunton station local trains run to Chard, a small Somerset town that had the luxury of two stations. Trains heads towards Cogload Junction from Taunton and after a short distance they head south through Hatch, Ilminster and into Chard GW. There is also a L&SWR station, enabling residents to travel to Chard Junction on the Main Southern Line.

We are now progressing steadily towards Norton Fitzwarren where there is a junction to Minehead through such places as Bishops Lydeard, Stogumber and Watchet, where travellers get their first glimpse of the sea. Another seaside junction at Norton Fitzwarren is to Barnstaple.

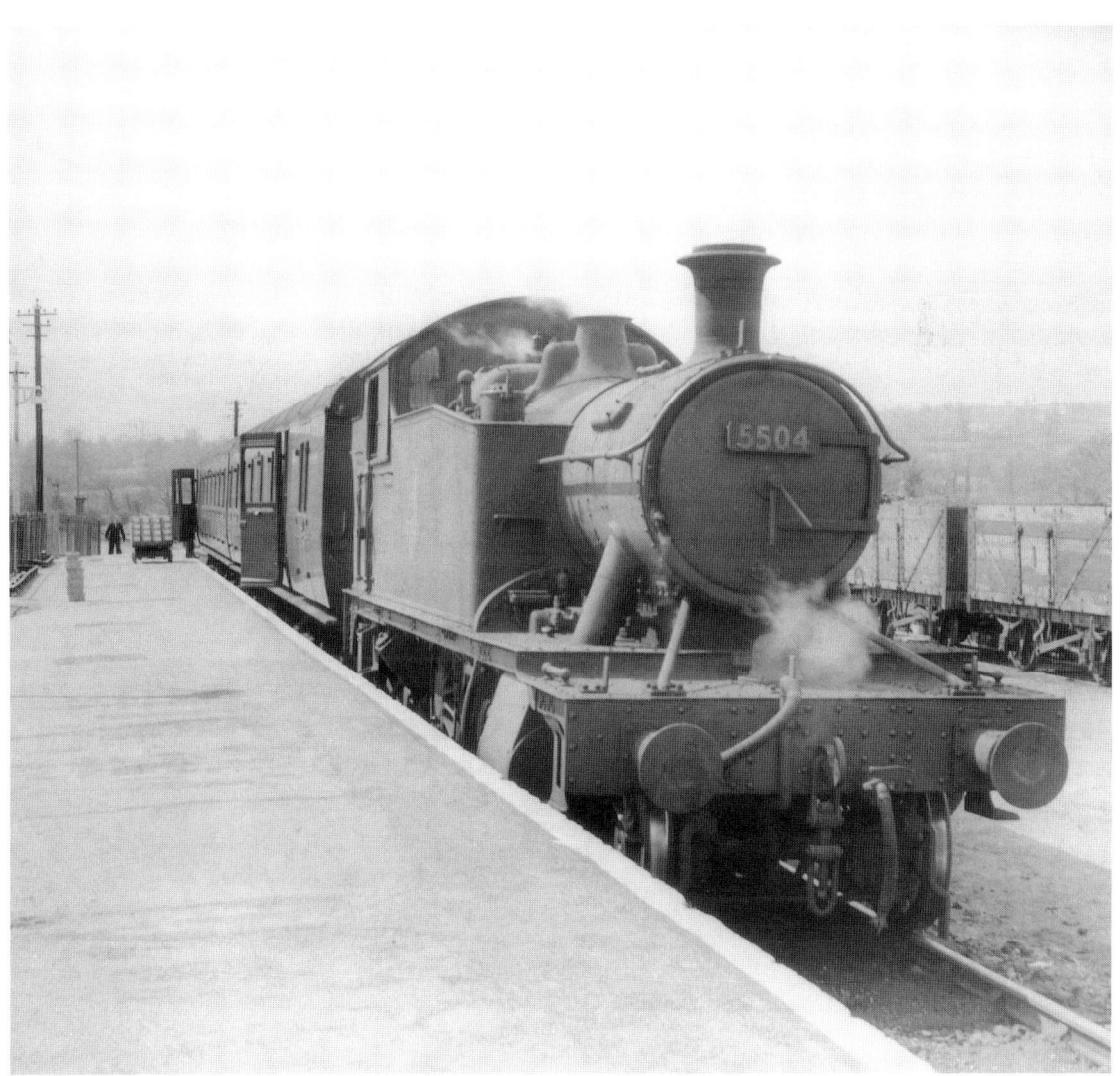

No. 5504 photographed at Chard GW station in 1954.

As we speed through Norton Fitzwarren we are reminded of the tragic accidents which have occurred at this spot. One took place in 1890, and another in November 1940, in which the Paddington–Penzance sleeper train was involved. The driver had forty years' experience and his fireman were Old Oak Common men. The driver who lived in Acton had suffered in the bombing, and shortly before this journey his house had been damaged. All was well until Taunton; driving conditions were very poor – very dark and wet – and there was a driving wind. He had driven this train many times and always, on leaving Taunton, had been routed down the main line. One can only imagine the poor man's state of mind; house bombed, blackout conditions and bad weather. He did not realise on that fateful night that he had been routed on the Down relief, with a train of thirteen carriages. He was working up a good speed with no. 6028 *King George VI*, when to his horror, another 'King' travelling a little faster than him, drew level on his right-hand side. This was a newspaper train with a light load and the signalman at Taunton had allowed this train to take the main line as it was faster. It was at this point that the driver of no. 6028 realised his mistake and that he was going too fast on the relief. He applied the brakes, but too late. No. 6028 came off the track at Catch Points. Many of the carriages telescoped and spread across the four tracks. There were nearly nine hundred passengers, many of whom were injured and tragically twenty-seven were killed. The fireman also died, but the driver escaped with cuts and bruises. The accident could have been very much worse – if the newspaper train had been a minute or so behind the sleeper, it would have ploughed into the many carriages and there would certainly have been a much higher death toll. The newspaper train was examined at Wellington, a short distance on, and was found to have scratches and pitting to the last carriage where 6028 had thrown up ballast on overturning. At the enquiry, it was found that the driver of 6028 passed a signal at red, and cancelled the ATC warning, which meant an accident was inevitable.

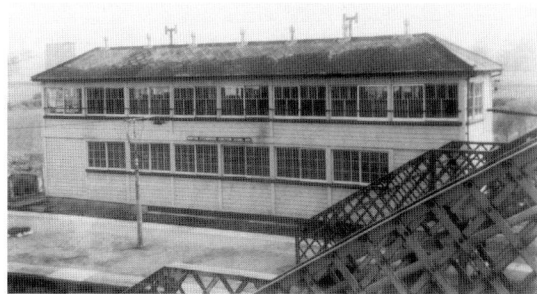

Above: Norton Fitzwarren station and signal-box. It was a few hundred yards beyond this point that the accident occurred.

Below: Signals at Taunton.

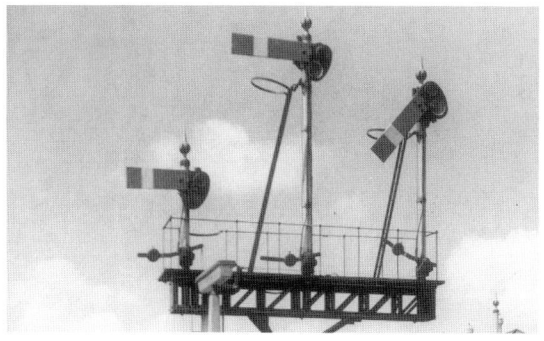

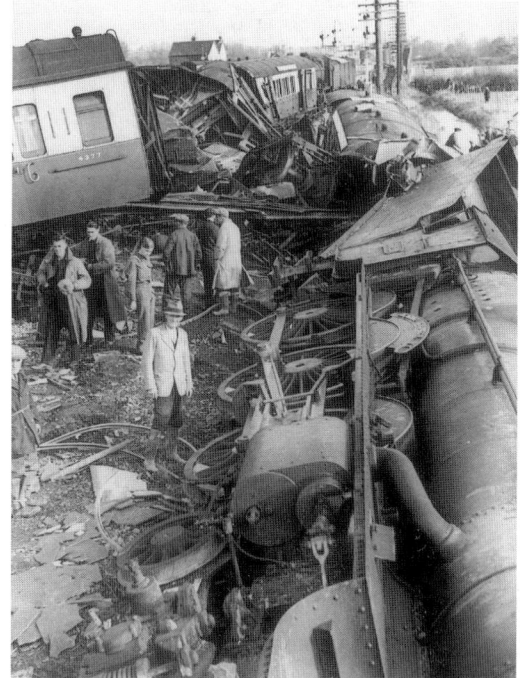

King George VI lies on its side after coming off the track at Catch Points. The extensive damage to the carriages is very clear.

We have now passed the accident blackspot at Norton Fitzwarren and the junction for Barnstaple, and will soon be approaching Wellington, where *City of Truro* broke the 100 mph barrier in 1904. Onwards towards Tiverton Junction we travel through the lovely Somerset countryside.

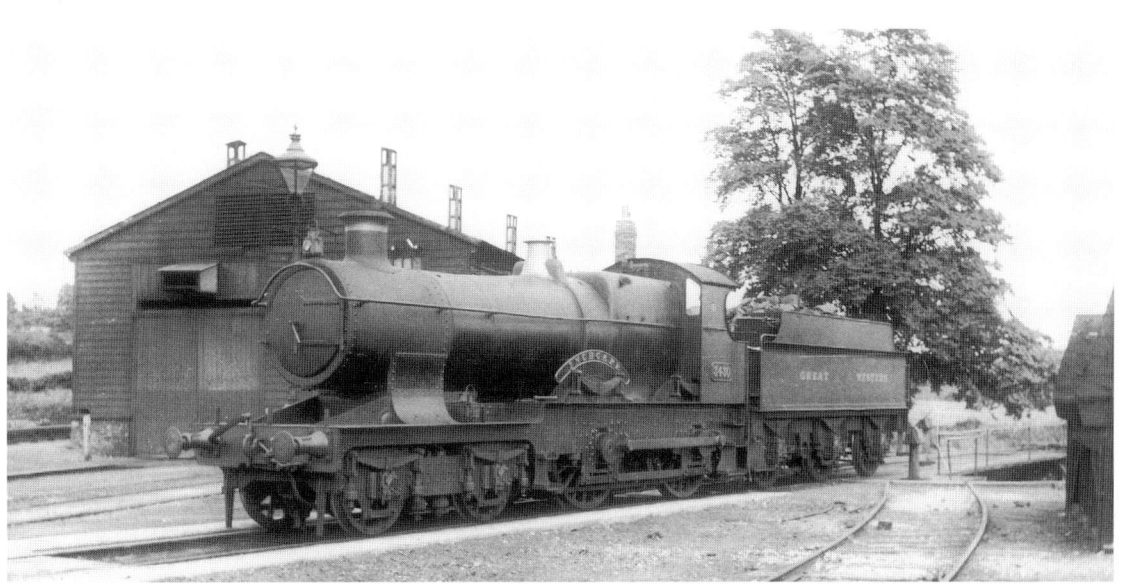

From Norton Fitzwarren the line to Barnstaple runs close to Lorna Doone Country – Exmoor. Through Wiveliscombe, Dulverton, Bishops Nympton, Swimbridge and many other West Country villages, until arriving in Barnstaple. Here 'Bulldog' no. 3430 *Inchcape*, with its tender full of coal, has come off the turntable and is ready to run back to Taunton in 1934.

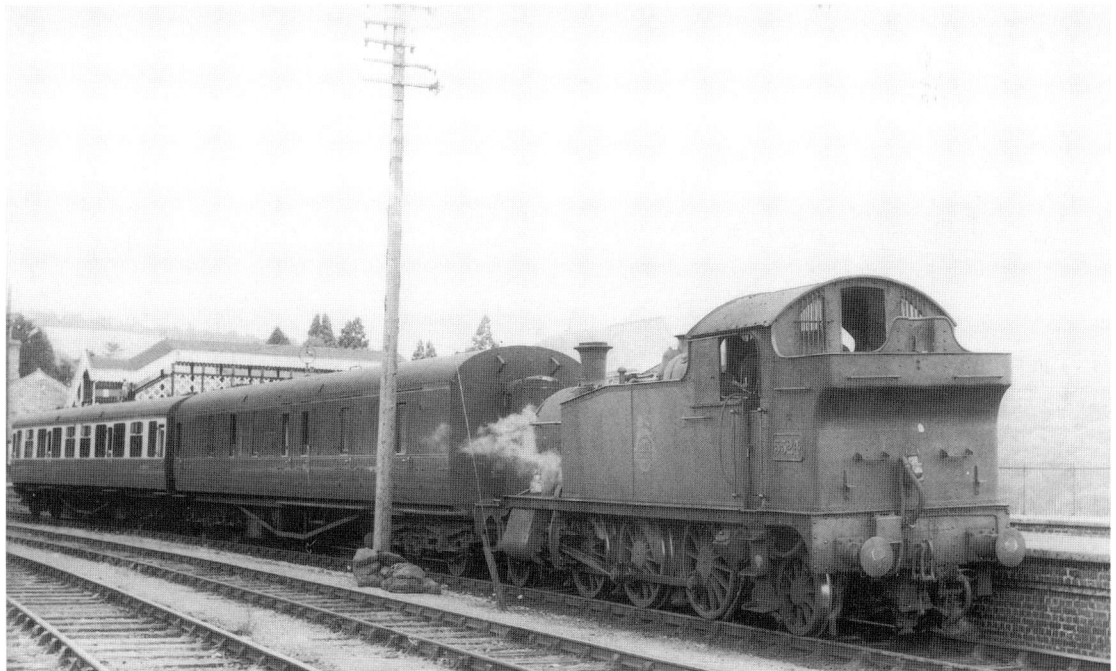

No. 5524 with a two-coach stopping train in Dulverton station, 1953.

Tiverton itself is a few miles away from the junction. Tiverton Town is on a line from Stoke Canon on the West of England Mainline to Dulverton on the Barnstaple Line. We are now picking up speed through Cullompton. The talk in the carriage is of our next stop, Exeter, where we may see some Southern Engines. We head through Stoke Canon and we are now slowing for Cowley Bridge Junction where the Southern Line from the North Devon coastal resorts joins the WR Mainline. Our engine is just pulling gently now, and we will soon be into Exeter St Davids.

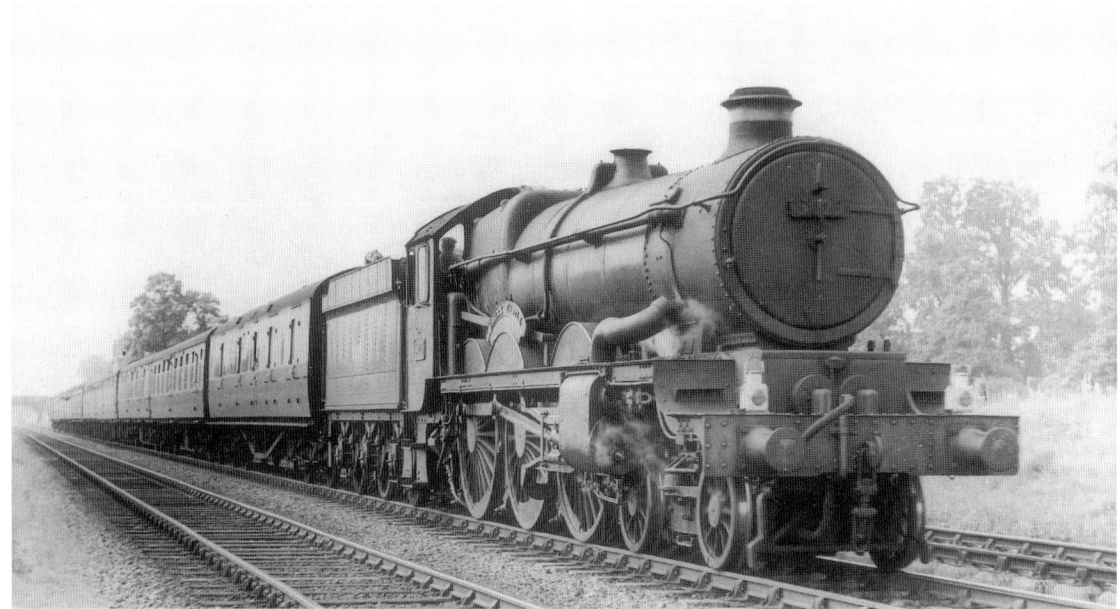

No. 5025 *Chirk Castle* near Cullompton. You may remember we saw this engine at the start of our journey at Paddington.

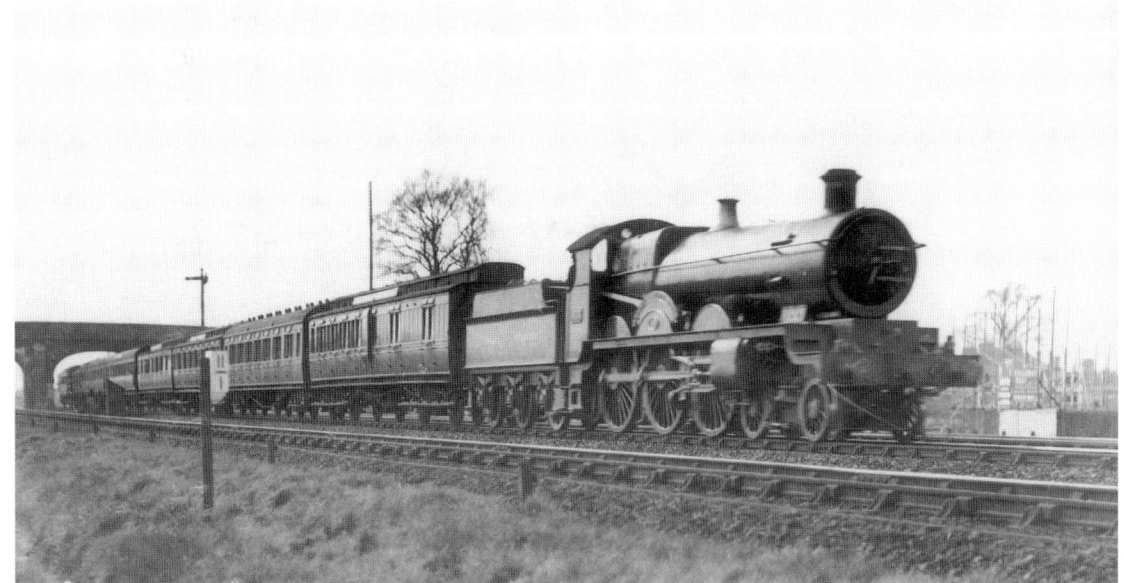

'Star' no. 4017 *Knight of Liege* near Exeter in 1912.

With that familiar squeal of brakes and carriage doors opening, we are into Exeter St Davids. From a railway enthusiast's point of view this is a fantastic station, particularly in the summer months when the holiday expresses arrive thick and fast. The Southern trains come in from Ilfracombe, Barnstaple and the North Cornwall coast at Bude. They stop at St Davids in the centre road for a banker to attach at the rear to push them up the 1:37 bank to Exeter Central. While this is taking place, the West Country holiday trains are arriving at the platforms from the North via Bristol, and London trains via Castle Cary. We are out of our carriage as fast as we can, cameras dangling on straps around our necks, record books in hand and pockets stuffed with unused film, down to the end of the platform just in time to see a 'King', several 'Castles', various 'Halls' and a few Southerns. It was so hectic we didn't have time to stock up with sandwiches.

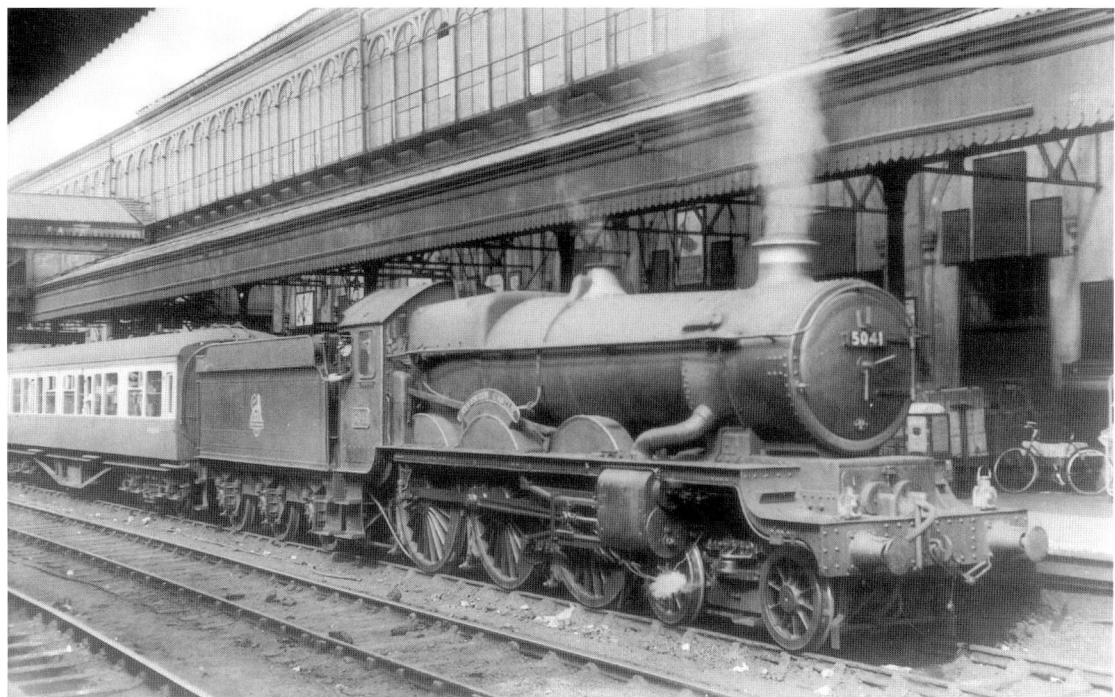

No. 5041 *Tiverton Castle* at Exeter St Davids.

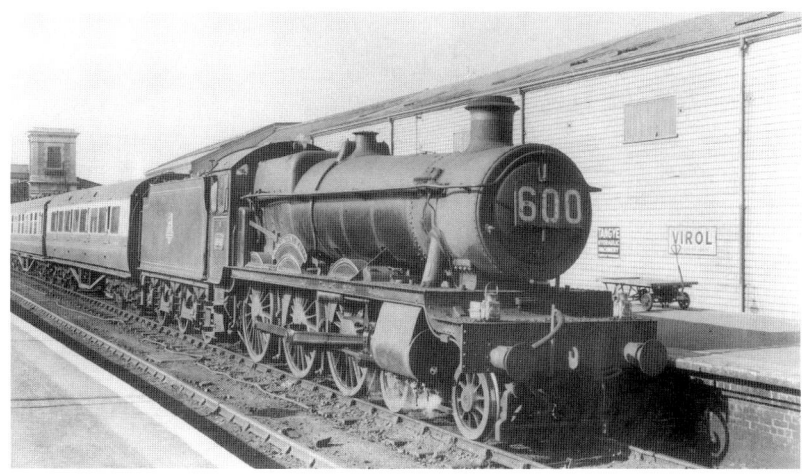

No. 6940 *Didlington Hall* also in Exeter St Davids, 1954.

Here we go again. I think we are all glad to have a rest, as that was a rather hectic stop in Exeter. In a few minutes we shall be through Exeter St Thomas and then we shall be on to that glorious stretch of the GW Mainline that at first runs along the banks of the Exe Estuary, and then the sea at Dawlish and Teignmouth. After all that we shall be into our next stop, Newton Abbot, where again we expect to be dashing around the platforms – so let us sit back and admire the Devon scenery.

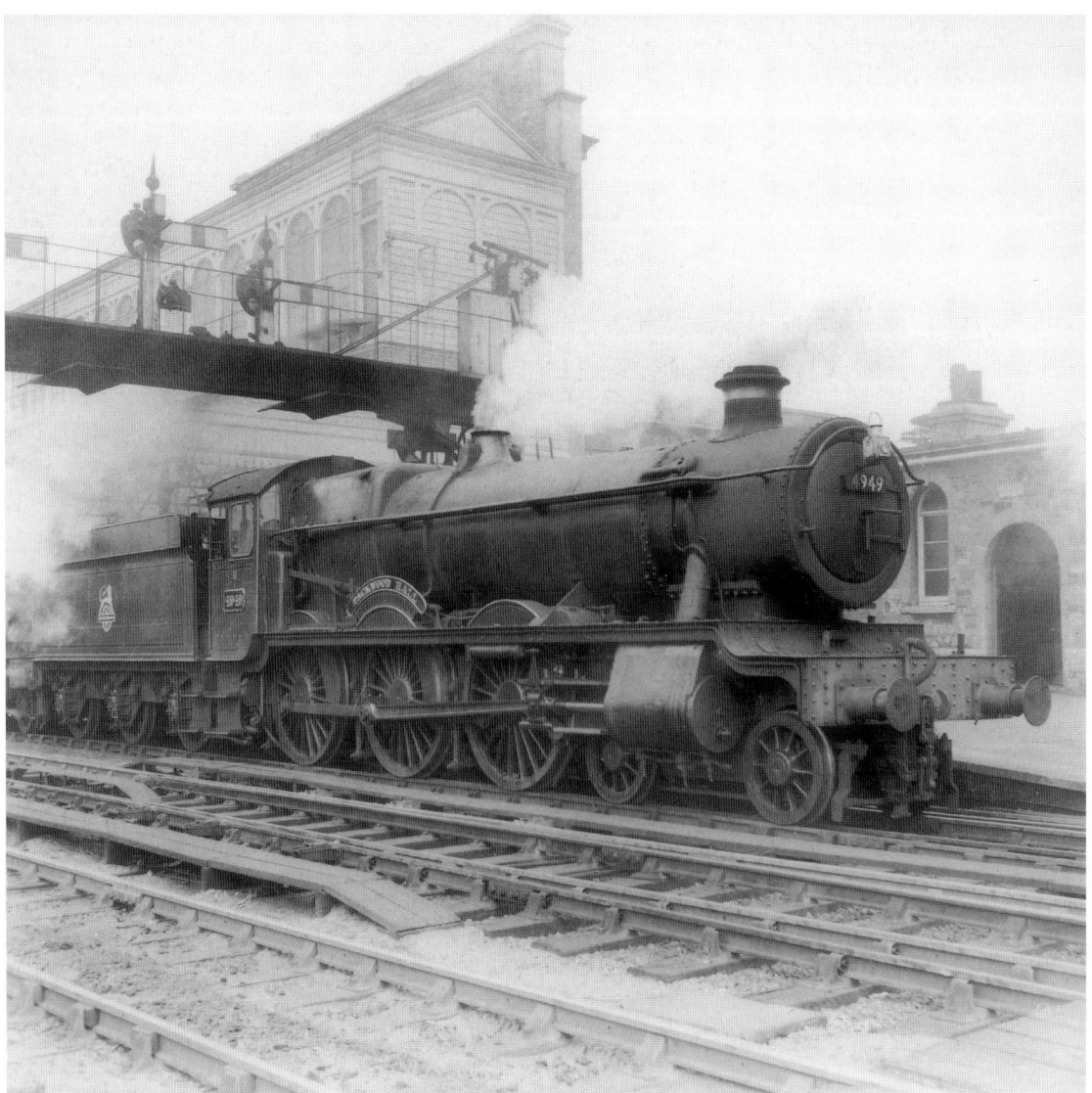

No. 4949 *Packwood Hall* departs from Exeter St Davids in 1953.

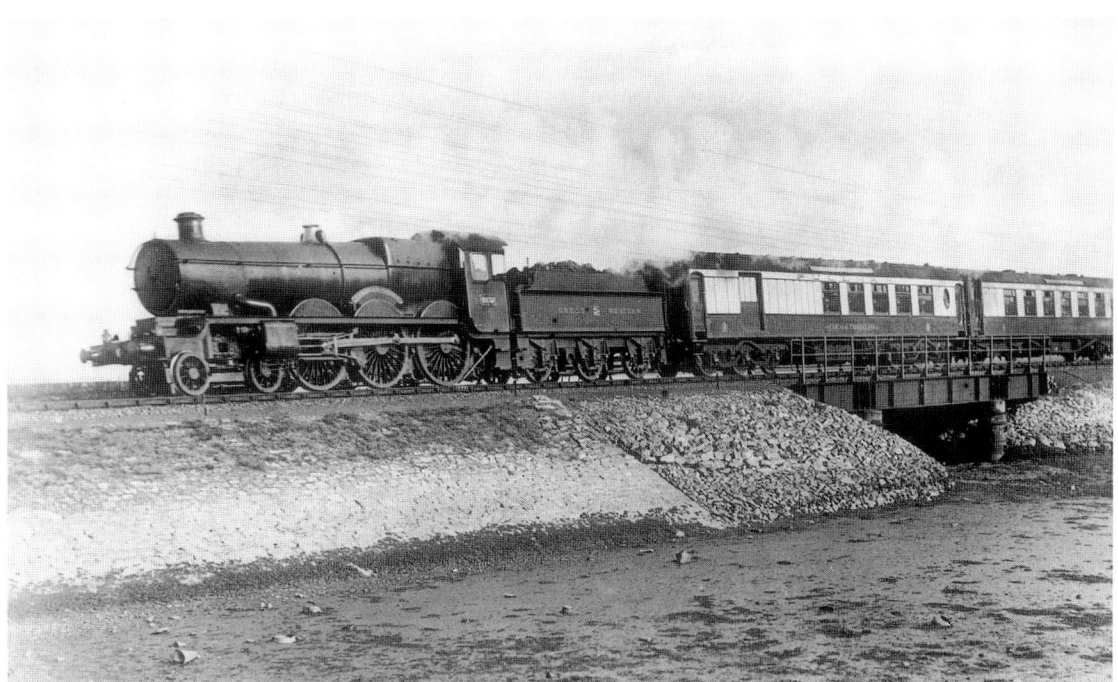

No. 4087 *Cardigan Castle* with a train of Pullman Coaches near Starcross in the 1930s. I have no information about this train and I would welcome any input from readers. At Starcross, of course, was what a lot of critics have described as Brunel's disastrous mistake – the Atmospheric Railway. I prefer to think of it as a design of a genius, way ahead of his time.

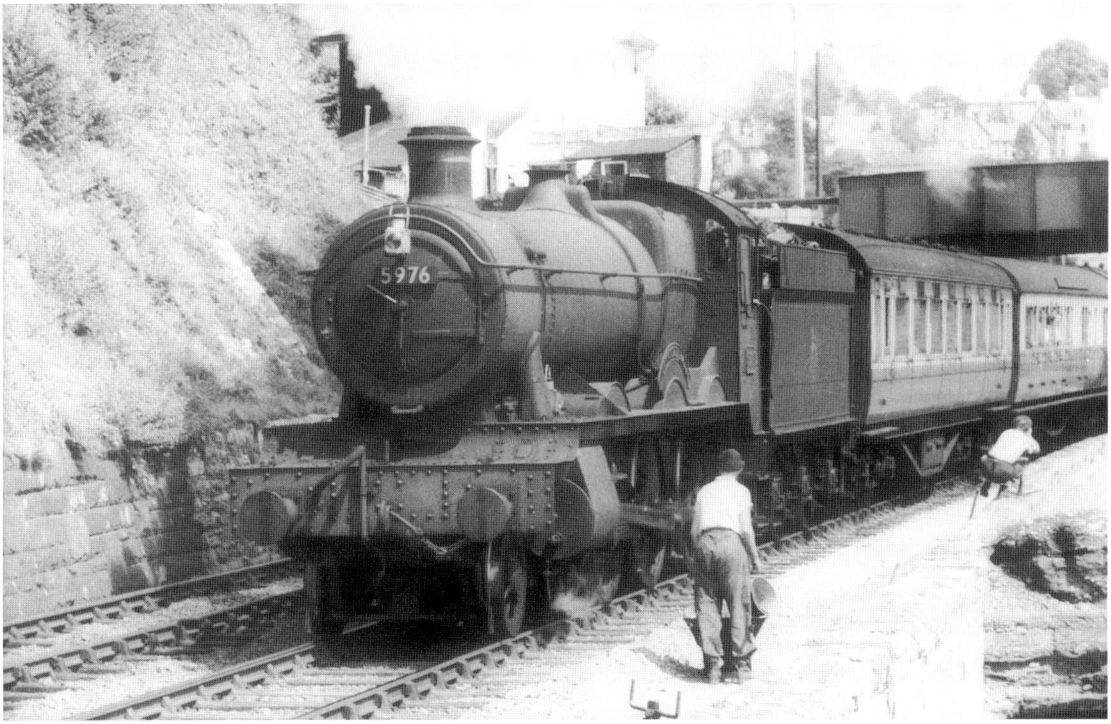

No. 5976 *Ashwicke Hall* heads south along the sea wall at Dawlish in 1953.

The area between Dawlish Warren and Teignmouth was an enthusiast's dream: sun, sea, and trains. Imagine the scene: a warm summer's day, the sound of the surf, there you are in your deckchair, when you hear the clang of a signal. You tell your wife and children you will just nip up and buy them an ice-cream. They give you knowing looks, but don't even ask why you are taking your camera – what a surprise! – 'The Cornish Riviera' suddenly appears with a gleaming 'King' at the head and you get a superb photograph.

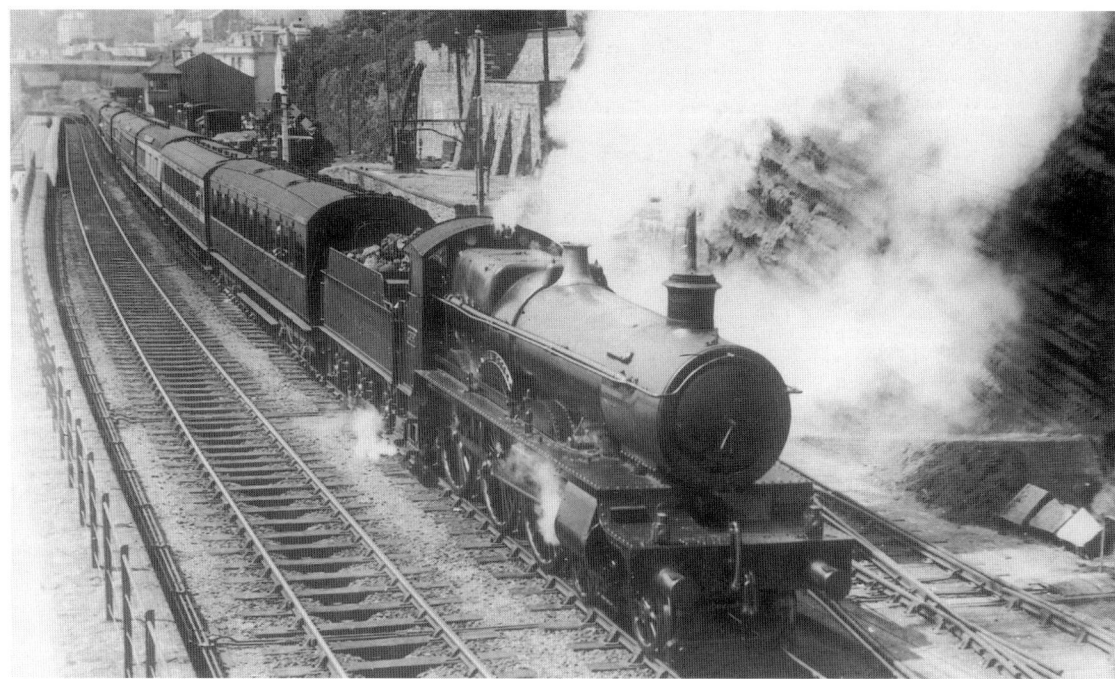

No. 2982 *Lalla Rookh* heads north out of Dawlish in the 1930s.

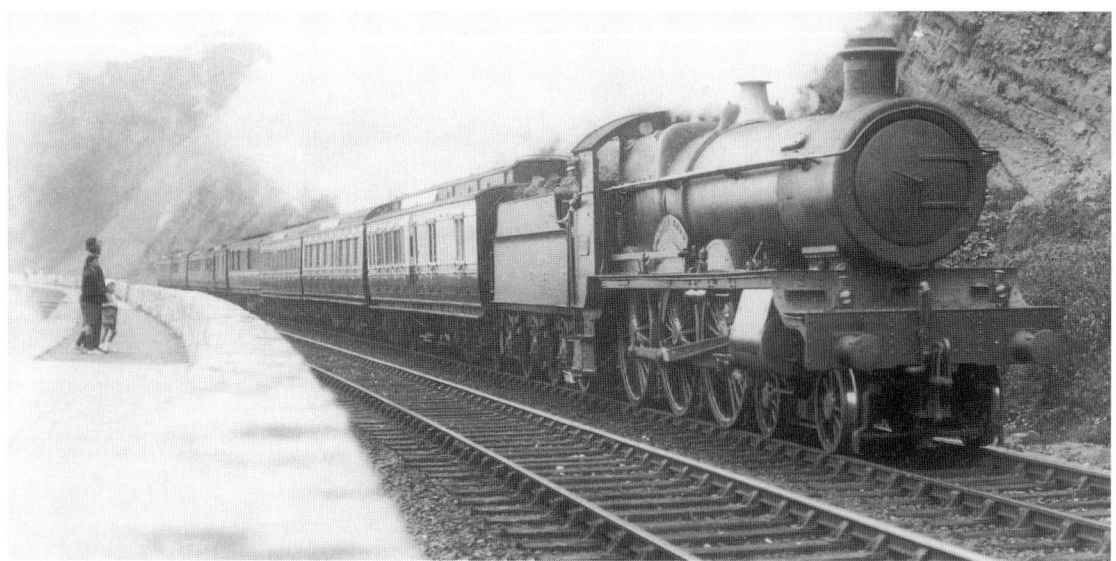

Holiday-makers get a wonderful view of no. 2986 *Robin Hood* running along the sea wall between Teignmouth and Dawlish in the 1930s.

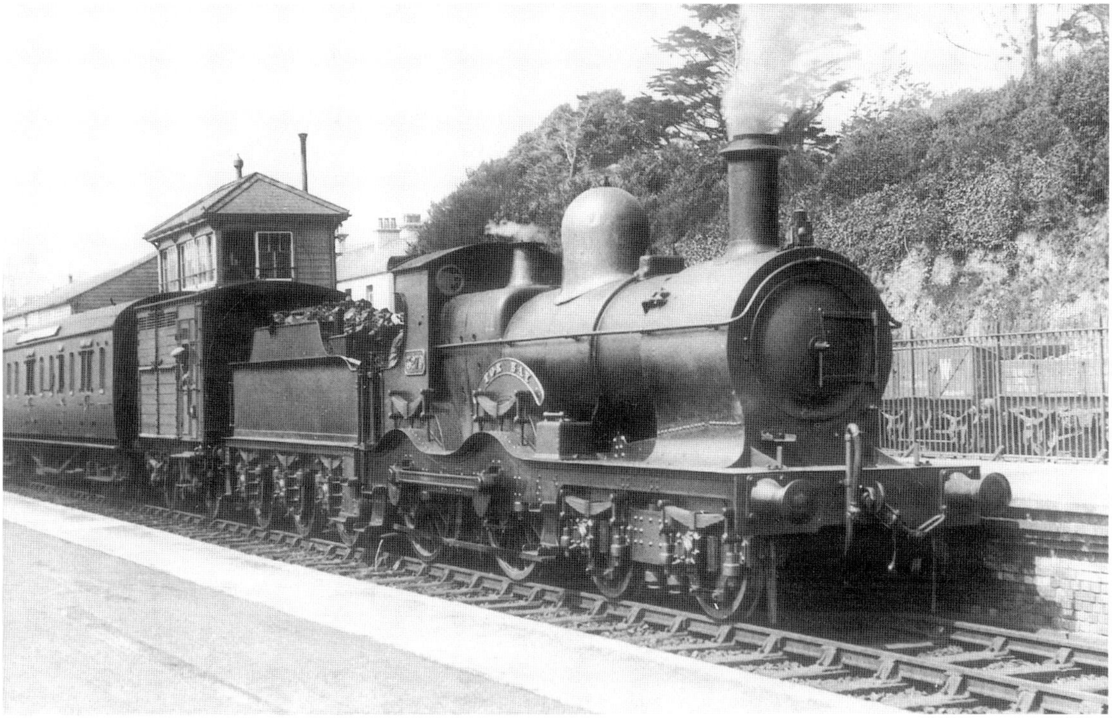

Another 1930s photograph, this time of 'Duke' no. 3279 *Torbay* at Teignmouth.

Twenty years later we see 'Castle' no. 4080 *Powderham Castle* leaving Teignmouth for the north in 1953.

Leaving Teignmouth we run alongside the River Teign and arrive at Newton Abbot. This is another station which in the summer months becomes a bottleneck with trains arriving one after the another, for the Paignton Kingswear branch, The Plymouth and Cornwall trains are just as frequent. There are specials to Newquay and St Ives from far away places in the north, and there are the branch lines to Dartmoor, so once more we will be busy with our cameras.

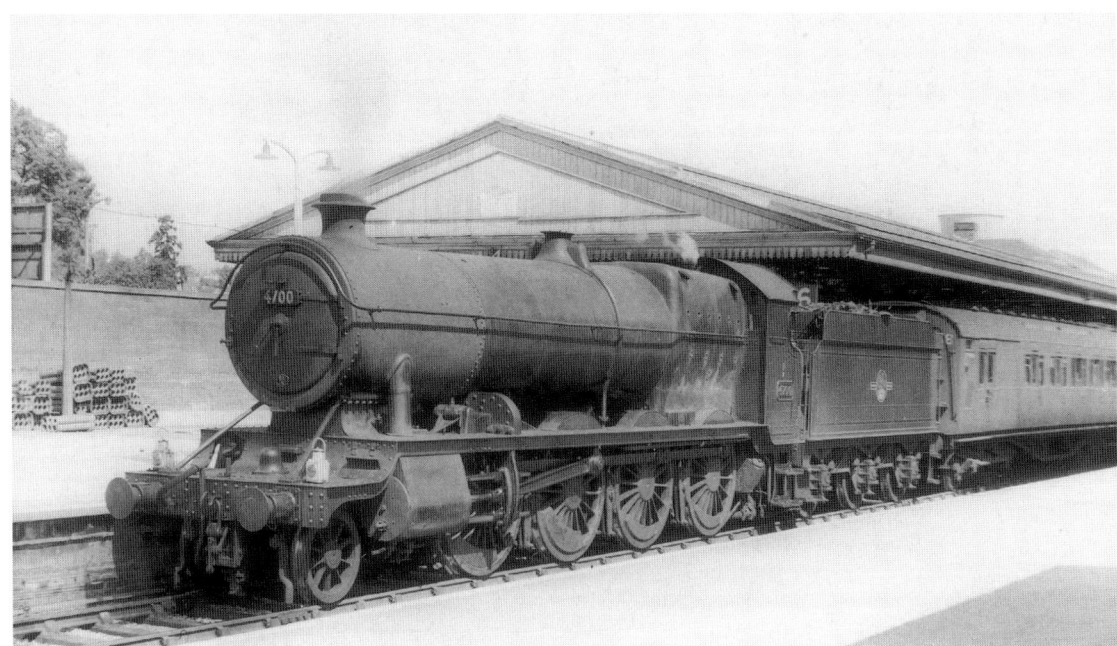

No. 4700 on a holiday special at Newton Abbot, 1961.

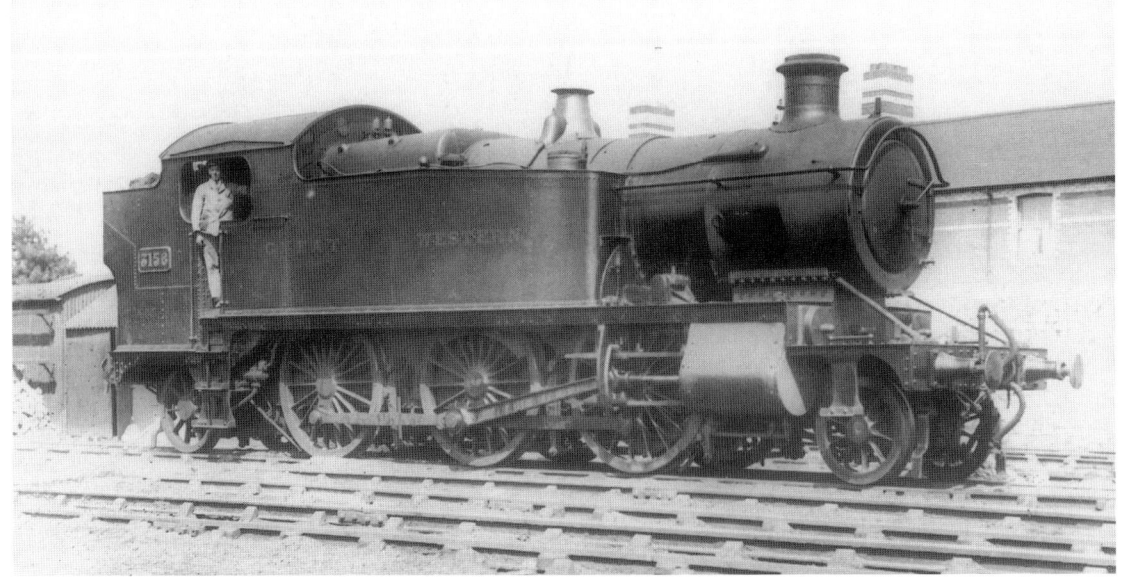

GWR no. 3156 waiting to act as pilot engine to an express that will need assistance over the South Devon Banks, 10 May 1923.

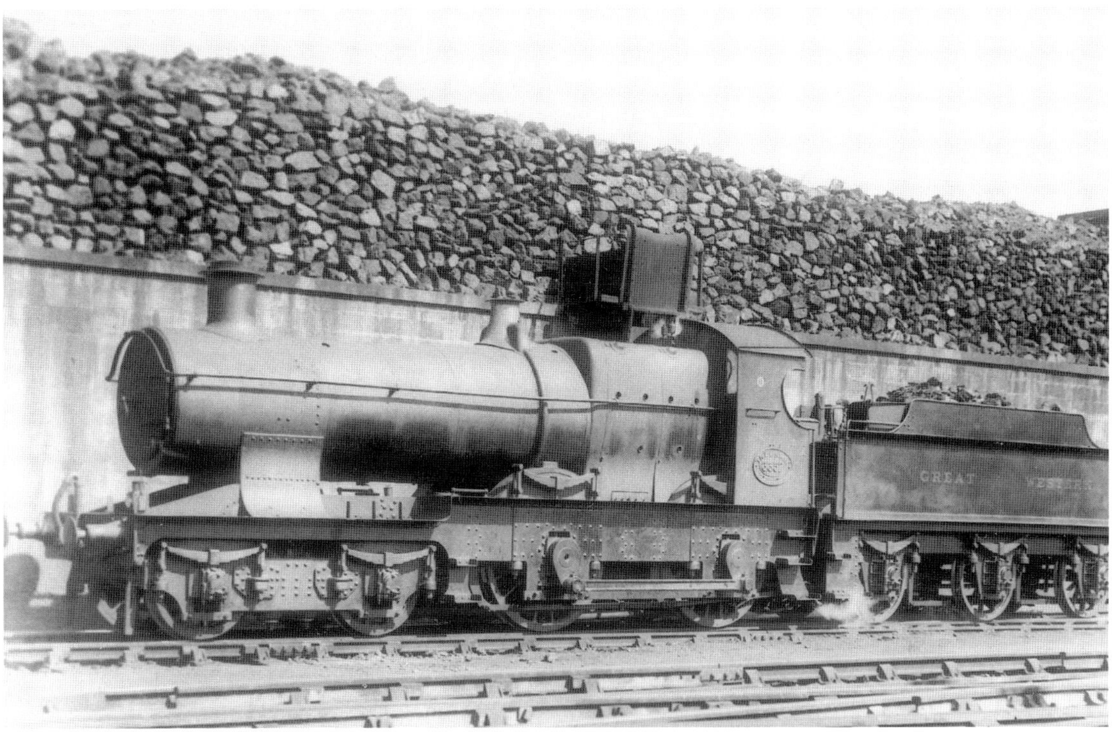

GWR no. 3357 *Trelawney* under a massive store of huge lumps of coal on Newton Abbot shed, 1924.

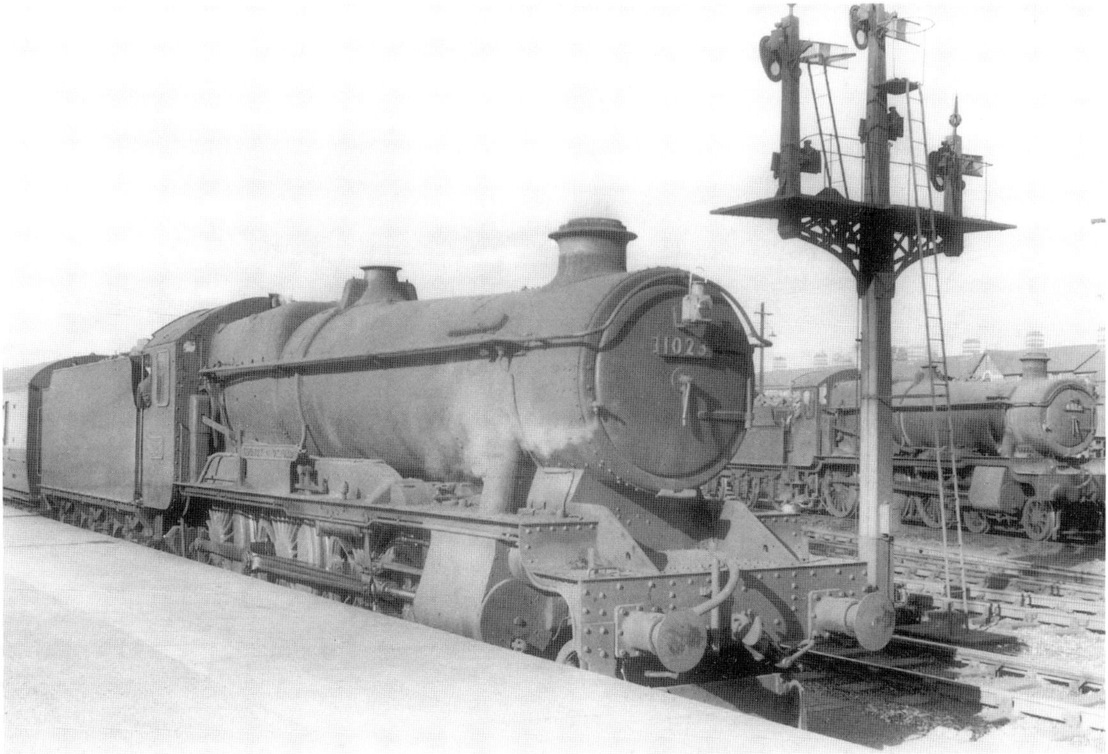

No. 1023 *County of Oxford* at Newton Abbot, 1954. In the background is 'Grange' no. 6813 *Eastbury Grange*.

On the move again, we have a pilot engine which we shall need, as with in a few minutes of leaving Newton Abbot we shall be at Aller Junction where the Torbay Line leaves to head south to Kingswear. We carry on double-headed, building up speed to attack the notorious banks.

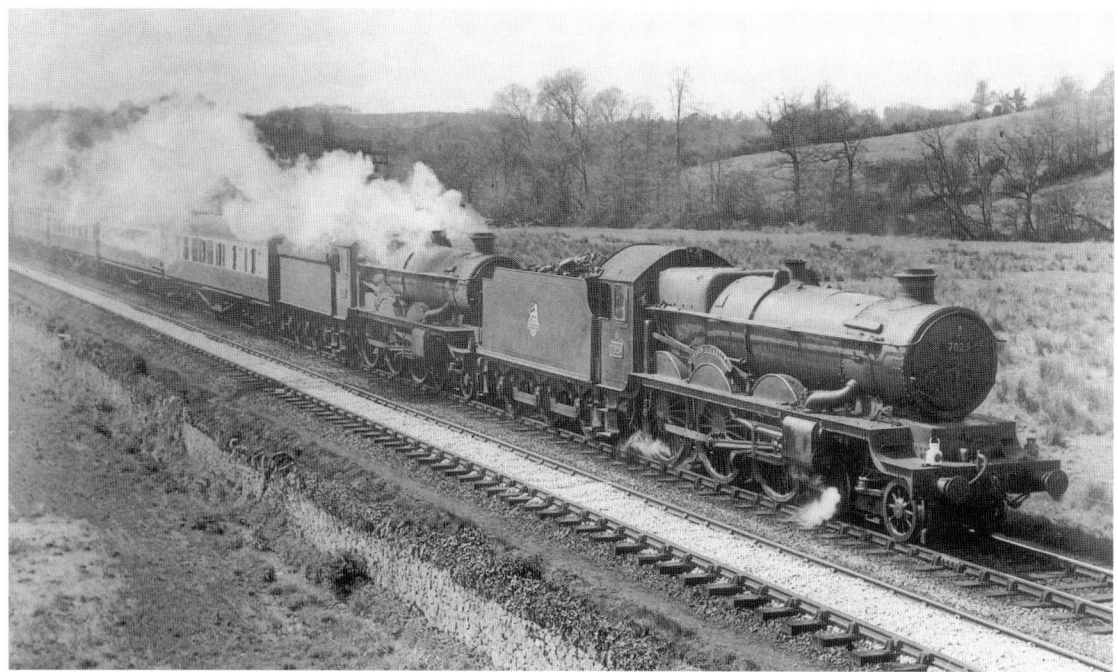

No. 7029 *Clun Castle*, and no. 5029 *Nunney Castle* near Aller in 1954.

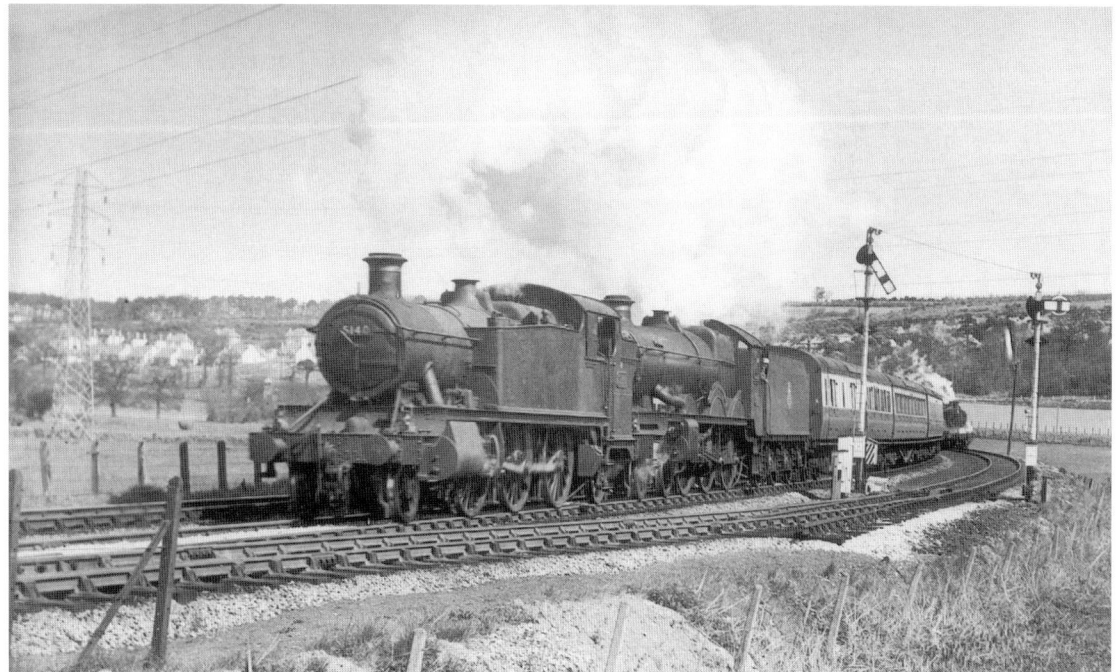

No. 5140 and no. 5012 *Berry Pomeroy Castle* working hard at Aller Junction in 1954.

The line to Kingswear catered for holidays by the sea all the way. First we arrive at Torquay, then Paignton, then Goodrington. At Churston is the branch to Brixham, then down to Kingswear, where a short ferry ride brings you to Dartmouth. Kingswear itself has quite extensive sidings, mainly for empty coaching stock, which during the summer months (especially on Saturdays) were full, as there were many trains that arrived early in the mornings, and had to be cleaned and sorted to convey holiday-makers home after a couple of weeks soaking up the sun.

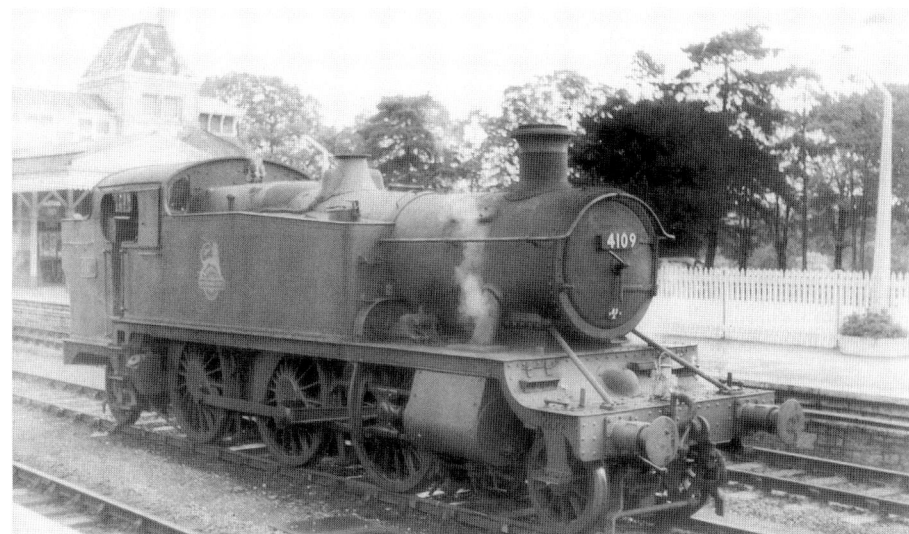

No. 4109 at Torquay carrying an 83A Newton Abbot shedplate, 1953. It has probably been piloting an express.

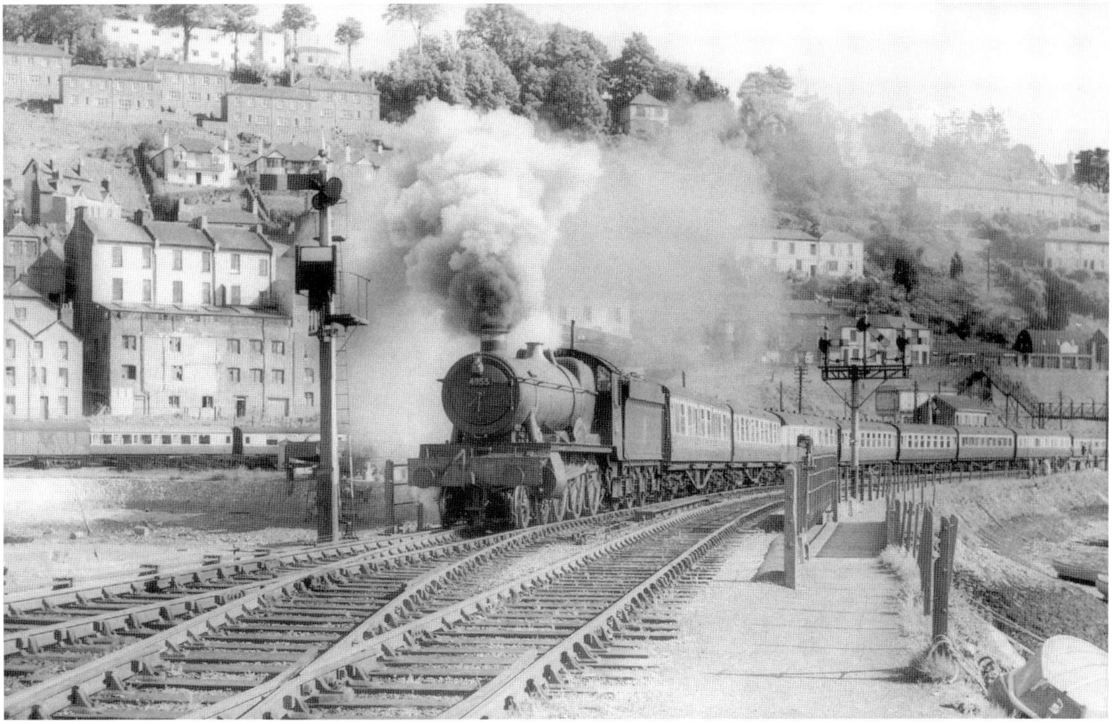

No. 4955 *Plaspower Hall* under full power as it leaves Kingswear. It has a steep incline to ascend before Churston in 1954.

We are now rapidly picking up speed, both engines are working hard and no doubt both sets of enginemen hoping they do not get a signal check at the approach to Dainton. All is well and the GWR bark from the two chimneys is music to our ears. For a short stretch on Dainton, the engines have to pull anything up to 450 tons up an incline of 1:36 – steeper than the well-known Lickey Bank. Once at the top of the incline, we have an easier ride to Totnes.

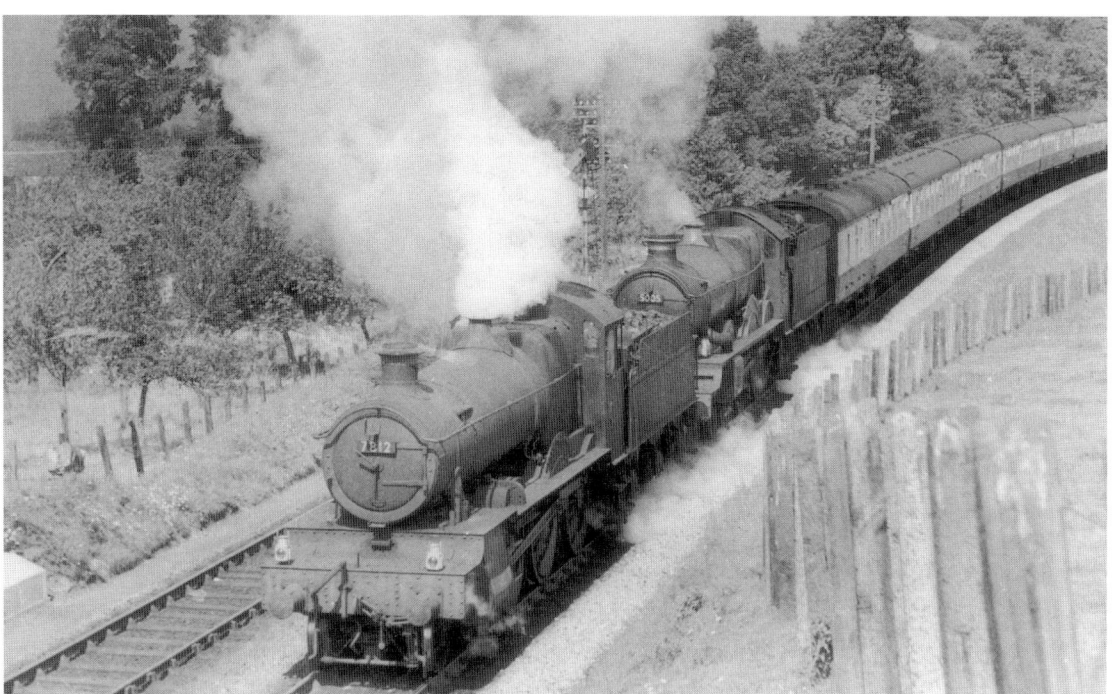

No. 7812 *Erlestoke Manor* as pilot and no. 5005 *Manorbier Castle* working hard on Dainton in 1953.

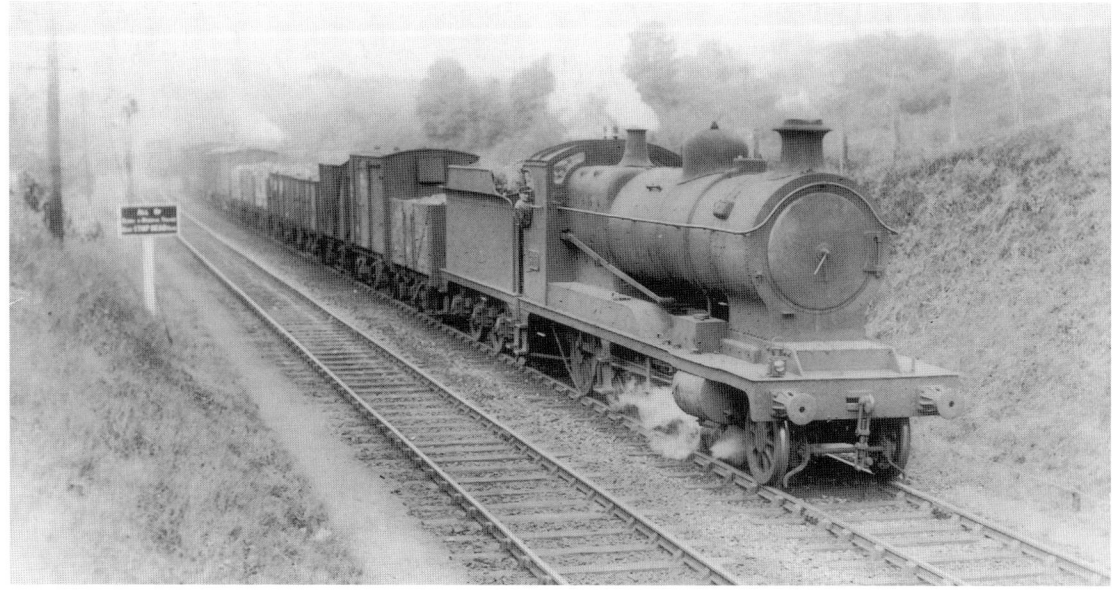

Rod no. 3040 on Dainton in 1929. Its speed at the top of the bank was probably not more than walking pace.

Here comes Totnes where we make a short stop. We might get a picture of the branch train to Ashburton, as they are usually held for arriving expresses because we are in a big tourist area.

No. 5009 *Shrewsbury Castle* with a stopping train, 1953.

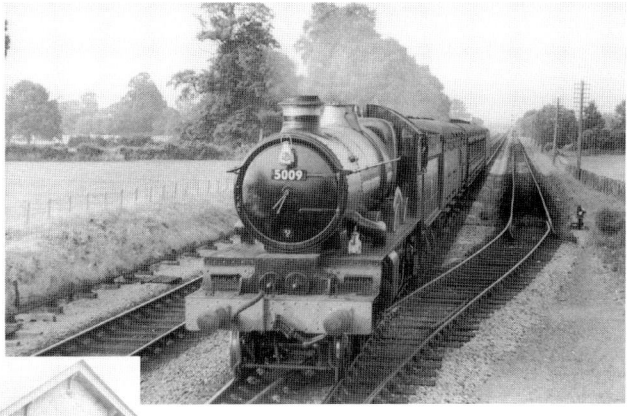

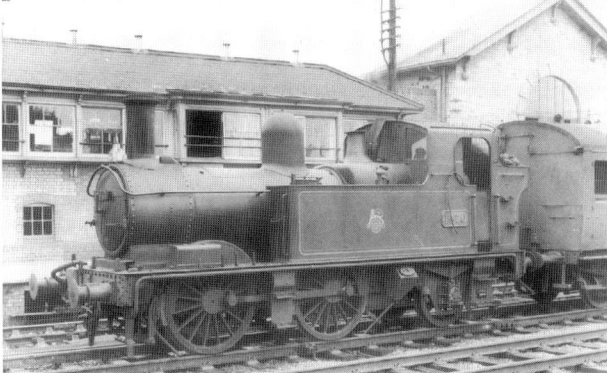

0–4–2T no. 1470 with the Ashburton branch train at Totnes in 1953.

GWR no. 830 in Totnes station with the branch train from Ashburton in the 1930s.

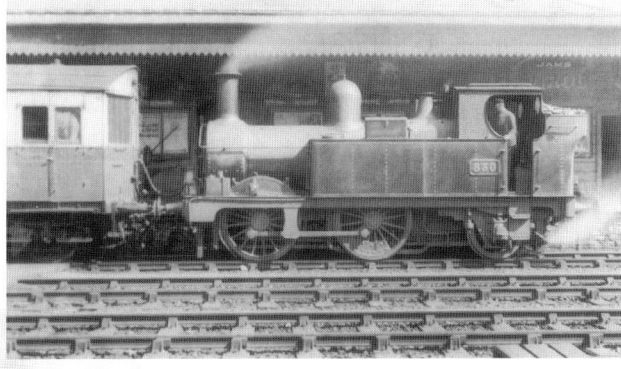

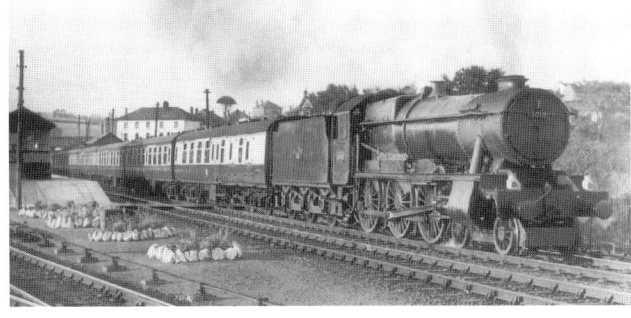

No. 1018 *County of Leicester* working hard as it pulls out of Totnes.

Talk in the carriage turns to the subject of another steep bank to come. We have all heard of Rattery, near Brent. One of our companions has looked it up in his book, and tells us that for the better part of a mile and a half, the line rises at 1:50, so we can look forward to that GWR sound again.

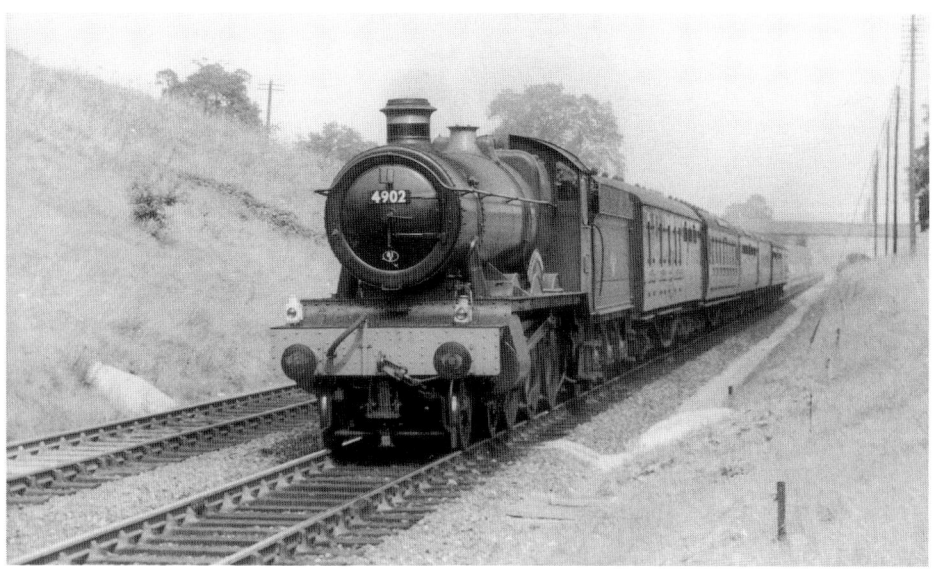

No. 4902 *Aldenham Hall* in the Devon countryside, 1959.

We are on Rattery now, with that wonderful sound ringing in our ears.

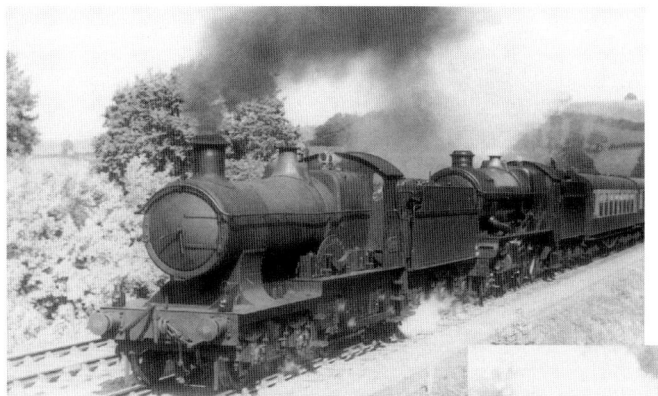

A 1937 view of no. 3449 *Nightingale* and no. 6016 *King Edward V* ascending Rattery.

Another 'Bulldog', no. 3398 *Montreal*, and an unidentified 'Hall' on Rattery Bank in 1937.

We will not be stopping at Brent on this trip, but we may catch a glimpse of a branch train, as a line to Kingsbridge goes off to our left. Yet again we not far from several holiday destinations in this part of the world.

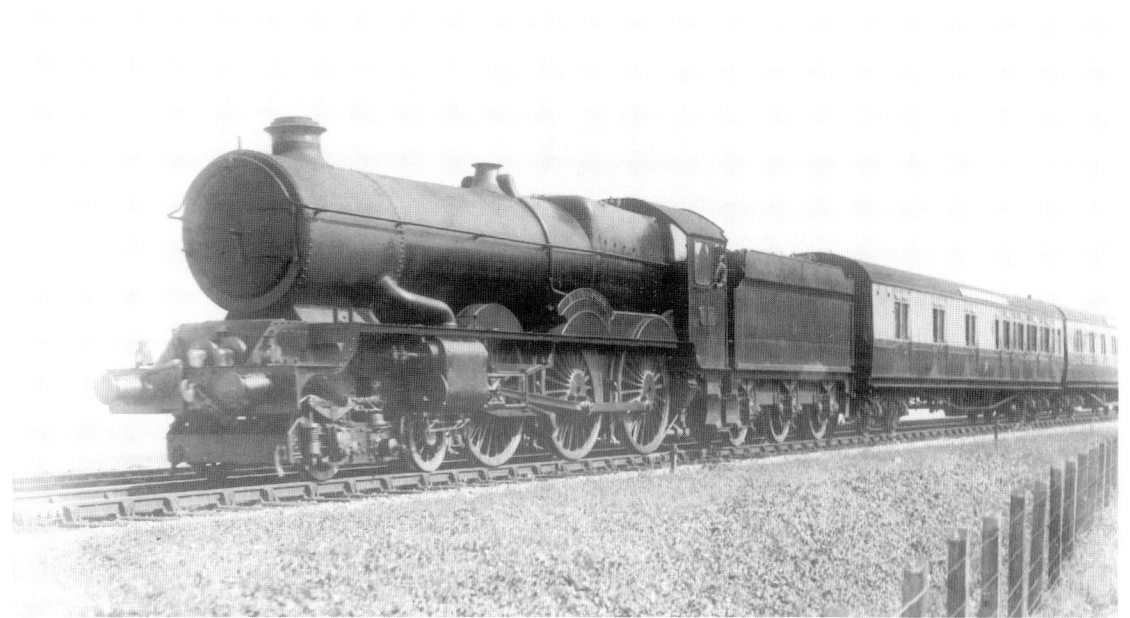

No. 6026 *King John* heads a pre-war express near Brent.

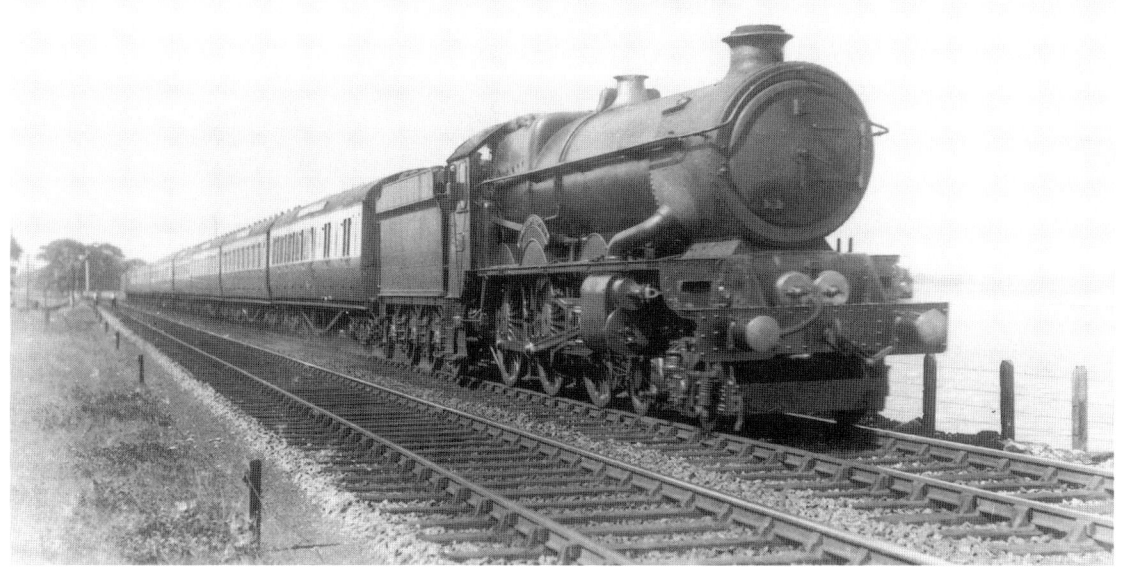

No. 6001 *King Edward VII* on another pre-war express in South Devon.

From Brent there are not many straight stretches of line, so there will not be any high speeds until we reach Hemerdon, where we have about a 2-mile straight line at 1:42 downhill. Even here we cannot be excessive as we shall soon be into Plympton. Just beyond Plympton there is a branch on our right, up to the desolation of Princetown, where of course many criminals will shudder at the reminder of one of Britain's grimmest prisons, Dartmoor.

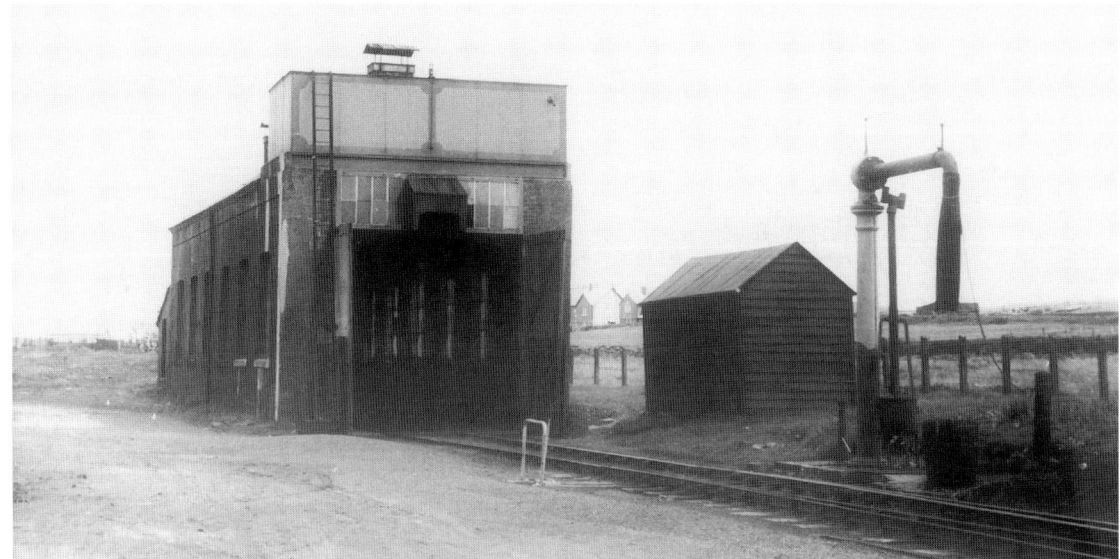

The exposed GWR shed at Princetown in the 1930s.

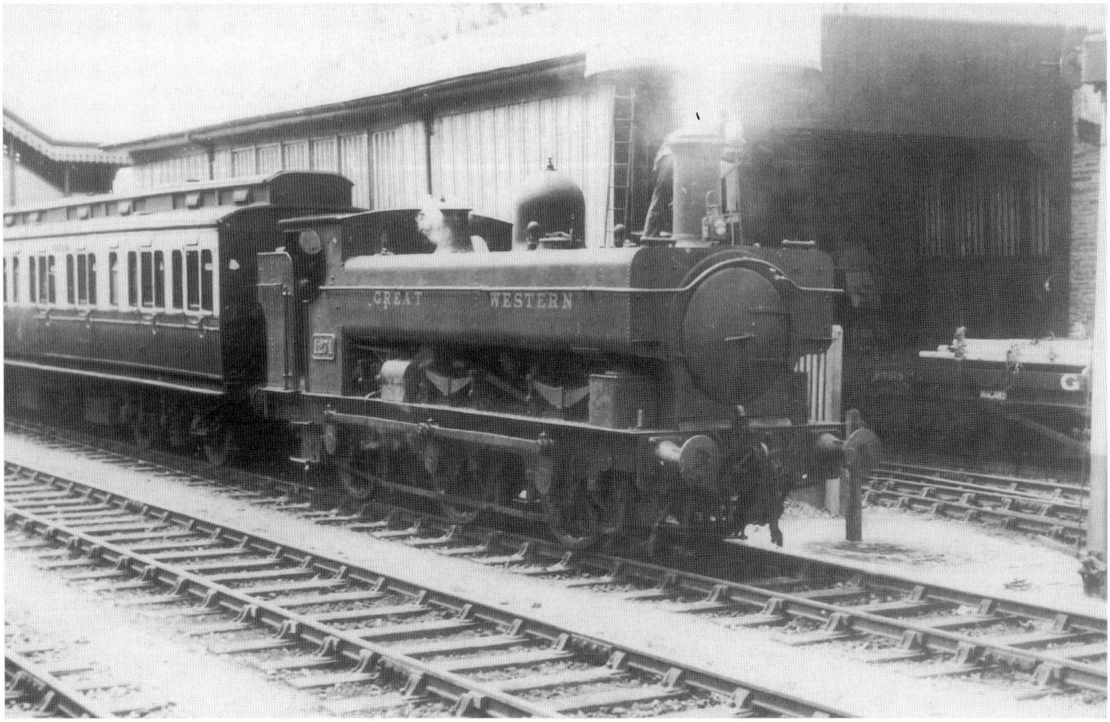

Another GWR view, this time of pannier tank no. 1271 at Tavistock in the 1930s.

Through Plympton and we cross the River Plym. We run alongside the river for a short distance, and then we come to Laira, the shed to visit in the South Devon area. We can only lean out of the windows and hope to see something, as the train does not stop at Laira. Through Mutley Tunnel we go and we come to a stand in North Road. After some of the stations we have been through, Plymouth seems to be quiet.

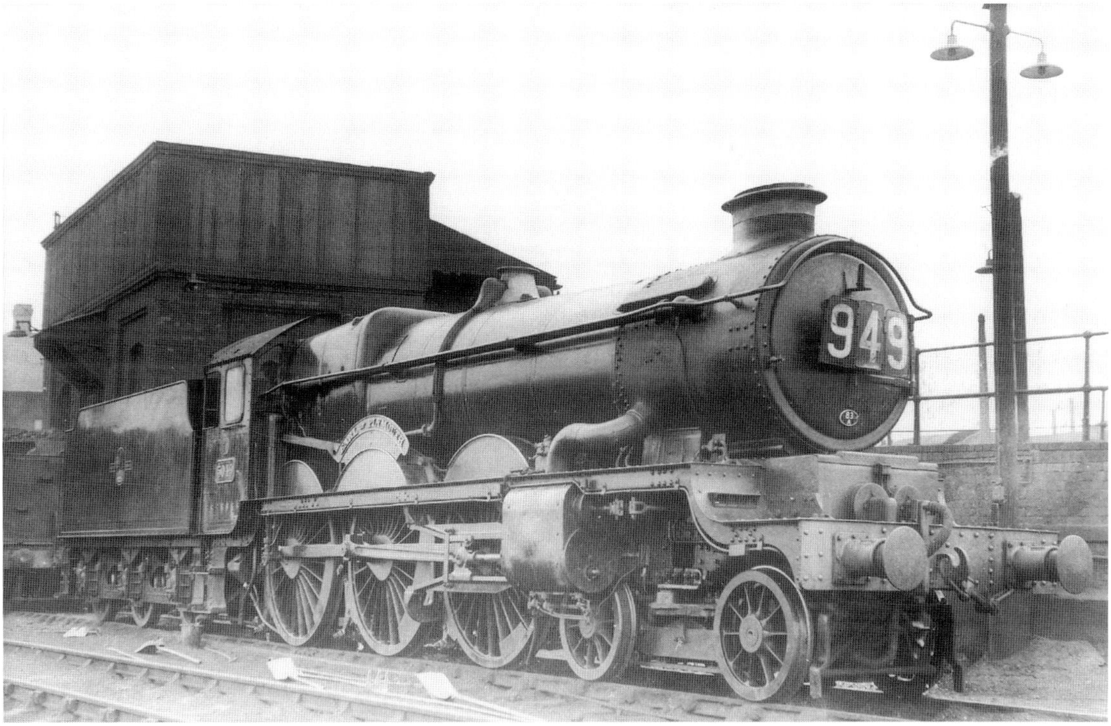

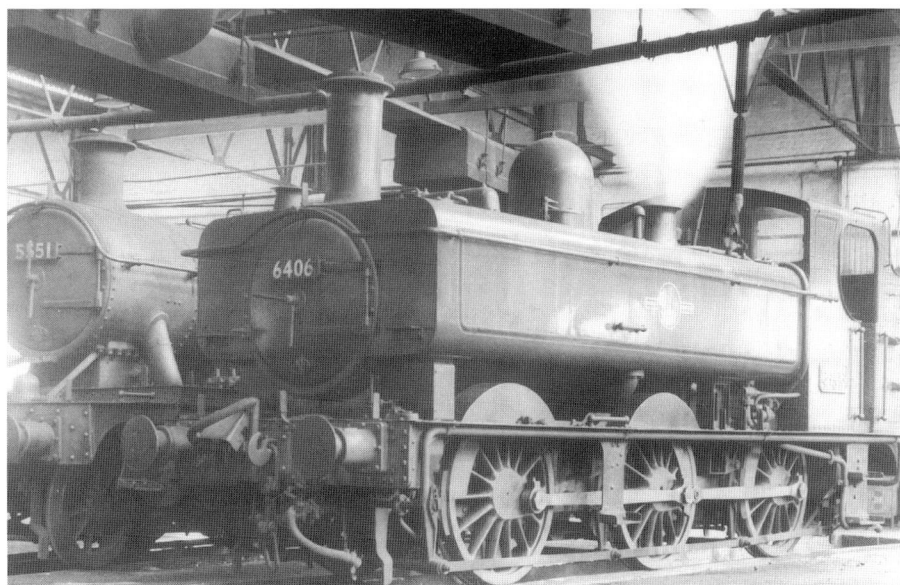

A very appropriate 'Castle' to photograph in Plymouth Laira is no. 5049 *Earl of Plymouth*, 1959.

Pannier no. 6406 in company with 2–6–2T no. 5551 on Laira shed in 1959.

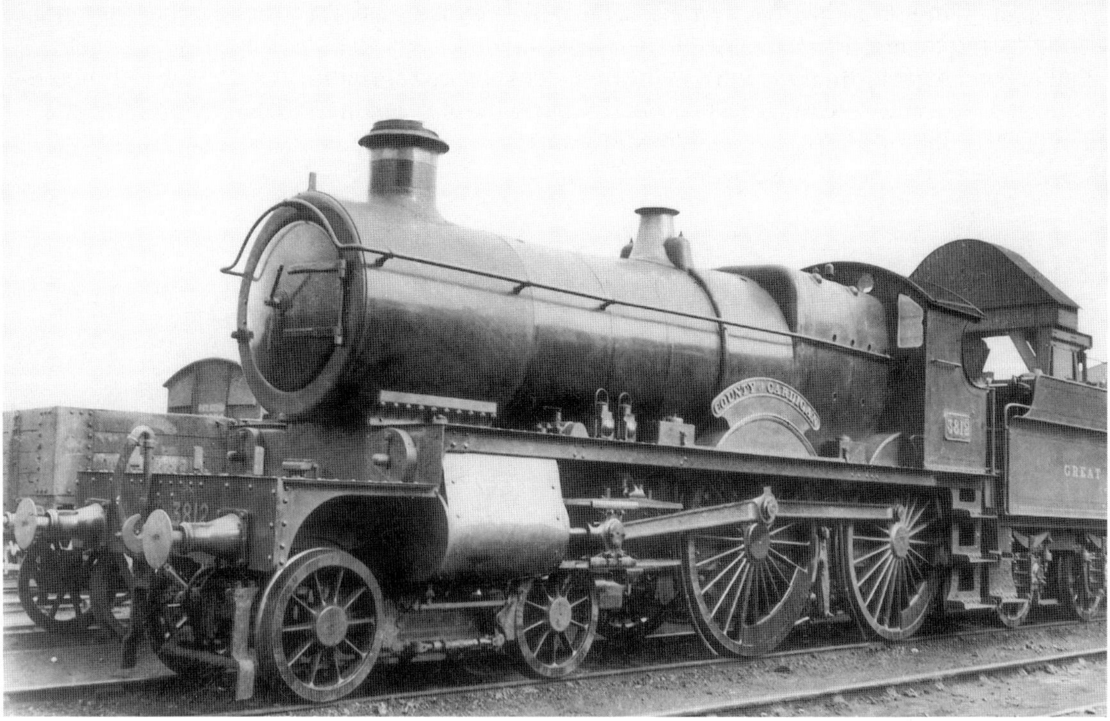

A prewar view of no. 3812 *County of Cardigan* on Laira shed.

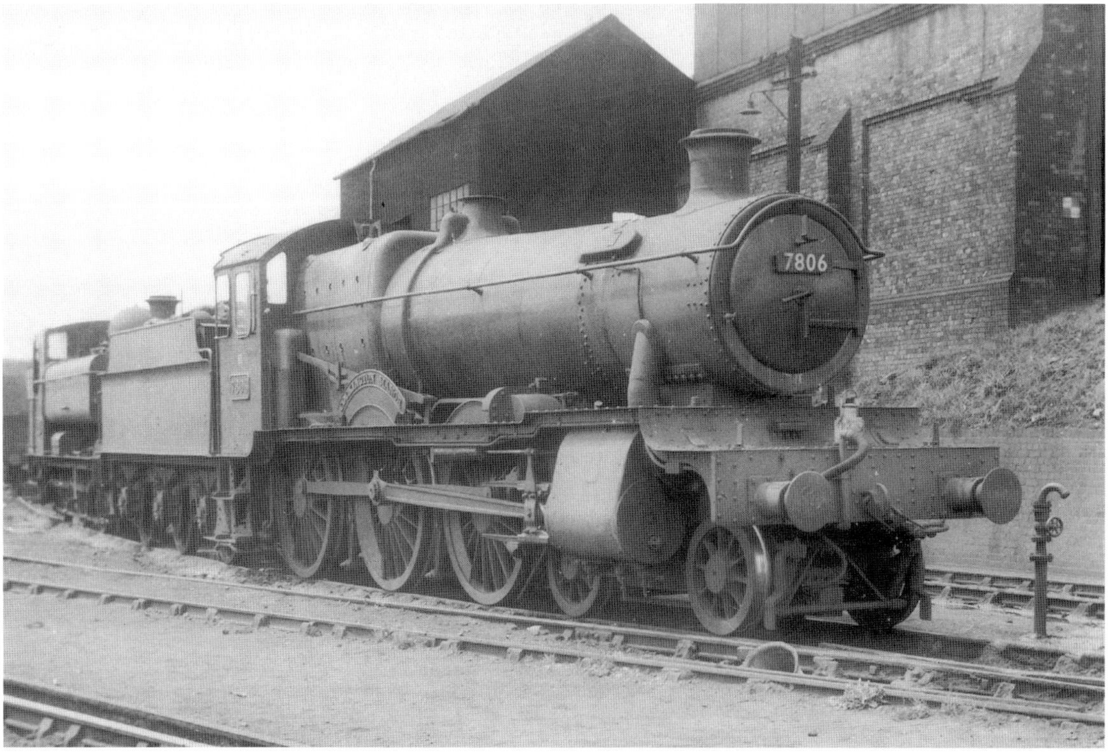

No. 7806 *Cockington Manor* on Laira shed in 1956.

Plymouth North Road station is the exchange point for expresses going to Cornwall. Trains like the 'Cornish Riviera', headed by a 'King', cannot go into Cornwall as there is a weight restriction on the Royal Albert Bridge, which means the heaviest engine permitted is a 'Castle'. Likewise the 'Halls', 'Counties', 'Granges', 'Manors', etc. do not pose a problem. In the city there is also Plymouth Millbay station, where the Transatlantic liners disgorge passengers and mail, and which brought about the race to London by *City of Truro* in 1904 when the 100mph record was achieved.

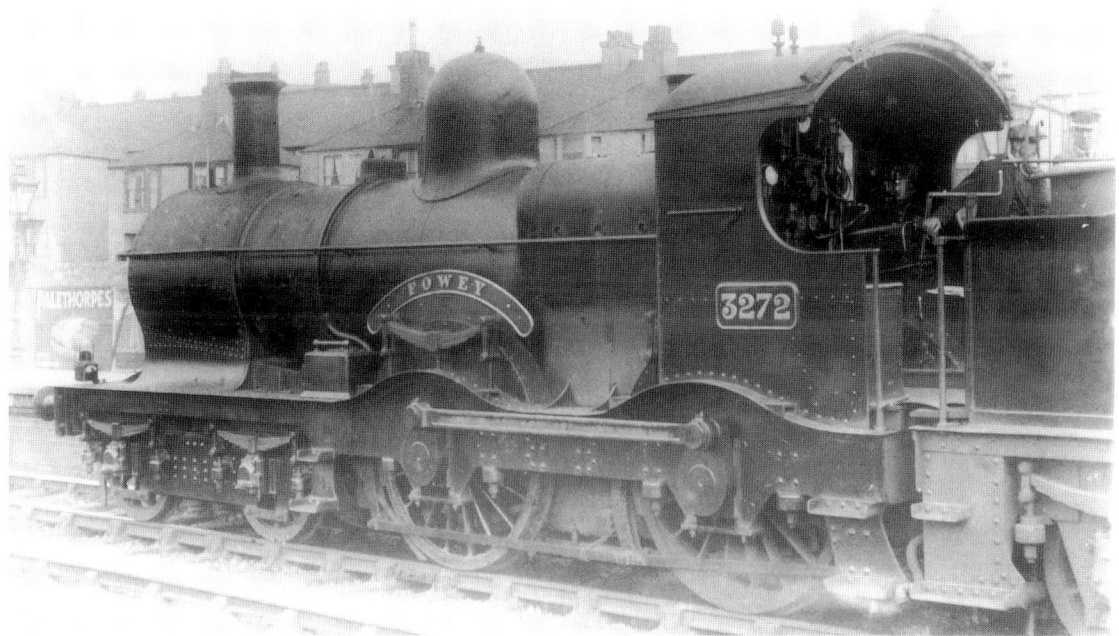

'Duke' no. 3772 *Fowey* in Plymouth North Road in 1920.

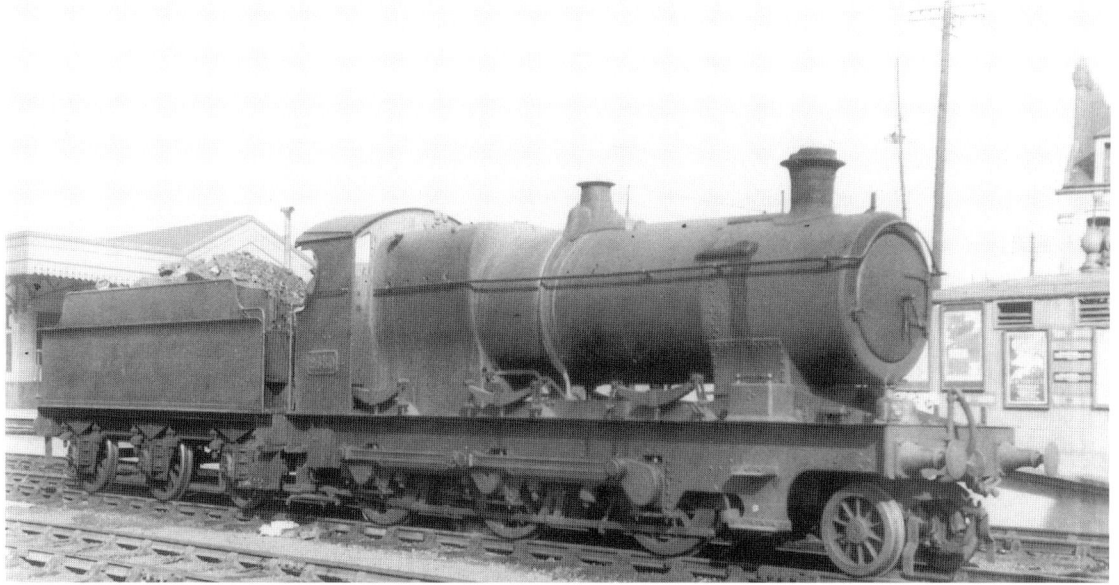

'Aberdare' class GWR no. 2680 in Plymouth North Road, 1920.

Leaving Plymouth we are now on our way to another of Brunel's masterpieces, the Royal Albert Bridge (or the Saltash Bridge as it is sometimes known). We pass the junction for Millbay, and on through Devonport where we can see some naval ships from our high point. Then comes St Budeaux and we get our first glimpse of the bridge. Started in the 1840s on instruction from the Cornwall Railway, it had to have a clearance of 100ft above river level to allow naval ships to pass beneath. There were a number of building problems which Brunel solved. The tubular trusses supporting the decking were floated out into position and jacked up into place: simple! I don't know about you, but with the issues involved in floating a construction 450ft long and several thousands of tons in weight, I am glad Brunel was organising it and not me! All was well and it was opened on 2 May 1859. Brunel was not in attendance; he was abroad owing to ill health and later a special train was arranged and he was taken across on his sick bed. He died not long afterwards.

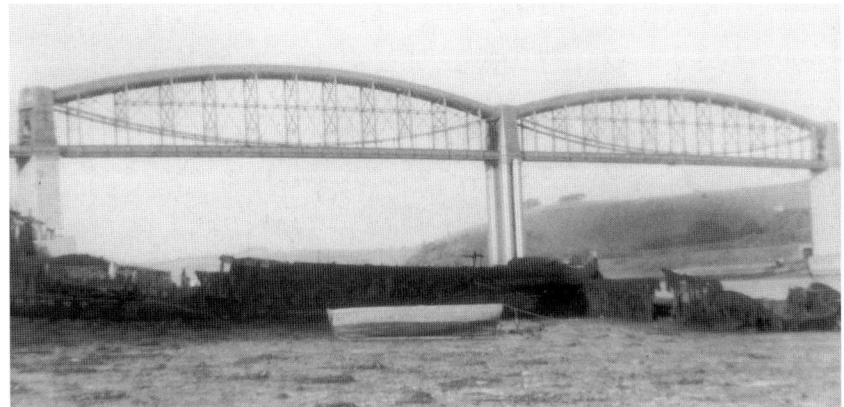

The Royal Albert Bridge in the 1920s.

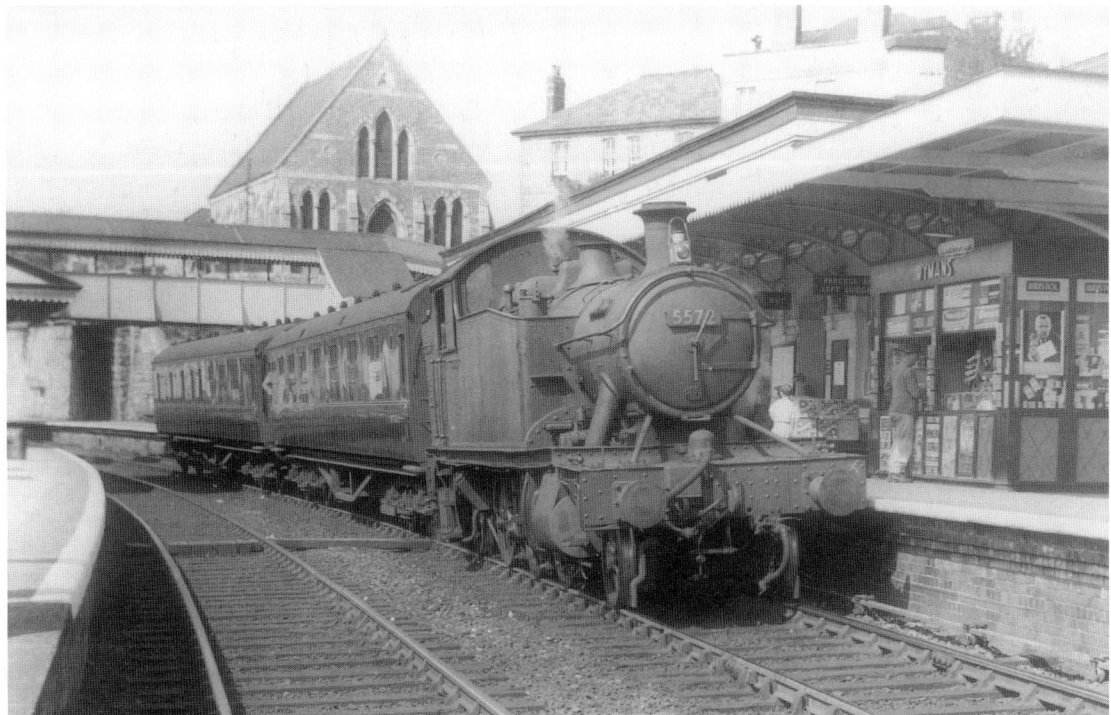

No. 5572 at Saltash on a stopping train to Plymouth.

We are now into Cornwall, thorugh Saltash, and back on double track. The Royal Albert Bridge is, of course, single track. We shall soon be crossing the St Germans Viaduct.

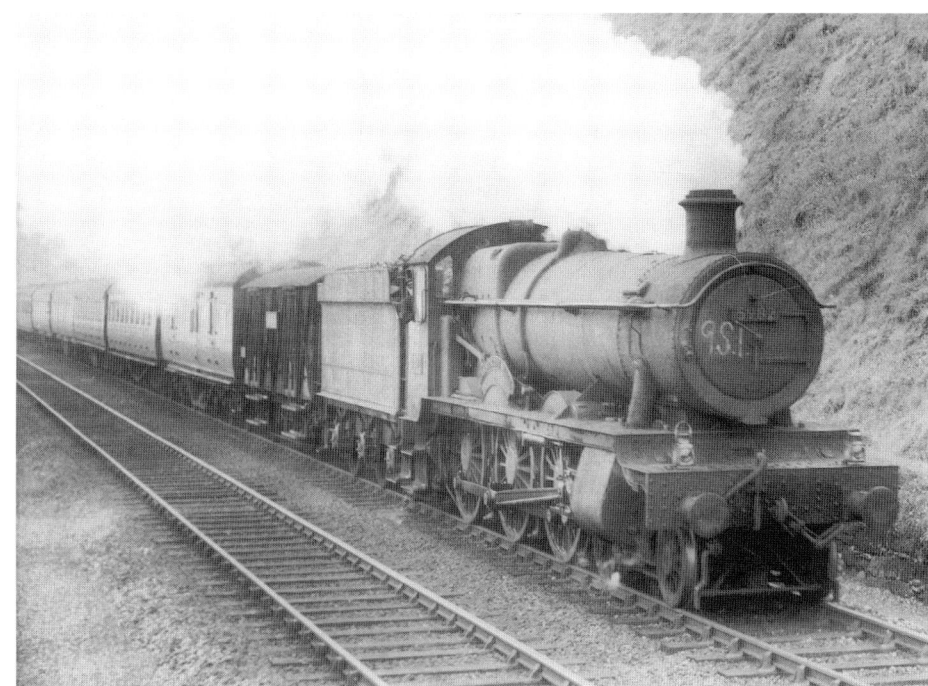

No. 5982
Harrington Hall
between
St Germans
and Liskeard
in 1954.

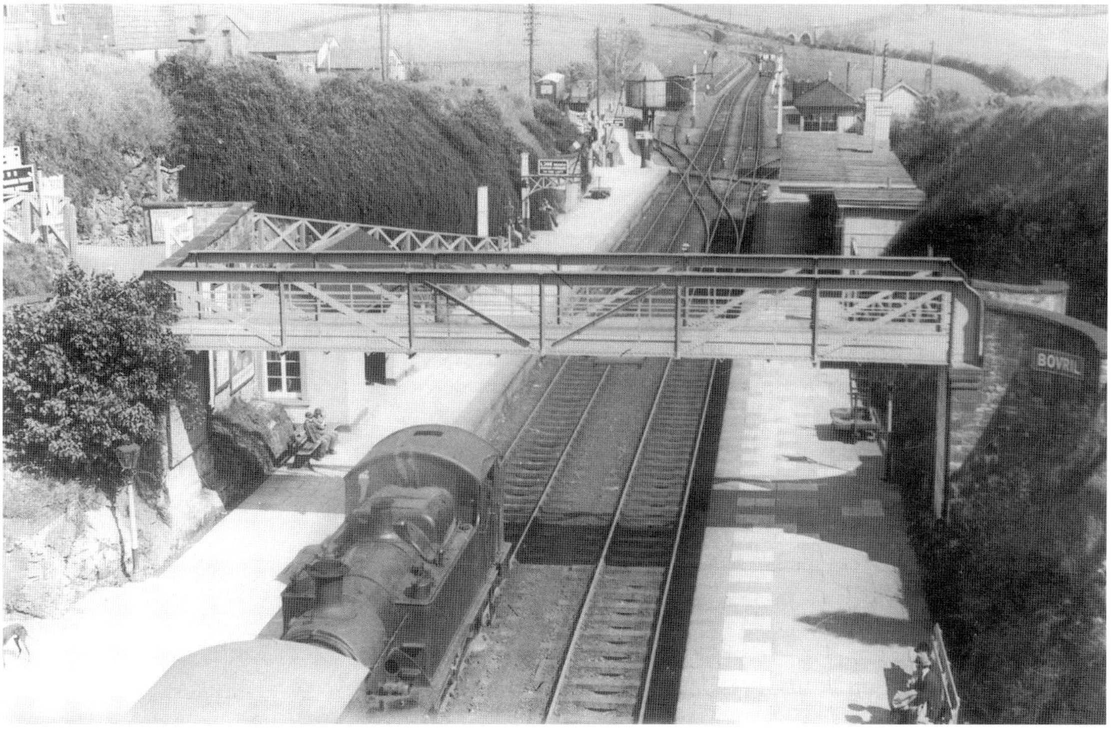

Liskeard in 1935. The branch to Looe is at the end of the platform on the left.

I wish we had time to visit some of the branch lines we shall pass, but expresses never stop long, just long enough for passengers to alight with their luggage. At Liskeard, the branch line to Looe has its own station at right angles to the main platform. Trains leave the station, drop down on a circular route, and pass under the main line. The track runs through pleasantly wooded countryside and into a lovely relaxing Cornish fishing village, somewhat crowded in the summer with holiday-makers.

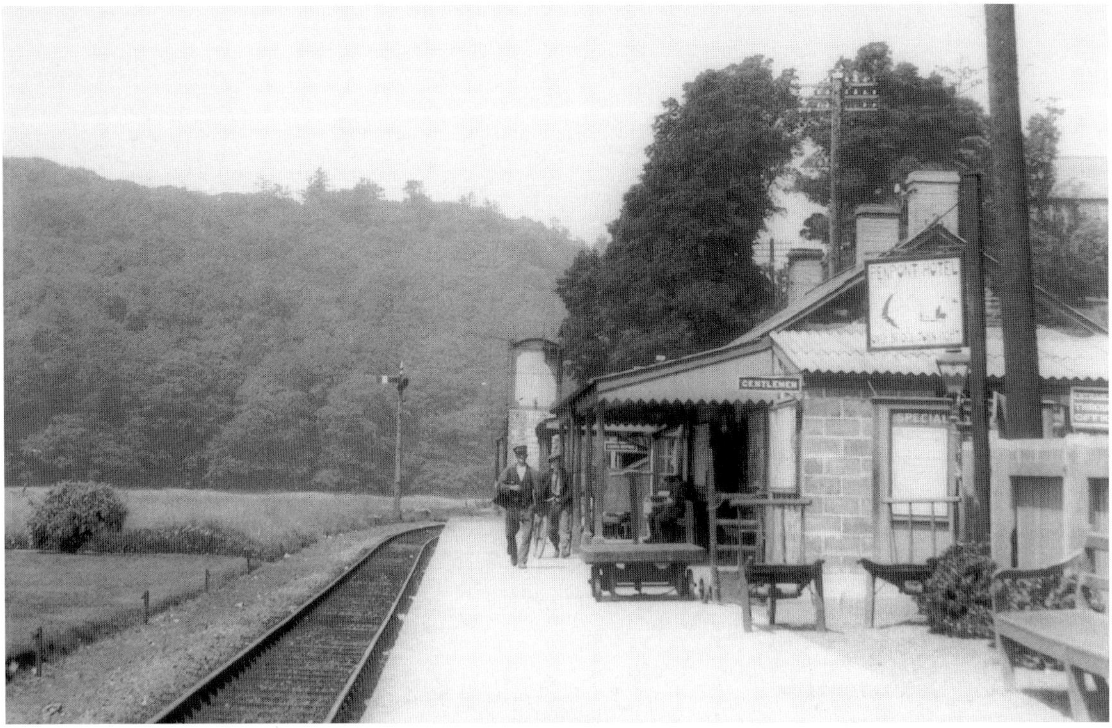

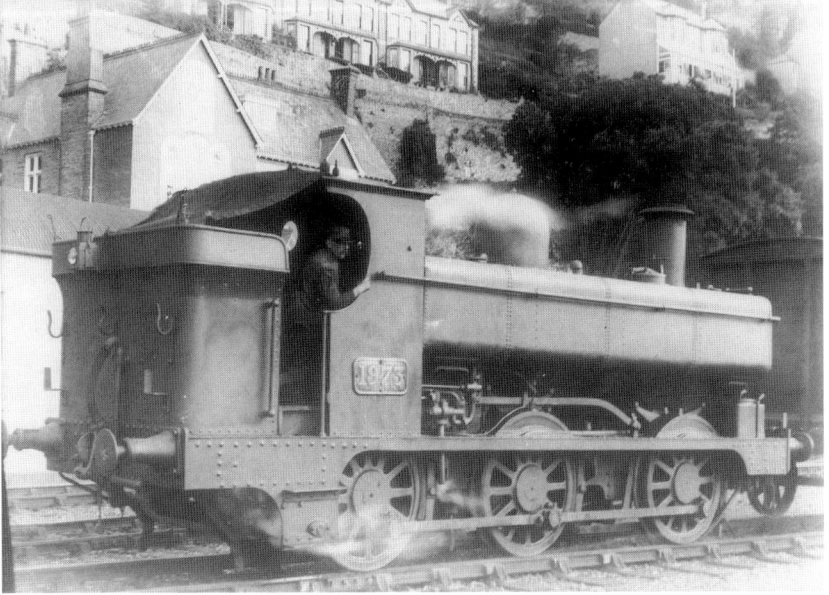

Looe station in the 1920s.

Pannier tank no. 1973 with a covered wagon, perhaps returning to the main line with freshly caught fish.

From Liskeard on we go to Bodmin Road. I remember returning from holidaying in Perranporth with my parents in the early 1950s, that I managed to persuade them to stop and have a picnic by the side of the railway near Bodmin Road. With camera, of course, I found a good vantage point on the banks of the railway at this particular place, where the area was covered with glorious rhododendron bushes. Around the curve came no. 5077 *Fairey Battle* pulling hard in lovely sunshine, the sort of picture one dreams of. I only had a cheap camera, so the result was not wonderful, and of course it was black and white. I still dream of that picture!

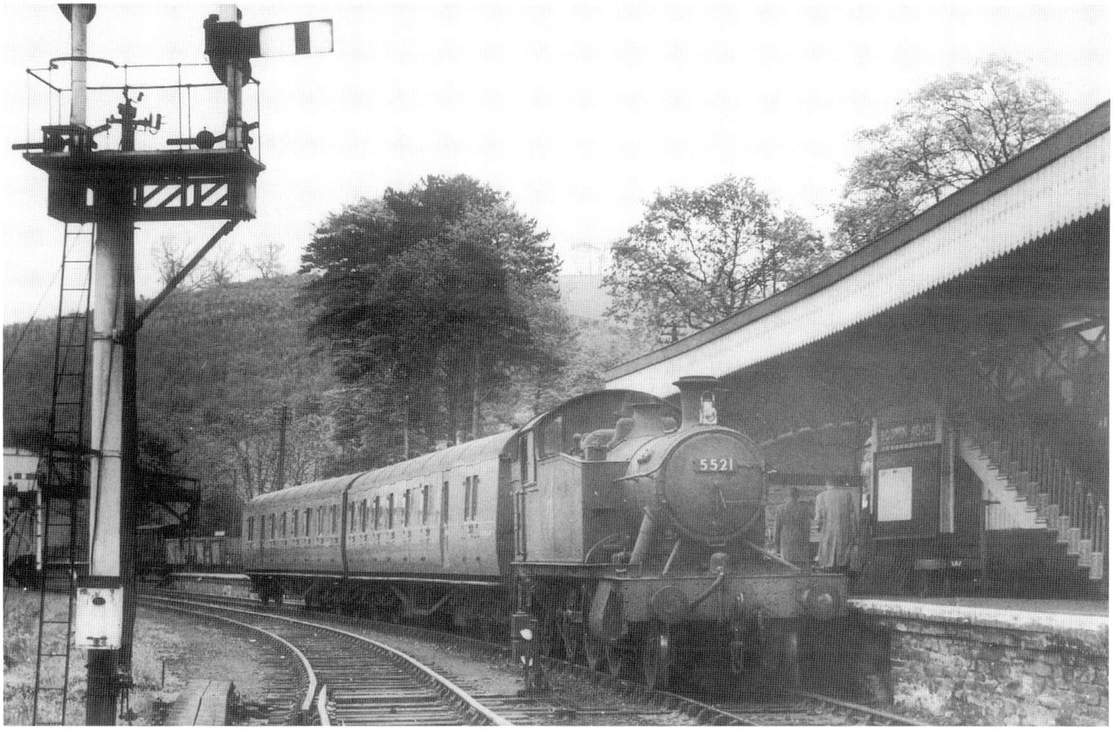

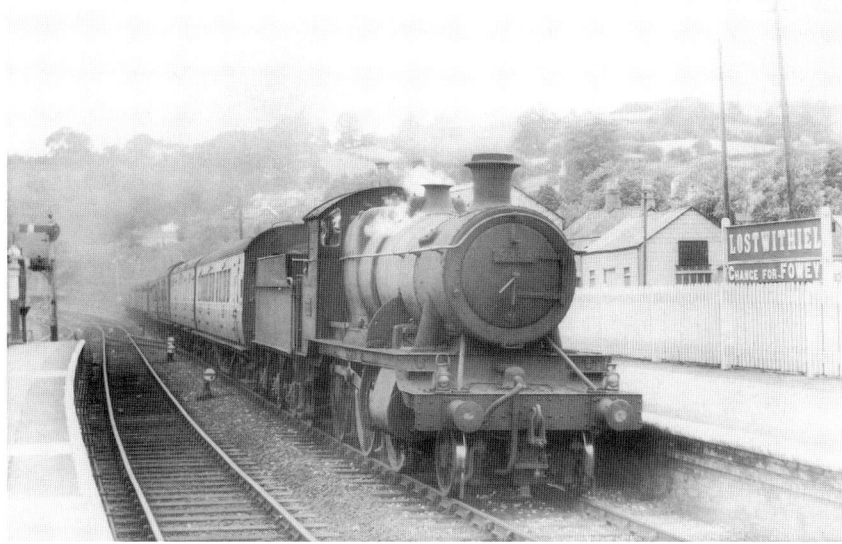

No. 5521 with a stopping train to Fowey collecting passengers at Bodmin Road, 1951.

No. 5336 with an express headcode, arriving at Lostwithiel in 1952.

Through Lostwithiel we shall soon run into Par Junction for the Newquay line, and also the shed of 83E St Blazey, near where the heavy freight tank engines for the China Clay industry were serviced. I knew the line for Newquay very well: most of my time as a conscript in the RAF (apart from initial training), was spent as a photographer at RAF St Mawgan, just a few miles from Newquay. The boundaries looked onto Watergate Bay. I used to catch the midnight Penzance train from Bristol Temple Meads. It was nearly always full of servicemen, army men for various stations, sailors for Plymouth, and a fair contingent of RAF boys for St Mawgan or St Eval. At Par, the train guard and station porters used to bang on the windows to wake us to change for the Newquay train which would be waiting and was usually a pannier or a prairie tank. We changed trains here and we were off. It is quite a difficult line, and engines have to work hard. We pass through Luxulyan and then Bugle; the porters shouting 'Boogle, Boogle'; then Roche, through St Columb Road, Quintrell Downs and finally Newquay. Everyone grabbed their luggage, and as soon as the train stoped we would make for the bus not far from the station and just about make it to camp on time.

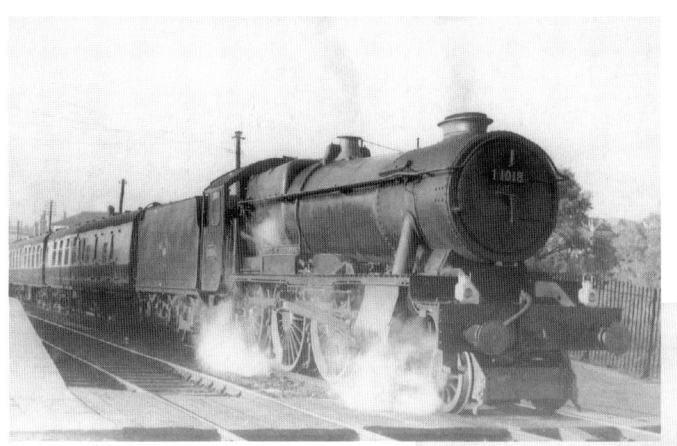

No. 1018 *County of Leicester* leaving Par, 1959.

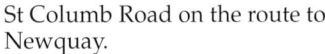

St Columb Road on the route to Newquay.

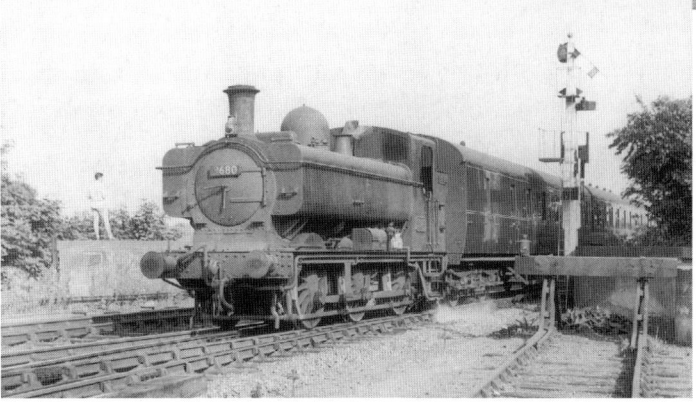

Pannier no. 9680 leaving Newquay on its way back to Par, 1954.

Once again the brakes come off, and we are on our way towards the end of our journey, through such well-known names as Burngullow, Grampound Road, and at Truro and we come to a halt again, just in time to nip out and see what's on Truro shed which is in sight of the station.

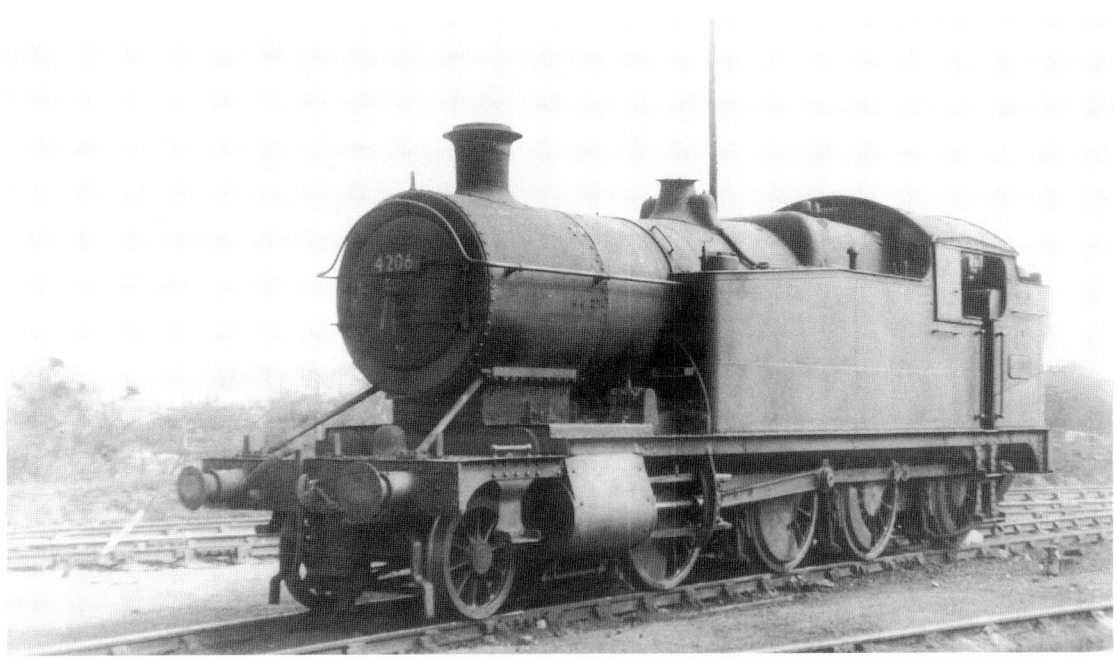

A heavy freight loco no. 4206, a 2–8–0T used for working the China Clay trains to the northern potteries, 1956.

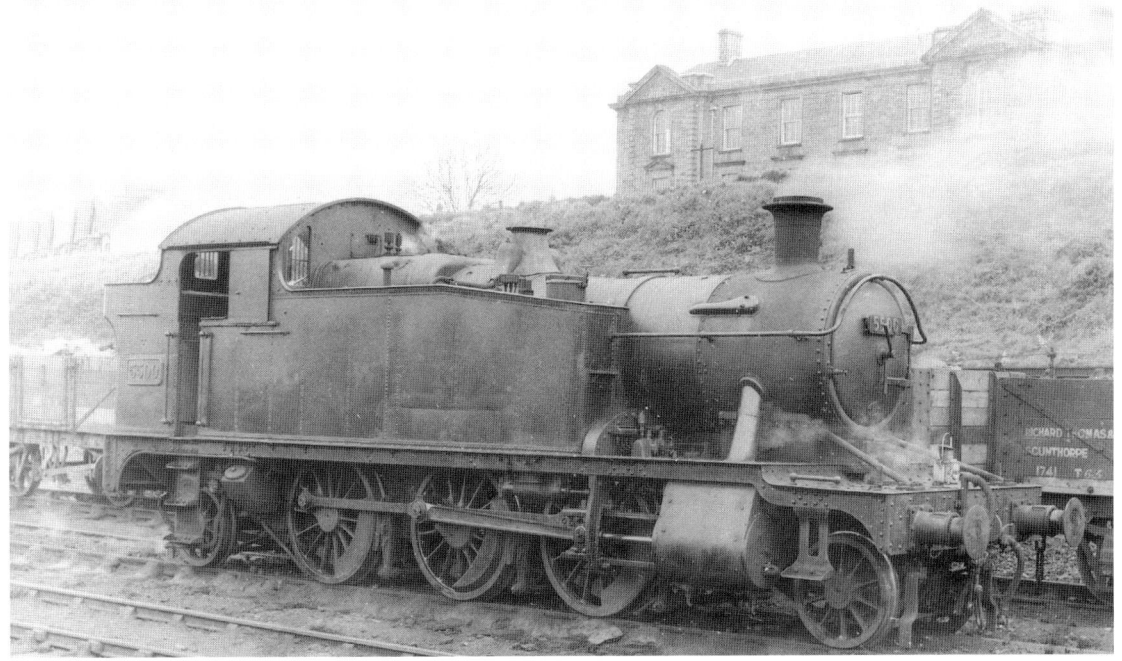

No. 5500 on Truro shed in 1956.

Just after Truro is the branch to Falmouth, a very busy commercial port which has its own small private port railway.

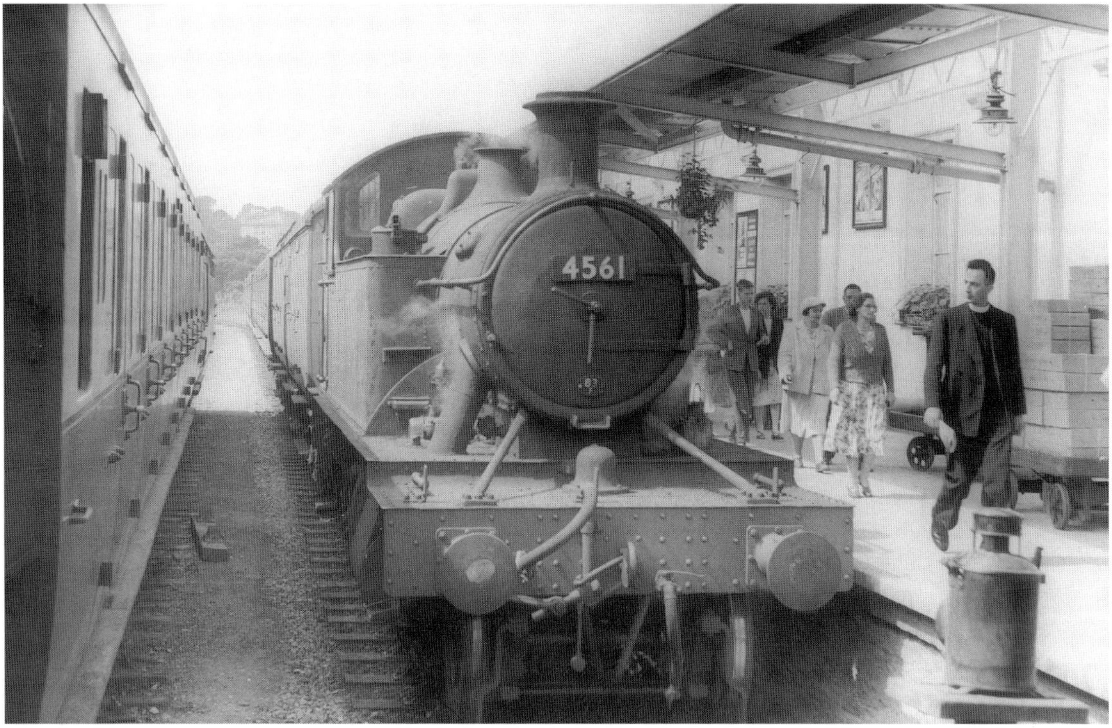

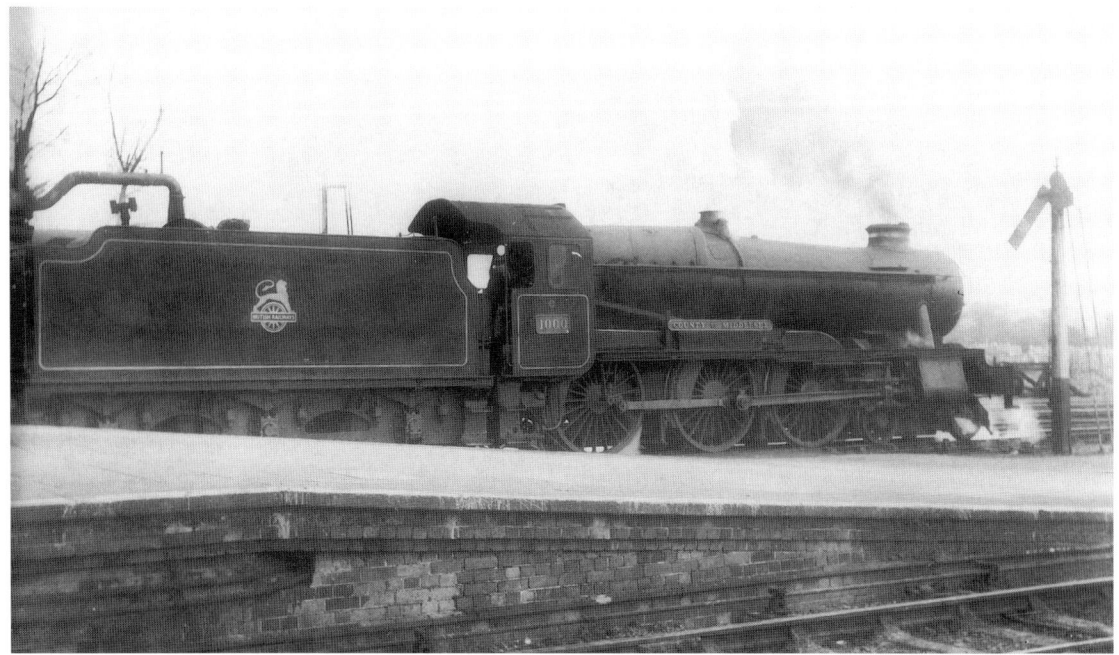

No. 4561 at Falmouth, being admired by the local vicar in 1952.

No. 1000 *County of Middlesex* leaving Truro. This was one of the original engines to have a double chimney.

Leaving Truro behind it is only a few minutes later that we run through Chacewater and then come to the junction for St Agnes and Perranporth. Both resorts were a favourite destinations for my parents, and we spent several holidays there. In the early 1950s it was a very quiet seaside village, far removed from the surfing centre it is today.

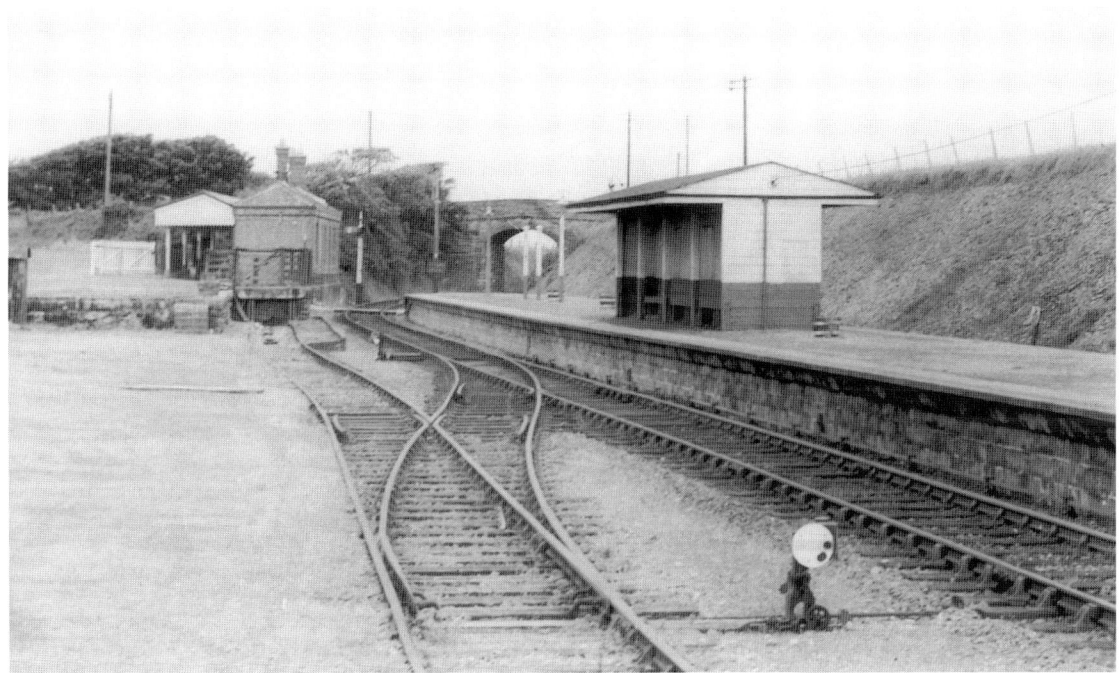

St Agnes station looking somewhat deserted, 1951.

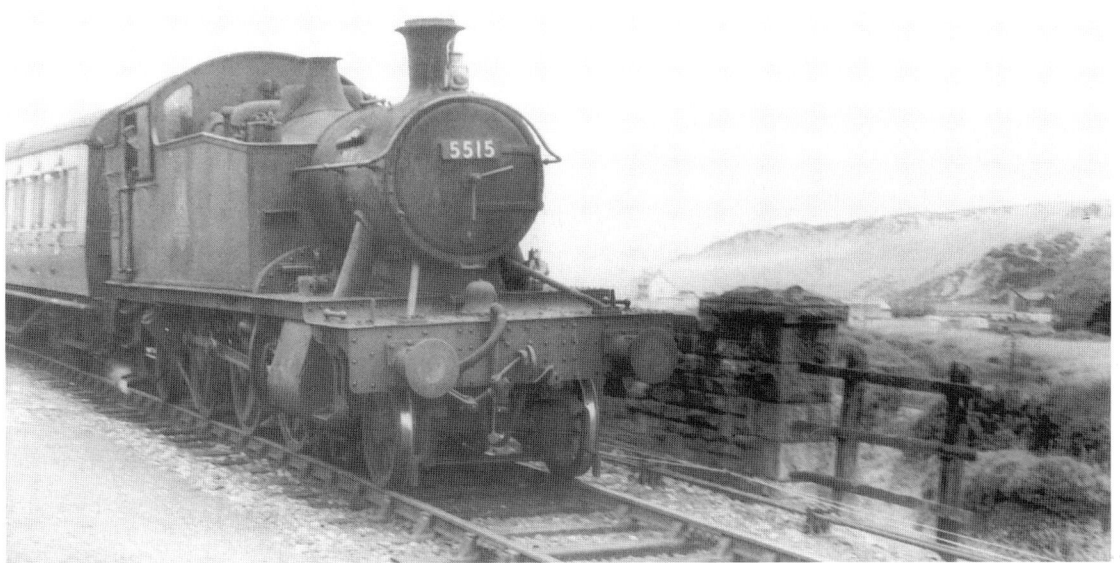

Prairie tank no. 5515 arriving at Perranporth from the direction of St Agnes. I had deserted my parents on the beach to take this photograph in 1953.

We are now passing through Redruth and the talk in the carriage is that the end of the journey is in sight – and what a fantastic journey it has been. I think we are all elated but very tired. Between us we must have taken hundreds of photographs and written thousands of numbers in books. Back to our journey and into Camborne – nothing much to see here – so on we go to Hayle and St Erth.

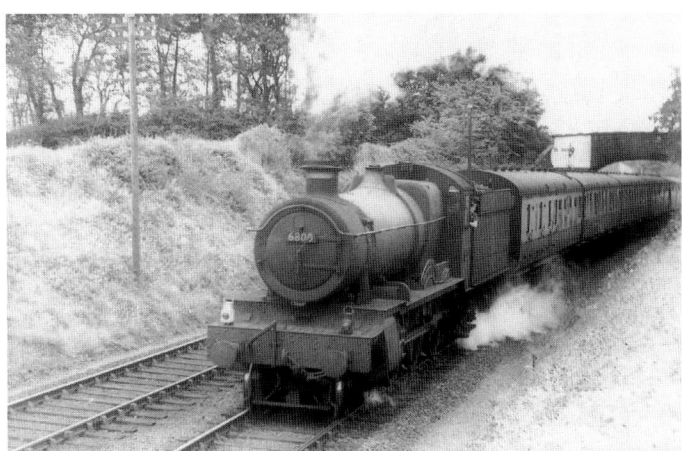

No. 6800 *Arlington Grange* approaching Redruth, 1954.

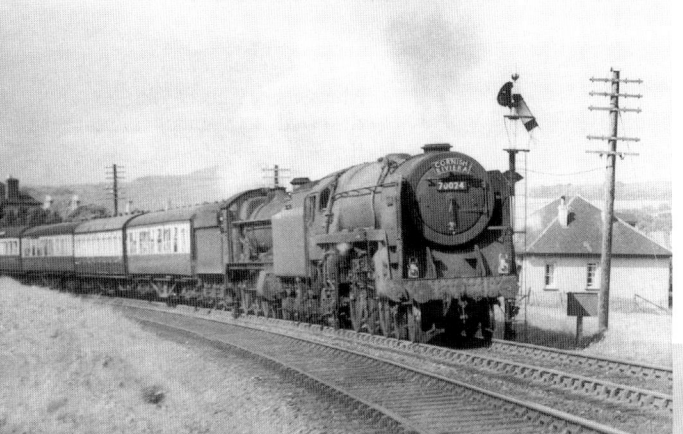

'Britannia' no. 70024 *Vulcan* is seen here as pilot to an unidentified 'Hall' leaving Hayle with 'The Cornish Riviera Express' in the early 1950s.

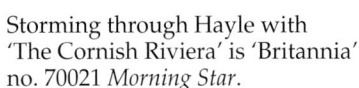

Storming through Hayle with 'The Cornish Riviera' is 'Britannia' no. 70021 *Morning Star*.

After Hayle comes St Erth Junction for St Ives and Carbis Bay, another popular destination for holiday-makers. You can board a train at Paddington and not change at all until you arrive at St Ives.

No. 4540 with an express headcode on a single track, and carrying a Penzance 83G shedplate. I believe this is either coming or going to St Ives in 1955.

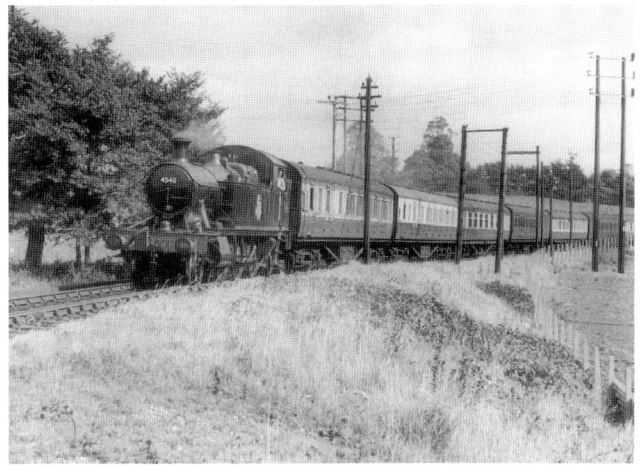

The penultimate station before Penzance, Marazion is a very popular seaside resort for visitors and also for those wishing to visit St Michael's Mount just off the shore.

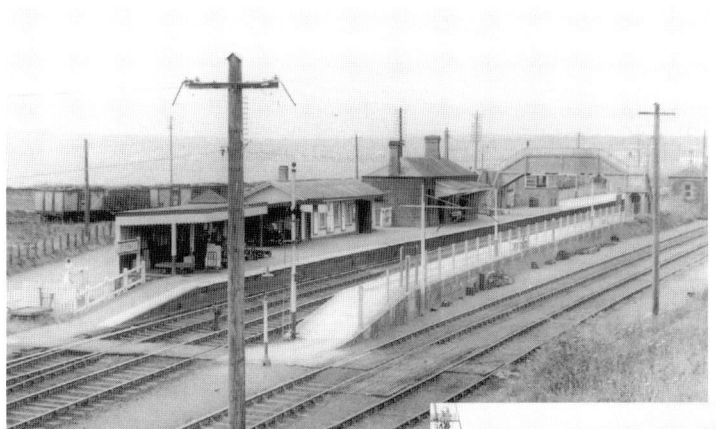

Marazion station looking very deserted, so perhaps it is early in the holiday season.

No. 6806 *Blackwell Grange* on its way back to Plymouth with returning holiday-makers.

On board, we enthusiasts are now looking out of the windows as we approach Penzance shed. We may be a little deflated at the end of this wonderful journey, but the adrenalin is still flowing. We are now passing the shed and our engine has shut off steam as we roll to a smooth halt in Penzance, there are no more tracks further than this.

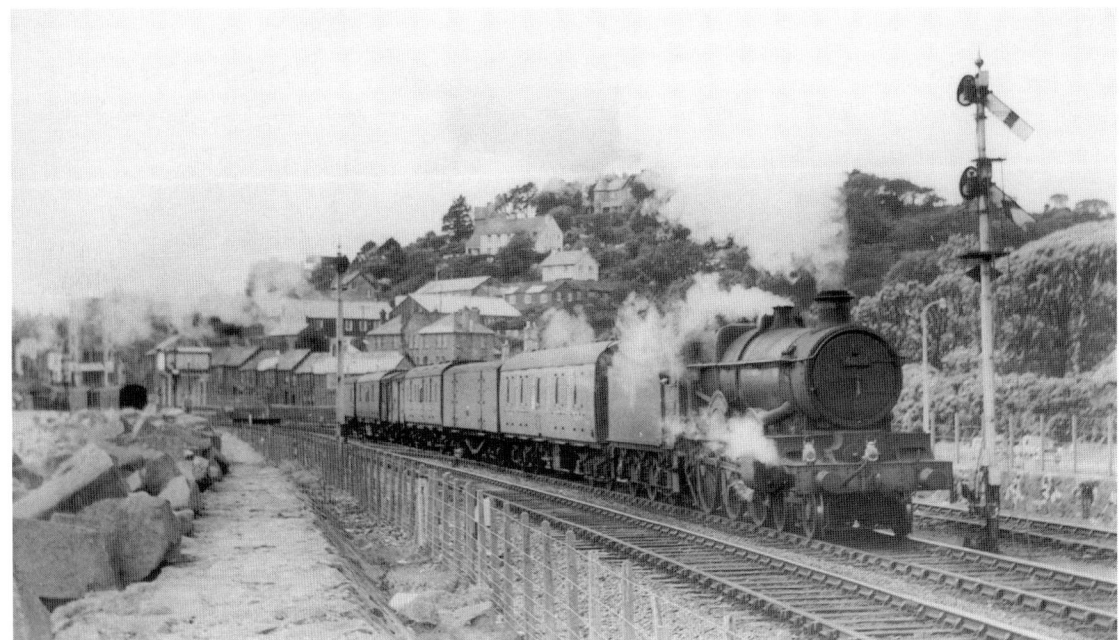

No. 4084 *Aberystwyth Castle* pulling out of Penzance in 1953.

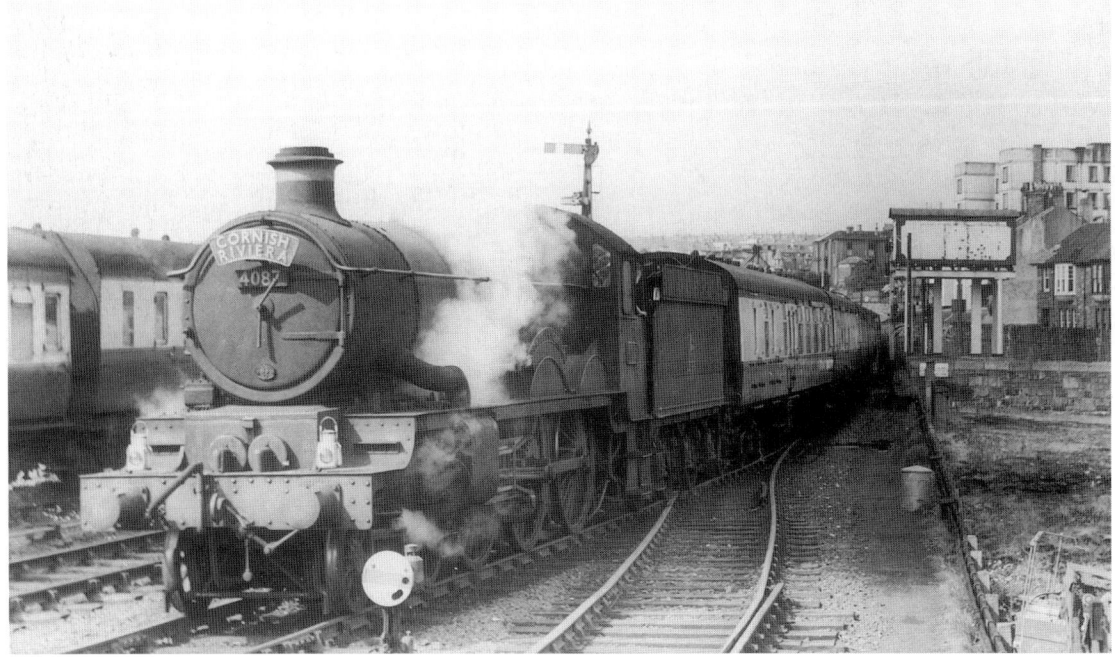

Slightly further on we see 'The Cornish Riviera' again, with no. 4087 *Cardigan Castle* in charge.

Penzance station terminus and the end of the line. Right on the waterfront, it can be a very wild place in winter, hence the overall roof to protect the passengers. Penzance is a favourite place for visitors and there are hundreds of little coves and fishing villages within easy reach, including Land's End, of course. It is time for us to collect our bags, record books and cameras and get off the train for the final time.

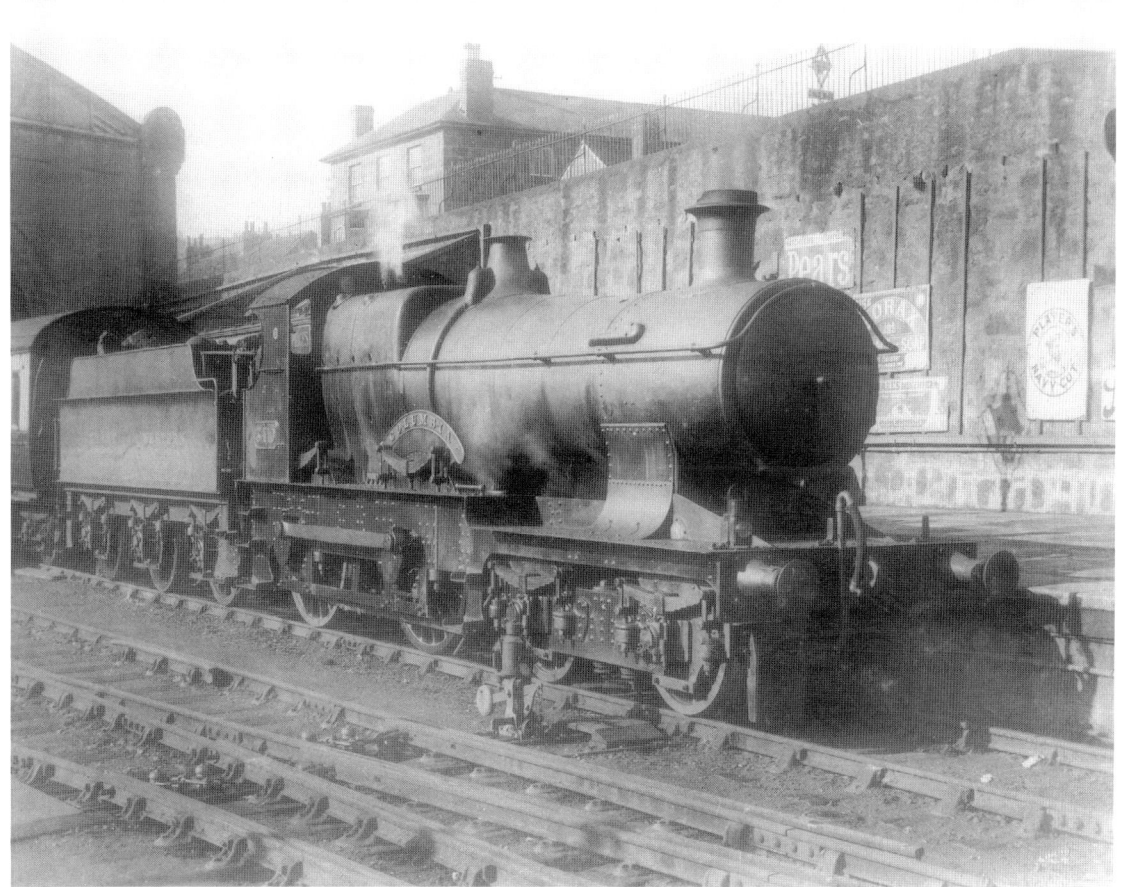

'Bulldog' no. 3410 *Columbia* has just backed on to its train in Penzance station in the 1920s.

I know this has been an imaginary journey and mention has not been made of hundreds of interesting locations, but it would take a great many volumes to go everywhere, and I would not have sufficient photographs to illustrate them. I have therefore tried to mention and show photographs of places where I have negatives in my collection. This is the one rigid rule I made for myself: I must have an original negative. I do not use copy negatives – to me, an original negative has actually had a form of contact with the engine and is a living image. My last railway picture is of no. 6988 *Swithland Hall* at the head of 'The Cornishman' (Penzance–Wolverhampton) about to leave Penzance. The signal is off, and we will watch it leave at the end of this very long day. I wonder if the return journey will be as exciting?

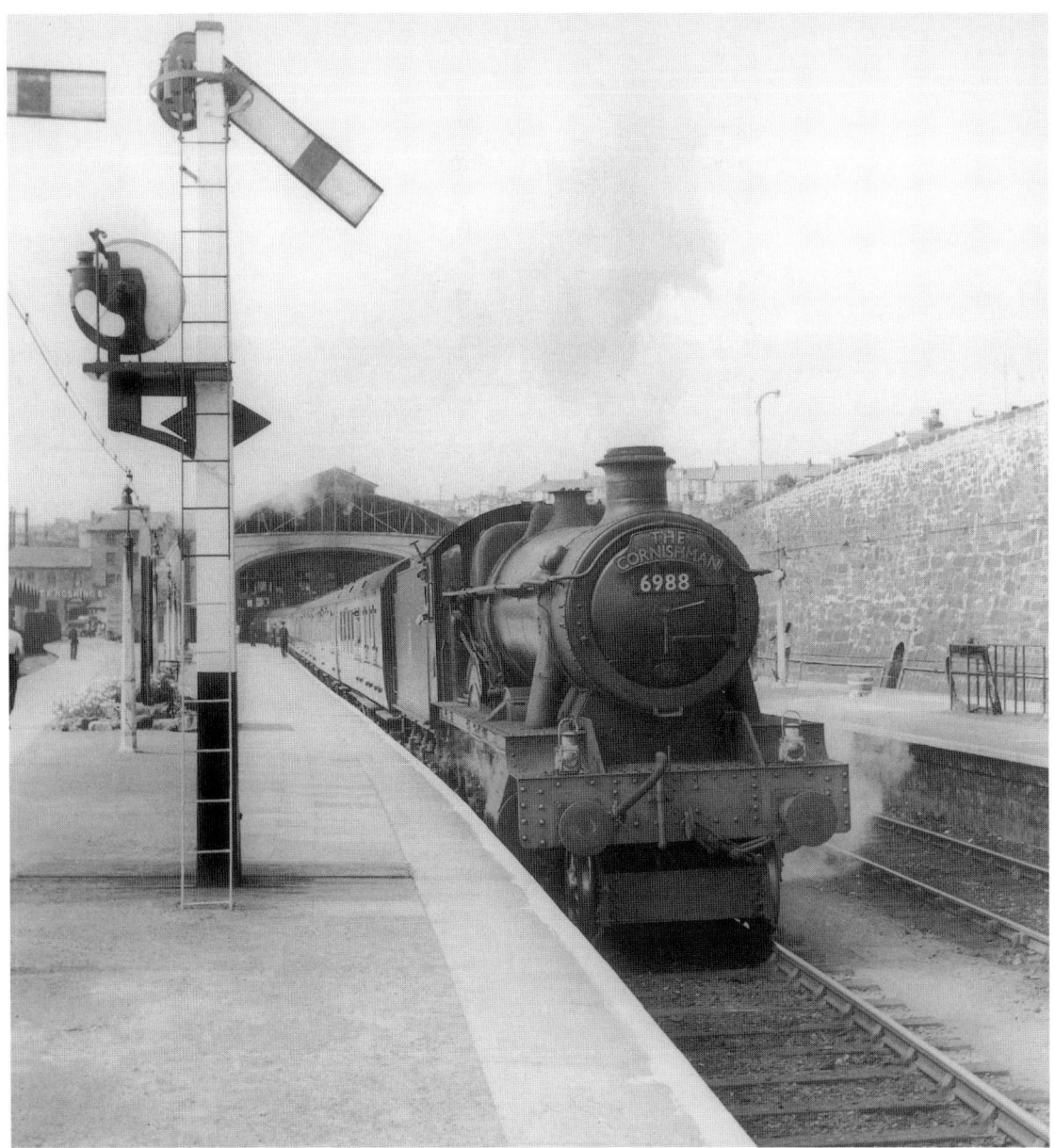

No. 6988 *Swithland Hall*